Latter-day Screens

Latter-day Screens

GENDER, SEXUALITY,
AND MEDIATED MORMONISM

Brenda R. Weber

DUKE UNIVERSITY PRESS   DURHAM AND LONDON   2019

© 2019 DUKE UNIVERSITY PRESS. All rights reserved

Designed by Courtney Leigh Baker
Typeset in Minion Pro and Helvetica Neue by Westchester Publishing Services

Cataloging-in-Publication Data is available from the Library of Congress.
Library of Congress Control Number: 2019943713

ISBN 9781478004264 (hardcover)
ISBN 9781478004868 (pbk.)
ISBN 9781478005292 (ebook)

Cover art: *Big Love* (HBO, 2006–11).

Publication of this open monograph was the result of Indiana University's participation in TOME (Toward an Open Monograph Ecosystem), a collaboration of the Association of American Universities, the Association of University Presses, and the Association of Research Libraries. TOME aims to expand the reach of long-form humanities and social science scholarship including digital scholarship. Additionally, the program looks to ensure the sustainability of university press monograph publishing by supporting the highest quality scholarship and promoting a new ecology of scholarly publishing in which authors' institutions bear the publication costs.

Funding from Indiana University made it possible to open this publication to the world. This work was partially funded by the Office of the Vice Provost of Research and the IU Libraries.

For Michael and Stacey,
my North Stars

CONTENTS

Acknowledgments ix

Past as Prologue. Latter-day Screens and History 1

Introduction. "Well, We Are a Curiosity, Ain't We?": Mediated Mormonism 13

1. Mormonism as Meme and Analytic: Spiritual Neoliberalism, Image Management, and Transmediated Salvation 49

2. The Mormon Glow: The Raced and Gendered Implications of Spectacular Visibility 91

3. The Epistemology of the (Televised, Polygamous) Closet: The Cultural Politics of Mediated Mormonism and the Promises of the American Dream 120

4. Polygamy USA: Visibility, Charismatic Evil, and Gender Progressivism 162

5. Gender Trouble in Happy Valley: Choice, Happy Affect, and Mormon Feminist Housewives 201

6. "Pray (and Obey) the Gay Away": Conscience and the Queer Politics of Desire 241

Conclusion. Afterthoughts and Latter Days 276

Epilogue. Mormons on My Mind, or, Everything I Ever Needed to Know about Hegemony I Learned in Mesa, Arizona 284

Notes 309
References 329
Media Archive 345
Index 361

ACKNOWLEDGMENTS

This book is not about Mormon people and history so much as it is about Mormonism as an idea, an image, and a way of thinking. While I have my own experiences with Mormonism that I detail in the epilogue, this book isn't really about me. Yet, it isn't *not* about me, in that growing up non-Mormon in the highly Mormon city of Mesa, Arizona, cultivated in me a certain point of view that, no doubt, led me to a career in gender studies and a commitment to social justice. Even so, this book is not meant as a critique of a religion or its adherents but as an examination of the way Mormonism as a meme functions as a symbolic stand-in, particularly with respect to gender and sexuality. I believe Mormonism serves as a lens through which to see a set of cultural operations and investments otherwise difficult to discern.

I recognize that religion is not, and never can be, only abstraction. And so I offer my thanks to the actual LDS folks who have been my friends over the past forty years, in real life and on social media. While some of those people have already unfriended me for being radically liberal, many others have remained. I hope those Mormon friends who become aware of this book might see it as a tribute to a way of seeing they fostered.

The LDS Church believes in a living doctrine, meaning some of the policies I discuss in this book have changed since 2019. Here's hoping for yet more advances!

I have two non-Mormon friends who have been with me since childhood. I first met Stacey when I was three and she was four, and our mothers were convinced we'd enjoy playing together. Were they ever right! Although we always liked each other, it wasn't until our families moved closer to one another that Stacey and I became inseparable. I loved and continue to love her ready laugh, her quick wit, her overall good-naturedness, and her capacities to go deep, all qualities that serve her well now as a physician. Stacey, I still owe you a nickel for believing my dog's hernia was a penis but tough crunchies.

Michael and I met in seventh grade, at Kino Junior High School in Mesa. I will never forget my first glimpse of him dashing down the hall in a furtive run-walk as he delivered messages for the nurse. Never was there a more conscientious or fast-moving aide than he—or a more talented scene partner in acting class or a smarter competitor in AP English. I loved and continue to love his intensity, his intelligence, and his loyalty. He is now a highly successful attorney and ever-ready flash mob participant in Los Angeles. Michael, I'm sorry for crushing your cookies.

When I first began to consider writing a book about Mormons, both Stacey and Michael thought I was, to put it mildly, making a big mistake. Why go back and think about those things? Why be immersed in the very culture that we had all worked so hard to flee physically and emotionally? Yet, both told me stories of such intimacy and pain that I was deeply moved and doubly convinced that I wanted to write this book. I won't repeat those stories here, except to say that both Michael and Stacey have been part of a lifelong conversation that has tried to make tangible something ephemeral that had enormous influence over us. Together we have the makings for a classically unfunny joke: A lawyer, a doctor, and a professor walk into a bar and ruminate on the cognitive dissonances of their childhood. We all learned to negotiate a series of invisible codes that we were never taught yet learned so well that we often internalized. Together we cut our teeth on the hegemonic structures of Mormonism, and we all have moments, even now, when feelings of discomfort or confusion emerge mysteriously in our lives—reminding us of those tender days of childhood. For these reasons, I dedicate this book to my two lifelong friends, Stacey Davis and Michael Graham. I'm not sure you even know one another, but together you're fused as the North Star that has guided my writing in this book. While I regret that neither Stacey nor Michael live nearby, I am so grateful that both offer me an immediate intimacy and a lifelong connection.

I also want to thank all of the media producers whose creative and often courageous work fueled this project. While I appreciate and am fully fascinated by big-budget productions like *The Book of Mormon* and *Big Love*, it is the voices of individuals trying to navigate their way to a new truth that affected me most strongly and offered the clearest clarion call for putting my own truth on the page. In particular, I want to thank Terry Tempest Williams, Judith Freeman, Emily Pearson, Cindi Jones, Tara Westover, and Martha Beck for memoirs so radically vulnerable that I felt honored to read them and changed through the process of spending time with their thoughts. My thanks, as well, to David Ebershoff, whose novel and our conversation together about Mormonism past and present continue to feed my imagination.

At Indiana University, I wish to thank my colleagues in the Department of Gender Studies, a never-ending source of encouragement, inspiration, and esprit de corps: Stephanie Sanders, Jen Maher, Colin Johnson, Sara Friedman, Justin Roberto Garcia, Freda Fair, Lessie Frazier, Maria Bucur, Laura Foster, Gabriel Peoples, Kate Livingston, Cynthia Wu, Amrita Chakrabarti Myers, Cate Taylor, Maria Hamilton Abegunde. You put the "there" there. I'm also grateful to the department's staff, which literally keeps the wheels on the machine: Nina Taylor, Decker Cavosie, Mateo Perez, and Andrew Hennessey. You are my friends and comrades in arms. I thank my excellent team of graduate research assistants: Xavier Watson, Ariel Sincoff-Yedid, Adam Fisher, Sasha T. Goldberg (ever the finder of the most obscure research threads), and, most particularly, the excellent content editor Elizabeth Gilmore. I also am grateful to Greg Waller, Sara Friedman, and Patti Peplow, who read the book in manuscript form and helped bring its many screens into coherency. Thanks also to Justin Garcia, Susan Lepselter, and Susan Seizer, who offered invaluable feedback on the memoir chapter. During the writing of this book, I stepped into an administrative role as the department chair, and I offer my thanks to the executive dean of the College of Arts and Sciences, Larry Singell, for his willingness to negotiate a chair-ship that allowed me to remain research active. My thanks to Dean Jean Robinson, for her belief and encouragement. Jean clicked on a Facebook post saying something like, "10 Surprising Things You Don't Know about Mormons!" She then told me about it at a dinner, and chapter 2 soon sprang forth. It's fitting that someone as glowing and brilliant as Jean Robinson might have inspired a chapter on the Mormon glow. Finally, I wish to thank the vice provost for faculty and academic affairs, Eliza Pavalko, and the director of the Campus Writing Program, Laura Plummer, who have spearheaded years and years of faculty writing groups. Without our weekly sessions, I fear this book would have been another six years in the making.

Thanks to the international network of scholars working in gender and media, who have very kindly invited me to give talks at their universities or who have attended conference presentations when I have presented this material. I so appreciate the encouragement you have offered. In particular, I thank (the incomparable) Sarah Banet-Weiser, (the brilliant) Helen Wood, (the inimitable) David Gerstner, (the sensational) Haidee Wasson, (the indefatigable) Dana Heller, (the indomitable) Misha Kavka, and (the absolutely fabulous and much-beloved) Georges-Claude Guilbert.

During the writing of this book, I had the opportunity to serve as the Muriel Gold Senior Scholar-in-Residence at the Institute for Gender, Sexuality, and Feminist Studies at McGill University, Montreal. My thanks to Carrie Rentschler and the institute for this opportunity. I also received funding from the Indiana University College of Arts and Humanities Institute and the IU New Frontiers Initiative, for which I am grateful. In addition, this work was partially funded by the Office of the Vice Provost of Research (OVPR) at Indiana University Bloomington through the Grant-in-Aid program and through OVPR and the IU Libraries. I thank Diane Negra for encouraging me to publish a portion of the book on *Sister Wives* and spiritual neoliberalism in *Television and New Media*.

I thank my broad circle of friends and family who have received this work with boundless interest, particularly Chantal Carleton, Regis Helie, Bill Yarber, Barb Klinger, Kathleen McHugh, Gardner Bovingdon, Charles Aclund, Paul Gutjahr, Katie Lofton, Mara Einstein, Scott Curtis, Kirsten Pike, Jeff Hartenfelt, Jennifer Meta-Robinson, Brynda Forgas, Suzanne Bresina-Hutton, Karen Tice, Jean Ward, Jennifer Westerhaus Adams, Patti Peplow, Judith Wenger, Andrea Waller, Beth Kamhi, Robert Weber, Heather Weber, Becky Weber, John Weber, and, as always, Donna Swaim. Special thanks to my parents, David and Mary Weber, who are more than a little concerned that I might have written a book critical of our good and kind neighbors in Mesa. Mom and Dad, I hope your pride in me outweighs your apprehension, and I'm sorry for all of the swear words in the book!

I especially wish to thank Courtney Berger at Duke University Press, who from the very first inkling of this project understood its vision. Courtney, thank you for your insights, your editorial magic, and your always spot-on point of view. Thanks, too, to the excellent editorial team at Duke, particularly Sandra Korn, Liz Smith, and Karen Fisher.

I thank my best guys and my closest family, Jake Waller and Greg Waller. Thanks for making the stars shine and the coffee strong and for so much special time.

Finally, no book on Mormonism would be complete without some attention to Mormon foodways. I do not have recipes for Jell-O molds, homemade root beer, or funeral potatoes, but I do have something better . . . our neighbor Mrs. Osbourne's fudge cake. It is not for the weak of heart or the calorie conscious, but it does deliver an almost foolproof dessert for even the most challenged of chefs. My favorite part is that the frosting goes on right when the cake is out of the oven. I'm sure this is a time- and labor-saving device for busy mothers with lots of children, but it's also a flavor-enhancing breakthrough, since the frosting caramelizes as it cools. I hadn't really planned to include a recipe in this book. But this morning as I prepared to finish the copyedits on the book and to make my son's annual birthday cake—nine years old!—it seemed fitting to include this much-loved recipe that I begged off Mrs. Osbourne when I myself was nine. I offer it to the book and to you, my reader, as a sweet token of thanks and appreciation.

JOSIE OSBOURNE'S FUDGE CAKE

Sift together in a large bowl:
- 2 cups sugar
- 2 cups flour

Mix in a saucepan:
- 2 sticks butter
- 4 T cocoa
- 1 cup water

Bring to a boil and pour over flour and sugar. Stir well and then add:
- ½ cup buttermilk
- 1 tsp baking soda
- 2 beaten eggs
- 1 tsp vanilla

Mix well and pour into a greased and powdered-sugared 11″ × 16″ pan.

Bake at 400 degrees for 20 minutes.

While cake bakes, boil:
- 1 stick butter
- 4–6 T buttermilk
- 3–4 T cocoa

Remove from heat and add:
- 1 box powdered sugar
- 1 tsp vanilla
- 1 cup chopped nuts (optional)

Beat with a spoon and spread over cake while it is still hot.

Mrs. Osbourne's hints: this cake is better just a bit warmed up, and it will feed a family of 12!

PAST AS PROLOGUE

Latter-day Screens and History

This book considers gender and sexuality as examined through a range of screens, each containing a compelling combination of images, narratives, sounds, and discourses that I call mediated Mormonism. Though each of the texts I examine are bounded—in some cases by covers, in others by opening and closing credits—their meanings far exceed the boundaries of before, middle, and end that we have been taught constitute the basic elements of a story. Indeed, this is the very meaning of latter-day screens. It is not a single image or the sound of one bell ringing alone that I try to capture in this book but a palimpsest of images and a cacophony of noises, many bells clanging at once in synchronicity if not unison. While the intermedial discourse about Mormonism is complex, it is also remarkably coherent. Mediated Mormonism reinforces over and over again a story about preparing not for the end of times, the latter days, but for living in modernity itself, in all of its complexity, temporal dislocation, speed, and mediation. Remarkably, doing so requires engaging with and actively contesting conventional meanings of gender and sexuality in all of their complexity and nuance.

My interest in this topic is both personal and intellectual. I grew up as a non-Mormon in a highly Mormon city: Mesa, Arizona. As I detail in the memoir that serves as this book's epilogue, Mormonism taught me everything I ever needed to know about the silent workings of power, desire, and consent that we call hegemony. I also come to this project as a scholar of both gender studies and media studies, interested in how culture simultaneously serves as a conduit of social instruction and a mirror of social relations. Because of my personal relation to Mormonism, I can't hope to sustain the pretense of the scholar's objective pose; my own dry immersion in Mormonism makes me as far from an impartial witness as one could imagine. Yet I decided to bring my subtle contact and contract with Mormonism to this study because memory, like mediation and narration, functions as an important filtering agent that shapes the power and meaning of ideas. Memory is its own medium and another form of screen on which these stories are projected. It thus seemed not only important but necessary to offer to this study of gender and media my own imperfect, distorting, and unreliable memory, that of a child who came of age in the shadow of Mormonism. If I had not lived a childhood on the fringes of the Saints, who themselves believe they operate on the margins of an American mainstream, I doubt very much that I would have even realized the veins of power and hegemony, alienation and belonging, obedience and independence pumping through the body of mediated Mormonism. And what is perhaps even more striking—the kind of mediated Mormonism I discuss in this book blossomed in the late 1990s and early 2000s, long after my period of growing up in Mesa in the 1970s and '80s. Yet, when I wanted to understand my own experiences more, I didn't go to a historical archive. Instead, I watched a lot of TV and surfed a lot of websites and read a lot of books. We might say, then, just like dusting for fingerprints, mediated Mormonism serves as a clarifying technology that makes the hegemonic markings visible. Latter-day screens require we look at what is projected not just on the screen itself but in the patterns of dust particles that swirl and dance in the light.

The primary source materials I use in this book are readily available and affordable through retail outlets such as Amazon, Netflix, and Hulu. Print materials span the publishing gamut, covering all literary classifications (novel, short story, memoir, biography, poetry, nonfiction) and all segments of the publishing industry, from vanity presses to major publishing houses. These materials are augmented by an increased awareness of Mormonism in journalism and academia, all of which have fueled the surge of interest in, and concern about, Mormonism. Although I did my research in the United States, and most of the materials I consider are produced in English-speaking countries, mediated Mormonism—much like the Mormon missionary—exists in an international polyglossic network, aided and augmented by worldwide media distribution and consumption at both professional and amateur levels. A complex multi-platformed media culture is thus critical to the dissemination of Mormonism as a meme, rich with information about social values in the present moment. It is precisely because so much of Mormonism earns its saliency and visibility through both conventional and new media forms that its study has something important to say about the circulation, intelligibility, and appeal of ideas and ideology.

In doing this analysis, I am not so much interested in actual Mormon people or history so much as the fusion of stories and images that blend together to represent these things, what I call in the book Mormonism as meme. I am also interested in how the governing logics of Mormonism as a meme, in turn, provide a mediated pedagogy about power and identity, specifically with relation to gender and sexuality. I call this Mormonism as an analytic. Consequently, this book is not a sociological analysis nor a historical treatment nor a religious discussion nor an ethnography. In fact, during the writing of this book, I had the opportunity to interview a number of notable F/LDS folk, including Kody Brown, Steve Young, Donny Osmond, John Dehlin, Terry Tempest Williams, and Elizabeth Smart. Though fascinated by the possibility of actually talking to people, I chose not to pursue these possibilities because I wanted to engage with the cultural function of mediated Mormonism as both a meme and an analytic. Doing so requires that I engage with impressions as they exist in the public sphere. Yet I am very aware that Mormonism cannot and does not function only as a metaphor, and I want to be very clear that I do not wish to denigrate or disrespect any aspect of the religion or its peoples but, instead, to chart the movement of an idea as it moves across the mediascape.

A History of Sorts

References to Mormon history and beliefs constantly bubble to the surface of contemporary mediation, and so it is important to have some sense of the backdrop for these allusions. As just one example, HBO's *Big Love* frequently cites Mormon history and religious beliefs—in ways both veiled and unveiled—from the schism between mainstream and fundamentalist Latter-day Saints to sacred endowment ceremonies to the wearing of garments to the forging of documents. The television show might still make sense if a viewer does not recognize the ghostly apparition of Emma Smith (church founder Joseph Smith's first and only legal wife, who was adamantly opposed to polygamy), but it certainly helps to know who she is. In this spirit of better understanding contemporary mediated Mormonism, then, I offer an overarching and very brief history.

By most accounts, the church was founded by twenty-five-year-old Joseph Smith Jr. in 1830 in Palmyra, New York. Smith originally called his creation the Church of Christ and then changed it eight years later to the Church of Jesus Christ of Latter-day Saints, to emphasize how fully his Saints lay in wait for the end of days. "Mormon" is a colloquial nickname for Latter-day Saints (LDS) folk. The early nineteenth century was a period of great religious revivalism, particularly in the American northeast, when evangelism held sway as a precursor to the perceived end of times. The United States was awash with swashbuckling Methodists and Baptists preaching a fire-and-brimstone theology, and Smith's new church offered a combination of spiritualism and rationality that appealed to a great many would-be saints eager to pledge fealty to a faith that promised salvation both here and throughout all eternity.

Smith founded his church after nearly a decade of religious questioning that began for him as a teenager. Biographical accounts are consistent in suggesting that while praying in the woods, Smith claimed a visitation from an angel—named Moroni—probably in 1821 when he was sixteen years old. At that time, Moroni considered the teenaged Joseph too immature for the weight of the heavenly message yet to be bestowed. So the Angel Moroni commanded Joseph to return again to the forest a few years later (some accounts say four years; others are more vague). In 1827, Moroni came again and revealed to the young Joseph the location of golden plates on which were inscribed what was later to become the Book of Mormon. These tablets, buried in the hills of western New York, were thought to be engraved in an ancient script (reformed Egyptian), and Joseph used seer stones, called in the biblical tradition the Urim and Thummim, set into a pair of his mother's old wire spectacles, to read/interpret/create this new religious tract. Making matters of authenticity murkier, Joseph peered through his homemade spectacles into the deep dark spaces of his stovepipe hat, since the darkness apparently helped the clarity of his vision but also kept other people from seeing what he saw. In the process of translation, only a very select few (all sworn followers of Smith) were able to view the plates. Upon completion of the book, Joseph returned the tablets to Moroni, thus removing the primary evidence on which the religion was founded and making Joseph Smith's Book of Mormon the only version of God's truth available for followers and scholars.

There has been a great deal of controversy about the veracity of Smith's vision and accounts of what really happened. Explanations cover many options from the possibility that Joseph truly was an earthly scribe for an angelic message to the prospect that Joseph was a delusional and deceptive genius, capable of manipulating people through the force of his imagination, charisma, and colossal ego. My point in venturing into this much-told tale is not to lay out a truth claim of my own or to demean the origination story of the Mormon religion but to try to account for, at some level, the appeal of this new faith in the historical moment in which it was birthed as well as in the almost two centuries it has flourished.

Mormonism, like all religions, requires an extraordinary leap of faith in its followers. In this case, the fact that Joseph Smith quite literally pulled his revelation out of a hat has helped to build Mormonism in the American imagination as an odd religion and Mormons as a peculiar people, easily mocked by similar scenes of visitation, stone-enhanced visions, and testimony in HBO's *Big Love* and the Comedy Channel's *South Park*. It's worth repeating that this moment in nineteenth-century American history was notable not only for the evangelism sweeping through towns and cities but for the fusion of spiritualism and science that manifested in séances, dowsing and divining rods, and displays of clairvoyant behaviors, all predicated on the appeal of a rational holiness galvanized and made concrete by a charismatic personality.

Smith was a magnetic leader and, as appropriate for a man who made a business of finding lost treasure, he himself became a divining rod for religious converts, attracting masses of fans and parishioners even as these "latter-day saints" were persecuted and ostracized within their communities. As a consequence of many factors, including rumors of polygamy, the suspicious disappearance of the golden plates, the Latter-day Saints' charismatic hold on new parishioners, and the Mormons' often aggressive and militarized retaliation to perceived oppression from non-Mormons, LDS people were not much liked in the mid-nineteenth century. In fact, Illinois, Missouri, and the entire United States were separately at war, both figuratively and literally, with Joseph and his followers. Due to these many confrontations, Joseph Smith moved the Saints from his home in New York to Kirtland, Ohio, in 1831, and he moved them again to Far West, Missouri, in 1838 and then to Commerce, Illinois, in 1839. He renamed Commerce to Nauvoo, a Hebrew term he understood to mean beautiful.

Some fourteen years after his church's founding, the thirty-eight-year-old Smith was killed in a gun battle in which he purportedly did not fight back, a passive victimization reinforced by my junior high school friends and informants but contradicted by historical accounts, which place a pistol in Smith's hands. It is Smith's fabled passivism, after all, that lifted him to Christly martyrdom. What my friends never told me, and what they themselves perhaps didn't know as children, is that Joseph Smith had actively outfitted a militia called the Armies of Israel and prepared it to fight. Smith was also the self-appointed leader of this army, and most visitors referred to him by the honorific of General Smith. Most accounts also suggest that Smith (and after him, Brigham Young) cultivated the secret vigilante force called the Danites, which governed through intimidation, force, and murder. Whatever the precise historical facts, there is no doubt that Smith was a shrewd leader and a fierce opponent, capable of galvanizing support in followers and controversy in those who did not believe in his revelations.

After Smith's murder in 1844, Brigham Young led the Saints to their American Zion, Salt Lake City. While their journey did not endure for the forty years that Jewish people wandered the desert wilderness, it did create the hard experiences of sacrifice, fortitude, and perseverance that are central to Mormon self-understanding. This peripatetic beginning based on violent social intolerance has led the LDS people to understand themselves as outsiders. It's a critical theme of aliens in America, or belonging-by-not-belonging, that runs through most discussions of Mormonism, even in a contemporary context where mainstream Mormons are arguably model minorities. Indeed, this notion of community and exile manifests across the mediated discourses about Mormons in the contemporary American imagination that I examine here.

Brigham Young governed the growing church for thirty-three years and gave it the foundation that led to its transformation from a home-grown American sect of the nineteenth century to a postmillennial world religion. Young's stamp is fully imprinted in contemporary Mormonism, from the university named in his honor to the machinelike political coordination and economic self-sufficiency that give Mormonism its worldly power and mysterious veiling. Joseph Smith and Brigham Young aren't the only influential figures behind the Church of Jesus Christ of Latter-day Saints, of course, but together they represent the heights of its patrilineal heritage. The Mormon Church has relentlessly been governed by white heterosexual (or at least not publicly gay) men, who claim an exclusive divine access to the Almighty and take for themselves a share of that blessing in the promise that they and other righteous Mormon men within the church can and will inherit a world of their own in a celestial heaven. The role of women and children within this cosmogony is simply to serve, happily and obediently. Mormonism is thus not only saturated with the ideological characteristics of Americanness as a political economy, it also has the gendered and sexed imprint of Americanness within its very DNA. It's not for nothing that Harold Bloom called Mormonism "The American Religion."

Two insistent questions adhere to contemporary members of the Church of Jesus Christ of Latter-day Saints: Are you Christians, and Are you polygamists? The church has answered without hesitation or equivocation: yes to the question of Christianity and no to the question of polygamy. As mediated Mormonism makes evident, however, those answers may not be quite so simple, since the notion that a man might become the God of his own planet troubles the Christian notion of monotheism, and the likelihood of plural marriage in the Mormon afterlife makes polygamy more central to the bedrock tenets of the faith than is typically discussed. Indeed, for our purposes, it's important to have a clearer sense of the relation between polygamy-adherent Mormons (FLDS) and their more modern cousins, polygamy-adverse Mormons (LDS), which I detail in the next section.

The LDS/FLDS Split

The present LDS and Fundamentalist Latter-day Saints (FLDS) grew from the same roots. Both Joseph and other early church fathers practiced plural (or celestial) marriage, though not always openly. *Doctrine and Covenants* 132 (revealed to Smith in 1842 and revered by both the LDS and FLDS) mandates plural marriage as a divine commandment from God. According to this edict, it is essential that men take at least three wives in order to be accepted into the highest level of the Mormon cosmogony, the Celestial Kingdom. Those who fail or refuse to achieve this number are relegated to the lower levels, the Telestial and Terrestrial Kingdoms, where they may only be angel-servants rather than Gods or, if women, the queens of Gods. There is no hell for believers, only this tripartite heavenly arrangement. In both LDS and FLDS contexts, hell, or outer darkness, is reserved for apostates—those who have followed the One True Church and rejected it.

When God spoke in 1890 and then again in 1904 to eradicate plural marriage, true-believing Saints split off into fundamentalist sects, themselves splintering according to various ideological conflicts or differences about which man was the true prophet. Both a specific sect and a generic label, FLDS is meant to indicate a number of fundamentalist groups that hold Joseph Smith's original version of Mormonism as the true iteration of the faith. As a result, the two faith systems share many common features and revere the same holy books and founding fathers, even while they hold each other in distrust and often open scorn. All Latter-day Saints consider themselves God's special people as reinforced by the Book of Mormon, but fundamentalists see themselves as purer and more righteous than the mainstream church, believing a fundamentalist set of beliefs more faithfully carries forward Joseph Smith's vision. The Fundamentalist Latter-day Saints are certain of their salvation in the imminent latter days—or at least, the most worthy of them will be saved—their fallen mainstream Mormon cousins sinking into oblivion.

It is not only polygamy that defines fundamentalism, but a whole host of doctrinal differences that include the Adam/God theory and blood atonement. The first holds that Adam, the first man of the Judeo-Christian tradition, was actually God, a flesh-and-blood man much like any other human, who came to Earth from another planet.[1] This philosophy sets the groundwork for two beliefs that are central to both LDS and FLDS scriptures and serve as insistent themes in mediated Mormonism: exaltation, or the idea that righteous Mormon men will themselves become Gods of their own planet, and eternal progression, or the idea that families can be sealed and thus stay intact through eternity. The ideas of eternal marriages and forever families are critical to the brand of Mormonism, both mainstream and fundamentalist, and the notion of male Godhead equally blends both faiths. The Adam/God doctrine (where Adam is God), however, has fallen to the domain of the fundamentalists.[2]

Similarly, blood atonement is a principle of salvation practiced in the nineteenth-century church that, in the twentieth-century fracturing, has accrued to fundamentalism. Blood atonement states that some crimes are so horrific that the conventional norm of Christian salvation does not apply. For those not familiar with the Christian tradition, the thinking is that God sent his son Jesus to be martyred and, in so doing, to absolve humans of their sin through his death. Mormon blood atonement takes this idea one step further, suggesting that for those sins not covered by Christly sacrifice (an idea sacrilegious to Protestant and Catholic thinking), the perpetrators of sin should be killed in a way that allows their blood to serve as a cleansing sacrificial offering. Jon Krakauer (2004) begins *Under the Banner of Heaven* with a description of a bloody scene of carnage, a woman and her baby daughter slaughtered at the hands of two fundamentalist men, who have enacted the commandment of ceremonial murder. Other mediated fare such as the feature film *Avenging Angel* (1985) or series of short stories in Shawn Vestal's *Godforsaken Idaho* (2017) show just how fully blood atonement is critical to Mormon history, both LDS and FLDS. Indeed, much of the mediated archive about fundamentalism fuses polygamy and ritual killing, the extreme beliefs of one reinforcing the radical possibilities of the other. In turn, the very real possibility of being blood atoned heightens the courage necessary to fight the prophet and his followers, who are willing to kill and to die as demanded. There are life-and-death implications for the holy wars being fought on and through these latter-day screens.

It is important to know this background as a way of understanding the fear and apprehension that haunts the memoirs and documentaries about fundamentalism. Danger is not an idle worry in a world where, as Brent Jeffs reports in *Lost Boy*, "Once Warren [Jeffs] was placed on the wanted list and the show [*America's Most Wanted*] aired, I was put under FBI protection. The violent history of Mormon fundamentalism combined with the nature of the charges that I'd made and the link between blood atonement and the building of a temple made them believe that I was at serious risk" (Jeffs and Szalavitz 2009, 222). Flora Jessop echoes these concerns in *Church of Lies*: "Why would Roundy [the Colorado City police chief] want to see me dead? Because I was rescuing his women and threatening his world. Besides, he was convinced I was working for Satan. Warren himself had said so, from the pulpit. I was a prime candidate for blood atonement—holy murder—an ongoing theme in Short Creek" (Jessop and Brown 2010, 256). Jessop places blood atonement at the feet of Joseph Smith, and indeed the concept originated with him. But media culture more fully attributes the violent justice of blood atonement to the dogmatic Brigham Young and, through him, to the branches on the polygamist tree that sprang forth in the twentieth and twenty-first centuries.

I should note at the outset that the term "Mormon" is claimed by the dominant sect of the faith, those headquartered in Salt Lake City, as exclusive to them, although in 2018 a new revelation required that Saints call themselves neither LDS nor Mormon but followers of the Church of Jesus Christ of Latter-day Saints. The mediascape has yet to follow this edict. Noted historian Jan Shipps calls mainstream followers "the Mountain Saints" (Metcalfe and Shipps 2014). But the nickname Mormon is discursively used to address all of the many sects that make up the LDS movement, both mainstream and extremist, including its splinter organizations. The Fundamentalist Church of Jesus Christ of Latter-day Saints is the name of an actual group run, at present, by Warren Jeffs (from prison), but FLDS is also a more general descriptor for those organizations that practice the principle of plural marriage and hold other dogmatic beliefs predicated on the early Latter-day Saints church. In this book, I use FLDS in this more generalized way except when specifically discussing Warren Jeffs and his followers.

The mainstream church's resistance has not changed the fact that many FLDS and independent fundamentalists of LDS extraction both self-identify and are popularly identified by the term "Mormon." Two examples from reality television evidence this point. *I Am Cait* features an episode when Caitlyn Jenner returns to Graceland University, the small Iowa college where she started her athletic and academic career. Caitlyn refers to the school as "very religious, very Mormon." Graceland is run by the Community of Christ, formerly the Reformed Church of Jesus Christ of Latter-day Saints (RLDS), or what Shipps calls "prairie Saints" (Metcalfe and Shipps 2014). Though not mainstream LDS, popular culture referents still position RLDS as Mormon.

In another occurrence, on *Sister Wives*, Kody Brown and his family (who are members of the fundamentalist Apostolic United Brethren, or AUB) go hiking during their vacation in Alaska. In the woods, the family meets a man, Mo, labeled in the diegesis as a "native American" and "an Eskimo." Kody gestures toward his brood, saying, "I have seventeen children; they aren't all here." The man looks both incredulous and impressed, asking Kody, "Are you a Mormon, or what?!" Mo's comments suggest that even in the remote wilds of Alaska, Mormonism and its valences are recognizable. Kody demurs and chuckles a bit: "Well, no, well, ha ha, it's funny. I have seventeen children and I do have multiple wives. They call that a fundamentalist Mormon, not a rank-and-file Mormon." So again, we see that the term "Mormon" is used more broadly than the Salt Lake City church approves to stand for identities and ideas that have relationship to, but may not be, LDS. In similar fashion, I follow this discursive trend, letting Mormon or F/LDS stand as the large umbrella covering the amalgam of LDS and FLDS peoples, practices, and philosophies.

Symbolic Proxies

A final point in this prologue needs to be reserved for the mainstream LDS church's participation in baptizing the dead and the degree of both consternation and panic it creates in nonmembers, angered they have been secretly involved in a process for which they did not give consent. As I've noted, both the LDS and the FLDS look forward to the imminent latter days, when the wicked will perish and the world will be made new for the righteous. The LDS Church teaches that salvation is only possible to those baptized into the One True Church, and so those who did not know or who died prior to the church's founding might be reclaimed through proxy baptisms, where a member in good standing goes through the process of baptism for another. By some accounts, the Mormon religious system also holds that the Kingdom of God cannot arrive until all living souls have been exposed to the faith, either through active recruitment in life or baptism in death, one reason why F/LDS families have so many children. Mediated Mormonism is rife with accounts of symbolic baptisms, since any Mormon in good standing who is at least twelve and holds a temple recommend is expected to be baptized upwards of thirty to forty times per year. This is the temple work to which many good Mormons allude.

This policy has led to a somewhat frenetic baptismal practice, whereby members have performed ordinances for a series of high-profile people, including the Founding Fathers of the United States, Joan of Arc, and Adolf Hitler (see "Baptism for the Dead" 2018). They have also performed proxy baptisms for many Jewish victims of the Holocaust, both living and dead. Indeed, when Elie Wiesel discovered that, though living, the Mormons had baptized him into their faith, he became livid. "I think it's scandalous," he said in the pages of *USA Today*. "Not only objectionable but scandalous" (Grossman 2012). The church's response has been twofold: (1) it has tried to calm the waters by telling folks that since the newly baptized person might refuse the offer of eternal salvation, it's a no harm, no foul scenario, and (2) the church has restricted its genealogy websites to members, asking Saints to submit proxy baptism names only for relatives. As with the lax policing of antipolygamy doctrine in the 1890s, however, for the most part the practice of random baptizing for the dead still continues, with LDS peoples increasingly looking for more leaves on their family tree that they might baptize into Mormonism.

It is for this reason that genealogy is such a critical linchpin of Mormon domestic labor, an obligation that often falls to women, since it is their job to ferret out lost family members who can be reclaimed through proxy baptism. Increasingly, however, genealogy has become a thriving business concern that has spilled far beyond the LDS confines, with perhaps the best evidence of this claim residing in the corporate juggernaut Ancestry.com, a privately held genealogy company based in Lehi, Utah, and founded by two male BYU graduates. Containing more than seventy million family trees, it is the world's largest for-profit genealogy company and a critical database for ancestry work.[3]

Ancestry.com is also a major corporate sponsor of *Finding Your Roots*, a documentary-style program on PBS, hosted by the esteemed scholar Henry Louis Gates Jr., that investigates the ancestry of "dozens of influential people from diverse backgrounds," mostly entertainment or political celebrities (*Finding Your Roots* website). While the program proudly acknowledges that "major funding is provided by" Ancestry.com (along with Johnson &

Johnson and AT&T), it does not explicitly make connections to Mormons or Mormonism. Indeed, Ancestry.com's ties to Mormonism are an open secret—not announced and yet not exactly hidden, given the BYU, Utah, and genealogical connections. Yet it is exactly this kind of archaeological investigation that fuels the historical treasure hunt narrative of the program and, really, of history itself, where over the course of time ideology becomes practice becomes product becomes mediated idea, seemingly absent the founding ideology. In all, we see a deferred and dispersed network of symbolic proxies that become visible when looking through a latter-day lens.

Given the controversies over proxy baptisms performed on Jewish victims of the Holocaust, *Finding Your Roots* offered a supreme irony in late 2017 when it featured the stories of politician Bernie Sanders and comedian Larry David, who brilliantly portrayed Sanders in *Saturday Night Live* skits. Both Jewish, David and Sanders discovered through the program the unspeakable hardships their grandparents and parents had endured in Russia and Poland, ending the segment with a surprise announcement of a biological link between the two men. They are distant cousins—pretty, pretty good! Yet this connection between David and Sanders, mediated through the auspices of *Finding Your Roots*, also lies at the crossroads of an LDS commitment to discovering familial links and to baptizing through proxy, the symbolic meanings of Mormonism engaged in a richly contested historical conversation about meaning, choice, and identity.

While it could well be argued that mediated Mormonism functions as a recruitment and naturalization strategy deployed by the Mormon Church to spread the brand of their faith, this book approaches the meanings of mediated Mormonism as a broader cultural discourse that uses the Saints as a semiotic signifier to work out a simultaneous attraction to and repulsion from what it thinks Mormonism is and does, specifically with relation to governing codes about sexuality and gender. *Latter-day Screens* is thus quite literally a book about ideas, about what's being communicated by the kind and degree of Mormon-centric concepts in the contemporary American mediascape. It is about collectivities and large-scale cultural attention in a microcasted world of media where individuals might organize and consume media content per their own design rather than as prescribed through mass media broadcasts. These many narratives offer a lens that allows us to perceive a set of codes and practices that distinctly shape debates about what constitutes (and should constitute) normativity and fairness in the contemporary moment. With this as context, let us begin the examination of mediated Mormonism across our latter-day screens.

INTRODUCTION

"Well, We Are a Curiosity, Ain't We?":
Mediated Mormonism

In September 2010, Kody Brown and his wives took a risk of phenomenal proportion. On a reality television show broadcast around the world through TLC/Discovery, the Browns exposed themselves as fundamentalist Mormon polygamists: one man, three women (as of 2010, four), and twelve children (as of 2018, eighteen) who together constitute the family at the heart of the reality show *Sister Wives* (2010–present). At the time of *Sister Wives*' premiere, the Browns lived in Lehi, Utah, a small, largely fundamentalist town in the north-central part of the state, which is itself predominantly Mormon. While marriages between more than two people are illegal in every state in the U.S., in Utah it was also against the law to claim one is married to multiple spouses. In this regard, to speak of multiple wives was a performative act made illegal by the state. The Browns and other families like them lived under an agreement of tolerance between law enforcement and practitioners of polygamy, basically allowing those in plural marriage to be free of prosecution if they lived a quiet life. Airing their twenty-two pairs of dirty underwear on international television was living a bit too large, apparently, and after *Sister Wives* debuted, the state of Utah began gathering evidence for a formal prosecution on grounds of illegal cohabitation through bigamy. Kody Brown argued in court that because he was only legally married to one woman (Meri) and his other unions (with Janelle, Christine, and Robyn) were symbolic-spiritual relationships, he was not in defiance of the law.[1] But the state of Utah viewed his long-term relationship with four women and their multiple children as evidence of common-law marriages and thus a violation of bigamy laws.[2] As Martha Beck has said about the rule culture of Mormonism more broadly, the eleventh commandment is "Thou Shalt not Commit Publicity" (2006, 207). In going public, the Browns violated this commandment against visibility.

Before the state could move on their findings, however, the Browns took a page from the book of their Mormon forbears, who—in the nineteenth-century context of their own persecution—quickly fled Nauvoo, Illinois, and headed west to the "new promised land" of the American Zion, the Great Salt Lake Basin.[3] The Browns' secret exodus (filmed by TLC's cameras) took them southeast to Las Vegas, where polygamy is illegal but publicity is not.[4] From their new home in the gambling capital of the world, the Browns sued the state of Utah in U.S. District Court in 2011. *Brown v. Buhman* argued that the antibigamy statute was unconstitutional since it prohibited the free exercise of religion and denied due process. In December 2013, U.S. District Court judge Clarke Waddoups agreed, striking down the case against the Browns and with it Utah's sanction on plural families. While bigamy—holding marriage licenses with more than one person—is still against the law, plural marriage of the type the Browns practice became lawful, reality television thus inserting itself as the thin end of the wedge for real-world legislative change as very much influenced by a larger social agenda.[5]

As the public face of modern polygamy, the Browns accepted the ruling with gratitude. Speaking on behalf of his wives and children, Kody reinforced a set of normative structuring codes that he claimed stood at the heart of their will to visibility. Free choice, individual determinism, and an American code of plurality and acceptance all justified their equal treatment under the law. Said Kody in a public statement broadcast across news outlets and internet blogs: "While we know that many people do not approve of plural families, it is our family and based on our beliefs. Just as we respect the personal and religious choices of other families, we hope that in time all of our neighbors and fellow citizens will come to respect our own choices as part of this wonderful country of different faiths and beliefs" ("'Sister Wives' Stars Win Legal Victory" 2013). The Browns' attorney, Jonathan Turley, further opined, "It is a victory not for polygamy but privacy in America" ("Legal Victory for Sister Wives" 2013).

As it was soon revealed, the ruling on bigamy also became a test case for marriage rights, and within one week, Utah—the most consistently conservative state in the nation—began issuing same-sex marriage licenses. Thirteen hundred marriages were performed in roughly three weeks, until the

Utah Supreme Court offered an interim stay that required citizens of Utah to vote on marriage rights through Proposition 3. This shift of marital rights and restrictions from the courts to the voters echoed a similar ruling against same-sex marriage in California in 2008 that was reinforced through the powers of Proposition 8, which prohibited future same-sex marriage rights but could not invalidate marriages that had already taken place ("Prop 8 Documentary" 2014). California's Prop 8 was largely, and at the time surreptitiously, supported by the mainstream Mormon Church in Salt Lake City, which sent its members on a door-to-door crusade across the Golden State to wipe out the right to marital unions between same-sex partners.

While marriage rights for same-sex people in Utah were themselves connected to *United States v. Windsor*, a landmark June 2013 Supreme Court case that invalidated the federal Defense of Marriage Act, the Browns' case inextricably linked Mormonism, polygamy, and same-sex marriage, both judicially and socially. This is fitting given that, as I demonstrate in chapter 3, the Browns and, like them, many other "progressive" polygamous families explicitly take their strategies from what might be thought of as a gay rights handbook for social change, arguing for freedom of choice among consenting adults and obligations for plurality within a democratic republic. In the transmediated archive through which their message of family is communicated—reality show, published memoir, Twitter, Facebook, tabloids, and talk show interviews—the Browns speak of oppression within the mainstream, of living a closeted life, of shouldering shame and retribution due to their beliefs, principles, and manner of loving, of deserving respect and freedom as citizens of the United States.

I use this case as a curtain raiser for a book on gender, sexuality, and mediated Mormonism because it nicely sets the stage for the many themes that come together under the banner of Mormonism. Importantly, in the word "Mormonism" I mean not specific or actual F/LDS people, practices, or histories as much as the multiple stories told and retold about these things. It is thus mediated Mormonism as both an idea (meme) and a way of thinking (analytic) that beats at the heart of my inquiry. I regard Mormonism as a lens for seeing American social investments in the meanings of justice, particularly with respect to identity. I argue in this book that the ideas of what constitute Mormonism—which are distinct from the actual mainstream LDS Church or its many fundamentalist sects' doctrine and social practices—function with rich symbolic meaning. "Mormon" is often used as a code word with respect to gender and sexuality, but the meanings of that code do not always tether to the same concepts. In some cases, "Mormon" means sexually chaste; in other contexts it denotes sexual lasciviousness; in other uses still, the term means sexually bizarre.[6] Gender functions as a similar sliding hermeneutic, given the contrasting expectation that adherents (across both LDS and FLDS groups) be simultaneously free agents and wholly obedient. In all cases, gender, sex, and sexuality speak very clearly about power, including how it is enforced and how it can be modified. Given that these mandates often find themselves enmeshed in cultural materials—from television to Broadway plays to feature films—to reference "Mormon" is to reinforce its various meanings as a hermeneutic that is ironically separate from yet wholly identified with the church/es and their followers, however broadly identified.

This American-born religion, conceived in the mind of its charismatic prophet, Joseph Smith, and nicknamed Mormon for its holy text the Book of Mormon, believes in love, optimism, meritocracy, family unity, hard work, and the ultimate form of gendered upward aspirationalism, whereby a man might inherit his own world and himself become a God. It is American through and through (even, one might argue, in its provocative polytheism). And yet Mormons have long held a contentious place in the American scene. From the very beginning in 1830, Joseph and his increasing flock of impassioned followers were perceived as threats to the establishment order, even amid a nineteenth-century backdrop of American religiosity, the Second Great Awakening, that fostered a number of new religions, from the Owenites (dedicated to separatist utopian socialism) to the Oneida Perfectionists (dedicated to sexual egalitarianism, or the idea that all men could be married to all women, and thus sex within marriage did not require monogamy). Mormonism struck its own rancorous chords for the way it consolidated the Saints into voting blocs, recruited new members, and formed monopolies in business and real estate. Throughout the early 1830s, there were also reports of "strange marital customs" among the Mormons, rumors of polygamy that threatened the staunch bourgeois sexual sensibilities of the American mainstream. As Nancy Cott's (2002) *Public Vows* illustrates, eighteenth- and nineteenth-century America created an ideological template whereby monogamy was linked to civilization and barbary to polygamy. This contract had deep roots in the U.S. political order and fed much of the antipathy toward Mormons. It was not LDS separatism, then, but a refusal to be separate combined with Mormons' popular and political influence and perceived disruption of mainstream moralities and governmental systems that upset the townspeople in Missouri, Ohio, and Illinois. This, in turn, triggered mutual violence, persecution, and death (including that of Smith in 1844) and ultimately forced the Saints to venture westward to Salt Lake.

In this, sex and gender mores have often marked the battle lines that offer intelligibility to Mormonism, shaping its headlines and branding its identity as played out through America's newly forming mass media, from penny dreadfuls and tabloids to the lecture circuit and the nation's august papers of record. In *Selling God*, R. Laurence Moore's capacious discussion of American religion and the marketplace of culture, he contends, "Mormonism served the 1840s until the end of the nineteenth century as a serialized best-seller for American readers, a story tantalizingly released over several decades in a multiplicity of ephemeral and diverse texts" such as pamphlets, memoirs, and tell-all exposés (1995, 128). For a nineteenth-century culture that often did not directly speak of sexuality but was deeply fascinated by it, the Mormon practice of plural marriage "gave Americans a rare opportunity to talk openly and publicly about sex" (128–29). "What people wanted," Moore claims, "was less the truth about the Mormons and other groups than a way to imagine sexual misconduct without feeling guilty about it" (134). Indeed, nineteenth-century versions of mediated Mormonism allowed just the right combination of religiosity and sexual nonconformity that might provide the "material for 'sensational' discourse" (129). Importantly, notes Moore, "Mormonism was not merely a new religion. It was a new religion that owed its success to cheap newspapers and their aggressive editors who relied upon controversy to stimulate public demand for their product" (128).

While Moore limits the cultural work of mediated Mormonism to the end of the nineteenth century, the dynamic is still going strong. The concept of Mormonism allows people not only to talk about sex, as Moore claims, but also to sort through complicated arguments with respect to gender, race, religion, nationalism, separation, and belonging. As one example, often in contemporary American culture, to speak of Mormons (both fundamentalist and mainstream) is also to invoke anxieties about Muslims, particularly in the fused fascination and fear that attach to religions that ascribe to orthodox practices around community, clothing, sexuality, food consumption, alcohol prohibition, and the possibilities for polygamy. Indeed, the mediascape is fascinated by the fact that both Muslims and Mormons anticipate heavenly rewards for righteous men meted out in the currency of desirable women. As a consequence, more than one mediated text refers to the Fundamentalist Latter-day Saints as the American Taliban and to its leader, Warren Jeffs, as the Mormon Osama bin Laden.[7] But the popular culture ties between

Mormons and Muslims are not exclusive to the FLDS. Indeed, in April 2017, a group of seven mainstream Mormon scholars made national news when they filed an amicus brief in the Ninth Circuit Court of Appeals, seeking to strike down Donald Trump's travel ban. Noted Carol Kuruvilla (2017), writing for the *Huffington Post*, "The scholars reached back into history to draw a striking parallel between how the United States government treated Mormons in the past and how Muslims are treated today.... Together, they urged the Court to make sure 'history does not repeat itself.'" As moments like these attest, Mormonism functions as a pulse point for the beating heart of America and its complex history with respect to race and religion.

This "peculiar people," as the Saints call themselves due to their separation from mainstream and non-Mormon—or Gentile—ways, continue to occupy a distinct location, particularly with respect to gender and sexuality. As the editors of *Mormon Feminism* write, "From its polygamous nineteenth-century past to its twentieth-century stand against the Equal Rights Amendment and its twenty-first-century fight against same-sex marriage, the Church of Jesus Christ of Latter-day Saints has consistently positioned itself on the frontlines of battles over gender-related identities, roles, and rights" (Brooks, Steenblik, and Wheelwright 2015, back cover).[8] Indeed, just as Joseph Smith used magical stones to decipher the meanings of golden tablets and thus to write the Book of Mormon, we might think of Mormonism as an interpretive guide, or even a touchstone, bigger than itself. As with touchstones of old—pieces of flint used to test the purity of gold or silver by the streak left on the stone when rubbed by the metal—Mormonism provides a ready tool through which we might assess the quality of a thing. That thing here is nothing short of cultural mores about the meanings of gender justice.

All of these dynamics, both tacit and overt, require the rich archive of contemporary media for their sustenance and saturation—a transmediated palimpsest of media platforms that I refer to as latter-day screens. Indeed, in this mixture of media forms and types—from big-budget feature films to independent documentaries and reality television, from memoirs and novels distributed by major publishing houses to books made available by vanity presses, from globally distributed television fare to local-access and amateur video production picked up and redistributed through video sharing services such as YouTube and Keek—mediated Mormonism itself provides a unique perspective on the size, shape, and expanse of modern media as well as the implications of gendered selfhood and modern standards of justice.

The vast cultural archive by and about Mormonism serves as a lens through which to perceive a distinctively gendered turn in the semiotics of value, from those more masculine (emphasizing tropes of rationalism, individualism, domination, authoritarianism, accomplishment, and competition) to those more aligned with queer-positive and feminist-friendly politics (emphasizing collaboration, liberation, and community). In this, I hope my book demonstrates the civil rights adage made resonant through Dr. Martin Luther King, Jr. that the "arc of the moral universe is long but it bends toward justice."[9]

This is quite an audacious claim, I realize, given the conservative constitution of F/LDS peoples. While progressive Mormons do exist, the mainstream LDS Church has consistently proven itself antifeminist and antigay through such edicts as the excommunication of the three greatest threats to the church: LGBT+ peoples, feminists, and intellectuals.[10] Most fundamentalist strains of the church fare no better, with pronouncements against people of color and sexual permissiveness. And though, as I have noted, fundamentalist Mormons do not follow the mandates of the Salt Lake City brethren, the great melting pot of the mediascape cooks LDS and FLDS in the same complicated stew, where one metonymically stands in for all, even while this same mediascape has afforded a degree of specificity and clarity to individual voices that has never before been possible. The attempt among progressive Mormon scholars to undo a Muslim ban notwithstanding, it is perhaps further difficult to believe that a conservative religious group might be the tipping point for dialogues on social justice in a Trumpian world, where forces of xenophobia, racism, sexism, and intolerance have found such a ready toehold in the mainstream operations of governmental and social power.

And truly, the progressive results of mediated Mormonism surprised me. When I first began to analyze the evidence, I was expecting to find something entirely different. But time after time, I encountered the antigay, anti–working woman, and highly conservative tropes that attach to mediated Mormonism, only to see their representation open conversations that advocated more progressive and pluralistic standards for justice. Contesting orthodoxy here produced progressive clarity. I want to be clear that I do not argue that Mormons themselves—as individuals or a group—are necessarily more liberally inclined. Instead, I contend that the amalgamation of materials that turns on Mormonism as a trope—and public conversation about those texts—has had the effect of opening more channels for progressivism, by which I mean a pluralized, diverse, and polylogic regard toward meaning and identity. This consequence is largely due to the social issues that attach to Mormonism—specifically, sexual economies, gender roles, raced and gendered power relations, same-sex attraction, forms of kinship, the meanings of immigration, and the obligations of families and communities to provide sanctuary—and to the proliferation and spread of media in the last twenty years.

It is my intention that the entirety of this book will illustrate such a hopeful claim about mediated Mormonism as a gauge for and accelerant of social justice, but a more specific example can be seen in the upswell of mediated Mormonism contesting the church's anti-LGBT+ stance. It is no secret that both mainstream and fundamentalist Mormons perceive "traditional" marriage (which is not always to say monogamy) as the cornerstone of their divine architecture as lived on earth. According to Mormon doctrine that I will explain in greater detail through this book, exaltation into the highest of heavens, the Celestial Kingdom, requires many acts of devotion and privation. Chief among these as Joseph Smith first revealed is the mandate that men marry at least three women, so that he and his wives might propagate an eternal world where he rules as God. While the commandment to live plural marriage was revised in 1890 (at least from the point of view of mainstream Saints), the commitment to polygamous marriage carries forward in both the mainstream and fundamentalist understandings of life after death. Those who are not heterosexual refute this design. Or as Emily Pearson more candidly puts it in the documentary *8: The Mormon Proposition* (2010), "Gays upset the Mormon plan for heaven." Pearson's life is intricately interwoven between LDS and LGBT+, a fact I discuss more in chapter 6.

The Mormons are not, of course, the only religious group opposed to gay rights, but their commitments to big families through heterosexual union have translated into larger politically contentious positions—for instance, in 2008 actively funding the drive to strike down California's Proposition 8, which allowed for same-sex marriage, and in 2015 declaring that children raised in LGBT+ homes would be disallowed from church membership until they were eighteen and had left the family home. In turn, teen suicide among LGBT+ youth in Utah has risen precipitously since 2008, a fact that has inspired many progressive Mormons, former Mormons, and non-Mormons to take action through support groups such as Mama Dragons (mothers of LGBT+ youth) and The Progressive Mormons (a website organized around inclusion and diversity) or documentaries such as *8: The Mormon Proposition* and *Believer* (2018). Indeed, both documentaries suggest precisely why political agitation around church doctrine matters—since the church's own history allows for significant, even massive, juridical change, as evidenced, primarily, by the divine revelations in 1890 to cease polygamy and in 1978 to allow black people to become members of the church and black men to hold priesthood status. Further, good Mormons have been trained by their church to speak out against what they consider unjust. Dan Reynolds, the lead singer of Imagine Dragons and one of the executive producers of *Believer*, reflects after the church's continuance of its anti-LGBT+ positions that he is resolved to out-Mormon the Mormon Church:

> There's one thing my Mormon values have taught me since I was young. It's that no matter what the world says about who you are, what you believe, still do it. A hundred percent. That spirit was the spirit that carried me through my mission. I felt like I was baring my truth regardless what anyone thought about me. That's all because of Mormonism and my parents, they all prepped me for this moment now. A determined Mormon is a scary thing, I will tell you that. Because they don't stop. I knocked a hundred doors to get into one door. I knocked a thousand doors on my mission. If there's one thing I can guarantee it's that I will continue to knock this door until somebody answers. (Argott 2018)

In 2019, LDS leaders announced a new revelation: LGBT+ Saints would no longer be apostates, though they are still considered sinners. The ruling did not sanction same-sex marriage and still bans extramarital sexuality. Media have been a clarion call for gender justice, yet there is more to be done.

The fundamentalist Brown family also offers a ready example of the feminist-friendly and queer-positive consequence of Mormonism as a meme and analytic, since the phenomenon that they represent (an oppressed marginal group forcing themselves into the public sphere to counter damaging stereotypes) has itself become a flashpoint for conversations and legislative advancement that constitutes an agenda for progressive social change. While it is noteworthy that the Browns speak in liberal terms about acceptance of others, it is not necessary that they be so inclined for the public discourse that attaches to them to have this effect. As one case in point, for instance, the putative opposite of Kody Brown is Warren Jeffs, the imprisoned president and prophet of the FLDS, made famous for trafficking in women, raping children, exiling boys and men, and engaging in sex parties (what he called "heavenly sessions") with his underaged brides at his temple in Texas. In 2006, Jeffs gained the notorious distinction of being the number one person on the FBI's ten most-wanted list. He is now serving life plus twenty years in federal prison. By most accounts—including and especially those of the Browns and other modern polygamous families—Jeffs constitutes evil incarnate, the personification of a combined egomania and perversity, fed by assurances of absolute godlike authority. One couldn't really find a less liberal, fluid, or progressive leader than Warren Jeffs. And yet his place in the mediascape demarcates something that he himself would never endorse, since the public conversation about Jeffs very much works to establish a protocol for social justice that gives women authority over their own bodies and all people the right to self-governance, a point I discuss at greater length in chapter 4.

In terms of mediated stories of this type, I would argue that both as a real person and a mediated figure, the polygamist patriarch steeped in his own perverse privilege and extreme egotism signifies deeply for a culture needing to work through the meanings of justice, religious commitment, fanaticism, intolerance, sexual regulation, and malignant narcissism. And this process works against monologic orthodoxies that allow for only one version of truth. That such a politically liberal and, frankly, optimistic outcome is possible in and through one of the more socially conservative religions, a religion premised on the imminent end of times—the latter days—is precisely what makes this study both fascinating and worth doing.

Mediated Mormonism, in Context

From Victorian pulp serials and early twentieth-century silent films that depicted Mormonism as a dangerous cult to Mormon-produced magazines and documentaries that feature the religion's zeal for international proselytizing and conversion, media have served as the chief tool for spreading the word of and the fear about the Church of Jesus Christ of Latter-day Saints, both by the Saints themselves and by a broader Gentile culture. This is perhaps fitting given that the prominence of Mormonism now can well be attributed to its birth at the nexus of American nineteenth-century media culture. Smith and his supporters (predominantly Martin Harris) took full advantage of the rise of cheap paper, ready printing presses, and close proximity to the Erie Canal, which was under construction at the moment of the discovery of the holy plates and would soon become the distribution superhighway of the time. Indeed, the banks of the Erie Canal are easily visible from the back door of the Grandin Print Shop in Palmyra, New York, where the Book of Mormon was first published. Fawn M. Brodie, Smith's biographer, astutely notes, "Joseph Smith dared to found a new religion in the age of printing. When he said, 'Thus saith the Lord!' the words were copied down by secretaries and congealed forever into print" (1995, vii). One might argue that media made Mormonism.

It has surely sustained it. As I briefly discuss in the prologue, from its founding to the early part of the twentieth century, Mormons were regarded with a mixture of what Mary Campbell terms "fascination, distaste, and outright horror" (2016, 29), largely due to their separatism and adoption of polygamy. Mormons, and through them the territory of Utah (statehood was conferred in 1896) were referenced in "Orientalizing vocabulary" of the "seraglio," "concubine," "Sultan," "Moslem," "Mohamed," "Turk," and "Arab," invoking racialized fears of a homegrown otherness (Campbell 2016, 31). Countering this notion required recasting the mold of Mormonism, using the powers of media to re-create Mormons as the very epitome of "civilized, cultured, and cosmopolitan" and thus, as the model of an idealized notion of American citizen (Campbell 2016, 23). As a consequence, the twentieth century saw a rise in Mormon-produced films, often called Mollywood, and television, which lead journalist Rollo Romig to quip, "Mormons are the filmmakingest of all faiths" (2012).

Media has also served a proselytizing message. In 1934, for example, Elder Joseph F. Merrill (1934, 568) wrote in the *Millennial Star* that "favourable publicity will open many doors now closed to the Gospel message," a publicity that church leaders cultivated in order to counter the negative stereotypes promulgated about Mormons by "evil people" (Neilson 2011, 2). In *The Book of Mormon: A Biography*, Paul Gutjahr (2012) notes the extraordinary measures that the mainstream Mormon Church has demonstrated in its efforts to disseminate Mormonism throughout the world, both in its relentless production and translation of their primary religious text, the Book of Mormon (presently available in 107 languages), and in the church's worldwide network of 55,000 Mormon missionaries made famous through a host of mediated fare. And lest we argue that Mormonism is anything but capacious in how it understands either media or proselytizing, *The Washington Post* reported a new variant—vending machines paid for by the Mormon Church that allow people to purchase "good things" as donations for various world charities (Iati 2018). After three weeks in operation in December 2018, the "giving machines," as they are called, had generated $1.3 million to be collected and redistributed by the church. These vending machines are not only altruistic; they serve a secondary purpose of evangelizing through image management. The article quotes a Mormon named Anthony: "A lot of times when people think about our faith, they think about the missionaries traipsing door to door and trying to change you in some way." The vending machines, by contrast, "can help non-church members better understand the religion's emphasis on serving others."

The media history of the American regard toward Mormons is vast, yet this present moment is unprecedented in terms of a U.S. fascination with and fear of Mormon people and practices, in some part aided by having in 2012 two Republican Mormon candidates, Mitt Romney and Jon Huntsman Jr., vying for the presidency of the United States (perhaps mirroring the religion's founder, Joseph Smith, who was a candidate for president in 1844).[11] These developments, joined with the 2002 Salt Lake City Winter Olympics, the 2002 Elizabeth Smart abduction, the 2008 raid on the Yearning for Zion Ranch, the 2012 arrest and conviction of FLDS leader Warren Jeffs, and the 2008 silent effort by the Utah-based Mormon Church to block gay marriage—and the public blowback the church experienced when this political machination was exposed—have all compelled the LDS Church to become more savvy in its public relations efforts. Thus, in 2011, the mainstream LDS Church launched an insistent internet and television PR campaign, "I'm a Mormon," featuring "Mormons with diverse backgrounds" who "share details about their everyday lives and their deep commitment to Jesus Christ," many of whom, conveniently, are beautiful models or successful professional athletes (Mormon Channel 2018). Radio podcasts and social media sites like Facebook and Twitter are also becoming increasingly popular new modalities through which to extend the message and image of Mormonism, at the same time as the internet has provoked a crisis of faith amid many LDS adherents (Goodstein 2013).

In this postmillennial moment, Mormonism exerts a strong fascination, as augmented by LDS cultural producers such as science fiction writer Orson Scott Card, fantasy fiction author Stephenie Meyer (writer of the *Twilight* books), or self-help and business management guru Stephen Covey (author of *The Seven Habits of Highly Effective People*)—to name just three—whose popular and seemingly religious ideology–neutral books solidly articulate a world of conventional gender patterns and orderly, optimistic ways of being, even for vampires. Brigham Young University Television (BYUTV) and BYU radio are now staples on most expanded cable or satellite packages, offering all subscribers programming such as *The District* (a reality series about missionaries) and *Studio C* (a sketch comedy show). In addition, BYUTV airs feature films such as *The Best Two Years* (2004) or *It's Latter-day Night! Live* (2003), produced by Halestorm Entertainment, which specializes in Mormon-themed media.[12]

In many ways, this insistent strain of Mormon-made cultural production takes very seriously a mandate in 1952 that LDS members actively engage in politics, the arts, and social services, so as to increase the prominence and visibility of the church more broadly. In this new millennium, being an active and visible thought leader often means running for office and living one's LDS principles publicly. As one example, Arizona senator Jeff Flake earned equal parts praise (from liberals and middle-ground conservatives) and opprobrium (from hard-line conservatives) when in 2017 he excoriated Donald Trump, declaring in a resignation speech from the U.S. Senate that he "would not be complicit" with "the indecency of our discourse," the "coarseness of our leadership," and the "compromise of our moral authority." He continued, "We must never regard as 'normal' the regular and casual undermining of our democratic norms and ideals. We must never meekly accept the daily sundering of our country—the personal attacks, the threats against principles, freedoms, and institutions, the flagrant disregard for truth or decency, the reckless provocations, most often for the pettiest and most personal reasons, reasons having nothing whatsoever to do with the fortunes of the people that we have all been elected to serve." Flake rose again as an independent thought leader when in 2018 he refused to follow his party in the confirmation of Supreme Court justice nominee Brett Kavanaugh until allegations of sexual assault had been more thoroughly investigated. While these stances need not be solely inspired by Flake's identity as a devout Mormon, one might readily discern Mormonism's adherence to a higher, better truth. Indeed, Flake's larger persona, what we might call his star text, is a monumental tribute to Mormonism, and the many forms of mediation that he engages in offer a mighty testimony to the religion—from speeches gone viral (like that cited above) to his memoir (*Conscience of a Conservative*) to radio programs (Zoe Chase's radio features on *This American Life*) to reality television (*Rival Survival*, in which Flake lives out his survivalist skills on a deserted island in a bipartisan effort with Democratic senator Martin Heinrich). Writing for *The Atlantic*, McKay Coppins (2017) describes Flake as "almost suspiciously good-natured" and possessing "preternatural niceness." Similarly, David Brooks (2017) describes Flake as being "sunny and kind," possessing a "serene courage" in a time when "politics has become a blood sport." "Assume the best. Look for the good"—it's a bromide often repeated when talking about Flake. This resolute pleasantness is coupled with a bulldog tenacity and unbending adherence to an ethical code, qualities that resonate with the associations evoked by the Mormon missionary.[13] Describing Flake as having grown up in a "giant Mormon family," Coppins (2017) quotes him in language that combines Flake's Mormon ancestors and the country's founders: "You can always find an excuse to not stand up for your principles. But if you don't risk anything, it doesn't matter as much." Here Flake's call to principle reinforces the masculinist qualities of resistance, independence, and fortitude that are believed to be the lodestone of American national character and make of Flake, in Brooks's words, the epitome of the "ideal public servant."[14]

There are other, equally gendered, ways for Mormons to live out their ideals in the broad spotlight of the contemporary mediascape. Sustaining a blog post is one of these. In fact, blogging is so common within the fundamentalist and mainstream churches that it constitutes a genre of social media, the Bloggernacle. The website Mormon Archipelago catalogs more than two hundred different blogs that constitute the ever-growing territory of the Mormon blogosphere, from big islands like By Common Consent to atolls like Mormon Life Hacker. By far, the most prominent land masses in the archipelago are linked together under a broader term that we might call lifestyle blogging, which includes mommy blogs and beauty blogs (and, increasingly, vlogs). Indeed, the domination of these sites by Mormons is a bit of an open secret, made visible in places like the mainstream beauty magazine *Allure*, which provides the answer to that age-old question: "Why are so many of your favorite beauty personalities Mormon?" The reason, says author Alice Gregory, is because lifestyle blogging reinforces notions of conventional gender attributes in women, particularly physical beauty, and this, in turn, ties directly to one's heavenly reward, in a logic of spiritual neoliberalism that I discuss in chapter 1. Gregory (2017) quotes Courtney Kendrick: "When you come from a patriarchal religion, your best bet for gaining power is to be appealing to the men in charge. It can be very hard for women who are outside of normative standards of beauty. In my religion you're not just asking about having to look good now. You're also talking about your eternal salvation. Ultimately these beauty standards are connected to what gets us into heaven." Gregory also notes that lifestyle blogging quite literally puts a good face on the religion itself, making "Mormonism look not just normal but enviable." This stance echoes Campbell's comments, through the figure of early twentieth-century LDS photographer Charles Ellis, about the LDS public relations machine historically and the workings of mediated Mormonism more broadly since media of this type cast "the Latter-day Saints as models of high cultural achievement and refinement, icons of modern American citizenship for the larger country to admire and even emulate instead of indict" (2016, 18). In the process, mediation such as this helps to fold "the church itself and its followers in the national body politic" (18), so that to speak of Mormonism is already to work through an idiom of Americanness.

Yet it is not only BYU-based media or independent production houses that have found Mormonism a rich vein for mining. Mainstream feature films such as *The Other Side of Heaven* (2001), produced by 3Mark Entertainment and distributed by Walt Disney Pictures, recounts the coming of age of Mormon boys through the mission process (and stars television actor Christopher Gorham and Academy Award winner Anne Hathaway). Best-sellers from major publishing houses such as Joanna Brooks's *The Book of Mormon Girl* (Free Press, a division of Simon & Schuster, 2012), Elna Baker's *The New York Regional Mormon Singles Halloween Dance* (Plume, a division of Penguin, 2010), and Nicole Hardy's *Confessions of a Latter-day Virgin* (Hyperion, 2013) offer "wickedly funny" and "homespun" witticisms about growing up Mormon in a non-Mormon society. Mormonism also relies on other major distributors, like Sony Pictures or Penguin, to forward their brand as a repository of family-friendly entertainment and educational media products. Conversely, as the *New York Times* noted, when Hollywood wants "good clean fun," it goes to "Mormon Country" for its writers, producers, and actors (Mooallem 2013). We've clearly come a long way from celebrity Mormons Donny and Marie Osmond and their homespun, toothy television show that ran on ABC from 1976 to 1979, though Donny and Marie continue to be fixtures of contemporary media thanks to YouTube, Las Vegas, and reality television, particularly *Dancing with the Stars*.

It's worth asking if Mormonism is alone in providing this touchstone on the nature of the object. Do other religions offer a similar set of optics or modes of understanding? Not to equivocate, but the answer is yes and no. Certainly, all religions function both as things and as ideas of things, as both signifier and signified. And many other religious traditions, for instance Judaism and Islam, have experienced and continue to experience parallel events—such as persecution, misunderstanding, and outright bigotry—that make their self-definition as marginalized outsiders similar to the F/LDS. Other religions, for instance Catholicism or evangelical Christianity, are also male governed and patriarchal; and other religions contain strong wellsprings for reform, tolerance, and renewal operating within them. Finally, other faith groups are American born and steeped in secrecy, with strong charismatic leaders, stringent rule cultures, and mandatory proselytizing. Some, like Scientology, have also fostered a significant amount of mediation. But no single religion carries all of these markers save the Mormons. And indeed, I would argue that the closest partner in the kind of cultural work the Mormon Church performs is not another religion at all but an entity such as the Boy Scouts of America or the United States Chamber of Commerce, two ideologically conservative enterprises that fly under the cover of patriotism and free-market principles to become what Alyssa Katz terms "influence machines" (Katz 2015; see also Jordan 2016).[15]

One final note on Mormonism and cultural influence, and this has to do with the regulation of the physical body that is so critical to the Mormon project. As with many faith-based organizations bent on purity, F/LDS Mormons are barred from any sexual activity outside of heterosexual marriage, its members pledged to virginity before marriage and monogamy after. While not all Mormons marry, marriage is required for heavenly advancement. As I elaborate in my discussion in chapter 6, the LDS Church does not recognize non-normative sexualities, though certainly Mormons possessing these desires and identities exist. Among fundamentalist groups, only heterosexual unions are permitted, and of these, only those that are sanctioned and called into being by the prophet are allowed. Often this might mean one man being joined in union with multiple wives, some of these merely girls. The higher the status of the man, the more wives he receives. Typically, fundamentalist cultures not only disallow but exile Saints who break the rules of the larger sexual economy, though more progressive families work out different accommodations—*Sister Wives*' Mariah Brown's coming out as lesbian at the end of Season 12 in 2017 thus stands as another moment of ground-breaking television with respect to Mormonism and progressive values. Within both mainstream and fundamentalist systems, certain (unwed) Mormons are never allowed officially to be sexual, and all Mormons might experience their sexuality only through church-sanctioned means. These tensions in the context of broader initiatives for gay rights and the purported transgender tipping point allow Mormonism to function as a place of critical mass with regard to sexuality studies in the mediascape.

Making the matters of the relation between religion and justice all the more germane, Mormonism is also a faith, unlike most other major religions, that builds flux and change into its very code of being. There are thirteen Articles of Faith to which LDS adherents subscribe. These are fairly standard declarations, particularly for those sects considering themselves to be Christian, such as "#1. We believe in God, the Eternal Father, and in his Son, Jesus Christ, and in the Holy Ghost." But the ninth Article of Faith sets the Mormons apart: "We believe all that God has revealed, all that He does now reveal, and we believe that He will yet reveal many great and important things pertaining to the Kingdom of God" ("Articles of Faith" 2018). This ninth article marks the faith as always about potentiality. It is ever possible that the church may change its stance. New revelations may come and have come to the church's prophets. In a twentieth-century social context, perhaps the most dramatic revelation was heralded in 1978, when the three members of the First Presidency, Spencer W. Kimball, N. Eldon Tanner, and Marion G. Romney, announced a new revelation on priesthood that allowed male members of black African descent to function as priesthood holders (see chapter 2). It's important to note, here, that these hopes for change as voiced in mediated Mormonism are always for more inclusivity and tolerance, not greater restriction and orthodoxy.

It is this very capacity for not only fluidity but downright reversal that allows outlying Mormons to be ever hopeful that divine revelation might allow for their legitimate inclusion in what they perceive to be the One True Church. As a character in one of Johnny Townsend's short stories on gay themes thinks to himself: "In the past, polygamy was a commandment. In the past, interracial marriage was against church teachings, and Blacks couldn't hold the priesthood. It was *possible* that at some future date, the prophet would have a revelation accepting homosexuality. At every General Conference, Jason waited to hear the announcement. But the words never came" (2009, 31).[16]

In practical terms, Boyd Packer's enemies of the church—"feminists, homosexuals, and intellectuals"—are a particularly literate group to alienate (Packer 1993). Indeed, I'd argue that this outward suppression of a significant group of highly educated and politically active people massively contributes to the aliveness of the Mormon mediascape in the present moment. Contemporary mainstream Mormons joke about those who leave the church but can't leave it alone, meaning the apostates who write memoirs denouncing the church or who build websites intent on incriminating the church. But put simply, there are a lot of people needing to process what they've experienced in relation to the F/LDS experience particularly and about conservative religious culture more broadly.[17] The expanded platforms for publication, internet conversation, and video capture and broadcast make it incredibly easy to put one's voice in the public sphere and to make common cause with others who, in an earlier time, would have been isolated and bereft of community.

How to Date a Mormon: Gender and Sexuality on Latter-day Screens

WikiHow offers a nine-step tutorial on how to date a Mormon, seemingly intended for the white, straight Gentile boy who is interested in the white, pure Mormon girl ("How to Date a Mormon" 2015). Their pointers include such admonitions as being open to prayer, refraining from consuming alcohol, tobacco, and caffeinated products, behaving modestly and respectfully (particularly to her parents), and remaining open to converting if marriage is a likely outcome of the romance. Point number 7, "Understand the Law of Chastity," offers the most detailed set of injunctions. The broader rule is "no sex before marriage," but just so everyone can be clear, the post details a series of other unacceptable forms of eroticism. Partners may not:

- Participate in passionate kissing.
- Lie on top of the other person.
- Touch private parts of another person's body with or without clothing.
- View pornography, before or after marriage. Viewing pornography is not acceptable, ever.
- Arouse sexual emotions in any way except having relations with their spouse, not even watching movies with nudity.

And while this advice is meant to cover the mainstream church's philosophy of regulation, it very much echoes the FLDS reality television father, Kody Brown, who tells his daughter and her boyfriend, "Kissing can be very dangerous. When you kiss, the person that you kiss, their hormones go into your mouth and it registers certain things that stimulate both the heart and the body for other reasons." While some might credit Brown for being familiar with the oxytocin hypothesis, his statements on the dangers of kissing have been picked up and rebroadcast throughout the world as "bizarre" ("'Kissing Can Be Very Dangerous'" 2014).

Tip number 9 of the WikiHow instruction, showing an attractive man and woman standing in front of the Salt Lake City Temple in silhouette, is illustrated by a wedding photo clearly drawn from teenage vampire juggernaut *Twilight: Breaking Dawn* (2011), here making Mormonism as a meme quite literal (see figures I.1 and I.2). As I have already mentioned, Stephenie Meyer, the author of the *Twilight* books, is a practicing Mormon, who lives in my hometown of Mesa, Arizona, and her best-selling trilogy detailing the star-crossed love between a vampire boy Edward and a human girl Bella has riveted millions. I wouldn't be the first to suggest that the code of chastity between Bella and Edward—a no-sex-before-marriage policy meant to keep him from eviscerating her with his monstrous strength—is a lightly veiled rendition of the Mormon law of chastity, as is their steamy postmarital sexual experience that results in the destruction of their beachside bedroom. Indeed, Edward's superhuman strength, Bella's conversion to vampirism, their resulting capacity to live as a family in perpetuity, and the fact that Edward is able (even as a member of the undead) to father a child, all evoke the broader codes of mediated Mormonism, which maintain not only that families can be sealed for all eternity, but that righteous fathers will become Gods, and the birthing of children will continue to take place in heaven, though only at the celestial level. The film version of Edward and Bella's honeymoon in *Breaking Dawn* actually features a canopy bed with long diaphanous white netting, thus allowing Bella and Edward in their romantic foreplay to flirt with the idea of going through the veil, an important part of the supersecret Mormon marriage sealing ordinance.[18] Indeed, I would argue that the parallels between the vampire idyll and the Mormon ideal are so strong that instead of being depicted in front of falling white flowers, Bella and Edward's wedding picture would be more appropriate if they too had the Salt Lake City Temple as their backdrop. Given these connections, it is perhaps fitting that this advice—for the Gentile boy and the Mormon girl, for the vampire boy and the human girl—is communicated through WikiHow and illustrated by *Twilight*, thus cementing a code of chastity and Mormonism in the popular culture imagination.

I will return to *Twilight* in chapter 2 on race, but here I want to focus more on the regulation of the body, which is so critical to Mormonism. Through the Word of Wisdom, a law of health revealed to Joseph Smith in 1833, members are expected to uphold a tight regulation of the body's desire. They are restricted from consuming alcohol, tobacco products, tea and coffee, and illegal drugs, though perhaps in reaction to these strict mandates, the strongly Mormon state of Utah leads the nation in prescription drug abuse ("Prevalence of Prescription Drug Abuse" 2012), antidepressant use (Leonard 2010), and candy consumption (Stephenson 2015). At the age of maturity—for boys, typically around eighteen, before the start of a mission, and for girls, typically before marriage—worthy adherents experience a temple endowment ceremony, which obligates Saints to the lifelong and perpetual wearing of garments, or holy Mormon underwear, a constant reminder of the regulated body's role in living a pure life that might qualify one for godly things. Many believe these garments have supernatural capacities to protect the wearer from evil spirits, fires, and even bullets. Garments also work to shield all erogenous zones of the body (and then some), since they cover the body from shoulder to thigh.

Mormons are not the only religion to put a high premium on righteous virginity, of course, and thus many conservative religions have earned a reputation as agents of repression and sexual frustration: think chastity belts,

FIG. I.1 "How to Date a Mormon" (2015, WikiHow).

FIG. I.2 Edward and Bella, *Twilight: Breaking Dawn: Part I.*

vestal virgins, immaculate conceptions, semi-celibate clergy, and dire pronouncements about the sin of spilling one's seed. But even in the age of reality television's fascination with religious extremism, recent Catholic pedophilic sex scandals, or evangelical Christian father-daughter purity balls (where fathers vow to be leaders of integrity by serving as celibate boyfriends, and their teenage daughters wear promise rings and lay white roses on a cross as a silent commitment to their sustained sexual purity), Mormonism's brand correlates with tightly regulated sexuality. Elna Baker writes, for instance, about Mormon dances in New York City that require men and women to retain a distance at least as big as "the standard works" between them. "So when you're dancing, the *Old Testament, New Testament, The Book of Mormon, Doctrine and Covenants,* and *Pearl of Great Price* should be able to fit in the space between you and your dance partner—or you're standing too close" (Baker 2010). In spite of the fact that Baker talks about this imposed distance between young desiring bodies with humor, the message is seriously rendered through her memoir as a whole: Mormonism mandates your absolute allegiance to the governance and suppression of bodily appetites, be that sexuality or cigarettes. Violating the Word of Wisdom is a slippery slope toward disloyalty to the entire faith.

The mandate placed on sexual purity was made all the more poignant when in 2013, ten years after her highly publicized abduction by a fundamentalist Mormon zealot intent on making the teenage girl his second wife, Elizabeth Smart spoke about why she had not tried to flee her kidnapper. She noted that her Mormon upbringing encouraged her to feel worthless due to her sexual experience, even in the case of rape. "Why would it even be worth screaming out?" Smart asked. "Why would it even make a difference if you are rescued? Your life still has no value" (Dominguez 2013). Smart's words raised a furor in the Mormon blogosphere, something I first became aware of when my outraged Mormon friends from high school began posting Facebook updates by the dozens, indignant that Smart would blame the church's stance on sexuality for her victimization. I saw only one blog post that readily acknowledged the emotionally coercive tactics that are often part of a young Mormon girl's religious and social education. Joanna Brooks wrote:

> We celebrate new official LDS Church curriculum for Mormon young women that eradicates the old chastity object lessons, even as we know that clearing them from Mormon culture will take much, much longer. . . . We're still not doing young women in Mormonism many

favors in the way we teach sexuality and particularly in a hyper-emphasis on modesty in dress that has emerged in many Mormon communities.

And then we read Elizabeth Smart, and we find ourselves once again in that place, that place of deadly stillness, that paralysis, that we lived in during those weeks in late spring 2002. When we wondered why she couldn't just run. But inside we already knew. (Brooks 2013)

In the larger mediascape, it is not just female chastity but the insistence that mainstream unmarried Mormon men must be sexually celibate that generates incredulity and also serves as the primary point of tension in any number of the mediated texts I examine here. This fascination with repressed sexuality for men, including the belief that it is not natural for men to thwart their sexuality, exerts itself in a range of materials, from *BuckleRoos Part II* (2004), a gay porn romp where sexually naive Mormon missionaries are coached in the ways of man-man sex, to *Tabloid* (2010), Errol Morris's documentary about the 1970s media circus that surrounded the abduction and rape of a male American Mormon missionary serving in England. In true Morris fashion, the documentary weaves a compelling narrative of confusion, where fiction and reality have an ambivalent relation to one another. But one major theme of the film amplifies the idea that the strict sexual economies of Mormonism preclude the possibility that a missionary might admit his willing participation in a sexual liaison (whether heterosexual or homosexual) for fear that he would be excommunicated for his sinful acts.

Lest we think these are exclusively the devices of fiction or artsy documentary, the notorious Mormon Murder Case (also known as the Jodi Arias trial) put the same ideas front and center as American talking points. In brief, the case centered on the 2008 murder in Mesa, Arizona, of salesman Travis Alexander by his ex-girlfriend Jodi Arias, both of whom were members of the LDS Church, though Alexander converted as a child, and he baptized Arias into the faith in 2007. After changing her story several times, Arias admitted to killing Alexander but said her actions were in self-defense. Arias testified about a complex sex life with Alexander, including oral and anal sex, which Alexander considered to be not real sex and so not against the chastity rules of the church. (Arias and Alexander were not alone in this thinking about forbidden forms of sexuality, as an "oral is moral" refrain from *Big Love* nicely mocked.) The Arias case became a cause célèbre, largely due to the live video feed that ran from the courtroom as well as to the development of a nightly cable show, HLN *after Dark: The Jodi Arias*

Trial, which discussed and dissected each element of the case. An American documentary television series, *48 Hours Mystery*, aired a feature story on the case in 2008, which was then used as evidence in the trial, making the already tenuous line between representation and reality all the more blurry. The *Huffington Post* deemed the case an "over-the-top media-spectacle" (Skoloff and Billeaud 2013) and the *Toronto Star* stated, "With its mix of jealousy, religion, murder, and sex, the Jodi Arias case shows what happens when the justice system becomes entertainment" (Quinn 2013). Postconviction of Arias, the media are still fascinated by the Mormon Murder Case, as evidenced by both a 2013 made-for-TV movie, *Jodi Arias: Dirty Little Secret*, and a 2018 three-part documentary retelling of the story in *Jodi Arias: An American Murder Mystery*.

In the Arias case, both mainstream and new media attention were, and continue to be, galvanized by three things: a woman's violent murder of a man, their steamy nonmarital sex life, and the "confusing conflicts" of a "devout Mormon," as *Radar Online* put it, who led a "secret double life" of rampant non-normative sex and perhaps even pedophilic same-sex attraction (Emery 2013). Tellingly, the devout double-life-living Mormon in question was not the woman, Arias, but the man, Alexander, since somehow his claim to Mormonism was considered more valid than hers. But more specifically, even in the context of Arias's acrobatic accounting of what had happened between herself and Alexander, the scandalous story centered on a grown man, pledged to celibacy before marriage and somehow, the logic went, driven to perverse sexual pleasures in order to claim virgin status. As in the case of Elizabeth Smart, the discursive logic indicated that LDS-induced sexual repression was at the heart of this American crime story.[19]

These sorts of tales about the surreptitious secret (sex) lives led by Mormon men and women make for riveting stories to an America steeped in the histories of Puritan asceticism and masculine heteronormativity. They are one reason why Mormon polygamy stories are so popular in the American mediascape, since polygamy tells the same tale of a regulated sexual economy in reverse. These stories do not ask how a man can stay celibate but how one man can please/service multiple women. The answer on *Big Love* is with Viagra. Indeed, whether the talking points focus on too much sex or too little, these stories allow for a paradigm where sex is central. Temptation stories position Mormons as objective correlatives where Mormon characters work out a nation's preoccupation with indulgence and regulation, with production and consumption, and with the normal and the abnormal, all decipherable through sex acts.

Mediated stories about regulation and repression do not stop with sexuality, of course, but extend to gender. Without apology, Mormonism sustains a politically conservative version of gender relations that idealizes women's nurturing, submissiveness, and other-oriented qualities, in pointed contrast to men's wage-earning potential, familial and church authority, and bravery. There are even nicknames for these idealized positions: Molly Mormon, or MoMo, a woman who is upbeat, church oriented, motherly, and obedient, and Peter Priesthood, a clean-cut man who upholds the stereotypical qualities of Mormon manhood.[20] From Mormon mommy blogs to newspaper feature articles on daring Mormon firefighters, stories abound in the mediascape that reinforce these normative extremes of gender performance as desirable qualities for both women and men.

Perhaps no moment illustrates this idea better than an August 9, 1978, interview Barbara Walters conducted with Donny and Marie Osmond (then twenty and eighteen, respectively; see figure I.3). In what would have aired in primetime to a significant percentage of the media share, Walters reminds her viewers, "To understand the Osmonds is to know that they are Mormons: Honor thy father and thy mother, family first, a strict code of conduct." In her interview, she directs the siblings over the heated terrain of both civil rights and the Equal Rights Amendment, asking about the church's refusal to allow black priests and women's status in the home and church. Donny fields the question on race, saying he is no authority, but he also isn't prejudiced. "They [black men] are not allowed to hold priesthood . . . right now. And I don't know why," says a somber and earnest Osmond. "But that's the way the Lord wants it" (*The Barbara Walters Special* 1978). On June 9, 1978 (after the Walters interview with Donny and Marie but prior to its airing), white male church leaders, particularly President Spencer W. Kimball, declared they had received a revelation from God, instructing them to reverse the racial restriction policy, an outcome that perhaps Barbara Walters and the combined pressures of the civil rights movement helped along.

Immediately following a discussion on whether Donny or Marie would marry a non-Mormon and if both intend to have only one sex partner for their entire lives (they answer no to the first question and yes to the second), Walters turns the topic to women's rights and says to a pixie-haired Marie, "Now, I have noticed here that you have no trouble speaking your mind. And yet, in the church . . . it seems to me that the woman holds a secondary role." Donny and Marie's mirrored stance is striking, their matching beige shirts, broad smiles, full dark hair, and earnest attention a visual assertion of agreement and harmony, as their right hands both clench in determination to make points about their religious beliefs (see figures I.3 and I.4). Marie responds to Walter's questions with a classic verve but an unfortunate choice of pronouns. "Secondary, no. But you have to remember that you need a patriarch at the head of the home. . . . The woman is equally as important, but as far as speaking her mind, that should be the man's job." While there is much to discuss in this interview, for my purposes the relevant point is that both Donny and Marie project a feminized position in relation to the authority of the church, even while occupying conventional gender roles with respect to one another. Their job is not to question but to believe and to follow. And to smile. And Marie's job is further to tease Donny, even while she upholds his greater authority to speak for her. This reinforces what Matthew Bowman characterizes as the mainstream church's emphasis on living a "tight moral code" rather than encouraging intellectual inquiry, where church governance "is designed not to promote theological reflection but to produce Mormons dedicated to living the tenets of their faith" (Bowman 2012, 206, 197). And while both men and women are implicated in this code of submission and subordination, the hierarchy of power reinforces a gendered power relation that masculinizes those who make the rules and feminizes those who must adhere to the rules.

To see the connection between mediated Mormonism and a fascination with sex, one need only follow the golden thread of the Osmond family through the tapestry of latter-day representation. One prime example occurred during Howard Stern's 1998 interview with Donny Osmond. The conversation ranged, in typical Stern fashion, from whether or not Donny ever sexualized his sister, Marie, to the kind of sex Donny would or wouldn't have with his wife (no anal or oral, no porn). "You are sexually repressed, Donald!" yells Stern. "No, no, no I'm not," says Donny with a smile on his face. "I'm happy." In interview after interview—from Barbara Walters to Larry King to Katie Couric to Oprah Winfrey—the Osmonds are genuine, decent, happy. Even in pain—as, for instance, during Marie's divorces, the death by suicide of her son, Donny's long struggle with depression, their father's death at age ninety—Donny and Marie are public Mormons, eager to speak of their faith, of forever families, of being happy in their ethical commitments. As Donny tells Ellen DeGeneres (2013) about Marie's remarriage to her first husband, "It's a Cinderella story with a lot of bumps in the road but a beautiful, happy ending." And as we shall soon see, this version of happiness is critical to the gender-sex dynamic of mediated Mormonism.

FIGS. 1.3–1.4 The mirrored stances of Donny and Marie Osmond.

Happy Valley and the Kingdom State of Deseret

Happy Valley is the nickname attached to Utah County, an area south of Salt Lake City that includes Provo (home of Brigham Young University) and is ringed by the majestic snow-capped mountains of the Wasatch Front. But Happy Valley is also a state of mind, a metaphoric descriptor of all of Mormonism and most of Utah, a term sometimes used mockingly and other times admiringly. While many Mormons living outside of the mountain West and the United States take issue with what they term Utah Mormons as the template for all of Mormonism, Happy Valley typifies a brand that applies to the idea of the mainstream church more broadly. Latter-day Saints are widely recognized for their upbeat, optimistic, big-smiled, high-energy personalities, affective qualities that link to the broader ideologies of Americanness. Mormons are often credited with being the happiest faith system in the world (or at least the most convincingly upbeat), and the growing number of international converts suggests a gospel of happiness has much appeal. I discuss this idea of happiness as brand more in chapter 1.

Mormonism is not only a religion born on American soil, it gains its sustaining values from the ideographies of space that bind Mormonism to Americanness, particularly to projects of imperialism. Utah became the Mormon heartland in 1847, largely because its emptiness and absence of arable land marked the space as both removed from and undesirable to others. This relative lack of popular and political interest in the vast desert spaces that Wallace Stegner calls "Mormon Country" are also why the literal and figurative fallout of atomic bomb testings figure so prominently in narratives about Mormon people, particularly Brady Udall's (2011) novel *The Lonely Polygamist*, which includes a scene of atomic detonation, and Terry Tempest Williams's *Refuge* (1991), a moving account of the natural history of the Salt Lake Basin region and her family's struggle with breast cancer.

Yet LDS folk didn't come to Utah with only the humble aspiration of settling exclusively in and near the basin. As historian Walter Nugent notes, "church fathers had in mind an imperialist vision in a kingdom or state of Deseret that would encompass not only Utah but also present-day Nevada, southern California to the Pacific, three-fourths of Arizona, and large chunks of Colorado, Wyoming, and Idaho" (Nugent 2004, 37; see figure I.5).

The Mormons founded many Western cities that otherwise seem now remarkably disconnected from their teetotaling ways (such as Las Vegas), and they laid the groundwork for infrastructure across the broad swath of the Mountain West, moving north into Alberta, Canada, and south into Mexico.

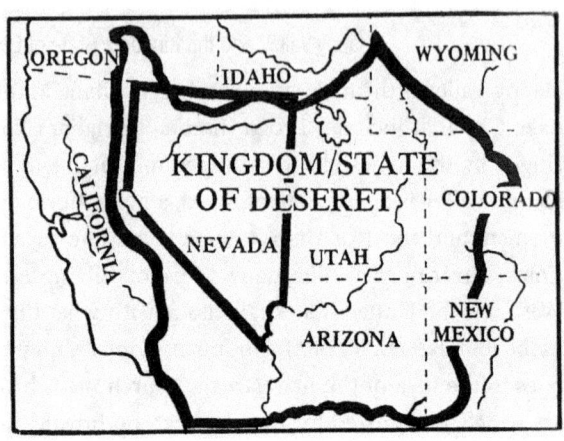

FIG. I.5 The Kingdom of Deseret.

Indeed, media are at the very heart of the expansionism, since Mormon outposts were established along telegraph lines that the church erected to create a communication network across the West.

Mormonism's holy story draws on the significance of place, and thus the Church of Jesus Christ of Latter-day Saints stands as the only major religion in which the Americas figure prominently. The Book of Mormon recrafts the broader story of Christianity so that the Americas (the United States, Mexico, and perhaps Central America—the specific geography is unclear in church stories) play critical roles in the divine project. Mormonism puts the American continent front and center in its cosmogony, claiming in the Book of Mormon that Christ came to North America after his crucifixion and resurrection, and the end of times, the second coming, will happen in the hallowed grounds of Jackson County, Missouri, not far from Mark Twain's boyhood home. Mormonism also pins its notion of heaven and earth on a philosophy of meritocracy and diligence that fully exemplifies an American ethos of hard work and can-do optimism, cementing all the more an ideology of Americanness to a credo of Mormonism.

In the nineteenth century, the West offered a remote space promising the church's safety where worshippers could follow the edicts of their prophet and live in peace, unmolested by the outside world. On the Mormon Trail as believers laboriously trekked with their loved ones across the Great Plains of the American Midwest—often on foot or pushing unstable handcarts to carry their possessions—Western meadows and grasslands beckoned as a place of rest.[21] On longer sojourns, they offered soils for cultivation of wheat or barley or oats. But meadows were also potentially a place of vulnerability, where those with harm in their hearts could isolate and wound. These associations are palpable even on contemporary television, as evidenced when an episode of *Walker, Texas Ranger* (1993—2001) features a flashback in which its protagonist, Cordell Walker, played by Chuck Norris, saves a vulnerable Mormon party making passage to the West.[22] The narrative of stalwart-but-ultimately-vulnerable Mormons is as well worn as the rutted Mormon Trail itself. Indeed, the great Western director John Ford committed the story of defenseless Mormons in need of saving to film in *Wagon Master* (1950).

The mountains of the West were, of course, about epiphanies and visions, about elevation and transcendence. But they also signified hardships, challenges, the enormous Rocky Mountain ridge, with its unforgiving coldness and unfathomable altitudes. The adversity of the trek westward gave Henry Hathaway (director) and Darryl F. Zanuck (producer) their American Zion, allowing them to create the romanticized *Brigham Young* (1940), in which a persecuted holy people flee injustice, cross a massive body of water (the Mississippi River rather than the Red Sea), and follow their holy leader through adversity—including a plague of crickets rather than locusts—in order to arrive in the promised land. The West called for hardscrabble perseverance and steely determination in the context of catastrophe. In many respects, these images of Western spaces gave the Mormons their backbone and their identity as outsiders and those who endure. For this reason, even contemporary cultural texts that take up Mormonism participate in an elegy to place: Salt Lake's Wasatch mountain range frequently rises majestically behind scenes in *Big Love*, *Sister Wives*, or *Escaping Polygamy*; the brightness of the desert's sunlight functions almost like another character in films such as *The 19th Wife* or *Prophet's Prey*, the striated layers of the Salt Lake basin in *Refuge*, swimming in immense manmade lakes surrounded by submerged canyons in *Dancing with Crazy*, the unforgiving cold of Provo's mornings in *Saving Alex*. As it concerns Mormonism as a meme, then, the American West in all of its many connotations lies at the heart of the cultural and ideological landscape it represents. Much like the Colorado River, which has carved a majestic path through the rock of the Grand Canyon, Mormonism cuts a broad swath through the ideographies of the West.

The Great (Normative) White Way

As anyone who has seen parodies of a milk-guzzling Mitt Romney on *Saturday Night Live* or freakishly loving families during family home evening on *South Park* can attest, mainstream Mormons are often portrayed as kinder, nicer, and purer than others, but also as both naive and old fashioned. Mainstream Mormons as a group and a social identity have come to take on the very characteristics most exemplified by two famous Mormon families: the Romneys and the Osmonds—attractive, seemingly stable and happy large families, financially prosperous, influential, kind but firm, conservative, with flashing smiles. By contrast, as evidenced by such fare as *Outlaw Prophet: Warren Jeffs* or *Breaking the Faith*, fundamentalist Mormon men are depicted as idealogues and their wives and children as duped, deceived, and desperate to escape. All of these factors are coded through an unrelenting veil of whiteness and Western hegemonic forms of masculinity and femininity. While the demographics of the mainstream church's global membership are quite heterogeneous and the church's public relations efforts make a case for Mormonism as pluralized in ethnicities, races, and other social identities, the idea of Mormonism and the way that meme functions in the American imagination largely hews to a hue of whiteness that insists on heterosexual desire and practice as a fundamental ingredient of both priesthood and godhood. Critical to these represented identities are a whole host of messages about marriage and morality, queer identities and politics, and postfeminism and contested/confirmed patriarchies.

In terms of gender progressiveness, women within the mainstream church are still lobbying for priesthood (as well as the right to wear pants to Sunday services), and while there are no longer official test labs at BYU designed to "dehomosexualize" Saints through means of electroshock therapy and other forms of extreme behavior modification, the church takes a hard stance against LGBT+ rights and people. It is for this reason that stories of the clean-cut Mormon man tempted by SSA (same-sex attraction) or even premarital and extramarital sexual desire provide such a titillating consideration in such fare as *The Book of Mormon, Angels in America, Latter Days, Orgazmo*, or even *Big Love* (if a homicidal fundamentalist false prophet can count as clean-cut). Indeed, as I noted, when Jodi Arias murdered her boyfriend in grisly fashion, the press made much of their shared Mormon faith and unmarried eroticisms, putting one more version of LDS sexual repression/perversion into public discourse. So while the representation of actual Mormon people tends to reinforce a whiteness of skin that correlates with heteronormative identity, one outcome we might see in the broader signifying system of mediated Mormonism is that the hegemonic hefts of whiteness and heteronormativity do not always prevail.

Chapter by Chapter: The Mediated Mormon Trail

Before laying out a description of the chapters in this book, I want to address the topic of trigger warnings. I'm of two minds about whether or not an author should warn readers about potentially traumatic materials, particularly those related to sexual violence. Trigger warnings can sometimes serve to create the very thing they seek to suppress: anxiety and trauma. They also make a priori assumptions about what might count as traumatic, often reinforcing feelings of alienation and misunderstanding for those people who have experienced violence outside of the purviews of the warning. Some people also feel that trigger warnings dull the necessary challenges that come with a call to critical thinking. With all of that being said, I feel it ethically important to note that the kind of violation and suffering experienced by children who are sexually abused is different in kind. I thus wish my reader to know that there will be many moments in the ensuing text during which I speak about sexual violence, including rape of children. I admit that this finding surprised me when I began to engage with the broad archive of mediated Mormonism, for it is a sad reality that many of the memoirs about being in and leaving the church (both LDS and FLDS) are also harrowing accounts by survivors of childhood sexual abuse. The patriarchal cultures of LDS and FLDS cultures, combined with the notion that children are innocent until they join the church at age eight, provide the perfect breeding ground for the abuse of young children. Further, patriarchal ethoses that emphasize obedience and sexual purity often reinforce the discursive codes of abuse. As the *Salt Lake Tribune* warns, "Teaching youth that it is permissible and appropriate for authority figures to ask personal, invasive sexual questions grooms them to not recognize abusive situations" (Dodge 2018).[23] This is not to say, by any means, that all or most Mormon children are abused, sexually or otherwise. But it is to say that sexual abuse is a major motif of mediated Mormonism and is addressed, sometimes in painful detail, in this book.

Chapter 1, "Mormonism as Meme and Analytic," demonstrates how the idea of Mormonism as a faith fixes the meanings of what I call spiritual neoliberalism, a gendered aspirational target that is marked by the imperative to make good choices and improve the self as fused with marketplace goals of financial success that have long been the hallmark of neoliberalism. The chapter examines how Mormonism is variously used by those within and outside the church and by both amateur media producers and professionals to reinforce and renegotiate codes that align with a democratic norm of the citizen-self, who believes in (and thrives due to) egalitarianism, meritocracy, self-actualization, self-determination, and seeming free choice. These investments manifest through an orientation toward screens, self-reflexivity, and the monetization of identity or self-branding. In fact, I argue that the politics of representation at play in larger popular narratives about Mormonism perfectly combine a cultural logic about neoliberalism and globalization that meshes well with the mainstream LDS Church's own logic of neoimperialism and new technologies of communication. The amalgam marks a period that mobilizes media savvy and manipulation of the image but that also requires the machinelike routinization that serves as the hallmark of industrialism, elements we see perfectly manifest in the worldwide missionary program that so emblematizes the LDS Church. Work ethos and business savvy are also critical to an F/LDS notion of financial and faith-based rewards. In this respect, Mormonism epitomizes the theoretical ground staked out in a post-Enlightenment democratic temporality, where concepts of rational individualism and meritorious labor, rather than aristocratic lineage, cohere over time to earn one success in its own version of the prosperity gospel. That this model of rational advance adheres to a religion and thus secures one a place in the ephemeral domain of a celestial paradise is only one of Mormonism's more brilliant contradictions—or contributions, depending on your point of view.

Crucially, these values are also augmented and authorized by an ideology of whiteness deeply imbricated in the F/LDS DNA. Chapter 2, "The Mormon Glow," takes up the idea of an epistemology of light—to borrow Richard Dyer's phrase—that reinforces goodness as the path to godliness. In this chapter, I consider the church's long-standing position on race, including the lived prophecy that stands as a founding principle of the religion. Because the basic articles of faith, specifically Article 9, allow for prophetic revelation not just in the past but in the future, the church's policies are amenable to change over time, thus leading to the hope and the distinct possibility that God will change his mind about same-sex marriage or women holding the priesthood. This chapter takes up these notions of good works, the Mark of Cain, and what is colloquially referred to as the Mormon Glow, or an embodied goodness in Mormons intelligible to others, arguing for the Mormon Glow as both phenotype and media spectacle.

Chapter 3, "The Epistemology of the (Televised, Polygamous) Closet," turns to a discussion on modern polygamy, including issues of privacy and publicity. If one of the undergirding modes of Mormon self-understanding is the church's separation from mainstream society, mediation and celebrity complicate the edict of separatism that has functioned as the backbone of the church's regard toward its own identity since its inception. Mainstream postmillennial Mormon polygamy stories have been largely grounded in HBO's critically acclaimed drama *Big Love* (2006–11). And while *Big Love* has arguably been the most respected and expensive venue for the portrayal of what one way of doing modern polygamy looks like, it has hardly been the only site for such depictions. Since 2010, reality television has offered its own point of view on anomalous family arrangements. *Sister Wives*, on TLC, presents a fringe group of Mormons—in this case the polygamous Brown family—as a composite family that neutralizes the extremes of FLDS. This depiction conflates mainstream Mormon and Fundamentalist Mormon alike under the big, if controversial, tent of polygamy. Both *Big Love* and *Sister Wives* have, in turn, created a market for other mediated fare that has linked itself to this new public fascination with modern polygamy. Rather than seeing these linked media/consumer networks as capitalism run amuck, I'm much more interested in the way these narratives position the modern polygamous family as the quintessence of contemporary American individualism, steeped as it is in entrepreneurial spirit, aspirational ambition, management efficiency, and image savvy.

Chapter 4, "Polygamy USA," considers orthodox forms of plural marriage that modern polygamists contest, as made visible in such sites as the reality shows *Escaping the Prophet* (2015) and *Escaping Polygamy* (2015–present), the 2005 raid on the Yearning for Zion Ranch, and the 2011 conviction of its leader, Warren Jeffs. That Jeffs is both separate from and elided with the original Mormon polygamists, Joseph Smith and Brigham Young, is also critical to the mediated discourses clustering around this topic. Through these accounts that range from Jeffs to Joseph—from dusty compounds to lushly appointed mansions, from sister wives to spurned male children—this chapter analyzes stories about fundamentalist polygamy that position it as retrograde, anachronistic, and evil. Yet narratives about the perversions of polygamy offer their own rendering of modern progressivism, particularly since they depend on a culture of celebrity to make their warnings intelligible. Indeed, if chapter 3 considers polygamy, or at least modern polygamy, as a savvy resource for modern living, chapter 4 provides a different point of access on voice, agency, and political action. These orthodox polygamy stories tell a consistent story about the worst abuses of patriarchy and male privilege, only to make the primary villain so uniform and one dimensional that he is pushed to the edges. It is those who have suffered and survived, escaped and evaded, the sons of perdition and the apostate sister wives, whose stories emerge as vibrant, complex, and compelling. Taken together, chapters 3 and 4 offer commentary on how gender and sexuality norms are established and contested within narratives about fundamentalist beliefs, even those stories that vary in terms of their relation to modern values and lives.

While the entire book engages with sexuality and gender as critical throughlines to understanding Mormonism, media, and identity in the modern moment, chapters 5 and 6 serve as capstone discussions. Chapter 5, "Gender Trouble in Happy Valley," looks very specifically at the role of women in both fundamentalist and mainstream contexts. This examination includes the affective imperative that women be happy as well as the feminist resistance long part of Mormonism. This chapter also considers the case of Elizabeth Smart, whose story captivated the nation, largely because it involved a kidnapping with a happy ending in that it did not end in her death. Smart's kidnapping allowed for another public and newsworthy display of the underbelly of American culture, articulated through the tale of a pretty, affluent blonde girl being stolen away from the upscale home of her parents by a polygamous homeless zealot bent on making her his second wife. This chapter thinks about women in both the mainstream and fundamentalist churches—about the affective demands that they be smiling, nurturing, and obedient and about their own needs for liberation and individuation within this extremely patriarchal system.

Chapter 6, "'Pray (and Obey) the Gay Away'" turns more specifically to a consideration of mediation about Mormons and not only LGBT+ lives but queer sexuality and desire more broadly. Both fundamentalist and mainstream Mormonism maintains that heterosexuality (though not always heteronormativity, as we see in the case of polygamy) is God's plan. But given how important personal truth—or testimony—is to the perceived validity of Mormonism, LGBT+ F/LDS peoples experience an excruciating tension between adherence to self or system. The examples that fill this chapter speak to a finely titrated formula of conscience in relation to culture, as filtered through needs for self-expression and amplified by social media and publicity. In turn, this exquisite tension between self and system reveals much about identity, orientation, desire, and conscience. When LGBT+ stories about identity and desire are mediated, packaged as consumer products, spread through social media as memes, and turned into complex semiotic codes of their own, they make visible the hegemonic workings of power in relation to norms of the self.

I close the book with a conclusion that summarizes the intellectual points and follow this with an epilogue that is a personal essay in which I detail my own vexed relationship to Mormonism, steeped as it is in the ambivalent teas of both admiration and anxiety that were so fully a part of my growing up in Mesa, Arizona. The state of Arizona is itself a place of social, geological, and climatic extremes, from the red and purple canyon lands and whispering pines and white-barked aspens of the north to the saguaro fields with their pink-tipped arms open to the sun of the Sonoran Desert to the south. The landscapes of the West are godscapes. On seriously weather-rich days, when luminous clouds slink low around the crags of mountains, the light is dramatic and spectacular. A natural chiaroscuro. Shafts of light beaming through the sunset are like incandescent slides. A darkened mound backlit with gold becomes the hiding place for a light-filled and playful God. *Tricks of sun and shadow.* The landscape is entirely surreal and otherworldly, too unlike the prosaic to be anything but lumen filled.

Arizona contains every stereotype imaginable about the Wild West, from gun-slinging cowboys to miners whose lungs have grown black with coal dust. Phoenix and Tucson even sport the occasional yuppie and hipster. And yet the Mesa of my childhood was remarkable largely for its blandness. While a large city, Mesa sits inconspicuously at Phoenix's elbow. In a former day, irrigated fields of alfalfa and cotton stretched for mile after mile, and just outside the city limits, orange groves perfumed the winter air with their sweet delicate aroma. But that sweet scent is now mostly a thing of memory, since most of those groves have been cut down to accommodate the population boom that struck the Sun Belt in the 1990s. Mesa is a city founded and largely run by Mormon people, and while the city also houses a diverse population of Latinos and Indigenous peoples, the tastes and temperaments of Mormonism rule the culture of the city. What this means in practical terms is that the Mesa of my childhood offered very few of the amenities and cultural stimuli that a comparable city of its size might support, since Mormon families spend so much time with themselves and each other, at family home evening, at church, at Sunday school, or in activities planned through their ward and stake centers. For the non-Mormon, Mesa was thus a city where one's presence felt attenuated, a vacuous place of absence belied by the flesh-and-blood reality of being. In offering this memoir of my coming of age in Mesa, I introduce yet one more version of mediated Mormonism as remembered through the lens of my own feelings of marginalization and judgment. I bring my voice here in memoir form to suggest that experience taught me something quite subtle and yet palpable about hegemony. I never needed to be instructed in these codes about morality and gendered behavior, and yet I knew them so well that I internalized them.

Overall, I'm intrigued by the tangle of ideas that wrap themselves around the meme of Mormonism. They weave a complex tapestry about lives in the present moment that are fractured, contingent, and even precarious in every way possible—by demands on personal time and energy, by imperatives to be competitive in a global marketplace, by moral and ethical concerns about the state of the family, by worried judgments about racial and ethnic plurality and multiculturalism, by injunctions that limit the body's desires and hungers, by an intense awareness of stigma and stereotype, and by the use of media to measure, counter, and circulate so-called misperceptions. In this, the latter-day screens of mediated Mormonism reveal much about the shifting meanings of contemporary U.S. gender politics and social justice.

1. Mormonism as Meme and Analytic

SPIRITUAL NEOLIBERALISM, IMAGE MANAGEMENT, AND TRANSMEDIATED SALVATION

Question: Why is it better to be Mormon?

Best Answer: Because you have a religion that teaches you that if you try hard enough, are good enough, and pay enough money, then you can ascend to a tier of heaven in which you can be a god of your own universe. God, after all according to Mormon doctrine, started out as a flesh and blood person like you and me, but he ascended to a high enough tier of heaven to get his own universe. It's sort of like Amway on a grand scale.

—Yahoo! Answers, "Why Is It Better to Be Mormon?"

Just as we wouldn't hesitate to learn another language, we shouldn't hesitate to work within the vocabularies of others to communicate our meanings.... We can teach and testify of many gospel principles if we are careful in selecting words which carry out meaning but come from [non-Mormons'] experience and frame of mind.

—Stephen R. Covey, *The Divine Center*

The ubiquitous figure of the smiling, clean-cut, pleasant-but-persistent Mormon missionary stands as a meme in itself, the symbolic gatekeeper for most public introductions to Mormonism. In a crisp white shirt, necktie, black pants, and black name badge emblazoned with the elder's name, the clean-shaven and short-haired young man (typically aged eighteen to twenty-one) is joined by a comrade in arms—a look-alike companion identically dressed and groomed. Together, they patrol the landscapes of most communities, from the bustling streets of Beijing to the cobblestone streets of Old Montreal. Most people have seen a missionary; many people have spoken with one, sometimes unwillingly. I personally have many childhood memories of these young missionaries, since they constantly came to our suburban home, hoping to convert my Presbyterian family. But perhaps my most vivid image is one I acquired recently. While in my car at a stoplight on Hurstbourne Road in Louisville, Kentucky, I looked over to the sidewalk to see two missionaries on their bikes, their black name tags, ties, and collared shirts marking them as conspicuously unlike any other teenagers on the street. Laughing with each other, they were perched precariously on their wobbly bikes—their legs lifted in the air, challenging one another to see who could balance longest without putting his feet down for support. The sight touched my heart for its reminder of the sheer youth of these boys, who serve as foot soldiers in the army of their church's salvation campaign.

The Mormon missionary program is a worldwide web of its own, spreading across the globe to 347 different sites, with an approximate 55,000 identically dressed Saints knocking on doors to testify of the One True Church. While young Mormon women and older married couples may also serve as missionaries, they are often assigned to permanent locations, like Temple Square in Salt Lake City or the Palmyra, New York, print shop where the Book of Mormon was first published. It is typically teenaged males (or those in their early twenties) who patrol urban spaces in the name of their faith. Males in the LDS Church are called elders, a status they gain at age twelve when they enter the Aaronic Priesthood. By the time of their mission, these teenage elders are also members of the Melchizedek Priesthood, which grants them authority to heal, receive revelation, and offer priesthood blessings. As I discuss at greater length in chapter 5, mediated Mormonism makes clear that Mormon women are barred from holding priesthood authority, and the few female missionaries are therefore limited in geography and responsibilities. If women missionaries get the golden ticket (a convert), men perform the rite of baptism to bring the new believer into the church.

Given that most of the missionaries circulating from door to door fit the type of clean-cut, young, white men such as those featured in figure 1.1, it is no wonder that the sociological omnipresence of the male missionary serves as a ready template for the imagination of Mormonism. It is also no surprise, given the missionary's always-there-ness, that he is an insistent mediated trope, cropping up in plays, books, films, and television—indeed, figure 1.1 comes from a Mormon-produced parody video about the many rejections and occasional euphoria of mission experience, set to Adele's now-famous

FIG. 1.1 Joseph and Smith, themselves former missionaries, parody the constant rejection and occasional joy that is the missionary's plight. The fellow on the left has a slightly pained expression because he is trying to sing and smile simultaneously, all while offering to do lawn work and then go away forever (Smith and Joseph 2016).

song "Hello" and released on YouTube. A quick search also reveals dozens of missionary parody videos. Clearly, no one is better at mocking the codes of Mormonism than Mormons themselves—particularly if karaoke and video equipment are involved (Marceil 2014).

On another media platform, the Tony award–winning Broadway play *The Book of Mormon*, itself both parodic and admiring, has become a veritable phenomenon, earning for its writers, Matt Stone and Trey Parker (creators of the hilariously ribald animated series *South Park*) and Robert Lopez (cocreator of *Avenue Q*, the tale of a queer *Sesame Street*), a windfall of cultural and financial capital. *The Book of Mormon* tells the story of two young Mormon missionaries sent to a remote village in northern Uganda, where a brutal warlord threatens the local population. Naive, optimistic, ambitious, and exceedingly high energy, the two missionaries attempt to share the meaning behind the Book of Mormon. But they have trouble connecting with the locals, who are more worried about war, famine, poverty, and AIDS than about religion. *The Book of Mormon* is both satire and comedy. It lampoons organized religion and traditional musical theater with more than one joke about anal penetration and bestiality, yet it ultimately regards the church in friendly terms that praise an all-American decency that is equal parts happy optimism and virginal repression.

I will return to the fusion of the parodic and the erotic—what we might well call parodica—and *The Book of Mormon* musical at the close of this chapter. Here I want to focus on the concentration of associations, images, and meanings made intelligible through the figure of the missionary, since he, in turn, is a helpful illustration of Mormonism as both meme and analytic. Across the mediascape, the Mormon missionary is an adaptable figure, available for the projection of fantasies and fears about whiteness, about masculinity, about raging hormones and bodily control, about ambition and perseverance, about faithful obedience, about sex. A small sampling from the world of film: in the Disney-produced high-budget film *The Other Side of Heaven* (2010), the missionary is a young hero off to serve his church and save the world; in the mafia adventure *Inspired Guns* (2014), he is the true-believing genius capable of outsmarting (and converting) two dumb mobsters; in the legal drama *Day of Defense* (2003), he is the lawyer surrogate who must defend himself and his church; in the dramatic thriller *The Saratov Approach* (2013), he is an innocent victim taken captive and beaten by Russian bad guys; in the feature film *Missionary* (2013), he is a crazed stalker and murderer; in the horror short *M Is for Mormon Missionaries* (2013), he is both a serial killer whose face is bashed in with a hammer and the victim of this assault; in the documentary *Tabloid* (2010), he is a manipulable rube, abducted, shackled, raped, and the center of a real *Sex in Chains* scandal from 1977; in the comedic film *Orgazmo* (1997), his door-to-door ramblings and naive virginity make him an unwitting participant in the porn industry; in the pornographic film *Buckleroos* (2004), he serves much better than a pizza delivery boy for a gay male sex fantasy about young men who suddenly appear at the threshold, friendly and eager to serve; in the feature films *The Falls: Testament of Love* (2013), *The Falls: Covenant of Grace* (2016), *Latter Days* (2003), and the documentary short *Elder: A Mormon Love Story* (2015), he is a young gay man finding love for the first time, a love forbidden and outlawed by his church. And these are just the film treatments—across television, novel, memoir, and blog, the Mormon missionary is a singular, if overdetermined, figure who, in his capacity to signify white male anxiety, functions as a screen to those fascinated by what they believe his image reflects.[1]

As the working of the trope of the missionary indicates, to say that Mormonism functions as a meme and analytic is thus to suggest that the idea of Mormonism is bigger than and separate from any single Saint or the particularities of the mainstream or fundamentalist churches themselves. As a meme, Mormonism can self-replicate, mutate, respond to selective pressures, and transmit socially. As an analytic, Mormonism reveals the vagaries of power and identity. In this, I use the term "Mormonism" much as historian Joan Scott understands the term "gender," which is to say that "gender is a primary way of signifying relationships of power" (Scott 1986, 1069). Just as, Scott notes, concepts of power may build on gender but need not always be literally about gender itself. Mormonism is similarly both indicative of a specific American religion/people and far abstracted from this literal referent. As such, I hope my readers understand not that Mormonism is everywhere, but that as both meme and analytic Mormonism provides a lens for perceiving an ongoing contestation about power, sexuality, and gender as expressed through the fine titrations of media that is, itself, malleable and moving.

Much like the notion of the celebrity or star, the meme is made salient both through the thing itself (the person, the object) and the points of reference, both socially and discursively, that animate the meme's relevance and lend it intelligibility. Here it is helpful to move sideways (theoretically speaking) to Richard Dyer's discussion in *Heavenly Bodies* of the factors that go into creating the phenomenon of the star. Dyer notes that the movie star is a composite that results not just from his or her films but from ancillary promotion in the form of "pin-ups, biographies and coverage in the press" (2004, 2). The star's image, he writes, becomes coherent through "what people say or write about him or her" as well as "the way the image is used in other contexts such as advertisements, novels, pop songs, and finally the way the star can become part of the coinage of everyday speech" (3). The star image is always "extensive, multimedia, intertextual," claims Dyer, relying on multiple forms of media for the saturation, intelligibility, and spread of the idea of a celebrity, who is a fusion of person and fable (3). Dyer suggests in both *Heavenly Bodies* and *Stars* that the concept of the star tells us something more broadly about personhood by making the "deep and constant features of human existence" tangible to audiences (2004, 17). The star, he argues, reifies the saliency of structuring belief systems, sometimes by reinforcing cultural values and other times by violating them. And because of this important cultural work, celebrity is never random or mercurial but historically specific and emblematic of deep cultural investments in notions of selfhood, meaning, and identity.

So too, I argue, is Mormonism. And perhaps beyond making the contours of what it means to be a human salient, Mormonism does a more historically specific work. In this new millennium, I argue that mediated Mormonism reinforces the defining qualities of the democratic citizen, born of the American republic, weaned on individualism, and nurtured in notions of meritocracy, where hard work rather than wealth or bloodline purportedly equips a person for success and where social privilege seemingly doesn't exist. While this category of the citizen is often referred to as a default, an everyman figure that any person might fill, he is quite clearly gendered and raced, his capacities to signify for all things a part of the privilege of his ontology. *All men are created equal.* In this respect, the Mormon commitments to self-definition, individual choice, being saved through personal action rather than God's grace, aspirationalism, regulation of the body, male authority, and a punishing work ethic often learned in the trenches of the mission make the faith inextricable from both masculinity and Americanness. These memetic impressions of the F/LDS do an epistemological work, carving cognitive pathways that create new knowledge with respect to identity and power. As such, the present abundance of stories, conversations, and fears about Mormonism creates an analytic through which we might better understand the workings of gender and Americanness in the current moment.

Spiritual Neoliberalism: The Prosperity Gospel and Mormon Meritocracy

If you make good choices, good things happen.—Halie's mom's advice, *Teenage Newlyweds*

In this chapter, I ground my analysis of Mormonism as a meme and analytic with a concept that is marbled throughout the entire book—spiritual neoliberalism. By this I mean a neoliberal regard toward self and systems emphasizing smart choices, care of the self, maximum efficiency, and reduced government intervention. But while neoliberalism often looks to marketplace success to determine its endpoint, spiritual neoliberalism mandates loftier, more spiritual, goals as markers of achievement—personal well-being, enlightenment, heavenly happiness, the godhead. The latter-day screens of mediated Mormonism project these ideas with remarking clarity.

To see this in operation, reality television offers a ready example. Airing on the FYI network, a subsidiary of A&E and Disney/ABC, *Teenage Newlyweds* follows three couples, who (unsurprisingly, given the program's title) marry as teens. One set of newlyweds in particular, George (twenty-one) and Halie (eighteen), is LDS, and the program frequently reminds viewers of their Mormonism by lingering on images of the gold-plated statue of the Angel Moroni atop the Salt Lake City Temple in Utah or the fortress-like temple in Mesa, Arizona (see figure 1.2). Though their love story is perhaps unusual in the broader context of American teen stories, in the Mormon

FIG. 1.2 George and Halie in front of the Mesa Temple, *Teenage Newlyweds*, 2016.

world, their experience is largely unremarkable. George is a returned missionary; Halie desires to be a wife and mother. They met while he was serving his mission in Mesa, and they became engaged quickly after his mission's completion (some newspaper reports say two weeks; others say four months). George and Halie were discovered when television producers read the announcement of their engagement on social media and approached the couple about participating in the reality program. The couple wed and were sealed—a custom of both mainstream and fundamentalist Mormonism that promises eternal marriage—in the Mesa Temple during the second episode of *Teenage Newlyweds*. The temple underscores their virginal bonafides (since only the sexually pure are eligible for temple weddings), but the diegesis does the same with its focus on their sexual anxieties during their wedding night, featured in exacting detail.

Deciding to appear on a reality show was a difficult decision, reports Halie's father, Robert, to LDS *Living*. "We spent a lot of time as a family fasting and praying if this is something we should be involved in. We felt a very strong impression that this would be an opportunity for the world to be exposed to how members of the LDS faith live their day to day lives, why

FIG. 1.3 Reciprocal advertising: wedded bliss and the fused LDS/FYI meme.

we believe so strongly in eternal marriage and families, and how living a Christ-centered life is the key to happiness in today's world" (LDS Living Staff 2016). For George and Halie, then, as for many of the F/LDS people featured on reality television and other forms of mainstream media, visibility serves as a tool for audiences to not only understand but accept the subjects depicted on screen. More broadly, being featured on the show functions as an extended commercial for the important dividends that are increasingly the recognizable brands of LDS living: virginal fortitude, forever families, and domestic happiness. In turn, George and Halie serve as the memetic brand for the television show, since it is their picture that one sees as advertising copy for the program and as identifying information at FYI, the brand of the church and the brand of the network here combining in a recognizable meme (see figure 1.3).

This is not to say that George and Halie are depicted as being in constant bliss. But unlike the other two teenage couples featured on the show, George and Halie have something unique going for them: a community of family and friends who support their decisions. Not only is it considered normal to marry as a teenager, it is smart. Within the unfolding narrative, when Halie's mom gives her a bit of advice about making good choices, she is not saying it is a bad choice to marry at eighteen or to forego college and a career. Instead, she reinforces the right choices Halie has already made to become sealed to her eternal companion and to begin living their forever existence together. Her life will be blessed because she made good choices.

As Halie and George continue to live together, to bear children, to continue in the church's mandate for its members, they will have more opportunities for making good choices—by tithing, by keeping the Word of Wisdom, by always being temple worthy, by performing temple ordinances—concepts I explain at greater length later in this chapter. And they will have the opportunity, indeed, the obligation, to prove to their church authorities that they have made these good choices, through personal worthiness interviews such as annual tithing settlement sessions (where members prove to their bishops that they have paid the mandatory 10 percent tax) or temple recommend conferences (during which members answer a series of questions about their ethical, sexual, and religious behaviors in order to earn entrance to the temple). They will also be interviewed regularly through the personal priesthood interview to be sure their choices do not veer too far from the acceptable route. Are George and Halie holding family home evening weekly? Are they tithing? Are they participating in proxy baptisms? Are they trying to start a family? Are they keeping the law of chastity? Do they know of others who are not keeping the law of chastity? Are they actively involved in promoting the primacy of the church? The community here serves as a mechanism for surveillance and surety, to remind George and Halie of the importance of their good choices.

The average viewer of *Teenage Newlyweds*—or most any kind of mediated Mormonism—will not be familiar with the stringent set of governing codes behind George and Halie's beatific smiles. They simply come off as sweet, young, über-white, and very nice kids, committed to a future they can scarcely imagine. The same is true for any number of media representations that feature Mormons—from the polygamous Henricksons of *Big Love* to the naively sweet new kid Gary on *South Park*, who is able to convert a playground ass-whipping into an invitation to family home evening. Yet, for those in the know, mediated Mormonism consistently traffics in the codes of neoliberalism—good choices, management of the self, communities that enact surveillance as a form of caring. An extended viewing of *Teenage Newlyweds* and George and Halie's life of family and church service also indicates another key element of neoliberalism—a reduced reliance on governmental systems. As *Religion and Ethics Newsweekly* describes it in their consideration of the Mormon welfare system, LDS culture is galvanized by the image of Deseret—the beehive—and its emphasis on "industry, harmony, order, frugality, and the sweet results of toil" ("Mormon Welfare Program" 2016). The program speaks glowingly of the church's canneries, giant warehouses stocked with food, and unending volunteer workforce: "It's huge, it's impressive, and gets zero funding from the government." The canneries also reinforce a larger tenet of the Mormon faith—the storing of food, usually a year's worth, as insurance against emergency or world's end and a way to retain self-reliance even amid catastrophe. It is for this reason that within mediated Mormonism, houses bursting to overflowing with children still reserve prime real estate for a provisions cupboard. The mandate to store food has also resulted in growing businesses for the F/LDS, as plainly evident in Janelle Brown (of *Sister Wives*), who owns EZ Pantry, a food storage company advertised through her social media that is made valuable by the publicity provided by the reality show ("Janelle Brown" 2015).

As a term to describe a political economy, neoliberalism stresses the efficiency of privatization, the reliability of financial markets, and the decentralization of government, often announcing itself in cultural terms through practices and policies that use the language of markets, efficiency, consumer choice, and individual autonomy to shift risk from systems to persons and to extend this sort of market logic into the realm of social and affective relationships. Under neoliberalism, the individual is the primary unit of agency, and personal choice reigns supreme as the reason one succeeds or fails. Neoliberalism is fueled by governmentality, a concept made salient through Michel Foucault (1991) to indicate the degree that systems such as government, religion, and mainstream culture produce citizens who are best suited to the policies of the state. Within the market-based logic of neoliberalism, governmentality colludes with other hegemonic factors to create the terms for a docile body, which is willing to write on itself the codes of success that will enable competition within a larger global marketplace. Critical to the idea of governmentality is the tacit regulation of micropractices—that is, self-control, guidance of the family, management of children, supervision of the household, and development of the self. Neoliberalism and governmentality thrive on the pedagogies offered in and through mediated Mormonism, particularly as such instruction is often labeled a form of care or, as in the case of George and Halie, of making good choices that will, in turn, yield good things.

"Good things" is here both aspirational and vague, slippery enough that the larger mechanism can evade blame should Halie and George fail to achieve good things, yet desirable enough that they will work to do so. The good choices/good things dyad implies a causal teleology that perhaps seems so obvious as to not even warrant writing out: good choices accrue to bring positive outcomes. Or, more precisely, we might read the formula as saying that good choices encourage righteous behaviors that, in turn, build one's putative claim for placement in the highest degree of glory: the celestial heaven. With apologies for the crassness of the simile, much like differences between economy, business, and first class, each level of F/LDS heaven offers differing degrees of benefit and cost.

According to the F/LDS doctrine that percolates through mediated Mormonism, Joseph Smith received divine revelation on February 16, 1832, that all people will be resurrected at the final judgment and will, in turn, be placed in one of three degrees—or kingdoms—of glory: the celestial, the terrestrial, and the telestial. A small number who commit the unforgiveable sin of apostasy will be banished to outer darkness, where they are termed Sons of Perdition, if male. Female apostates do not seem to carry a nickname. Celestial heaven is the highest reward and requires being sealed in marriage, which might only happen in the temple, which, in turn, requires several levels of worthiness, including tithing, chastity, and obedience. The smiling image of George and Halie in front of the Mesa Temple therefore not only serves as a memetics of marriage, it offers a signifier that testifies to their purity and worthiness. They passed their worthiness interviews—they were virgins and made regular donations to the church.

In nineteenth-century iterations of the church and present-day FLDS teachings, admittance to the celestial heaven also requires that a man have at least three wives. While the mainstream church has done much to distance itself from its polygamist past, living the principle of plural marriage is very much an open possibility in the afterlife (C. Pearson 2016). As I have noted, celestial heaven offers a Mormon man the greatest of all possible dividends for good choices: he might inherit a planet of his own and become its omniscient and omnipotent God, his wives and children serving as divine subjects. The terrestrial heaven occupies the middle ground of the Mormon cosmogony. Its occupants are still in heaven yet serve as "ministering angels" to those in the celestial levels. They are the also-rans of the heavenly trifecta, having been exposed to the truth of the reformed gospel but failing to live out its mandates in their earthly lives. The telestial kingdom is the lowest order. It is meant for those who did not receive the truth as well as for "liars, and sorcerers, and adulterers, and whoremongers, and whosoever loves and makes a lie." Telestial dwellers "suffer the wrath of God on earth." They are cast down to hell and "suffer the vengeance of eternal fire" (*Doctrine and Covenants* 2018, section 76, verses 103–5). In other words, for those familiar with *The Book of Mormon* Broadway musical, they live out the "spooky Mormon hell dream."

Now obviously, the idea of heaven and hell existed long before Joseph Smith. But this three-tier system of heaven, whereby one might earn different dispensation through good choices and right action, strikes me as a model of aspiration perfectly in tune with a neoliberal ethos. Indeed, the good choices/good things dyad is important to parse precisely because of what is not said: if good choices and righteous living bring good things, both here and in the afterlife, it also implies that someone who experiences bad things on Earth is being punished for bad choices and bad actions. Bad choices, in turn, forfeit the possibility of eternal happiness. We might ask: is bad luck or even tragedy a recognizable sign within spiritual neoliberalism of those who are not so righteous? If good choices bring good things, then bad things are clearly the result of bad choices.[2] The Saints are not alone in adhering to this version of a binary moral code or what Marie Osmond calls the "Santa Claus principle, that good is rewarded with good and bad brings on bad" (Osmond, Wilkie, and Moore 2001, 186). They are also not singular in pushing a larger ethos of meritocratic aspirationalism, where one rises or falls based on worthiness and work. These principles are built into the bedrock of Americanness, a connection perhaps not surprising given that the religion was born early in the life of the American experiment. What is surprising is that this most American of religions initially structured itself in more communal ways.

Even given the tripartite heavenly balloon payment that awaits the obedient followers in the afterlife, the Latter-day Saints' early days under Joseph Smith and Brigham Young were marked by a governing code seemingly more similar to communism than free enterprise. Both Smith and Young inveighed against earthly riches, even as historical reports now indicate that both men desired to amass them. The early church enacted what was called the United Order, a redistribution system of shared goods and monies so that all would be equal. Said Smith, "If you are not equal in earthly things ye cannot be equal in obtaining heavenly things" (*Doctrine and Covenants* 2018, section 78, verses 5–6).

Writing for *Salon*, Troy Williams (2012) notes both the promises and perils of material wealth: "The prophetic message of the [Book of Mormon] scripture is sharp; if Americans are obedient to God, we will be blessed with riches. If Americans set our hearts on riches and ignore the poor, we will be destroyed." Williams contends that in the face of an "existential threat of federal disincorporation" in the late nineteenth century, "the LDS Church responded by seeking assimilation at any cost. They began to privatize their cooperative business ventures throughout the 1880s and publicly abandoned polygamy in 1890. The course was set. To survive in America, Mormons would transform themselves into patriotic citizens. The quest for Zion would be replaced by the American dream. The rhetoric of communalism exchanged with a reverence for the free market." Clearly, Williams sees Mitt Romney's 2012 Republican nomination for president of the United States as an affirmation "to Mormons that their faith is finally authentic—that they are the indisputable Horatio Alger of American religions."

Arguably, the religion has deserved the sobriquet of Horatio Alger and its ties to meritocratic individualism from its beginnings. Here is one reason why: the communal ideal of the United Order is not extinct; it simply lives in a new form, in the privatized Mormon welfare system that is Deseret Industries (a church-backed thrift store) and the Bishop's Storehouse (a system of 130 church-owned grocery stores where people shop with promises for labor), both of which are frequently depicted or referred to across the latter-day screens of mediated Mormonism. Rather than seeing the early church as being committed to socialism, then, we might well understand Smith's United Order as instrumentalizing earthly suffering as the necessary sacrifices one makes for massive rewards in heaven. Certainly, we might see this notion of a teleology-based altruism in the present mediation of a doctrine that suggests prosperity is the reward for hard work.

The prosperity gospel is the idea that God rewards the righteous with earthly as well as heavenly gifts. Typically identified with Evangelical and Pentecostal Protestantism in the United States, the prosperity gospel preaches that health, wealth, and good fortune are given by God as rewards—or payments, if you will—for faith, positivity, good works, and donations to church-endorsed causes (Bowler 2013). Kate Bowler notes that the prosperity gospel sprang, in part, from the American metaphysical tradition of New Thought, a late nineteenth-century ripening of ideas about the power of the mind. It's a bit like the new age philosophy of *The Secret*: Positive thoughts yield positive circumstances, and negative thoughts reap negative circumstances (Bowler 2016). But here, that notion is turned to more practical ends: thoughts create choices; choices govern behavior; behaviors earn rewards.

While mediated Mormonism suggests that more fundamentalist Latter-day Saints are still called to give all to the prophet's central receiving house, more mainstream Saints are mandated to give 10 percent of their income. What they make over and above this amount (minus other mandatory incidentals like a 5 percent fast offering) remains their blessing. If they fail to give unto the Lord the mandatory 10 percent tithe, lore suggests that Saints will experience bad luck and financial ruin. Mormonism does not contend that it is a sin to be wealthy, but rather that it is a sin to be prideful about wealth. As Andrew S writes as part of the blog on *Mormon Matters*: "Blessed is a loaded term because it blurs the distinction between two very different categories: gift and reward. It can be a term of pure gratitude. 'Thank you, God. I could not have secured this for myself.' But it can also imply that it was deserved. 'Thank you, me. For being the kind of person who gets it right'" (S 2009). Failing to be prosperous is thus not the fault of the godly machine or the religious system but user error. "*The Book of Mormon* foretells this," says Andrew S. "The Book of Mormon can be essentially summarized as a process by which righteous living *does* net you economic blessings."

Religion and commerce have long been bedfellows, of course, yet advanced capitalism has shifted these dynamics to new ground so that churches now compete in a crowded field of brand culture. As Sarah Banet-Weiser writes, even in light of religion's long commodification, "the contemporary political economy of advanced capitalism encourages a shift from commodification to the branding of religion, where brand strategies intersect with consumer activity and content to create a brand culture around religion, and where capitalist business practices merge with religious practices in an unproblematic, normative relationship" (Banet-Weiser 2012, 171; see also Einstein 2008). In this symbiotic relationship between branding and religion, Mormonism lends itself as a ready lens through which we might see a different organization of neoliberalism, what I'm calling spiritual neoliberalism.

In using this term, I reference a phenomenon at work even beyond the neoliberal exploitation of religion under advanced capitalism. Indeed, at stake in the term "spiritual neoliberalism" is less the co-opting of religion and more the establishment of spiritualized goals—such as salvation, peace, and fulfillment—as best (or only) achievable through neoliberal methods requiring free choice and open markets. This domain in which spiritualism and neoliberalism fuse constitutes what might be viewed as a neoliberalism 2.0, where financial success in the market must be matched and bettered by benchmarks in both self-improvement and spiritual aspirationalism.

There is an important distinction to make here between earthly rewards and heavenly dividends, and when the Bloggernacle turns its attention to wealth and prosperity, it hums with disagreements. Some, like the consortium of writers who post to *By Common Consent*, contend that notions of material wealth and spiritual reward should not be conflated. Blog poster JKC reminds readers of Elder Dallin H. Oaks (one of the Twelve Apostles, an LDS leadership group), who publicly admonishes: "Those who believe in what has been called the theology of prosperity are suffering from the deceitfulness of riches. The possession of wealth or significant income is not a mark of heavenly favor, and their absence is not evidence of heavenly disfavor" (Oaks 2015). Yet JKC (2016) also notes a broader Mormon culture that sees "material prosperity as the result of righteousness," a connection often reinforced when callings to church leadership positions are made to men earning high salaries, while those less financially successful are overlooked. University of Tampa sociologist Ryan Cragun told the *Huffington Post* that the LDS religion "appeals to economically successful men by rewarding their financial acuity with respect and positions of prestige within the religion" (Henderson 2012a).

"As far back as I can remember," says the anonymous author of the *Post-Mormon* blog, "the leaders have promised that if a person has the faith to pay tithing, then 'the Lord will open the windows of Heaven and pour out his richest blessings'" (Postmormongirl 2012). The "windows of heaven" reference comes from Malachi 3:10.[3] In the Mormon context, the phrase is made salient through a speech given by Lorenzo Snow, fifth president of the LDS Church (1896–1901). *The Windows of Heaven* (1963) is also a very popular historical drama produced by the mainstream LDS Church that follows Snow as he deals with drought and the church's increasing debt. As the film demonstrates to twentieth- and twenty-first-century viewers, individual tithes to the central LDS Church bring both material prosperity and nature's bounty (in this case rain), reminding Saints of every generation that tithing is mandatory if they expect to enjoy blessings on Earth or in heaven. Again, we see that the founding inequities of Americanness express themselves in and through Mormonism as meme and analytic.

Indeed, across the internet in both pro-Mormon and ex-Mormon forums, an explicit connection is made between tithing and wealth, so much so that entire memoirs turn on traumatic memories when children recall going hungry so that parents could satisfy their tithing mandates. For those still in the church, these stories are evidence of their parents' devotion. The LDS Church asks members to fast once a month, foregoing food and drink for two meals and donating the monies they would have otherwise spent on the LDS world mission program. This fast offering makes a point about discipline in the name of devotion. The fast offering is also a donation over and above the standard 10 percent tithe, an obligatory payment that members are required to offer not only so that they might be temple worthy but so that they might be eligible for the flood of riches from the windows of heaven.

The anonymous author behind *Post-Mormon* writes, "Leaders talk about how you can't afford *not* to pay tithing. They give examples of people who paid tithing and were miraculously able to make ends meet. They promise—

over and over—that having the faith to pay your tithing will result in blessings." By contrast, those who do not pay or cannot pay are told they will suffer. Miss O responded to the blog post, saying:

> It's not only the LDS church that preaches that blessings are in the form of material things and so on. BUT it's the LDS church where you will hear stories of folks getting loans to pay tithing or paying tithing rather than feeding their family and then having to go [to] the Bishop's Storehouse.
>
> What better way to get people's money though right? Start young and create this HUGE desire to want to go to temple, have their whole reputation dependent upon it once they reach adulthood.... Then once they are there, they must pay in order to go and not disgrace or shame their families by threatening that status. To find out someone is NOT temple worthy is almost as bad as all the babies that atheists eat. ;) (Postmormongirl 2012)

Miss O is remarkably prescient in pointing to a complex organizational relationship that historian D. Michael Quinn traces in exacting detail: the psychological and structural interconnectedness between doctrine, cultural practices, social interrelation, and financial stewardship that is part of the Mormon Church. Indeed, Quinn makes the case in his three-part *Mormon Hierarchy* tomes that the structural corporatization of the LDS Church reveals a state within a state, a privatized sovereign nation that operates its own goods and services, regulates its own medical and welfare systems, and engages in a highly politicized and bureaucratized management of its adherents (see Quinn 1994, 1997, 2017). Within the complex world of Mormonism in the intermountain West, members are encouraged not only to worship with one another but to purchase products from one another, invest in one another, and vote for one another. This interconnection leads to a wider network of multilevel marketing (MLM) businesses with strong F/LDS connections such as LuLaRoe (modest clothing) and Young Living (essential oils) that rely, much like the missionary, on word-of-mouth testimonials, new recruits, and endless perseverance.

The interconnection also makes members extremely susceptible to manipulation. According to Mark W. Pugsley (Clarkson 2017), a member of the Securities Litigation Group at Ray, Quinney and Nebeker Attorneys at Law and a person interviewed on the *Mormon Expositor* podcast, the in-group economy leads to an extremely high rate of "affinity fraud," or members who trust those like themselves and are then duped in elaborate Ponzi schemes.[4] While I would not charge the broader faith culture itself with affinity fraud, NBC News Investigations has reported that the mainstream LDS Church has immense financial holdings that are very much due to the contributions it receives from its members. "The church can rely on $7 billion a year from tithing," reported the news site. In addition, "It owns about $35 billion worth of temples and meeting houses around the world, and controls farms, ranches, shopping malls and other commercial ventures worth many billions more" (Henderson 2012b). The aggregate value stands at nearly $35 billion globally, though no one can be certain of the exact figure since religious organizations in the U.S. are not required to disclose full financial holdings. Although the church has pledged itself to a new form of transparency—as I discuss at greater length in the next section—I want to leave this discussion by reflecting on a moment that has rattled many, Mormon and non-Mormon alike, for its overt ties between commercialism and religion. In March 2011, the church opened a hugely ambitious—one might even call it a mega—project, City Creek Center, a shopping mall of gigantic proportion. Perhaps using LDS temples as architectural models, City Creek Center features, in the words of Caroline Winter (2012) writing for *Bloomberg Magazine*, "a retractable glass roof, 5,000 underground parking spots, and nearly 100 stores and restaurants ranging from Tiffany's to Forever 21. Walkways link the open-air emporium with the church's perfectly manicured headquarters on Temple Square. Macy's is a stone's throw from the offices of the church's president ... whom Mormons believe to be a living prophet." The cost of building the mall was roughly $2 billion, and the church was able to pay for it, and indeed all of its building projects worldwide, through membership tithes and thus without incurring debt. In her article, Winter quotes Keith B. McMullin, long-time church official and present CEO of Deseret Management, Inc., about the spiritual value of the megamall. "The Church of Jesus Christ of Latter-day Saints attends to the total needs of its members. We look to not only the spiritual but also the temporal, and we believe that a person who is impoverished temporally cannot blossom spiritually." According to McMullin, the church expected to profit only a small amount from the mall. Its larger purpose was humanitarian: urban renewal for Salt Lake City and "furthering the aim of the church to make bad men good, and good men better" by revitalizing downtown business. As so succinctly expressed, we see a clear articulation that establishes earthly prosperity as the meritocratic building block to celestial eternity.

MLMs: Buy More, Be More

Multilevel marketing (MLM) businesses offer one extended example of this three-part working of spiritual neoliberalism, meritocracy, and the prosperity gospel. While they are highly popular across the United States, MLMs predominate in the Mormon populations of Utah and Arizona, both mainstream and fundamentalist. They sell their products not in stores but person to person, meaning that individual testimonials can also be sales pitches, and friends and family members are clients to be cultivated. Sales reps make money through commissions and by recruiting other people to be representatives within their structuring umbrella. Thus, MLMs are like a pyramid scheme, in that the closer someone is to the top of the organization, the more money they are likely to make. The further downline a distributor resides, the costlier the dalliance with the MLM. It's the business model of Mary Kay or Amway—the American Way. Yet to call an MLM a pyramid is to disallow the fact that these companies often sell wares that customers consider high quality and effective. As former Utah congressman Jason Chaffetz, and also former head of the MLM skin care company Nu Skin, argues, "Well if you're a pyramid that's illegal, in fact you should be prosecuted for that but sharing a product and being compensated for that is fair game and that's the American way" (Roth 2015).

For structural and ideological reasons, MLMs have particular appeal in Utah. As Stephanie Mencimer writes for *Mother Jones*,

> There's a reason why MLMs, many of which peddle natural health products like NuSkin's dietary supplements, have thrived there. Mormon scripture encourages the use of herbs as God's medicine, and the faith has a strong tradition of turning to alternative medicine. Its founder, Joseph Smith, reportedly shunned traditional doctors, believing a physician had killed his brother. The tight-knit Latter-day Saints community, and the trusting nature of its adherents, have made Utah a lucrative terrain for multilevel marketers. Mormons, who typically spend two years serving as missionaries, are also natural recruits for companies that need salespeople with a high tolerance for rejection. And finally, MLM firms often pitch themselves to women as a way to stay home with their kids while still earning substantial incomes. (Mencimer 2012)

There is a further neoliberal ethos supporting the availability of supplements, herbs, and other nutraceuticals. As N. Lee Smith observes about Utah's attempts to regulate "quackery," the enforcement of "laws restricting unproven methods" is perceived as a violation of "free agency," since it works against "'an individual's freedom to choose between God's methods and man's methods' of health care" (Smith 1979, 38, quoting Gillespie 1976, 62). As the epigraph that begins the chapter attests, MLM companies are structured very much like the Mormon Church itself, in an amalgam of meritocratic effort that promises big payoffs if a recruit works hard enough, tithes enough, and is good enough. Further, the structuring codes of MLMs, particularly the several dozen located in Utah, make use of an appeal to upward progression that operates through a combined logic of marketplace prosperity and enlightened self-development, or spiritual neoliberalism.

While there are many companies I might identify to make my point, I will focus on the essential oil company dōTERRA because I have an active and ongoing relationship with the company. In full disclosure, I began using dōTERRA essential oils in January 2016, after a string of five colds over an eight-month period made me desperate for some kind of relief. I hacked and sniffed my way through a yoga class that used an atomizer to disperse dōTERRA oils. Feeling better at the end of the session, I reasoned that perhaps dōTERRA could help cleanse my environment and thus my respiratory system. Although I was writing this book at that time, I did not know dōTERRA was largely a Mormon concern. I made the connection when, after joining, I saw on the website that the company's headquarters is in Pleasant Grove, Utah, and its two founding executives are the fathers of seventeen children (chairman and CEO David Stirling's bio lists nine children, and president and chief financial officer Corey B. Lindley's bio claims eight children). A quick Google search confirmed the connection.

Joining dōTERRA made me a sales rep, or in their words a "wellness advocate," and technically enables me to recruit other wellness advocates and thus to decrease the cost of my monthly fees as well as to earn money relative to my recruits' sales. But I've never been much interested in that part of the cycle. I like the oils well enough mostly for their smell. Though I haven't really experienced the uptick in health that my own wellness advocate promised and still suffer from an inordinate number of respiratory infections, I like to atomize the oils and find they help me concentrate while writing. (Guess what's floating above my head right now?)

Because I am a member and can access the website through a username and password, I receive regular in-group messages from dōTERRA International inviting me to attend their annual conventions in Salt Lake City, where I can commune with a loving, glowing community of like-minded people dedicated to wellness. I also receive promotions encouraging me to take advantage of their Empowered Life Series that will introduce me to dōTERRA's founding executive team, medical advisory board physicians, and top wellness advocates, who will "educate and inspire" me to "create an abundant life of wellness." *You won't want to miss this!* Every month, I am eligible to take part in an Empowered Life Series dedicated to using essential oils, perhaps on my baby or my elderly parent. And lately, I have been receiving invitations for dōTERRA's Wellness Prosperity Summits, which will "educate and empower" me and teach me how to "prosper physically, emotionally, and financially with dōTERRA" ("Wellness Summits" 2017). In 2017, thirty-four Wellness Prosperity Summits took place across the United States, eight conducted in Spanish. Eight summits were also held in Canada. This is no small enterprise.

I am hailed by dōTERRA as pretty much what I am: a white, middle-class mother (okay, and also a suspicious academic), who rarely believes the promises of big business or big government or big medicine, who likes the idea of plants being healing, and who wants to help her family avoid sickness. dōTERRA's customer service agents are relentlessly pleasant and cheerful, encouraging me not to despair when I have trouble negotiating the website. They LOL along with me when I make a joke in Instant Messenger about how confusing the many acronyms on the website are. We all write with an abundance of exclamation points and smiley face emojis. "What are LRPS?!!" I type. "How do I know the amount of PVs in a 15 ml bottle of Wild Orange essential oil?" When I modify my LRP, which I now know means Loyalty Rewards Program, and my PV, which means personal volume, I am sent a friendly but coercive automated message, asking, "Are you sure you want to save this order process with less than 100 PV?" (see figure 1.4). If I only increased my order to 100 PV, I could earn commissions and accelerate in rank. And if I ordered 125 PV, I could get dōTERRA's free product of the month. This is why so many MLM customers have cases and cases of product filling their living rooms, I grumble, yet add more to my LRP. I have 143.16 rewards points remaining, and I'm not at all certain how to spend them. But I want to pause to reflect a bit on the genius logic of this naming system, since a PV, or personal volume, is nothing less than a newly calibrated currency system. The beauty is in convincing the consumer, in this case me, that increasing my dōTERRA PV will, in turn, expand my literal personal volume. I'm becoming a better person! I'm living my best life!

As another demonstration of this fusion between spiritual neoliberalism, Mormonism, and what we might call human potential enhancers, consider

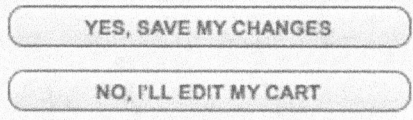

FIG. 1.4 Buy more, be more.

Marriott International. The hotel chain was founded as a root beer stand in 1927 by J. Willard Marriott, Jr., whose two years as a Mormon missionary in Washington, DC, convinced him that what people wanted most was a place to get something cool to drink. The family opened their first hotel in 1957, and as a commitment to spreading the word of the LDS Church, Marriott (and Courtyard) hotels have long included both the Bible and the Book of Mormon in each of its rooms. In 2016, Marriott acquired the tony Ritz-Carlton hotel line (Starwood, Westin, Sheraton, St. Regis, and W), and it is now the world's largest hotel conglomerate. From all I can gather—but cannot get Marriott International to confirm—Marriott does not now insist that each of its hotels in this prodigious chain place a copy of the Book of Mormon in every room. But on a 2017 splurge-stay at the Westin Chicago River North, I found something equally indicative of Mormonism: a small vial of lavender essential oil, inserted into a card that asked me to "sleep well" and promised that, with its help, I might "wind down naturally" and "foster good sleep," all "for a better you™" (figure 1.5). While I have spoken

FIG. 1.5 Westin Hotels and Resorts' trademarked slogan: "For a better you."

with several people at Marriott's corporate headquarters, no executive will tell me who makes the oils placed in Westin rooms and sold in their online gift shop. Marriott also will not tell me when or why the decision was made to put essential oils in their higher-priced properties. But they are awfully nice in their refusals of information.

The possibility of these optimistic promises notwithstanding, there is an insistent message wafting through the air as sure as the droplets of On Guard or lavender oil I breathe in: If I buy more I might be more—the aspirational logic of wellness delivered in bright vials that I can tuck in my pocket or purse. Their message sews wellness to empowerment, and both of these are stitched tightly to material prosperity. Until I start making money through my own string of wellness advocates, dōTERRA encourages me to feel good about buying hundreds of dollars' worth of essential oils because of the charitable donations they make through their Healing Hands Foundation. I hear the words of Margene, Bill's youthful, exuberant third wife on *Big Love* when she discovers Goji Blast and her own MLM venture. She gushes,

"You can't make money unless you help others prosper too! Do well by doing good!" Prosperity here beckons, but prosperity cannot be achieved without helping others. As such, what is positioned as altruism serves as the ticket one purchases in order to board the first-class cabin of the heavenly train.

I am also hailed by dōTERRA in a way that does not feel familiar to me as a feminist and a professional. dōTERRA speaks to me as a woman lacking agency. The oils will allow me to express a power otherwise lacking in my ordinary life. An introductory film, "Our Story," makes it all clear. The video opens looking up at a grove of trees, much in keeping (I find myself thinking) with the vantage point of a young Joseph Smith in the grove when he was first visited by the Angel Moroni. A guitar plays in the background as we peek in on a prosperous white family of five: a mother and father and three little girls, all bathed in light from the full-length windows of their upscale home, their whiteness a glowing beacon of happy contentment. The mother is holding one of dōTERRA's starter kits, which range in price from $99 to $794. All attention is on Mom, who moves a vial around for the family to smell, everyone delighted by the scent. The video advances to more families and more uses of dōTERRA. A young man's white hand rolls PastTense on a young white woman's back; a mother puts Peppermint in the white hands of a child (but don't let that toddler touch her eyes!); a black father and son play catch (though they are not depicted using dōTERRA, we assume they do). And here it's important to note a broader racialized logic to "Our Story," in that of the thirty people depicted in the 3:47 film, twenty-two are white (glowingly so) and eight, or 26 percent, are darker skinned—what appears to be Hispanic, African or African American, and Southeast Asian. This 3:1 ratio seems fairly salutary until you consider the ratio of screen time for the people of color is 27 seconds, or .08 percent. The number of speaking roles for this group? Zero.

The film suggests that the oils might serve as ablutions of intimacy and togetherness, binding forever families in a pluralistic vision of utopic wellness that bears an uncanny similarity to testimonies for the One True Church. "We didn't even know," says one mother in direct address, "that the power of essential oils existed." Another offers her testimony: "It was amazing. Especially knowing what we had gone through and feeling, for once, that I was able to help my child. It's a mom's dream. It was very empowering and that was kind of my moment when I knew, why wouldn't it work." As viewers, we do not know what this mom experienced, though she seems genuinely happy not to be going through it any longer. "I didn't know that I had another option," confesses another mom. "I didn't know that I could have the power or the choice. dōTERRA has given me the ability to make those decisions and to see that you don't have to give up all of your power. You can actually do it yourself." These statements seem a bit puzzling. To whom had she given up power? Why do the oils offer it back? Can lavender essential oil really work that kind of empowerment miracle?[5] In some ways, the answer is a resounding yes. In fact, I'd venture to say that the women featured in the video are talking back to the very patriarchal culture of their church, here dōTERRA commodifying the gendered power relations that lie at the heart of Mormon hierarchical structures.

While, clearly, not all customers of dōTERRA are Mormon (myself as Exhibit A), the public relations materials speak in a coded idiom that most LDS folk would recognize. Oils are a critical part of both mainstream and fundamentalist culture, a secret element of F/LDS life that is increasingly mediated. Wikipedia, for instance, tells us this:

> **Washing and anointing** (also called the **initiatory**) is a temple ordinance practiced by The Church of Jesus Christ of Latter-day Saints (LDS Church) and Mormon fundamentalists as part of the faith's endowment ceremony. It is a purification ritual for adults, similar to chrismation, usually performed at least a year after baptism. The ordinance is performed by the authority of the Melchizedek priesthood by an officiator of the same sex as the participant.
>
> In the ritual, a person is sprinkled with water to symbolically wash away the "blood and sins of this generation." After the washing, the officiator anoints the person with consecrated oil while declaring blessings upon certain body parts. The officiator then declares that the person is anointed to become a "king and priest" or a "queen and priestess" in the afterlife. ("Washing and Anointing" 2017)

Anointing with oils is part of an elaborate and highly secret temple endowment ceremony, and those who experience the process—during which they also receive a new name and their garments—must promise never to speak of the ritual upon penalty of an extremely painful death. It is worth noting that I have read or viewed detailed accounts of secret endowment ceremonies upward of twenty times as part of the research for this book, readily accessible through memoirs, YouTube videos, and even *Big Love*. While both men and women might anoint supplicants in temple endowment ceremonies, it is only through the authority of the male priesthood that women are allowed such privileges. Other patriarchal blessings might be conferred only by men.

Upon receiving entrance to the Melchizedek Priesthood (typically at age sixteen), men are vested with patriarchal authority, which allows them to

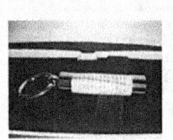
LDS Oil Vial - Olive Wood from the Holy Land - for Priesthood - Chrome Pen Striped Style
by MajestiCrafts
$20.00 (1 new offer)
☆☆☆☆☆ ▾ 2

Product Description
... This *oil vial* is beautifully hand crafted using Olive Wood from the ...

LDS (Mormon) Priesthood Holder Consecrated Oil Vial - Pre-sale for Father's Day
by Cheboski
$18⁵⁰ + $4.49 shipping

FIG. 1.6 LDS oil vials on Amazon.

"preside over posterity in time and eternity" (Smith and Smith 1993, 323). They are also vested with authority to offer blessings and to heal the sick. As I understand it primarily through published memoirs, LDS men in good standing carry at all times a vial of consecrated oil in case they are called upon in time of emergency to anoint or heal someone. These vials are small and discreet, often fitting on a keychain. While sold at specialty stores, they are also available on mainstream websites like Amazon (see figure 1.6). Oils thus function as a token of priesthood authority, a power explicitly denied to women. Mediated Mormonism renders these scenes of blessing visible. In QR, for example, former NFL quarterback Steve Young (2016) remembers a car accident he was involved in and expresses his thanks that he had his oil vial in his pocket and could bless the driver of the car before she died.

The testimonials in the dōTERRA video featuring multicultural mothers newly energized by their own curing power thus begin to make more sense. Particularly as combined with a gender code that expects women to be unpaid caretakers of the home, dōTERRA, specifically, and MLMs, more broadly, offer a helpful alternative to the gendered paradigm that denies women prosperity, both earthly and in the afterlife. She might have her oil and heal with it too—Dr. Mom—and if she is industrious, she might also earn a passive income. Do well by doing good.

The Great Plan of Happiness

In addition to fostering the culture of MLMs, Mormonism as a mediated ideology holds several grounding principles that make it the perfect screen on which to see the workings of spiritual neoliberalism. The most salient of these is the idea that the individual and the religious community are sovereign to the federal government and the conviction that action accumulates in ways knowable, measurable, and rewardable, both on Earth and in heaven. Indeed, central to the F/LDS Plan of Salvation, also called the Great Plan of Happiness, is a series of beliefs that essentially provide a worldly road map offering epistemological, ontological, and spiritual navigational certainty to "guide our path in mortality" (Oaks 1993; see also Church Educational System 2003). Included in this plan is the idea of "eternal progression," which holds that humans are the "spirit children of heavenly parents" who, before birth, live in a preexistence as "sons and daughters of the Eternal Father." In order to move to a higher level of existence, spirits require embodiment and are thus birthed into a mortal frame so that they might face Satan's temptation, fear death and failure, and undergo the process of self-improvement necessary for full celestial apotheosis.

As the official webpage of the LDS Church states, Satan has a very specific agenda, particularly with regard to gender identity and gendered roles:

> Satan seeks to discredit the Savior and divine authority, to nullify the effects of the Atonement, to counterfeit revelation, to lead people away from the truth, to contradict individual accountability, to confuse gender, to undermine marriage, and to discourage childbearing (especially by parents who will raise children in righteousness).
>
> Maleness and femaleness, marriage, and the bearing and nurturing of children are all essential to the great plan of happiness. Modern revelation makes clear that what we call gender was part of our existence prior to our birth. God declares that he created "male and female" (D&C 20:18; Moses 2:27; Gen. 1:27). Elder James E. Talmage explained: "The distinction between male and female is no condition peculiar to the relatively brief period of mortal life; it was an essential characteristic of our pre-existent condition" (*Millennial Star*, 24 Aug. 1922, p. 539). (Oaks 1993)

The Great Plan of Happiness is clear on social mandates that many would argue inform the culture wars and certainly create the core of how and why this faith system speaks directly to gender and sexuality in a modern moment: correct principles require proper self-governance; "confused" gender and/or homoerotic relations between men and women work for Satan and against God; the command to "be fruitful and multiply" is absolute—there is no one way to opt out of it; righteous marriages are not only for all of time but for all of eternity, meaning that single and working mothers violate the divine design of marriage and thus perpetuate "rising numbers of abortions, divorces, child neglect, and juvenile crime" (Oaks 1993).

In this respect, not only does Mormonism speak of the broader temperament and perceived characteristics of the faith—relentless cheerfulness, homespun modesty, and upbeat optimism, like a whole state populated by the smiley Osmond family—it also announces one of the basic identifiable brands of Mormonism. To strive for perfect obedience and continued self-improvement under the Plan of Happiness functions as a meritocratic system promising ultimate power for men and a diffused form of bliss for women. Technologies of self-making are central to the spiritual neoliberal goal of establishing a kingdom where one might be God. Those humble and smiling missionaries patrolling the world for converts have a long game in mind: if the meek shall inherit the Earth, the righteous Mormon man shall inherit his own planet.[6] And so shall the missionary's memetic counterpart: the polygamous patriarch, who in his own way uses earthly practices to store up credit for celestial rewards through the Great Plan of Happiness. As the British program *Three Wives, One Husband* tells its viewers: "Like many fundamentalists, Abel believes that having a big family with lots of wives will help take them all to the top level of heaven."

As in broader discourses of neoliberalism, those who work hard are perceived as worthy of success and those who do not succeed have only themselves to blame. The spiritual neoliberalism of Mormonism requires an exacting meritocratic commitment to behavior and affective norms, often expressed through the marketplace idiom of industry and efficiency and the social conscriptions of happy heterosexual marriage and fertility. Those who cannot or will not play according to the rules of the Great Plan of Happiness deserve their dismal depression, thus making happiness itself critical evidence in the teleology of progression.

Happiness as a Technology of Spiritual Neoliberalism

The *New York Post* wants to know, "Are Mormons the Happiest People in America?" (Dawson 2016). Beneath a photo banner chock-a-block full with smiling Mormon celebrities (figure 1.7), reporter Mackenzie Dawson uses Mormonism to speculate more broadly on happiness and Americans' obsession with it. She cites the work of British journalist and documentarian Ruth Whippman, whose book *America the Anxious* and her addictive

FIG. 1.7 Happy Mormon celebrities: (*clockwise from left to right*) entertainer Marie Osmond, novelist Stephenie Meyer, actor Jon Heder, politician Mitt Romney, entertainer Donny Osmond, actor Katherine Heigl, rock musician Brandon Flowers, actor A. J. Cook, and professional athlete Bryce Harper.

consumption of Mormon mommy blogs—where authors are dedicated stay-at-home moms and children are beatific and well behaved—compel her to visit Provo, Utah. Provo is the heart center of Mormonism and "the happiest town on earth," as determined by the 2014 Gallup poll. In a classic British stance to all things American, Whippman is at once fascinated and shocked, and in a chapter specifically addressing Mormonism, she conflates the American credo for optimistic happiness with the Mormon way of being, writing:

> Not only are religious people in the United States generally significantly happier than nonreligious people, but if the studies are to be believed, Mormons are the happiest of all. On almost every measure, Mormons appear to be outpacing the rest of America. Around 90 percent of Mormons rate their communities as excellent or good, compared with just 70 percent of Americans generally. Mormons have some of the lowest rates of unemployment in the country and according to Gallup polls, Provo, Utah, where close to 90 percent of the population identifies as religious Mormon, is officially the happiest town in America.

So is it that simple? Could all the books in the personal development section of the bookstores be condensed into one single three-word e-book? How to Be Happy: The Definitive Answer. Become a Mormon. The end. (Whippman 2016, 130)[7]

In order to understand the affective appeal of happiness and religion, Whippman devotes a good deal of her book to mainstream Mormons. They are, "as a group," she writes, "highly conservative. They don't drink tea or coffee, let alone alcohol. They overwhelmingly vote Republican. The church advocates strict gender roles, with men out providing and women at home looking after the (many) children. Black people were not permitted to hold the highest religious honors within the church until 1978. Women still aren't" (2016, 131). Whippman confesses to "cognitive dissonance" when it comes to the Mormons and the larger modern project of happiness. "The statistics seem to point clearly to the idea that I would be much happier doing a lot of things that don't sound as though they would make me very happy at all. Spending lots of time in church. Having several more children. Giving up alcohol. Submitting to the patriarchy. Joining the Republican Party. Would I really be happier if I were a Mormon?" (131). Another way to ask Whippman's questions: Do reduced personal choices about how one consumes, how one behaves, and how one acts actually yield greater happiness? *Is the examined life not worth living?*

Writing for the British *Sunday Times*, Valerie Segal called Whippman's book "a funny yet unsettling book about the modern quest for happiness." Segal (2016) notes with a kind of uncanny clarity:

> This is not merely a personal voyage of enlightenment . . . nor an extended eye-roll at wacky Americans. The book's serious underpinning is a warning about how happiness is being weaponized by governments and employers, directed towards their people to make them work harder and longer. . . . Happiness, Whippman suggests, instantly becomes "happiness" when filtered through corporate interests, a shiny simulacrum far removed from genuine well-being or the old-school satisfactions of sometimes leaving the office. . . . There are no problems, just "problematic thinking." Its appeal to austerity pushing governments is clear: "If circumstance is of little consequence to happiness, why worry if people are struggling?"

With Mormonism as a prime example, these considerations of the desire for self-improvement and affective betterment in turn reveal their own kind of affinity fraud. Through an appeal to purported normativity and sameness—we all want to be happy—these models create a scripted economy of personal enhancement that metes out spiritual devotion with material rewards and punishments.

Salvation through the Screen: Image Management as a Technology of Spiritual Neoliberalism

Happiness notwithstanding, Mormonism has long faced and been working on the problem of its "weird image" (Kirn 2011). Terryl L. Givens notes, for instance, that in the nineteenth century Mormons were the objects of ridicule and hostility due to their theological differences with mainline Protestant groups of the time. "The earliest recorded complaints," he writes, "concerned the church's religious peculiarity based on ongoing revelation and additional scripture, and the threat its phenomenal missionary successes posed to mainstream churches. In addition, Mormons preached an irksome doctrine of exclusivity and engaged in communalistic economic practices. Unlike the Shakers, who considered their unconventional way of life a higher order of existence but only for those who felt the call to so live, the Mormons claimed a monopoly on the path to salvation" (Givens 1997, 3). Then add polygamy, politics, and theocracy, Givens says, and "the Mormon problem" comes into vibrant focus.

Perhaps most striking for our purposes is how self-aware Mormonism is of its own brand management. Jan Shipps argues that Mormonism was considered a radical sect in the nineteenth century and into the twentieth. After World War II, however, church authorities created a new identity: "those amazing Mormons," possessing all of the Boy Scout virtues of loyalty, honor, and fidelity, but honed with the capitalist savvy and shrewd consumerism that epitomizes the American marketplace (Shipps 2012).[8] Indeed, mainstream Mormon leaders moved not only to change their image in the public mind but to reorganize around the concept of correlation, or the idea that the Salt Lake City–based LDS Church should be structured, as Matthew Bowman (2012), author of *The Mormon People*, writes, in conscious imitation of American corporations. What this yielded in sociological and historical terms was a contradictory position where Mormons were poised as able to take care of their own and not be dependent on government at the same time as they used tax-supported public aid to make their businesses prosper. The FLDS, in particular, eschews the government yet relies on welfare assistance for its many legally unwed mothers and government contracts for its sustenance, a strategic accommodation it calls "bleeding the beast."

While both LDS and FLDS folk have long referred to themselves with pride as a "peculiar people," a term to indicate their separation from worldly ways and their chosenness by God, the thought that non-Mormons perceive them as weird stings just a bit. In *How Americans View Mormonism: Seven Steps to Improve Our Image*, Gary Lawrence (2008) cites polls that contend 43 percent of the country believe the LDS Church treats women as second-class citizens; 39 percent think Mormons use pressure tactics; 38 percent said the church is pushy; 16 percent see it as racist; and 16 percent say it is a "church to be feared."[9]

Given that self-improvement and attentive labor toward personal perfection stand as important technologies of both modern self-making and Mormon ideation, it is fitting that Lawrence's book on the Mormon image problem is a self-help primer for change. His seven-step improvement regime includes that Mormons listen before commenting, avoid LDS jargon, speak plainly, follow the Golden Rule, and eliminate pressure tactics from missionary outreach. "Telling people that force has no place in the church and that we are committed to freedom of choice and the principle of individual agency is critical to allaying fears and improving our image," Lawrence (2008) writes. It is corporate religion on-message as both telegenic and friendly.[10]

While Lawrence advocated inward reflection and personal modification, the mainstream church followed its well-worn path by seeking to alter public perception. In 2014, the church released *Meet the Mormons*, a documentary, says member Blair True, "originally produced to give people, especially those that are not of our faith, a little glimpse into who we are, what makes us tick" (Prescott 2016). *Meet the Mormons* was originally intended to be screened in the visitors' center at the Salt Lake City Temple. "But that's not what happened," said True. "An outside consulting firm from Los Angeles took the film out and tested it specifically with those who are not of our faith—individuals and families who don't know much about Mormons. The reviews were positive, so ultimately the First Presidency decided to expand the film's audience." The documentary screened in 100 of 317 nationwide locations and ranked number ten in national total box office sales that week, in-group media thus serving mainstream distribution ends ("'Meet the Mormons' Pulls in Audiences" 2014).

By way of concluding this section, I want to hone in on the church's stance on social media in the consolidation of their image, since the internet has been a more powerful change agent for the church's stance on secrecy and exclusivity than anything before it.[11] On June 23, 2013, leaders of the church announced that the brave new world of social media might, in turn, offer an expansive new set of heavenly converts. At a major meeting held at the

Mormonism as Meme and Analytic 79

FIG. 1.8 LDS Worldwide Broadcast.

20,000-seat Marriott Center at Brigham Young University in Provo, Utah, white-haired and dark-suited church leaders instructed their young charges amassed in the assembly hall (see figure 1.8). Thomas S. Monson, the church's president, and Boyd K. Packer, president of the Quorum of the Twelve Apostles, the church's most exclusive and prestigious governing council, spoke to the crowd. Together, these massive talking heads intoned what must have surely been a radical message to the ears of the faithful gathered under the Marriott's dome: the Latter-day Saints might now use social media to herald a holy message—available easily, affordably, and in a familiar context.

L. Tom Perry, a member of the Quorum of Twelve, took the podium and explained to the crowd, "During less-productive times of the day—chiefly in the mornings—missionaries will use computers in meetinghouses and other Church facilities to contact investigators and members, work with local priesthood leaders and missionary leaders, receive and contact referrals, follow up on commitments, confirm appointments, and teach principles from [the missionary guide] *Preach My Gospel* using Mormon.org, Facebook, blogs, email, and text messages" (2013). Home churches were instructed to friend visiting missionaries on Facebook, and even those not actively serving missions were encouraged to make their experiences of Mormonism more broadly known through social media means like Twitter or blogging.

The images documenting this gathering and published by the church on their website (lds.org) are uncanny enough—those looming heads levitating above the hordes, glowing like transmediated deities, transmogrification in the digital age. But also surreal is the fact that the vision for the new age was voiced by three elderly men, all of whom were born in the 1920s and very near or older than ninety at the time of the meeting (Packer, eighty-nine; Perry, ninety-one; Monson, eighty-six). Aside from offering new possibilities for nonagenarians, the conference reinforced the very things that the Mormon Church, and really organized Western religion more broadly, has come to resolutely signify: whiteness, aged masculine authority, emotional distance, stodgy traditionalism. In short, patriarchal governance.

Indeed, to understand why this message was so radical, it's important to fill in a bit of history about notions of regulation within Mormonism. As I have mentioned, the LDS Church is quite famous for its political conservatism and commitments to family.[12] Popular entertainment is also restricted. While there is not an official censored list of popular culture materials members must avoid, there is a general understanding that Mormons do not attend R-rated films (or worse) and Mormons do not listen to music that is violent or sexualized. As with many orthodox systems, adherents to the LDS religion dedicate themselves to upholding a rigorous behavioral code—perhaps not the 613 mitzvot of Judaism or the Ten Commandments of the Judeo-Christian Old Testament, but exacting expectations nonetheless. Importantly, however, most of these codes are not written down in the church's juridical volume, *Doctrine and Covenants*, which lists the revelations received by the church's presidents. Instead, codes function as expectations imposed by censure, scrutiny, and surveillance. Writes former missionary Jeffrey Draga (2011) on his blog, "I know that they are not actual commandments, but you know as well as I do that every single item on this list is expected of the members. . . . I think that they overwhelm their members on purpose to make sure that everyone has that inadequate feeling. That will keep them inline." For many cultural theorists, this sort of move is all too familiar—it is the governance of neoliberal culture.

According to mediated Mormonism, the church itself takes these principles for proper behavior quite seriously, with biannual exams of members to determine temple worthiness. The church also maintains a Strengthening the Church Members Committee, which is charged to "pass on public information to local leaders about members participating in abuse, fraud and other activities that may endanger others" ("Strengthening Church Members Committee" 2017). Quite often, to do this work the committee lurks on members' Facebook pages, examines members' search histories, and keeps track of members' public and private activities, looking for Saints who are not functioning in perfect obedience to the religion. Indeed, one of my research assistants for this project, a very capable and left-leaning PhD student, who is also a five-generation Mormon tracing his roots to Joseph Smith, felt quite squeamish about doing some of the web searches and other forms of research on LGBT+ rights, sexuality, and feminism that I needed for this project. His objection was not intellectual or political but practical, since he feared that his internet usage for me would out his gay- and feminist-friendly inclinations to the church and thus jeopardize his membership. We agreed that the best way for him to proceed was to avoid certain hot topics, so that church leaders would not misinterpret the work he was doing for me as evidence of his wayward liberalism, a censoring of self that is hardly self-censorship.

Those members who do defy the church's teachings are called to tribunals, called Councils or Courts of Love. As Martha Beck writes,

> Mormon Church courts (officially referred to as Councils of Love) are major tribunals, in which a panel of twelve local men, called the High Council, convenes to try and sentence a Saint who has confessed to or been accused of some infraction. Six men are chosen by lottery to plead the defendant's case, while the other six argue against him. The defendant is rigorously questioned by both sides, the content and quality of the answers duly noted. (Did the accused weep remorseful tears? Did he or she acknowledge the authority of the Church to define moral behavior?) After both sides have been heard, the council votes on a consequence, which may range from nothing at all (if the defendant is found not guilty) to the ultimate punishment: excommunication. Another possible sentence, "disfellowshipment," drastically reduces a person's status without actually cutting him loose. (Beck 2006, 206)

In tightly knit Mormon communities, like that at Brigham Young University about which Beck is writing, excommunication and disfellowshipment would equally result in a person being ostracized by the community. Any employee of BYU would also lose his or her job with little chance of finding another, if faculty. Crucially, the mediascape represents these Councils of Love as Orwellian and totalitarian. As media spectacles, they function as high points of fascination, from Barb's tribunal and excommunication for practicing plural marriage as depicted on *Big Love* to Marnie Freeman's (2014) trial for lesbianism in her memoir *To the One*. These scenes play out the worst fears about Mormonism: behind the toothy smiles lies a cutthroat authoritarianism that demands perfect obedience to its rules.

If media culture perceives the Saints as ominous, the same is also true in reverse. The LDS Church believes in the harm of popular culture to such a degree that it puts extra limitations on how much and what type of media its missionaries might consume while on their missions. *The Missionary Handbook* entirely bans television and popular movies, disallows personal cell phone use, and restricts going online to once a week (and then only so that an elder might blog about his religious testimony). Until 2019, phone calls home were allowed only twice a year, typically on Christmas and Mother's Day. A missionary's time is highly quantified and tracked with elaborately coded time sheets that testify to the use of the days and hours and minutes spent in prayer, in studying the scriptures, in tracking (knocking on doors), in speaking to investigators (people interested in joining the church—or in just talking to two nineteen-year-old boys on their front porch). That research assistant of mine I mentioned above served a mission in Japan and told me he was extremely proud that during those two years in the field, his time spreadsheets indicated he had only wasted thirty minutes. There is a reason why FranklinCovey, the maker of schedules and values-based planners and founded by devout Mormons Stephen Covey and Hyrum Smith, leads the booming industry of efficiency-based wellness journals designed to help people be their best selves as a necessary stair step to happiness and prosperity.[13]

Missionaries are assigned a same-sex companion, formally addressed as "Elder" if male and "Sister" if female. Companions are charged never to leave one another's presence, except when an individual uses the bathroom. According to the missionary handbook, companions are meant to protect one another against "spiritual and physical" danger. But companions are also accountability agents who prevent personal time (and reflection) and who guard against wayward behaviors, such as masturbation (these are usually nineteen-year-old boys, after all). Given these many restrictions and limits to free agency, online proselytizing opens a worldwide web of possibilities for conversation in the name of conversion. While missionaries are not allowed to surf as they please, they are encouraged and allowed to perform their ministry across a broad platform of mediated possibilities in the name of the church.

It is this composite—the restrictions on behavior and embodiment and the Janus-faced reality of welcome and warning—that combine to solidify Mormonism as a meme and analytic. Even if often understood differently than the church intends, these codes circulate in the public imagination as part and parcel of Mormonism and as cautionary tale on authoritarianism.

It's for this reason that Sam might joke on *Cheers* that Mormons don't dance (although they do) or an FBI character on the Russian spy show *The Americans* complains to another character about how Mormon it is to have early morning meetings.[14] It's also for this reason that mediated stories about polygamy so often follow a model of abuse and corruption. Even the über-secret sacralized underwear worn by worthy Mormons has achieved a veritable cult status in the twenty-first-century imagination that far outstrips its role as a textile chastity belt. Indeed, the unauthorized circuit of semiotics positions garments as everything from gay fetish wear to secret markers that only the initiated might discern, hence the game of spotting the magical underwear, also known as "the Mormon smile," on Mitt Romney during the 2012 presidential campaign (see figure 1.9). Cross-platform media play a crucial role in sustaining this critique.

"For centuries," says Joanna Brooks in a *Daily Beast* exposé on the fate of progressives within the church (Joyce 2015), "Mormon leaders have tightly controlled all messaging about Mormonism. In 1993, the church excommunicated a number of critical intellectuals who became known as the 'September Six,'" a group of scholars (three women and three men), who were excommunicated or disfellowshipped by the church for publishing scholarly material that was perceived as harmful to Mormon religious doctrine. "The hierarchy's monopoly on church image began to change with the advent of the Internet," writes the *Daily Beast*, "as progressive Mormons were able to connect with one another in unprecedented ways." Brooks notes that the surge in new media has led to a "decentralization of perspectives about the church, and far broader public engagement among the laity about difficult aspects of Mormon life." Social media have also led to an increasingly visible stage on which to play out the social agenda of this world religion.

The church has always tightly regulated information about itself, but it has also played along with the publicity game of the modern era. Indeed, Moore tells us that Brigham Young encouraged early Saints to enjoy "amusements" such as dancing and the theater, largely because culture, in Young's words, "can be made to aid the pulpit in impressing upon the minds of the community an enlightened sense of a virtuous life, also a proper honor of the enormity of sin and a just dread of its consequences" (Moore 1995, 97 fn 20). From the stages of the 1860s to the screens of the 2000s, we see a similar logic in operation. Early reports suggest that missionaries have been 80 percent more likely to win over curious nonbelievers through devices such as instant messaging, email, and Facebook than they were through face-to-face and door-to-door encounters, largely through insomniacs who

FIG. 1.9 The Mormon smile: spotting the visible garment lines of Mitt Romney's magic underwear.

instant-message missionaries in the wee hours of the morning (Bosker 2014). The internet is now an approved place for the worldwide web of Mormon missionaries, largely because their behaviors are tightly scrutinized, the penalties for misuse are threateningly clear, and because the accessibility, visibility, and sociability provided by social media attracts new Saints ripe for salvation through the screen.

Taking It in the Missionary Position: *The Book of Mormon*, the LDS Brand, and the Divine Politics of Cultural Appropriation

As a conclusion, I offer a gentle reminder that my purpose in writing this book is not to critique or challenge Mormon people or beliefs but to demonstrate how the idea of the faith underlies and reinforces a set of structuring values and inequities that are taken as American commonplaces. Those values speak to notions of independence, free choice, unfettered agency, and divine reward. It's a credo of spiritual neoliberalism that underscores a teleology of action and free agency: good choices bring good things; do well by doing good. So my final point of this chapter is a small demonstration of how this process works. Let's go back to that term "parodica," the union of parody and erotica. At first blush, parodica doesn't seem a whole lot different from a camp aesthetic that forces rupture through exaggeration, irreverence, self-reflexivity, and a gay sensibility. But parodica, as I use the term with respect to Mormonism, turns from camp (or out-camps camp) in its conservative co-optation of both parody and erotica.

Allow me to set the scene. In their perceived earnestness, sincerity, and commitment to decent all-American heteronormativity, mainstream Mormons are an obvious group on which to center a satiric comedic send-up, such as those created by Matt Stone and Trey Parker in the television show *South Park*, the feature film *Orgazmo*, and the Tony award–winning Broadway musical *The Book of Mormon*. Mormons have been the butt of many jokes (gay sexual double entendre most absolutely intended), as they take it in the missionary position over and over again. Consider, for instance, the satiric website *Mormon Missionary Positions* (DaCosta 2018), which starts off with a modified image of the Book of Mormon and moves into images of two clean-cut and exceedingly white young missionaries, only to be followed by a cavalcade of Kama Sutra–inspired sex positions from, of course, the missionary position to hanging bow. My personal favorite: bicycle position (see figures 1.10 and 1.11). Indeed, when *The Book of Mormon* musical began using an advertising motif in 2018 that mirrored these comedic Kama Sutra poses, media culture moved one step closer to parodica (see figure 1.12). On the more explicit side, there's Mormon Boyz.com, which promises that Mormon boyz are Mormon boys, real Mormon men engaged in same-sex online pornography organized around (what I believe but don't know are) faux secret insemination ceremonies that the website explicitly labels as Mormon. And, of course, *The Book of Mormon* musical makes jokes about anal penetration and gay desire, featuring one character in particular, Elder McKinley, plagued by his same-sex attraction and committed to turning it off. These ideas participate in their own ideological undoing through a process of reversals so queer we might call them camp.

It is not exclusively these scenes of semicloseted same-sex desire or of tap-dancing and pink-sequins-wearing gay fabulousness that lend *The Book of Mormon* its camp flair; it is the overall tenor of deep ridicule (and self-mocking), coupled with a relentless and audacious irreverence, all taking place amid an in-your-face display of what Susan Sontag calls "camp vulgarity." The fourth song of the musical, for instance, is a full-ensemble number called "Hasa Diga Eebowai," translated to the missionary characters' horror as "Fuck You, God." One lyric line goes, "When God fucks you in the butt, Fuck

FIGS. 1.10–1.11 *Mormon Missionary Positions.*
Photographs by Neil DaCosta.

FIG. 1.12 *The Book of Mormon* ad, *New York Times*, April 15, 2018.

God right back in his cunt," a sort of gloriously irreverent gesture of resistance to a gender-complex version of God. Rory O'Malley, who originated the role of Elder McKinley on Broadway, calls the show "not necessarily offensive to Mormons, I think it's equally offensive to all human beings" (Pellot 2014).

Enter parodica. While it might be understandable to look to Mormons as the butt of these jokes, they hardly seem to be the place to look for the production of camp itself. "DID YOU KNOW?" says the online advertising for the touring company of *The Book of Mormon*, "Instead of picketing Broadway or theaters nationwide as originally feared, The Mormon church has taken the good-natured and risqué lampooning of *The Book Of Mormon* with a wry grin and have instead taken out advertisements in the show's playbills across the world, under the heading 'The book is always better.' Now that is what we call a darned good sport!" (*The Book of Mormon* 2018). That, and the fact that the LDS Church also bought up prime advertising space to run in advance of and conjunction with the musical's international touring company, is also what we call darn good marketing (figures 1.13–1.14).

Indeed, the LDS Church's reaction to the camp sensibility of *The Book of Mormon* musical, where missionaries pretend to perform queer sex acts, and song-and-dance numbers center around sexual repression and same-sex desire, is nothing short of remarkable. The church's stance evinces a shrewd capacity to appropriate the discourses and idioms of the very things it considers to be perverse, turning these counterveiling critiques to its own advantage. As such, the church has managed to convert the attention given to *The Book of Mormon* musical into converts for its most holy of religious texts, the Book of Mormon. They've done so by capitalizing on the extreme version of Mormonism promulgated across media sites, turning the codes of camp back on itself to undo its irony. That is what we call darn good appropriation, or what I'm calling here parodica.

It's worth thinking more about the politics of parodica connected to *The Book of Mormon*, described by Clark Johnsen, an original cast member and

FIGS. 1.13–1.14 London public spaces advertising the "I'm a Mormon" campaign in advance of *The Book of Mormon*'s premiere in the West End, 2012. Photograph courtesy of the author.

himself a former Mormon missionary, as a "hyperbole of ridiculousness" (Dehlin 2015a). If the very logic of cultural appropriation is that one person or group has taken something (an identity, a mode of being, an aesthetic style) that rightfully belongs to another person or group, then we must ask how ownership, legitimacy, and authenticity are determined, and if, indeed, these are even the right modalities to consider. For all of its earnestness and godly seriousness, religion is itself a gathering of impossibilities as truth. Religion, particularly orthodoxy, states a demand for unswerving authority, yet in its reshaping of tradition and custom, its retooling of ritual to support new systems, and its mandate for a fantastic buy-in or leap of faith on basic beliefs, religion is itself appropriative and over-the-top, outlandish, ridiculous, often queer, and, well, camp.

The mixture of parody and erotica often creates an explosive tincture that shatters its definitional boundaries. Here the brand culture of spiritual neoliberalism invites progressive possibility where you least expect to find it—in the hallowed and hetero grounds of conservative religion. This strikes me as a fusion of incommensurabilities that ups the game of what camp might mean and do. And to my mind, that's the best trick yet that has been pulled from Joseph Smith's magical hat.

2. The Mormon Glow

THE RACED AND GENDERED IMPLICATIONS
OF SPECTACULAR VISIBILITY

Mormons make me nervous.... They just seem to be a slightly *superior* breed of human: they seem taller and more bright-eyed. Mormon kids have straight teeth. The women are all pretty. They are a wholesome, better breed of people. Never mind that Mormons wear more than their fair share of Dockers. Never mind that Utahans consume more porn than anybody else: that just speaks to their superhuman testosterone levels.... Salt Lake City is Mormon Mecca, spiritual and administrative home of the Church of Jesus Christ of Latter-day Saints. SLC is LDS, and being there can make you feel like you are on LSD.

One of the games I have always enjoyed playing when visiting SLC is "spot the Mormon." It's easy. You just look for anybody who looks happy. I can't explain it. Maybe it's the lack of alcohol. Maybe it's just that structure makes people happy. Maybe, ironically, in a country that prides itself on being the free-est in the world, strict guidelines actually make people happier.

—Michael Ian Black, *America, You Sexy Bitch*

Mormonism is one of the fastest-growing religions in America. Whatever criticism is made concerning some of the more atypical Mormon traditions, radical undertones, and beliefs, no one can suggest that this religion isn't hitting some kind of chord with Americans.... The appearance of being an extremely conservative throwback to a time when America was different seems to be the defining characteristic of the Mormon lifestyle, one that appeals mightily in a world where everything can feel a little too fast and somewhat scantily clad. Maybe American culture has gotten to the point where we are so over-stimulated, sent so many sexualized messages from the media, and desensitized in our reaction to overly bad behavior, that in comparison Mormonism can appeal as something that is safe.

—Meghan McCain, *America, You Sexy Bitch*

In 2011, as a lead-up to the U.S. presidential election, conservative princess, talk show radio host, and Fox news pundit Meghan McCain went on the road with liberal comedian and sitcom actor Michael Ian Black to tell their version of America. As the epigraphs that start this chapter attest, taking the American collective temperature means reckoning with the Mormons, their unique and recognizable visibility, and their massive appeal. By the time of their book's publication in 2012, Mitt Romney was poised to become the Republican nominee for president, and Mormon visibility was high, leading Walter Kirn (2011) to announce in *Newsweek* that the United States was in a Mormon Moment. These factors combined to put the Salt Lake City church in a position as a cultural authority that betokened a new mainstream status for Mormons and Mormonism.

That period of time was itself fleeting—by generous measures, about three years. In the wake of Kirn's declaration and Romney's loss of the race for president, many pundits decried the end of Mormon prominence. In 2014, for example, Cadence Woodland wrote an opinion piece for the *New York Times* declaring "the end of the Mormon moment," based on the "crackdown" against a number of church liberals and intellectuals, including Kate Kelley, who lobbied for women to hold priesthood status within the church, and John Dehlin, who founded *Mormon Stories*, a podcast interview program that gives voice and amplitude to Mormons struggling in their faith journey. For Kirn in 2011, to be in the Mormon moment suggested a level of unique influence and visibility to those things and people marked by Mormonism; for Woodland in 2014, to be out of the Mormon moment indicated a failure on the church's part to make good on the social justice opportunities its visibility provided.

In truth, public visibility did not begin for the Mormons in 2011 and it did not end in 2014. As one example, a 2007 posting in the online magazine *Pop Matters* reported that Mormons were at that time already "growing used to [being in] the spotlight," a beacon powered by both politics (Romney's first run for president) and art (in such feature films as *Georgia Rule* and *Napoleon Dynamite*, television shows like *Big Love*, novels with Mormon themes written by Mormon people, and music ranging from the Killers to the Mormon Tabernacle Choir). Explained Gregory Hahn (2007) in the *Pop Matters* article, "Mormons are 'in,' but that attention has brought an at-times-uncomfortable spotlight and a renewed pressure to maintain the uniqueness that has defined the religion since it started in 1800s America."

The real point about spectacular visibility, then, is that Mormonism has consistently operated within the spotlight to play a clarifying role with respect to broader U.S. understandings of itself precisely through the debated role of its own prominence and the implications of such status. If Mormonism has often walked the razor's edge between marginalization and the mainstream, between persecuted outsiders and American everyman figures, this has only enhanced its centrality as a hinge in the American hermeneutic. Media—in all of its new and old forms—are central in the cultural (and divine) politics of F/LDS Mormonism.

Consider, for instance, Kristine Haglund, the editor of *Dialogue: A Journal of Mormon Thought*, who wrote for *Slate Magazine* in 2014 that with the "unprecedented attention" generated by Mitt Romney's political bids for president, "Mormons hoped that becoming better known would mean becoming better liked." Much like Woodland, Haglund does not feel that the SLC church made good on its moment in the spotlight. Instead, she argues, "Media attention was a megaphone for the voices of Mormons who might ordinarily find themselves on the fringes of their congregations—academics, feminists, LGBT+ Mormons, and Mormons questioning their own beliefs" (Haglund 2014). Yet this consequence, she argues, is a step forward, since the elevation of marginal voices to mainstream positions largely through cross-platform mediation has advanced a more inclusive discursive culture where progressive members of the LDS persuasion might find common cause with one another, amid an "idealized America" governed by a "pluralistic creed." "Even as Mormons recognize their continued, unwilling exile from that America," she reflects, "we are affirming those ideals by learning, haltingly, to cope with our own messy history and to tolerate, albeit imperfectly, difference and dissent within the faith" (Haglund 2014).

Haglund gathers many of the outliers whose voices fill this book—academics, feminists, LGBT+ Mormons, questioning Mormons—as critical agents in a salutary social agenda. In this chapter, I want to focus very specifically on a different set of people who have been involved in one of the larger controversies faced by the mainstream Mormon Church and, to a lesser degree, fundamentalist LDS groups—those marked and affected by the F/LDS regard toward race and racialization. Let me start by coming back to that lyric line from *The Book of Mormon* musical: "I believe in 1978 God changed his mind about black people!" In the show, Elder Price's ballad, "I Believe!" is meant to be a moment of hyperbole that adds to and punctuates the increasingly outrageous positions these fictional Mormon missionaries, and the actual F/LDS churches, preach—"ancient Jews built boats and sailed to America," "God lives on a planet called Kolob," "Jesus has his own planet as well," "The Garden of Eden is in Jackson County, Missouri," and so on.[1]

But it is the divine mind change about black people being eligible for LDS Church membership in 1978 that centers this discussion and puts it in my own analytical spotlight.

Mormonism as a visual spectacle indicates that as a meme, it marks something extraordinary. This concept accords with the ideas raised in the epigraphs from McCain and Black (as well as a host of other bloggers, writers, and cultural producers), that Mormons, as a people and a faith, can be spotted, visually recognized by the radiance clean living confers. Across mediated Mormonism, this spectacle is called the Mormon Glow. Given the very clear associations between glowing and light, between light and white—what Richard Dyer has termed in *White* an "epistemology of light"—and given the rather large social and cultural history that conflates sin with darkness, and darkness with blackness, the racialized logics of the Mormon Glow key to an increasingly global preoccupation with those things "fair and lovely" as a signifier of whiteness and modernity. The racialized logics that come together under the broad sign of "Mormon" illuminate (and I choose this word specifically) a broader set of concerns about race and gender that link to norms of value and behavior. In this chapter, then, I consider the raced and gendered valences that are part of Mormonism's messy history with visibility, a set of complicated relations that continue, by most accounts, in an equally fraught present day.

The Mark of Cain: Historical Context

To better understand the implications of both visibility and race in and to the church, some historical context is helpful since one of the major issues the LDS Church has had to tackle in terms of its public mis/understanding has had to do with race. In the early days of the church, prior to Joseph Smith's death in 1844 and prior to the LDS/FLDS split, social tensions were often due to Mormons' perceived permissiveness and overall friendliness toward people of color, specifically Africans and African Americans held in bondage. Before the Civil War, black people—both bonded and free—were admitted as members, and black men were able to hold priesthood authority. Indeed, Joseph Smith was a public abolitionist, and part of his presidential platform in 1844 included the nationwide eradication of slavery. It was largely, though not exclusively, due to this stance on slavery that Mormons elicited such widespread animosity in the pro-slavery state of Missouri in the late 1830s.

It should be noted, however, that Smith and the early church founders (and most of white America) were highly racist by today's standards. Consider, for instance, that in 1836 when the Mormons were located primarily in Missouri, Smith entered the charged racial rhetoric of the antebellum South by writing a position statement that favored a time-released manumission of nearly twenty years. Smith did not support immediate and universal abolition due to concerns that it would "set loose upon the world a community of people who might peradventure, overrun our country and violate the most sacred principles of human society, chastity and virtue" (Smith 1836). Oliver Cowdery (1836), the first baptized Latter-day Saint and scribe to Joseph as he interpreted the golden tablets that would become the Book of Mormon, was more contemptuous in his racial dislike:

> Let the blacks of the south be free, and our community is overrun with paupers, and a reckless mass of human beings, uncultivated, untaught and unaccustomed to provide for themselves the necessaries of life—endangering the chastity of every female who might by chance be found in our streets—our prisons filled with convicts, and the hangman wearied with executing the functions of his office! This must unavoidably be the case, every rational man must admit, who has ever travelled in the slave states, or we must open our houses, unfold our arms, and bid these degraded and degrading sons of Canaan, a hearty welcome and a free admittance to all we possess!
> ... And insensible to feeling must be the heart, and low indeed must be the mind, that would consent for a moment, to see his fair daughter, his sister, or perhaps, his bosom companion, in the embrace of a NEGRO!

So though Joseph and early church leaders might have been open to converting those with dark skins, the ruling brethren were hardly convinced of black people's equal personhood.

This is somewhat surprising given that, as W. Paul Reeve has convincingly shown, early church members—the inheritors of a white-skinned Anglo-Scandinavian bloodline—were themselves racialized and denounced as historical throwbacks in an emerging United States challenged by its own vertiginous plurality. Reeve argues through scholars such as David R. Roediger that "race operated as a hierarchical system designed to create order and superiority out of the perceived disorder of the confluence of peoples in America" (Reeve 2015, 3). As such, the predominantly white-skinned Mormons (as well as Irish and Jewish people) were perceived as racialized subhumans in the nineteenth-century American imagination, a "new race" of devolved people. Mormon devolution was tied to the rumors of polygamy and inbreeding, and the Saints were often depicted as "distinct, peculiar, suspicious, and potentially dangerous outsiders" (Reeve 2015, 14). When their polygamous ways were publicly confirmed in 1852, Reeve notes that "Mormonism represented both a religious and a racial decline," thus solidifying the notion that the Latter-day Saints betokened atavism rather than modernity. It's remarkable, given these ties to both racialization and devolution, that Mormons today might be linked with both hyperbolic whiteness and modernization.

Mormons in the 1800s were also racialized due to their close trading and social ties with Native American peoples, whom they perceived as their "red brethren" and the remaining inheritors of the dark race of Lamanites, who had been, according to the Book of Mormon, "cursed by dark skin" for their treacherous ways against the Nephites, the godly whiter race in Joseph's holy book. Indeed, some Judeo-Christian traditions and Mormonism attribute the Curse of Ham as the mark of God's censure for iniquity (Genesis 9:25–27; 2 Nephi 5:21–23). According to LDS theology, the Lamanites were a "chosen people fallen into decay"; their darkness made them suspect—the mark of Cain—but their chosenness also made them worthy of sympathy and salvation (Reeve 2015, 55; see also Bushman 2005; Givens 2002; Skousen 2009; Mauss 2003).

Under Brigham Young, the Mormon relation to "people of color" intensified into the racist position that would mark the church for nearly 130 years. In 1849, Young announced that black men were disallowed from attaining priesthood status. Young was no nobler in his regard for Native Americans: "There is a curse on these aborigines of our country who roam the plains and are so wild that you cannot tame them. They are of the House of Israel; they once had the Gospel delivered to them, they had oracles of truth; Jesus came and administered to them after his resurrection and they received and delighted in the Gospel until the fourth generation when they turned away and became so wicked that God cursed them with this dark and benighted and loathsome condition" (*Journal of Discourses* vol. 14, Discourse 12, 87). Young's justification for racial intolerance stemmed from the social eugenics so popular among white elites in the nineteenth century. Young noted that "some classes of the human family that are black, uncouth, uncomely, disagreeable and low in their habits, wild, and seemingly deprived of nearly all the blessings of the intelligence that is generally bestowed upon mankind" had been purposefully marked by God as sinners. "The Lord put a mark upon him, which is the flat nose and black skin. Trace mankind down to after the flood, and then another curse is pronounced upon the same race—that they should be the 'servant of servants'; and they will be, until that curse is removed; and the Abolitionists cannot help it, nor in the least alter that decree" (*Journal of Discourses* vol. 7, 290–91).

In similar fashion, Native Americans, Polynesians, and other darkened peoples bore God's punishment, Young argued, so that skin color betokened God's long-standing punishment of an age-old sin, though Pacific Islander men were able to hold priesthood standing within the church, as opposed to those with African lineage. As these peoples became more holy, they would also become "a white and delightsome people" (*Journal of Discourses* vol. 7, 335–38), literally growing lighter as their commitments to Mormonism grew, the holy glow replacing the mark of Cain.[2]

As I've noted, Young's decree stood as official church policy from 1849 until 1978, 129 years of formal—many believed God-inspired—racism. Twentieth-century brethren changed the tone of Young's invectives against dark-skinned peoples, so that it was no longer inherited sin that brought the mark of Cain but a more neoliberal motif of personal failing. In 1954, Mark E. Petersen, member of the Quorum of the Twelve Apostles, put these feelings into words when he referenced a major teaching of the church—that all people who live on Earth had at one time lived in a preexistence where there is free agency. "We could be lazy there or we could be industrious. We could be obedient or careless. We could choose to follow Christ or to follow Lucifer" (Petersen 1954, 6). As such, dark skin marked poor choices in the preexistence—an individual punishment for an individual wrong. Writes Petersen, "We cannot escape the conclusion that because of performance in our pre-existence, some of us are born as Chinese, some as Japanese, some as Indians, some as Negroes, some as Americans, some as Latter-day Saints. There are rewards and punishments, fully in harmony with His established policy in dealing with sinners and saints, regarding all according to their deeds" (10). This logic establishes the terms for spiritual neoliberalism, in that it imposes a recalibrated market logic not only working in tandem with religion but using a religious ethos as its endpoint for racism.

The insidious logic of causality, virtue/vice, and race clearly indicates that if dark skin is the punishment for sin, white skin must be the reward for good deeds. *Do right and be white.* Or in the words of the Book of Mormon about Lamanites who convert: "And then shall they rejoice; for they shall know that it is a blessing unto them from the hand of God; and their scales of darkness shall begin to fall from their eyes; and many generations shall not pass away among them, save they shall be a white and a delightsome people" (2 Nephi 30:6).

In all fairness, I should note that there is some difference of opinion about the wording here. The phrase "white and delightsome" was included in the original translation from 1830. In 1840, the phrase was changed to "pure and delightsome," though European editions used "white and delightsome" until 1981. To my mind, there is little difference in the connotations behind the words "white" and "pure"—or for that matter, my word "fairness"—since these words often naturalize the racialized meanings that link purity with lightness and virtue with pale complexions. In the ideology of mediated Mormonism, "pure and delightsome" serve as adjectives for goodness, enlightenment, and God's blessing, while those things dark indicate impurity, sin, and collusion with Satan.

As it concerns 1978, cultural matters might well have helped God along in the change of opinion. In the lead-up to the 1978 decree on "those of African descent," black leaders in the civil rights movement had organized boycotts of the state of Utah and all Mormon Tabernacle Choir products. "The NAACP brought discrimination charges against the Utah Boy Scouts for prohibiting a black member from assuming a senior patrol position. College athletes refused to play Brigham Young University teams. Groups protested at the church's twice-yearly general conferences in Salt Lake City. Mormon leadership finally acknowledged that many, perhaps most, of the converts to the Church in Brazil had some degree of black ancestry. While their donations helped build the São Paulo Temple, they were not permitted to attend it" (Bennett 2011). By some accounts, the church handled the situation by declaring not that God had changed his mind about black people but that the injunction and prejudice against people of color had been a policy (rather than a prophecy) and thus amenable to new social conditions. In discussing the terms of the change, the church president at the time, Spencer W. Kimball, spoke of his continued requests to God for a new revelation. None was forthcoming. His solution was to tell God that the church planned to change its edict and to ask for a sign if God disapproved. Absent that sign, the new revelation was conferred (Young and Gray 2009). The website lds.org, the mainstream church's primary public relations tool, now considers the 1978 change a matter of divine revelation that is canonized in the *Doctrine and Covenants* as "Official Declaration 2." So, God changed his mind on racial matters when human provocation made the mainstream church's stance untenable.[3]

Coming into the Light

It wasn't until 2013 that the mainstream Mormon Church officially denounced the racial policies of its history, an announcement that made worldwide headlines. The *Guardian*, a major UK newspaper, quoted from the church's broadside: "The church disavows the theories advanced in the past that black skin is a sign of divine disfavour or curse, or that it reflects actions in a premortal life; that mixed-race marriages are a sin; or that blacks or people of any other race or ethnicity are inferior in any way to anyone else.... Church leaders today unequivocally condemn all racism, past and present, in any form" ("Race and the Priesthood" 2017; "Mormon Church Addresses Past Racism" 2013). As historian of Mormonism Armand Mauss surmises, this announcement may indicate a "new church commitment to greater transparency about its history, doctrines, and policies" ("Mormon Church Addresses Past Racism" 2013). Yet it also continues to give evidence for why there is a growing niche of mediated Mormonism dedicated to working through, and not always forgiving, the racist positions the church has held and still promulgates.

One case in point is the array of media fare discussing race and the mainstream as generated by two active LDS members, Darius Gray and Margaret Blair Young. Gray is one of the founding members of the LDS Genesis Group, established in 1971, an advocacy group for black people within the mainstream church. Though the pronouncement on race in 1978 allowed men of African heritage to hold the priesthood and all worthy Saints, regardless of sex, to participate in temple ordinances, the Genesis Group continues today "based on a perception that African Americans still had unique issues and could benefit from a chance to affiliate with one another, especially because many were the only members of African descent in their local wards [local congregations] and even in their stakes [geographical collection of wards]" ("Genesis Group" 2017). Young is a white author, filmmaker, and writing instructor, who taught for thirty years at Brigham Young University. Together Gray and Young have authored three historical novels on black Mormon pioneers under the broad title *Standing on the Promises*. They also created a documentary film, *Nobody Knows: The Untold Story of Black Mormons* (Young and Gray 2008), which received respectable circulation, including airtime on PBS and the Documentary Channel. *Nobody Knows* recounts the historical record of the church's prohibition on black men holding the priesthood, and, perhaps more importantly, it details the emotional toll of racism.

Tamu Smith, a young black woman featured in the documentary, poignantly recalls a moment when a white sister in the ward approached her with praise: "You're so sweet," she exclaimed, seemingly in friendship. "But I don't know how I'm going to recognize you in the Celestial Kingdom. I try to imagine you white, but I just don't see that." Smith's story puts a fine point on this sliding scale of value, whereby whiteness marks those who are worthy and thus in the highest of heavens, the Celestial Kingdom, even if that person's earthly body has dark skin. If Tamu earns her way to the Celestial Kingdom, the belief system reinforces the idea that her skin will lighten as a result of her righteous living. These ideas reinforce a racist presumption that dark skin is a temporary curse that will be replaced with the more divine glow of whiteness, both on earth and in the afterlife. Darius Gray told a *Washington Post* reporter that "at church functions," he and other black Mormons were reassured, "you will have the priesthood in the world to come." They were also encouraged to believe that if they lived worthy lives, they would "become lighter and lighter" (Horowitz 2012). In his memoir *Black Mormon*, Russell Stevenson (2014, iii) similarly suggests that the "Mormon tradition is built on the hope that Zion—the city of the Saints—could transcend the racial divisions of this world," not through radical inclusivity but through universal deracination. Smith's and Gray's experiences indicate such racial transcendence is actually a substitute for whiteness, as indicated both by skin tone and by social arrangements.

Probably one of the more influential contemporary Mormon bloggers and blogs is Jana Riess's *Flunking Sainthood*, distributed by the Religious News Service web network (*Flunking Sainthood* is also the name of her 2011 memoir about her year of spiritual experimentation and failure). In 2015, Riess featured "African American convert" and Relief Society president Bryndis Roberts in a guest blog post. Roberts argued that the church owed its members of all races a fuller accounting and apology for its racist past. She argued that the church's 2013 Gospel Topics statement acknowledging racial mistreatment did not go far enough to stem the ongoing tide of racial wounding among mainstream Mormons. She includes four examples:

- In 1977, an African American woman was ready to join the church. When she learned of the priesthood/temple ban, she did not join.
- In 1997, a white teacher told a young African American man that the reason for the ban was that "Blacks were less valiant in the premortal realm." The pain of that statement ultimately resulted in him becoming inactive.

- In 2007, an African American woman was investigating the church. She was repeatedly informed that the priesthood/temple ban had come from God and that her faith simply needed to be strong enough to accept that fact.
- In 2014, an African American woman was told that the "Race and the Priesthood" essay did not mean that the church had been wrong; instead, God had simply changed his mind about the "worthiness" of people of African descent (Roberts 2015).

In this blog post and other online forums—such as Mormon Press, a conglomerate of liberal Mormon voices and opinions—Roberts asks that the mainstream church do more than acknowledge its past with respect to race; it must actively reteach members through a proclamation from the First Presidency (the group of three men who helm the SLC church), including translating this document into every language spoken in the church worldwide and clarifying that neither the ban on black people nor its justifications came from God. Further, Roberts insists that the proclamation be read in every ward worldwide and incorporated into the church's curriculum and teachings. While church leaders have been reluctant to heed her call, mediated Mormonism has taken up the banner of racial equality, moving candid conversations on race to the forefront.

As one example, when Darius Gray and Margaret B. Young were featured on a two-episode podcast of *Mormon Stories*, listeners expressed gratitude for their frank disclosures on race. Wrote one respondent:

> I am so grateful to have found this podcast. I have been asking this question since I was 12 years old and I am going to be 50 next year!!!!! I have had debates, arguments, shouting matches (not the most effective mode of communication), and just plain cried many tears over this issue. Even as a young girl, the whole "fence sitter, seed of Cain" just seemed a smoke screen for racism. I left the church for 25 years and this issue was a large part of the reason that I left, when I returned with my family that is an interracial family, my husband is Black and my kids are mixed, I was not sure what to expect. I am ashamed to tell you that I have searched and studied, and searched for a reason that the priesthood was denied and I have never been able to find an answer. Today I know why. I am listening to Darron Smith [coeditor of *Black and Mormon*] as I am writing this response to your Podcast. My kids and husband have asked me and I have given them my own theory, which had nothing to do with any of the "folklore" that the Church had put out there. (Dehlin 2006b)

Here we witness a conversation on race and racialization unfolding amid media cross-platforming—a woman writing a public response on a website to a podcast featuring two people who are novelists and filmmakers—all illuminated by the spotlight on Mormonism.

The mediated public sphere has been a force of visibility, compelling answerability in the church. While those troubled by the priesthood ban and continued racism have pushed for the mainstream church to "come into the light" by speaking openly about race, their very provocations have forced much of the transparency they seek. If the overall codes of the LDS Church or the political temperaments of Mormons have not radically shifted, the mediated public culture around Mormonism has allowed atypical Mormons (people of color, LGBT+ Mormons, those excommunicated or apostatized from the church) a place to find and talk with one another.

In some ways, this is progressive political change 101, whereby revolutionaries use publicity as a means of leveraging new legislative and social positions. The media is one of the many tools women used to gain the vote in the early twentieth century, for example, and the court of public opinion continues to be essential in determining the threshold for domestic equality. It is perhaps more important (and also more depressing) to realize, then, not that media/image/visibility are used for political ends but that there is little, if any, consolidated political ideology or unifying goal attached to much of mediated Mormonism. Indeed, while any number of the social controversies—from gay marriage to the ban on black people to polygamy— elicit the words and responses of True Believing Mormons (TBM), the aggregated discourse on these topics represents a fusion of anonymous, amateur LDS and Gentile media producers, wanting to join a conversation about something that they consider to be important but not political. The progressive outcome is thus not a planned revolution but the political change that arises through the clustering of mediated conversations, both professional and amateur, all bent on understanding fairness and truth.

In concluding this section, let me come back to Kristine Haglund, who has argued that media attention put Mormons otherwise on the fringes into a more mainstream position, allowing them a megaphone to amplify their voices. The result has been to disrupt a public image of Mormonism as homogeneous and unified. Doing so has forwarded a progressive end, Haglund argues, in creating the terms for a complex diversity that mirrors the idealized codes of American plurality. The mainstream church, however, has disallowed these uses of media, often, as we shall see in later chapters, excommunicating those who bring public attention and scrutiny. Responding in

Slate to Haglund's ideas, Miriam Krule (2015) noted the catch-22: "The only way to effect change is to get the media involved, but if you get the media involved, you may face excommunication." If part of the dazzle of the Mormon moment, then, is to shine a brighter light on Mormonism, a darker shadow threatens active members who point the spotlight at the church itself.

The Mormon Glow

As you seek to know the will of our Heavenly Father in your life and become more spiritual, you will be far more attractive, even irresistible.—James Faust, general conference president, "Womanhood: The Highest Place of Honor"

We have been taught that "the gift of the Holy Ghost . . . quickens all the intellectual faculties, increases, enlarges, expands and purifies all the natural passions and affections. . . . It inspires virtue, kindness, goodness, tenderness, gentleness and charity. *It develops beauty of person, form and features.*" Now, that is a great beauty secret! . . . It is the kind of beauty that doesn't wash off. It is *spiritual* attractiveness. Deep beauty springs from virtue. It is the beauty of being chaste and morally clean. . . . The world places so much emphasis on physical attractiveness and would have you believe that you are to look like the elusive model on the cover of a magazine. The Lord would tell you that you are each uniquely beautiful. When you are virtuous, chaste, and morally clean, your inner beauty glows in your eyes and in your face. . . . There is no more beautiful sight than a young woman who glows with the light of the Spirit, who is confident and courageous because she is virtuous.—Elaine Dalton, president of the Young Women, "Remember Who You Are!"

As the almighty Bloggernacle teaches, Mormonism very much reinforces a notion that true believers are not only special people, but they give off an aura of blessedness, called the countenance, or in a more colloquial parlance, the Mormon Glow. The glow is believed to be a sign of God's (or some say Jesus's) divine presence, the Holy Spirit oozing from human pores and legible on Mormon families (see figure 2.1). Those who convert to Mormonism are thought to lighten in complexion, and those who leave the faith, the apostates, are thought to take on a darker countenance. The glow is also perceived to be a magnetic tool that draws others to true believers. Missionaries can use their glow to recruit investigators, and singles, particularly women, might lay claim to their glow to recruit potential spouses, who serve as eternal companions. Writes LDS blogger Malcolm Ravenclaw (2014): "Developing the Mormon glow isn't easy and it doesn't happen overnight. But when we have the image of the Savior in our countenance, people recognize

FIG. 2.1 Glowing, the Mormon way: dōTERRA promotional film, *Our Story*.

it. In an increasingly dark world, we have a responsibility to bring light to everyone we meet. As LDS single adults, having the Mormon glow is especially important because it helps us attract people who can add value to our lives." As the racial plurality of the I'm a Mormon Campaign indicates, the mainstream church tries very hard in its present iteration to suggest that the Mormon Glow is not about skin tone—all true believers, regardless of race, might possess the glow. But equally, references to the Mormon Glow make it impossible to strip the associations of the glow from its commitment to whiteness, since, as we have already witnessed through earlier discussions in this chapter, closeness to God is thought to materialize and be manifest on the (increasingly lightened) skin.

Ravenclaw is not alone in believing that Mormons have a special light shining in and through them, and this light operates as a divine cosmetic that makes believers whiter and, thus, according to the perverse logic of racialization, more attractive. Brigham Young taught, "'Mormonism' keeps men and women young and handsome; and when they are full of the Spirit of God, there are none of them but what will have a glow upon their countenances; and that is what makes you and me young; for the Spirit of God is with us and within us" (*Journal of Discourses* vol. 5, 332). The Strangites, an LDS splinter group that emerged after Smith's death and in opposition to Young, literalized the Mormon Glow. Led by James Jesse Strang, the Strangites thrived in their remote outpost on Mackinac Island from 1844 to 1856. During ordinance ceremonies, believers would be anointed with a mixture of olive oil and phosphorus, a combination that not only produced a heavenly glow but also, on occasion, caught fire (see Van Noord 1997; Beam 2014).

In a present-day context, two of the many LDS MLM companies based in Utah, dōTERRA (essential oils) and NuSkin (youth-enhancing skin products), make much of the light of inner calm and, one presumes, health that emanates from those who use their products. dōTERRA literalized its claim to health, wellness, and whiteness with the 2017–18 introduction of a brightening gel, meant to reduce age spots and maximize "skin tone and brightness." I discuss these and other MLM companies in chapter 1, but as notions of health, complexion, and the glow relate to race, it's important to note that the ties are so obvious that the *BunYion*, a Mormon version of the satiric paper and website the *Onion*, mocked the glow—and its instantiation of whiteness:

> "Here I was, thinking they were total suckers for buying all that crap from NuSkin and dōTERRA," said Draper resident Ashley Summers. "But now that 'Mormon glow' is all the rage, I guess I'll have to buy some too."
>
> "I remember my friend Lucia Escobar, a sweet, Lamanite girl from Mexico, who stopped using dōTERRA about a year ago," continued Summers. "It was so sad. All at once her foundation went away and she grew dark and loathsome in complexion. But I guess it serves her right for leaving the true path of essential oils. And, you know, for not being white." ("New Dermatological Study" 2015)

In quite a different context, psychologists Nicholas Rule, James Garrett, and Nalini Ambady decided to test the hypothesis that Mormons give off a heavenly light and that others could detect their brilliance. In 2010, they published "On the Perception of Religious Group Membership from Faces," which argues that Mormons could indeed be identified by face alone (Rule, Garrett, and Ambady 2010). The researchers structured their experiment by asking people to look at gray-scale photos of people in emotionally neutral poses. The photos had been cropped "to the smallest frame that included the sides and tops of targets' hair and the bottom of their chins." The experiment asked subjects to determine which of the people thus imaged were Mormon and which were not: respondents were slightly better than 60 percent accurate in their determinations, a percentage superior to guessing. Because the images were blocked so as not to show major distinguishing details, the researchers concluded that respondents used skin texture and tone in making their determination. The study further linked the smooth skin texture of Mormons to the overall longevity of LDS peoples, as augmented by the health codes that ban alcohol, restrict most forms of caffeine, and outlaw cigarettes and a social culture that prevents them from consuming "toxic media" such as R-rated movies.[4] "In conclusion," wrote Rule, Garrett, and Ambady, "Mormons and non-Mormons subtly differ in their facial appearance and perceivers are able to perceive these differences in a way that allows for accurate categorization. The two groups are distinguished by differences in apparent health, which appears to be expressed in facial cues signaling skin quality." It didn't take long before this scientific study appeared in popular magazines such as *Psychology Today* and from there on the internet. Now to Google "Mormon Glow" is to find a cache of articles citing the study as proof that, as lds.net put it, the "Mormon Glow is real" (Hampton 2015).

My point here, as with so much in this book, is not to come down on a side for the glow or against it. Instead, I hope to illustrate the resonance of this luminous metaphor as a salient and racialized signifier of a state to be desired and, in turn, to demonstrate how a host of media platforms sustain the intelligibility of the Mormon Glow. I believe the debate about the glow as expressed in mediated Mormonism is itself evidence of deeper investments in the meanings of raced personhood and embodiment, whereby those who are blessed with qualities of lightness, brightness, and whiteness are positioned as being in holy alignment with human perfection and godliness. I also hope to demonstrate how these ideas about race—the whiter you are, the closer to God—find their way into mainstream ideologies that seemingly have little to do with race or religion. In this ideological creep—from the actual bodies of Mormons to the aura that surrounds mediated Mormonism—the glow functions simultaneously as phenotype and media spectacle.

The captivating allure of the glow finds full expression in the spectacular vampire alluded to in the introduction, Edward Cullen from the *Twilight* series. Stephenie Meyer's sexy vampire family are unlike those who have populated literature and film in that they hunt and consume the blood of animals but do not drink human blood, thus calling themselves vegetarian. Importantly, *Twilight*'s vegetarian vampire coterie does not turn into dust when exposed to direct sunlight. Instead, with Edward as their primary representative, the Cullens sparkle like diamond-encrusted marble. In the novel, Meyer describes it as focalized through Bella: "Edward in the sunlight was shocking. I couldn't get used to it, though I'd been staring at him all afternoon. His skin, white despite the faint flush from yesterday's hunting trip, literally sparkled, like thousands of tiny diamonds were embedded in the surface. He lay perfectly still in the grass, his shirt open over his sculpted, incandescent chest, his scintillating arms bare. His glistening, pale lavender lids were shut, though of course he didn't sleep. A perfect statue, carved in some unknown stone, smooth like marble, glittering like crystal" (Meyer 2011, 260). Edward is here the perfect über-man: strong, immortal, impervious to human weaknesses, and, in Meyer's words, "white," "sparkl[ing]," "incandescent," "scintillating," "glistening," "pale," "perfect," "glittering." I've already made the point that in an oversimplified parallel, Edward represents the True Believing Mormon and Bella the investigator drawn by Edward's charismatic and embodied glow, desiring the dividends Edward can offer, for both time and eternity, but also, quite literally, desiring his body. Here, Edward as the godlike former human neatly fits with an LDS cosmology of the Godhead, particularly since a unique feature of the Mormon notion of God is that he used to be a man and continues to propagate children with a Heavenly Mother (or several) in a sublime afterlife. For his part, Edward seems to be a monogamist.

Due to the immense popularity of Meyer's novels, young adult fans expressed deep investments in the scenes they wanted to see reproduced on the screen. The filmmakers anticipated some of these: Edward and Bella's first kiss, Edward's lullaby for Bella, Edward and Bella at the prom. Yet director Catherine Hardwicke told the *Los Angeles Times* that she was surprised when fans were so vociferous about a key scene in the first book, in which Edward reveals the truth of his vampirism to Bella by allowing her to see him sparkling in sunlight as they lie together in a secluded flower-strewn meadow. Hardwicke notes that it was "super challenging" to make Edward glow on screen: "We had probably 10 special effects companies trying out experimental ideas on some footage we had to see how we can make him dazzle and sparkle and shimmer. . . . You know, the description in the book is a tiny bit contradictory. On one level, he is supposed to look like cut diamonds, on another, he's as smooth as marble. So you're like OK, when you think of encrusted cut diamonds that's faceted—and when we first did that it almost looked like acne, like a skin condition. And you want it to be smooth" (Martin 2008). Hardwicke also acknowledged that given *Twilight*'s extremely passionate fan base, if she didn't get the meadow scene right, "people [were] going to stone me in the streets!"

This deep investment in things that sparkle, glow, and are luminous—as here represented by a hunky shimmering vampire—are both about Mormonism and completely detached from it. Without speaking its name, the Mormon Glow comes to personify the special qualities of this new breed of the undead, but it also eclipses (excuse the pun) Mormonism as a media spectacle. In this respect the Mormon Glow is bigger than itself, since it is not only a signifier of value on the individual body, but a marker of passionate investment among a collective, a passion so strong that it constitutes media innovation. Indeed, if we let them, Bella and Edward can offer another point of access into these light-filled metaphors, what we might call luminosity, that will be very helpful throughout the consideration of *Latter-day Screens*.

Luminosity and the Raced and Gendered Politics of the Spectacle: The Glow as Phenotype

Another way to think about these matters of race and the glow is through two light-filled metaphors that we inherit from French philosophers to indicate both the emergence of consciousness and new, if fleeting, knowledge: Gaston Bachelard's notion of shimmering and Gilles Deleuze's idea of luminosity. Bachelard (2014) uses the word "shimmering" to indicate an endless vacillation in the "duality of subject and object," a dance between forms that he calls "iridescent, shimmering, unceasingly active in its inversions." Gilles Deleuze describes luminosity as "visibilities" that are "not forms of objects, nor even forms that would show up under light, but rather forms of luminosity which are created by the light itself and allow a thing or object to exist only as a flash, sparkle or shimmer" (1988, 45). In this respect, luminosity is not a thing so much as an experience-made-thing through media.

In this book, I talk about Mormonism as an optic, a gathering of ideas projected onto a set of overlapping screens, amplifying and making clear a network of social relations that might not otherwise come into visibility. In this—and just like the Mormon origination story, when a young Joseph Smith created a new media technology by putting seer stones in his mother's spectacle frames—Mormonism is both mediated and media. Yet, given the emphasis on screens and their shifting form in the twenty-first century, the Mormon Glow as media spectacle is situated not in the flatness of the screen itself but in the ephemera of dynamic particles that dance in the shafts of light projecting toward those screens.

I should note, here, that not everyone has such optimistic regard for either shimmering or luminosity (or for Mormonism, for that matter, but that is the stuff of another conversation). Several major feminist media theorists have decried luminosity for the way it keys to consumer-driven mandates, as Guy Debord (1967) argued so persuasively in his Marxist critique *The Society of The Spectacle*. In more recent scholarship, concerns about consumerism and spectacularization are expressed about girls, who receive countless pitches urging them to make themselves passive and glamorous spectacles for the male gaze (Kearney 2015). Sarah Projansky writes, for instance, that "media incessantly look at and invite us to look at girls. Girls are objects at which we gaze, whether we want to or not. They are everywhere in our mediascapes. As such, media turn girls into spectacles—*visual objects on display*" (2014, 5, emphasis in original). In *The Aftermath of Feminism*, Angela McRobbie similarly writes that "luminosity captures how young women might be understood as currently becoming visible" (2012, 60). Girl power of this sort, argues McRobbie, is no power at all, particularly since such logic of spectacularization colludes with marketplace goals that require young women to become neoliberal agents in the policing of their own image. "It becomes increasingly difficult to function as a female subject," argues McRobbie, "without subjecting oneself to those technologies of self that are constitutive of the spectacularly feminine" (2012, 60). In turn, these technologies of the spectacle, what McRobbie terms the postfeminist masquerade, "implicitly re-instate normative whiteness" through "violent exclusion of diversity and otherness." In effect, as we saw in earlier discussions in this chapter, light and luminosity function as the constitutive corollaries of whiteness, goodness, and valuable personhood, instantiating an epistemology of light that both "underscores white masculine domination and resurrects racial divisions" since it excludes "non-white femininities from the rigid repertoire of self-styling" (McRobbie 2012, 70). Indeed, the epistemology of light underscoring the Mormon Glow makes the rigid repertoire of self-styling relevant not only for the earthly frame but also for the afterlife.

But rather than simply turning our backs on what is clearly a fraught metaphor, I believe it important to consider how the ephemeral glitter and sparkle that Deleuze and Bachelard theorize might be of benefit. Indeed, many recent cultural theorists, particularly those who work in gender studies–related fields, have adapted these theories of shimmering and luminosity. Ben Singer's work on the transgender sublime, for instance, references shimmering for the way it "proposes a reading practice that allows holding incongruent registers of meaning in mind at the same time" (2011, 29). For Singer, shimmering allows not only for an oscillation in the object of consideration but a wavering of "interpretive movement" that, in relation to transgender embodiment, creates a "disorienting encounter . . . that unsettles familiar ways of seeing enough to enable a 'new kind of subjectivity'" (2011, 56, quoting Phillips 2009, ix). Shimmering thus heightens agentive possibilities within a larger inchoate field and promises power in the context of the objectifying spectacularization of modern mediation.

Mary Celeste Kearney (2015) further regards both shimmering and luminosity as key components in what she terms the "sparklefication of late modern life." Kearney calls for a "taxonomy of sparkle" or, in the words of Mikkel Bille and Tim Flohr Sørensen, an "anthropology of luminosity" to account for the specificity of light's meanings: how it is used, what modes it appears in, its various social manifestations and experiences (Bille and Sørensen 2007). Through this taxonomy, Kearney (2015, 268) argues, we might better glean sparkles' "semiotic and discursive power," since the participation in sparkle culture may not be the entrapment that postfeminist scholars have posited. She believes that scholars who critique luminosity "do not dig deeply enough into a compelling part of [the] arguments, which is the pronounced superficiality, theatricality and ironic knowingness of postfeminist glamour" (Kearney 2015, 156). These are the watchwords of camp, and they signal what to my mind is a necessary move to queer theory, particularly as related to the light-filled spectacles we are discussing. Kearney advocates that feminist media scholars resist the "moral panic discourse often asserted in the face of spectacular bodily displays" so that we might perceive a delight in illumination through a critically conscious engagement with its function.

In the context of this discussion, the Mormon Glow functions as a bodily distinction or phenotype, by which I mean it is malleable, individual, and conditional, and yet still codes as a stable and seemingly lifelong indicator of social identity expressed through and read on the body. As such, the Mormon Glow is also a condition of embodiment that keys very specifically to race. The biological meaning of phenotype suggests that it is visually available information made legible on a body, a signifying system that rises from a combination of environment and genetics. The phenotype can include not only the physical appearance of an organism but also its behavior. Colloquially, however, phenotype often stands in for its opposite: as a synonym for the natural body, or a form of immutable embodiedness born in the blood—much like the social understanding of race. Biologists have argued for years that race has no meaningful relation to genetics—there can be more genetic variation between people within the same national and skin-tone groups than those across racial types. The meanings of race also vary across time, nation, and place. It is for this reason that most scholars consider race to be constructed, even while the social investments in race as a reliable marker of identity are very real. In its connection of goodness, lightness, and godliness, the Mormon epistemology of light is complicit with a larger Western notion of enlightenment, both of which participate in a process of racialization whereby the glow (of knowledge and of spiritual purity) functions as both phenotypic ideal and as a way of knowing.

Whiteness under Siege

I want to turn briefly to another case study to make these points about race, the body, media spectacle, and the functions of light clearer, particularly as they are focalized through the latter-day screens of mediated Mormonism. Between 2016 and 2018, U.S. news outlets were agog over the right-wing siege of a federal building in Burns, Oregon, a small town in a remote southeastern section of the state. Most of the speculation about the reasons for the takeover pointed to long-standing tensions between the U.S. federal government and protesting ranchers, many of whom felt they had ancestral rights to use the land as they saw fit. The family behind the siege, the Bundys, traveled from their homes in Idaho to stage the takeover of buildings at the Malheur National Wildlife Refuge in protest of what they considered to be the unfair sentencing of Dwight and Steve Hammond, a father and son imprisoned for arson due to fires they started on their own land that spread to federal property (the Hammonds had served some time in prison and were released, only to be incarcerated again so that the minimum sentence could be served). The Bundys—father Cliven, son Ammon, and son Ryan—had been involved in their own anti-FBI and Bureau of Land Management (BLM) resistance in 2014 and felt inspired to launch the protest in support of the Hammonds.

What wasn't much mentioned about the siege was how fully it was supported by an ideology of Mormonism that perceived armed resistance as the right and obligation of God's elect. Indeed, in the larger mediascape, Mormonism as a meme often carries these valences of righteous resistance to government oppression. For instance, David Brooks describes Senator

Jeff Flake in terms that correlate with Mormon separatism: "As a Mormon he learned to be wary of the government, and especially the way it can persecute minorities" (Brooks 2017). Many of the key players in the siege were multi-generational Mormons—primary among these being the Bundys, Robert "LeVoy" Finicum, and a supporting player named Dylan Wade Anderson, who would only identify himself to the press as Captain Moroni, a military figure who fights for justice in the Book of Mormon. Ammon Bundy spoke of receiving heavenly confirmation of the holding of the government facility. In his words: "I clearly understood that the Lord was not pleased about what was happening to the Hammonds." In a YouTube posting, Bundy spoke of being concerned about their arrest, of lying in his bed fatigued, only to hear a push notification on his phone. When he looked down to read the news, he saw it was about the Hammonds, and he "knew he was supposed to write something." His emotions were clouding his thoughts, he says, so he asked God for clarity, "and [he] was able to write." He then composed a letter to "individuals and government officials" arguing for justice and calling supporters to meet together to protest in Oregon, "so that they could get back to prospering again." He promptly posted these reflections to his Facebook page, and they are now available on YouTube (Hatewatchblog 2016). The video is a callout to sympathizers, asking them to join the militia in their Oregon siege.

In much the same way that Joseph Smith asked converts to reflect within themselves on whether Mormonism was the One True Church and to be guided by their internal testimony, Ammon Bundy appealed to his fellow patriots: "I am asking you to come to Harney County, to make the decision right now of whether this is a righteous cause or not, whether I am some crazy person or whether the Lord truly works through individuals to get His purposes accomplished. I ask you now to come to Harney County to participate in this wonderful thing that the Lord is about to accomplish." It was a patriarchal vision as good as the brethren in Salt Lake City might have offered.

For its part, the LDS Church denounced the militia and their use of Mormon theology. The Hammonds, who were the metaphorical damsels in distress in this scenario, also distanced themselves from the Bundys, seeing the tie between their arrest and the Bundy-led siege as a publicity stunt. The occupation of the Malheur Refuge lasted for forty days, finally ending after one of the members of the antigovernment militia, Robert Finicum, was shot and killed by federal authorities after refusing to comply with authorities, an altercation caught on video from the backseat of his truck by a passenger with an iPhone. The footage is now available on YouTube as posted by the newspaper *The Oregonian*, as yet one more element of the latter-day screens of mediated Mormonism ("Shawna Cox" 2016). For roughly six weeks, the international news cycle and social media chronicled and commented on the comings and goings of the siege, reporting on the militia men as "rebel cowboys" (Levin 2016) and patriotic upstarts, who, according to James Purtill (2016), writing for the Australian Broadcast Company, "seemed to welcome the blurring of spectacle and entertainment with political protest." For many, the siege represented the quintessence of both Americanness and Westernness, given that the United States was founded by patriots fighting a revolutionary war against a much more powerful state. Noted Carol Bundy, matriarch of the Bundy clan, "The west was won by people standing up. It runs deep in our blood. Do you give up on something that is born in you?" (Levin 2016). The Oregon siege thus announced a conjoined patriotism and rebellion, a defiant antigovernment act as national birthright and obligation, just the way the country was founded. It also worked to reinforce the central place Mormonism had in these values of Western Americanism, a Mormonism recognized by those who could see its valences and knew the Moroni connection or the call to testimony issued by Ammon but unannounced for those who did not.

The siege was fomented by a larger political unrest at work in the United States today but fueled through media technologies: God's message sent through push notifications, a prophet's call to arms announced on Facebook and YouTube, a patriot's (or domestic terrorist's) death captured on phone video, satiric and comedic reactions on network nightly talk shows, an endless number of blogs commenting and critiquing, international coverage in newspapers, magazines, and on television news. And much as Mormonism was simultaneously visible and invisible in this media spectacle, so were the workings of whiteness, of settler colonialism, and of ethnic cleansing, which often assert themselves in absence. As journalist Aaron Bady thoughtfully commented, the Bundys' "libertarian fairy tale" required an extraordinary revisionist history that accounts for no history prior to 1870. No indigenous Paiutes, no Spanish exploration, no French Canadian trappers, no British occupation, no nineteenth-century government intervention to create a railroad that itself makes cattle ranching possible. Writes Bady (2016):

> Western militia-types like to fantasize that they are oppressed by a "foreign" government. They like to play dress-up, to pretend that they are entrepreneurial family farmers who built it all themselves. But you

can tell the story of Harney County as a morality tale about the evils of big government only if you leave most of it out. And so they do. The story the Bundy brothers tell is mostly empty space, like the Western frontier of their imagination. And perhaps this is fitting. After all, what is American history if not a history of unspoken violence, told by erasure?

Indeed, behind Ammon's desire to "go back to prospering" was a more sinister message about white privilege and a sense of dispossession. Cliven Bundy's beef was not just with the U.S. government but with black and brown people. As the *New York Times* reported in 2014, Cliven's resistance to the Bureau of Land Management made the "rancher a celebrity." And when his resistance to the government failed to generate crowds, his daily press conferences turned into "a long, loping discourse" on topics such as abortion, welfare, and race. During one of these rants, Cliven spoke in "appalling and racist statements" about black people, suggesting that they "are better off as slaves" (Nagourney 2014). In the Oregon siege, Cliven's sons reinforced this racist epistemology, and their white/right to prosperity, Mormonism here made to play the role of handmaiden in their quest for celebrity and rebellion.

The protestors made news again in October 2016, when a jury acquitted them of wrongdoing, their racial privilege as wronged white men evidencing a disaffected alt-right movement. Writing for the *Los Angeles Times*, Melissa Batchelor Warnke explicitly characterized the acquittal as a form of racial injustice. The militants, whom she described as "extremist Mormons with messiah complexes," disputed a notion of mandatory minimum sentencing, a regulation that seemed fair when the "right" people, meaning those of color, were held to these restrictions. "When people of color are locked up for minor crimes—X time in jail for carrying Y amount of weed, for instance—that's the application of law and order," Warnke wrote, channeling the voice and ideology of the alt-right. "But when white people are locked up for substantive crimes—setting fire to 100 acres of land owned by the government, for instance—that's an infringement of rights they believe they should have." Her own opinions come through loud and clear: "Can you hear how entitled, how insane, how racist that is?" (Warnke 2016).

The siege in Oregon is not alone, either in its connection to the white colonization of Western lands or the Mormon connection to disputes about history, space, and identity. In 2017, for instance, a new land grab controversy emerged, in the form of Bears Ears, Utah, a protected national monument in southeastern Utah run by an intertribal coalition made up of the Hopi,

Navajo, Uintah and Ouray Ute, Ute Mountain Ute, and Zuni nations. The monument, encompassing 1.35 million acres, had been targeted for reduction through a presidential order issued by Donald Trump. The order would thus open the land for cultivation. Coverage by NPR specifically labeled Bears Ears a part of "Mormon Country," and Terry Tempest Williams, while not making overt connections to Mormons, made pointed ties to Utah's LDS "bellicose politicians" Orrin Hatch, Rob Bishop, and Jason Chaffetz, who, with Trump, were engaged in a "new colonialism," moving the country back a hundred years (Siegler 2017; Williams 2017).

Conclusion: The Holy Glow

In sum, the Mormon Glow is both a symbolic and a literal racialized conglomerate denoting spiritual purity, whiteness, boundless energy, and limitless success—all fused through the meme of Mormonism and animated through media spectacle. Given this, I'd venture to say there is no better example to end this chapter than the smiling superstar siblings, Donny and Marie Osmond. This is particularly true since both Donny and Marie repeatedly serve as New Year's Eve poster children for youthful energy and good looks, their glowing and "age-defying" images designed to capitalize on the renewal projects that are so much a part of new year's resolutions. In 2018, for instance, both Donny and Marie appeared on separate January covers: Donny smiled forth from the cover of *Healthy Living Made Simple* (figure 2.2), a lifestyle periodical circulated free for Sam's Club, and Marie appeared hand-on-hip in *First for Women*, a periodical dedicated to health and wellness (figure 2.3). *First Magazine*'s back cover also featured Marie in her capacity as the spokesperson for Nutrisystem, a weight loss meal plan (this time with both hands on hips), making her the literal beginning and end of glowing health.

Healthy Living's feature article on Donny argued that a "lifetime spent in entertainment" provides him with the "motivation to stay in shape," his life in the spotlight thus both an inspiration and rationale for his "boyish good looks" (Marsh 2018). Yet his story is also about the Mormon Glow. His life, the magazine tells us, is one of faith, family, and constant personal reinvention, augmented by a dietary discipline that restricts sugar, alcohol, and tobacco. The accompanying image of Osmond in the spotlight reinforces the glow of good choices and scrupulous self-management, in an arms-outstretched pose that fuses the iconography of religion and celebrity as amplified through and in the whiteness of his literal glowing (figure 2.4).

FIG. 2.2 Donny as glowing cover boy. *Healthy Living Made Simple*, January/February 2018.

Interviews with Donny similarly work to sustain these connections between wellness, whiteness, and goodness, and Donny's glow is often referenced as evidence of what good choices might bring. Although he has been public about his struggles with depression and the family's bankruptcy, his present-day successes and youthful appearance are considered to bear witness to his right choices, scrappiness, determination, and resilience.[5] In a 2007 interview with BT, British Telephone's online magazine, for example, Donny notes that he was mocked mercilessly in his early career because he never drank, smoke, or took drugs: "My faith ... and my upbringing kept me on a pretty straight path." But Donny makes clear, "I think I've had the last laugh" (Fagan 2017).

Indeed, Donny reinforces these readings of himself as a signboard for glowing wellness, even offering "testimony" for products that enhance his appearance, such as the dietary supplement Protandim (manufactured by LifeVantage Corporation, a Utah-based MLM company), which promises

116 CHAPTER TWO

FIG. 2.3 Marie as glowing cover girl. *First for Women*, January 15, 2018.

FIG. 2.4 Beatific Donny.

to reduce metabolic aging by 40 percent. In 2012, he offered his personal testimonial on his blog: "I feel compelled to share it," Osmond posted. "Whenever I have the opportunity to discuss health and wellness, I mention Protandim because it has made such a difference in my life" (Osmond 2012). "Look at you!" exclaims Dr. Phil on his talk show when Osmond is a guest. "You don't ever get older." Donny flashes his trademarked pearly whites and speaks in the language of the missionary: "People are quite shocked when they hear I'm fifty-four years old. They say, 'How do you keep your youth.' I have found something, Dr. Phil! I think it's the closest thing to the fountain of youth. It's called Protandim, and it works. I'm telling everybody about this" (McGraw 2012).[6] What is perhaps obvious—but goes unmentioned—in this exchange of personal revelation and rejuvenation is that Osmond was contractually obligated to endorse the product as a paid spokesman for the MLM company.[7]

For her part, sister Marie similarly monetizes her celebrity brand through personal endorsements for products that make much of salvific selfhood—saving oneself through the power of personal change. In addition to being the celebrity spokesperson for Nutrisystem since 2013, she is also the designer and creator of a series of collectible dolls sold on QVC, the home shopping network. She has since 2010 put her domestic knowledge to fuller use through a series of crafting businesses and a how-to book called *Marie Osmond's Heartfelt Giving*, which offers patterns and other projects, including that for paper roses (the name of her hit song in the 1970s).

As with her brother, magazines make much of Marie's amazing agelessness and boundless energy. *First for Women* writes, Marie is still "WOW at 58!" With Marie featured on both the front and back covers of their January 2018 issue, the magazine's feature article calls her "slim, energized, and happy as she go-go-goes," and it offers various forms of "instant inspiration," ranging from Marie's "radiance secret" to her "loving mantra" ("Marie Osmond" 2018). Marie's struggles—and victories—with her body position her as both relatable and transcendent, both good girl and wonder woman. "It's time to take control!" she insists, in ad copy for Nutrisystem. In interviews, she often refers to weight loss as a feminist intervention, of finally learning to put herself first. Indeed, Marie remembers the last words of advice whispered by her mother, Olive: "Lose weight. Take care of your body. You're like me. We take care of everybody. If I could do it over again, I'd take care of me. Love yourself enough" (Hahn 2011). But Marie also talks about weight loss as a way to better meet feminine demands for other-orientedness, telling *Parade* magazine: "Take care of your body—for yourself, and for the people you love that depend on you" (Stephens 2014). In this case, while brother

Donny perceives looking good as a requirement for his job, sister Marie sees it as part of her devotion to others, both statements reinforcing codes of conventional masculinity and femininity in the larger meme of Mormonism.

While celebrity endorsements are perhaps as American as apple pie, in Donny and Marie Osmond we see an additional connection between an ideology of Americanness and spiritual neoliberalism as manifested through media spectacle. The glowing celebrity is taken as proof not only of looking good but of being good. The Osmond glow, I argue here, also bears witness to a semiotics of whiteness.[8] Indeed, within the broader logic of the Mormon Glow, whiteness is a sign of their good choices with respect to self-management, all made visible through boundless energy, youthfulness, and luminosity. It's fitting given Joseph Smith's early career as a diviner of lost treasure that the religion he created positions the self as the shining divining rod to the "white and delightsome" spirit.

3. The Epistemology of the (Televised, Polygamous) Closet
THE CULTURAL POLITICS OF MEDIATED MORMONISM
AND THE PROMISES OF THE AMERICAN DREAM

Most Utah women in polygamous marriages are indistinguishable from other women. They take jobs or work from home to help support their families. They don't wear prairie dresses or put their hair in braids or a bun, the style consistent among FLDS women.

In black dress pants and a white blouse with a charcoal-colored jacket, Heidi Foster looks like any other 36-year-old suburban Salt Lake City mom, albeit with 10 children in her home. The youngsters' father is an occasional visitor who acknowledges another woman as his only legal wife.

—Fox News, "Many Polygamists Blend into Modern Society"

The well-kept yellow house sat on the corner of a tidy cul-de-sac called South Bonner Circle surrounded by a black wrought-iron fence. From the outside it seemed like a typical suburban home, offering few clues of the secrets that were contained inside. A passerby might catch a glimpse of children in the windows, but for the most part, the Young family kept to themselves. Their neighbors had no idea that the family were prominent members of the Kingston clan, the most powerful polygamist cult in America—and one of the most dangerous.

—Jesse Hyde, "Inside 'The Order,' One Mormon Cult's Secret Empire"

"We aren't the polygamists you think you know," says Kody Brown, father and patriarch of the Brown family and male star of the reality series *Sister Wives* (2010–present). And who are the polygamists we think we know? The holy-haired and prairie-dress-wearing women and aged prophets we see on the news or, as Brady Udall (1998) describes it, "wide-eyed wooly-bearded zealots" and "ruddy-faced women with high collars buttoned up to their chins." These vestigial folk haunt the edges of film and television fare such as *Big Love* (2006–11), *Follow the Prophet* (2009), *Polygamy USA* (2013), and the *19th Wife* (novel 2009, TV movie 2010). According to these mediated texts, polygamists live in small, dusty locations (both actual and fictional) like Colorado City or Juniper Creek, way beyond the edges of civilization. They keep to themselves as they populate their compounds with hundreds of big-eyed children, scores of downcast women wearing big bangs and long braids and even longer pastel dresses, and a handful of wild-eyed patriarchs who command their circle of wives and children with an iron fist (and usually a rifle). These are the people, we are reassured in our mediated stories, who are made safe by their exceptionalism, their difference plainly legible on their unadorned, even homely, bodies.

By contrast, the first thing we need to understand about progressive polygamists—as those who live the lifestyle often describe themselves—is that they stand in pointed contrast to those they recognize in the stereotype of the old-world, isolationist, and evil polygamists, a version of orthodox fundamentalism that I discuss at greater length in chapter 4. Orthodox polygamy produced modern polygamy but is no longer commensurate with it. In this telling, what marks modern and contemporary very distinctly fissure, since there are many present-tense instances of non-modern polygamy, as those aforementioned people in dusty compounds more than attest. Unlike his all-knowing, godlike, isolationist counterpart of conventional polygamy, the progressive male polygamist is plugged in, upwardly mobile, eager to provide college educations for his many children, plagued by self-doubt, and in need of marriage therapy and perhaps performance-enhancing pharmaceuticals like Viagra. He is unsure about how to lead. His wives wear makeup and can support themselves financially, they have opinions and disagree with him openly, they make fun of him for not following directions or for his forgetfulness, they chide him for his attempts to dominate. Their children can be high-strung and difficult, boy/girl crazy or resistant, by turns showing their love or turning a cold shoulder to the five parents who raised them. *Like any other American family.*

In this distinction, modern polygamists must contend with a serious image issue, since popular misunderstandings about them perpetuate a bigotry and intolerance they consider to be unfair. But because their lifestyle, as they term it, is illegal, they also struggle with potential arrest and incarceration for being public about their beliefs, lives, and loves. Modern polygamy thus draws upon the most basic features of modernity itself—individual choice, rights to personhood, strategic mediation, and the power of the image—to reshape public opinion about private behaviors. Judith Stacey notes that soon after *Big Love* started airing in 2006, "the clearinghouse website for polygamy advocacy groups credit[ed] media interest in *Big Love* with reporting 'around the world' their conviction that 'polygamy rights is the next civil rights battle'" (2011, 116). Since that time, other mediated fare, such as *Sister Wives*, equally contribute to, if not a civil rights battle, then a rebranding of FLDS polygamy. And both *Big Love* and *Sister Wives* have inspired a rash of polygamy dating websites, including Sister Wives, polygamy subthemed groups in POF (PlentyOfFish), 4thefamily.com, and Polygamy.com. While not all of forms of mediated polygamy are by and about Mormons, Mormonism remains a theme that all sites address.[1]

Building new semiotic associations for progressive polygamy is front and center on the agenda. In the opening minutes of the first episode of *Sister Wives*, for instance, the television text bends over backward to present the Browns in a way that is personal and relatable. In addition to smiles of welcome and direct address to the camera, each of Kody's three wives (Meri, Janelle, and Christine) introduces herself, her home or living area, and her children, their names and ages in titles at the base of the screen (fourth wife, Robyn, joins the cast/family by the end of Season 1). The slow and almost painstaking introduction to the family and the text onscreen reinforces the kinder and gentler brand of polygamy the Browns are meant to represent, while establishing each wife's role as the domestic nucleus of Kody's nuclear family palimpsest. As each uniquely spelled child's name—Aspyn, Mykelti, Paedon, Gwendlyn, Ysabel—flashes across the screen in connection to that child's birth mother, the message is both overtly and covertly uttered: Kody is no Warren Jeffs, the infamous leader of the FLDS, who in 2012 was convicted for arranging marriages between adult men and underage girls, as well as sexual misconduct including rape and incest. Indeed, at a public forum in 2010 held at Tufts University that was also folded into a *Sister Wives* episode, Robyn notes in tears: "We don't believe in child brides. We don't believe in forcing marriages.... I was so upset, I just wanted to go rescue every girl. I think [Warren Jeffs] deserves to rot in hell. I really do."[2]

Bad polygamy exists, the Browns concede. But so does good. And in that difference and that oversimplified dichotomy, modern polygamy looks a lot like normal. But normalcy, as we all know, is complicated. In this case, as the quote from a Fox News segment that begins this chapter makes perfectly clear, the perceived normalcy of modern polygamy, its sheer unmarkedness, makes this version of polygamy even more ominous for its lack of being obvious. Many of those people practicing polygamy, it warns, are not visually distinctive, and thus, they can be anyone, anywhere, at any time. Heidi Foster looks like any other thirty-six-year-old suburban Salt Lake City mom. And if a normal mom lives a secret life, then what does that say about normalcy? Can a sister wife be an all-American mom? Can a fundamentalist Mormon man with four score and seven wives and children be an American everyman? Or is there something about a secret life that, itself, makes one American? Is the great code of Americanness defined as much by what we don't say, we won't say, as what we do?

Mediated stories about progressive polygamous families regard multiple wives and extended families as the quintessence of a contemporary American ideology of entrepreneurial spiritualism, aspirational ambition, management efficiency, and image awareness. As I discuss throughout this book, one of the governing principles of self-understanding within the Mormon Church (both mainstream and fundamentalist) has been its separation (as opposed to exile) from Gentile society. Indeed, this theme of Mormon difference and differentiation is often reinforced across the archive of mediated Mormonism. For purposes of shorthand, Joanna Brooks (2012, 15) puts it best: she was a "root beer among the Cokes," she writes.[3] It was a "sparkling difference" she relished but also a difference she, and many other like-minded Mormons, relied on to help establish her identity.

Yet what happens in an economy of visibility that predicates its raison d'être on an appeal to sameness rather than difference? In many ways, modern polygamy stories turn on the conceit that these are families just like ours (however singularly "ours" is understood), normal families pushed to an extreme that dips into and requires the public relations power of celebrity to confer social justice through mediation. Throughout the course of *Sister Wives*, for example, whenever the discussions get serious, the Browns keep coming back to this refrain: they are using reality TV to counter demeaning and cruel stereotypes about polygamy. Justice through visibility is also a central claim of *Big Love*, and the "freedom to be himself" stands as the primary reason why the lead character, Bill Henrickson (played by Bill Paxton), runs for a state senator position, thus outing himself and his family in a bid for social justice and political power.

Like most narratives about extremes, those characters/subjects/citizens who are able to survive and even thrive in the context of immense sacrifice and challenge earn new privileges and exalted status as model figures. For even as modern polygamy stories underscore the financial, emotional, temporal, and logistical demands of nuclear families comprising twenty to thirty people, and even as they push on a politics of oppression that seeks to give voice to the oppressed, they suggest that the ability to cope with and cultivate the temporal fluctuations and fluid kinship models that this lifestyle entails not only marks but successfully creates the kind of neoliberal savvy necessary for prosperity and celebrity in the global marketplace. In short, modern polygamy serves as the ideal proving ground for twenty-first-century success American style, where flexibility, adaptability, and the capacity to change tactics as situations arise yield dividends both divine and earthly. But as I note in chapter 1, this is not your grandfather's neoliberalism. Indeed, these stories about living "the principle of plural marriage," as it is called within F/LDS Mormonism, directly enforce a logic of spiritual neoliberalism keyed to a promised dividend of an afterlife where the man who has married the most women and begotten the most children might look forward to his own divinity.

I take up these ideas of separation and difference, of similitude and citizenship, of flexibility and community promulgated through a gospel of modern polygamy in this chapter, factoring them very specifically through the gendered identities of the male patriarchs and the female sister wives as well as the sexual politics of polyamory. Doing so reveals a fascinating strain of queer and feminist discourses about social and sexual behaviors, the rights of consenting adults, kinship by choice, conscientious lawbreaking, and model citizenship. Specifically, I hone in on three primary texts in different genres that offer complex portraits of modern polygamy: the TLC reality series *Sister Wives* (2010–present), the HBO serial drama *Big Love* (2006–11), and the novel *The Lonely Polygamist* (Udall 2011), arguing that each offers a glimpse into a seemingly normal American family, dedicated to ethical living and pushed to social extremes. It is along these edges that resources for futurity are found.

In varying ways, a composite portrait of modern polygamy positions it as quintessentially progressive, American, and normal, in pointed contrast to the foreign polygamies of the Middle East, Asia, or Africa or atavistic polygamies lived in contemporary times by premodern peoples, primarily the Warren Jeffs types of fundamentalist Mormonism. Modern polygamy stories also suggest an added benefit that accrues to plural families—in their commitment to community, they transcend the atomization that is so often taken as concomitant with modernity, suturing the wounds of modern living with the threads of consent, care, and kinship. This genre of polygamy stories thus indicates that the complex structural dynamics of polygamous families' homes and lives create individuals who can thrive in a neoliberal milieu where good choices matter more than governments and where the capacity to make media work for you yields currencies that are monetary, cultural, and also spiritual.

Of Modern Families, Modern Love, and Modern Problems

In this family, you were never free, you couldn't do anything on your own, because there was always somebody who had a dentist's appointment or volleyball practice or Deannae would have one of her epileptic seizures and there went everybody's Labor Day picnic down the tubes. It was like they were all connected by the same invisible string . . . and when one person wanted to do a certain thing or go a certain way, they yanked on all the others, and then another person tried to go in another direction, and so on, and pretty soon they were all tangled up, tied to each other, tripping and flailing, thrashing around like a bunch of monkeys caught in a net.—Brady Udall, *The Lonely Polygamist*

Here's the setup for Brady Udall's novel *The Lonely Polygamist*. Golden Richards is anything but a golden boy—the son of a deadbeat wildcatting dad, bent on discovering oil, who leaves Golden and his mother in small-town Louisiana when Golden is three. Golden, we are told, "grew too fast, his pants at perpetual high water, his shoes pinching his toes. He was a boy at odds with his own body: top-heavy, always stumbling, reeling suddenly like someone on the deck of a storm-tossed ship, breaking things, knocking pictures off the walls and whimpering apologies while his mother shrieked her dismay" (Udall 2011, 43). Golden somehow manages to mature and to migrate, moving from Louisiana to the Southwest, where Mormonism soon claims him. The story offers a Mormon Bildungsroman, showing how a hapless, miserable, isolated little boy can convert to the structures of FLDS (though still without faith) and become the husband to five women and the father to twenty-eight children. Yet this transformation in circumstance hardly translates to a transformation of character, and Golden ends the novel as he began it—as a woebegone, awkward, often incompetent, broke, confused, and suffering man, imbricated in family systems beyond his comprehension and control. The narrative is both sympathetic to his plight and merciless in depicting his misery, suggesting that in the midst of his hectic, insanely populated life, Golden longs for connection, understanding, and appreciation. And thus, for a brief time—and in the midst of sleeping with five separate wives—he toys with the idea of taking a Guatemalan mistress.

For my purposes, what matters most about this portrayal is the degree to which *The Lonely Polygamist* has been heralded as a novel about "the quintessential American family" (Alameddine 2011), and Golden has been taken as the personification of an American everyman figure that "makes us recognize the polygamist (and sister wife) in all of us. Golden Richard's [sic] struggles and desires are no different from ours, he just has them in multiples of four" (Houston 2011). As I have noted, Golden is more than woebegone in his role as patriarch and everyman figure. But this, in itself, does not exempt him from a position of being what S. Paige Baty (1995, 8–9) has termed a "representative character," who "embodies and expresses achievement, success, failure, genius, struggle, triumph," or, in other words, a string of often contradictory affective states and outcomes that make aspirational goals clear, even if manifested through flawed characters, who sometimes violate the hierarchy of achievement those goals are meant to represent.

The serial drama *Big Love* plays by the same rules, only holier. Bill Henrickson is husband to three wives (a fourth is sealed to him but leaves the marriage after a day) and father to eight children. He is also a successful but often challenged businessman (owner of building supply stores and a casino). Unlike Golden, Bill's everyman qualities stem not from a sense of existential alienation but from his desire to do good and to be good in the context of his growing business success and more-than-growing ego, both of which require stroking, the narrative implies, so that Bill might be a good provider and potential prophet. Bill grew up in fictional Juniper Creek, a polygamous old-world compound seemingly near Salt Lake City but far enough away that the narrative device of getting back and forth between the city and compound (or being stranded in one place or the other) factors into a good deal of the five-season series. This trope of the old (polygamous) world being nearby but still removed leans on the devices of modern media for connection: cars, mobile telephones, even self-help tapes that characters listen to during the long and tedious drives are critical links between the old world and the new. Mediation about modern polygamy shifts back and forth between these positions of the marginal and the mainstream with remarkable speed. In this movement, it is the interstitial getting there, the long slow passage through the open roads of the West, that is both inessential and inescapable to the larger plots these stories unfold.

Like many young men who grow up in polygamy, Bill is expelled from the compound by his father, abandoned in the city and left to fend for himself at the age of fourteen, an occurrence so common in FLDS culture that there is a lost-boys genre within mediated Mormonism. In Bill, we have the ingredients for a true American self-made man, who forges his way without the aid or hindrance of his father or family. After some years living on the streets of

Salt Lake and stealing to stay alive, Bill meets and then marries Barb (Jeanne Tripplehorn), a mainstream Mormon woman, who helps him solidify his new adult masculinity. They live a conventional mainstream LDS life, until a cancer crisis for Barb requires the family return to the compound for help. Bill and Barb take Nicki (Chloë Sevigny) into their home, first as a nurse and then, as authorized by Bill's prophecy, as a second wife. Some years later, Bill also has a prophecy about the babysitter, Margene (Ginnifer Goodwin), and she enters the family as a third wife (we later find out that Margene is sixteen when Bill marries her). The Henricksons, we are made to understand, live the principle of plural marriage in accord with their religious beliefs, yet it is also clear that religiously motivated polygamy is driven by the patriarch's prophecy, not explicitly by plurality consensus. *Big Love* thus nicely illustrates how male egotism masked as (and coterminous with) male prophecy fuels the patriarchal machine, which often engages in the hegemonic practice of compelling women's "free will" and "consent" to authorize its workings of power. *Big Love*'s creators, Mark V. Olsen and Will Scheffer, themselves a married couple, have noted that their ambition as gay men in mediating a story about Mormon polygamy was twofold: they wanted to show what a complicated, messy, and ultimately successful marriage looked like in all of its many permutations, and they wanted to provoke a larger conversation on the meanings of marriage. "We're dramatizing these people in a way that really does go toward asking, what is a good marriage? What is not a good marriage?" (Lee 2011).

Sister Wives similarly offers commentary on the state of contemporary marriage through a reality television version of modern polygamy. Like Bill Henrickson in *Big Love*, Kody Brown considers himself to be called by God to the principle of plural marriage, and his vision shapes how his wives and children experience the configuration of their domestic world. Unlike Bill, however, Kody was not raised in a plural family but rather in the mainstream Mormon Church. After he returned home from his mission at age twenty-one, Kody converted to a splinter group of the fundamentalist Latter-day Saints, called the Apostolic United Brethren, aka the Work, the Priesthood, the Group, or the Allred Group (his parents had been excommunicated from the mainstream LDS Church due to their interest in living the principle while Kody served his mission). Perhaps riding the coattails of the media and popular enthusiasm for *Big Love* and all things Mormon, *Sister Wives* began airing in 2010 and continues strong as of this writing. Since the reality show depicts real people living an illegal lifestyle, it generated a good deal of scrutiny, scandal, and celebrity for the Browns when it first began airing. It also drew the attention of state and federal authorities, and by the show's second season (spring 2011), the Utah-based family had fled the state for the more welcoming nearby city of Las Vegas, cameras documenting their secret passage. Subsequent seasons have featured the Browns as they attempt to bring their holy lifestyle to Sin City and as they try to establish a financial livelihood in the context of their reality celebrity.

Sister Wives often plays as a parable in modern loving and living, showing marriage in all of its messy glory. The producers focus on the domestic tensions that lie at the heart of all marriages, in this case multiplied by a factor of four but also intensified by worldwide celebrity. When first wife Meri, for instance, became entrapped in an emotional affair with an online lover, multiple forums from Twitter to Facebook commented on her cheating heart. When it was later revealed that Meri's mystery man was actually a woman who had catfished her, social media could not contain its delight, and *Sister Wives* could not refuse to comment on the scandal. Meri's catfishing has thus become one of the major plotlines of the reality show diegesis, and it is featured prominently as, by turns, a rupture of marital trust as well as a signifier of loneliness in an empty-nesting woman, who only has a husband one day in four. The program has also used the catfish scandal (and the loneliness that led to Meri's vulnerability) to suggest a motivation for Meri's desire to leave the family and open a bed and breakfast in a house in Utah that used to be owned by her great-grandfather. In episodes in 2019, Meri is questioned by Kody whether she cares more for the Utah property or her house in Las Vegas, enmeshed as it is in the compound of their four collective houses. "The value of both homes is equally important," she says defiantly. Meri then comments about the irony of his question in a direct-address response to the camera. "I don't think Kody should be questioning me about this. At all. I love both of the homes just the same," she says dissolving into laughter. "If he can say that about his wives, then I can say that about the two houses." Meri here reveals the open secret at the heart of this family's truth: love is not always multiplied as it is divided.

The show also, however, reinforces the basic functionality of the Browns' version of polygamy, spending as much screen time on reconciliation and conflict resolution as on conflict itself. After an episode in which the Browns participated in a contentious panel discussion about the relative merits of polygamy at the University of Nevada at Las Vegas (UNLV), for example, the show ended the episode with UNLV anthropology professor Dr. William Jankowiak, whose academic work deals explicitly with plural families. He noted in direct address to the camera (a visual cue to enhance his credibility as a scholar), "I estimate 25 percent or one in four [plural] families were able to achieve a satisfactory marriage or living arrangement, about 35 percent of families were in some state of ongoing, albeit manageable, conflict, and 30 percent were dysfunctional or in complete disarray" (Rodriguez 2013). While UNLV's digital newspaper, *The Virtual Rebel*, reprinted these statistics, it did not reprint Dr. Jankowiak's subsequent comment that these figures of 25 percent good, 35 percent average, and 30 percent bad are basically the same demographic spread experienced in the U.S. population as a whole. As such, much as Kody and his wives claim, there isn't much difference between polygamous couples and monogamous couples in terms of the day-to-day affective and domestic labors, struggles, and triumphs of relationship building.

There is a significant difference between polygamous and monogamous arrangements, however, in that the intensity of plural marriages' structure, the demands of the large family environment, and the complications of so much emotional and physical caretaking make polygamy an exquisite balancing act that only the strongest will survive. "Polygamy," jokes Robyn Brown, "it's not for amateurs." A sympathetic regard for polygamy thus credits it with being complex, difficult, and draining, yet portrayals also praise polygamy, in all of its excesses and triumphs, as a creative and complex way of loving. "Living in a monogamous lifestyle would just not be full enough for me." Positive portrayals establish polygamy as an important cornerstone in a twenty-first-century marriage debate presently ongoing in Westernized countries where nontraditional marriage is a polarizing double-coded signifier standing for both modern progress and devolution. As I discuss in the next section, modern polygamy stories mindfully use a language of consent and choice to authorize their structures, making common cause with what many consider to be the civil rights issue of the present moment: same-sex marriage.

The sexual contract articulated by and through modern polygamy stories demonstrates how fully regulation of the body and its hungers factors into the kind of modern citizen that polygamy of this form yields, a citizen who is able both to acknowledge emotions and to control them. In these stories, for example, each of the sister wives contends with varying degrees of jealousy in relation to one another and frustration in relation to her husband. Udall typifies the sister wife in *The Lonely Polygamist* as "a burning spotlight of attention and need" (2011, 17). In a broader mediated context, talk shows and special news hour episodes with sister wives frequently include discussion on how women contend with jealousy, particularly the sharp pangs at night when a woman is alone in her bed but knows her husband is down the hall or one house over making love to his other wife. Says Rosemary, wife number three of Brady Williams in the reality show *My Five Wives*, "Jealousy for me is like a wild animal [chuckles]. You've got to keep it in the cage, or it will tear you up [laughs]." Invariably, these women affirm that jealousy is natural, but if they are able to "set aside emotion" they can thus "communicate objectively," in turn heightening the functionality of the family (Ling 2011). Coping with these challenges is positioned in the narratives as part of the structural payoff of polygamy. In an LDS and FLDS religious context, strife in the earthly domain allows a woman to work through her biggest emotional hurdles as a form of self-improvement and a preamble to placement in the Celestial Kingdom, the highest stage of a tripart arrangement in the Mormon cosmogony. If she can forfeit her need for exclusivity, the logic goes, she can live in submission to God. Men must also learn to submit their will to that of a heavenly patriarch, who asks for sacrifices in the name of servitude. But a man often shows this devotion to the divinity through his leadership skills rather than his subservience.[4]

Modern polygamy stories carry these valences of religion, but they also make appeals to more secular, even workplace, values. For instance, "objective communication" could well be taken as the watchword of human resources managers, who encourage employees to transcend emotional upset in service of a more harmonious and efficient business setting. *The Lonely Polygamist* mocks this tie to corporatism with the installation of a suggestion box in the Big House, so that members of the household can register their concerns anonymously. Modern sister wives talk less about feeling their feelings than about suppressing them in the name of rational talk and overall familial well-being. Doing so has its payoffs. According to these stories, when modern polygamy works well, women are able to transcend both the edicts of patriarchy and the work/life dilemma while governing their lives by choice, a critical, though certainly not uncontested, element of contemporary feminism. Depending on inclination rather than obligation, FLDS women might stay at home or go to work. Says Kody, "Each of my wives has come into our family of her own free will. Choosing to join a plural family has been their choices, their preferences" (Brown et al. 2012, 6). On *Sister Wives*, this means that the third wife, Christine, can stay home with the children while second wife Janelle works outside the home. And while the freedom to work for money represents a major tension between Barb, Nicki, and Margene on *Big Love*, the extended family network makes room for a gigantic plot of free-range murders, lost boys, nosy neighbors, and homicidal patriarchs, each woman able to pop away from the domestic sphere of child rearing and dinner preparation into a bigger world of intrigue simply by leaving her young children with one of the other wives or older kids. On these programs, the sole man faces management challenges and has concerns about the best way to inspire confidence and to lead his family, who are, by turns, made synonymous with workers, troops, and pilgrims.

In this context, the man's task is to govern, seek consensus, and spread himself evenly across the wives and children who desire his time, attention, and affection. "It's a whole lot of work," laments patriarch Michael, talking to Lisa Ling (2011) on the modern polygamy episode of *Our America*. One of his wives acknowledges, "I'm sure it appears easier than it really is. It's living *la vida loca* for the guy, right? . . . The reality of not only providing for those women but trying to meet their physical, spiritual needs is huge. It's a huge responsibility." "Believe me," said an unidentified polygamist to the *New York Times*, "there are cheaper ways to have sex" (Williams 1997). As Emily Nussbaum (2007) joked about *Big Love*: "Bill may be trapped in every man's dream—three naked ladies!—but he's also living every man's nightmare: relationship processing so endless it might paralyze a seventies lesbian cooperative." In fact, it is precisely this impediment on masculinity and male sexuality—the fact that polygamy obligates men to cultivate committed sexual relationships through marriage rather than engaging in promiscuity (as if male sexuality can manifest only through one of these polarities)—that leads modern polygamy to consider itself committed to women's welfare rather than opposed to it.

But what may on the surface appear to be a woman-friendly system could in fact be seen as a new domain for cultivating masculinity. A good deal of gender theory contends that masculinity often establishes its contours on the edges of civilization and through certain kinds of excess—think the Western frontier, the demands of war, the challenges of Arctic exploration. In each of these cases, however, masculinity must absent itself from a feminized domain of home, child rearing, and emotional labor. As Michael Kimmel (1997) puts it, manhood is established in those places where it perceives itself as free of the feminized lassitudes of domesticity. In stories about modern polygamy, however, the home space establishes the alpha and omega of experience. While men like Bill or Kody or Brady or Golden might work outside the home, the narrative pull is always back to wives and children, to making ends meet, to the extremes and excesses represented by the home itself, and to a modern masculine frontier of emotional attentiveness that the man must cultivate in himself.

It's a most extraordinary set of circumstances and challenges for an otherwise quintessentially ordinary American family. Writes Kody in *Becoming Sister Wives*, "The demands on a plural family are far greater than those on a monogamous couple. Since we have to consider the sensitivity of other wives and other marriages on an everyday basis, plural marriage consistently challenges us. It makes us confront our shortcomings and overcome them. We have to learn to handle our jealousy, contain our aggression. We have to check our selfishness. There is no room for ego in plural marriage" (Brown et al. 2012, 5). I would argue, quite in opposition, that rather than there being no room for ego in plural marriage, it is precisely the ego of self-making that fuels the domains of modern polygamy. In many ways, this level of personal challenge is presented as a gender-neutral circumstance. In the language of my son's preschool, problems help us become mindful, and mindfulness is critical to our success. I don't dispute these ideas. In fact, I engage daily in my own efforts for self-awareness, self-regulation, and mindfulness, but the point here is the way such disciplines of awareness and behavior constitute a pedagogy of gendered being that positions the excesses of modern polygamy as the perfect incubator of neoliberal selfhood, where masculinity and femininity are both reified in fairly conventional ways. Men emerge as natural leaders; women choose their place as followers.

Visibility as Justice: Success as Vindication

The common academic template for understanding polygamy (both Mormon and not) is that it has grown less prevalent worldwide as more societies have modernized. Judith Stacey argues, for example, that monogamy has historically been the outsider, since "many more societies have practiced polygamy than have prohibited it" (2011, 124). In a contemporary context, polygamy has moved to the margins, and many scholars credit this subordinated and often alienated position to the fact that, says Stacey, "in industrializing societies . . . few male wage earners can afford to support more than one wife and children" (127). While this rubric may be true for real families, in the mediated world tales abound of large families that must exploit innovative cost-cutting and money-earning strategies to not only survive but thrive in tough economic times when large families attenuate an already-strained budget. Whether polygamous or not, those people who face extreme challenges and yet learn how to prosper in a challenging economic climate are deemed survivors, in the basest of social evolutionary thinking. In this case, survival of the fittest is not about the glacial time of natural selection but about finding the right sort of immediate self-management strategies that can offer instant payoffs.

This rapid-paced care and operationalizing of the self rings with the hegemonies of both modernity and spiritual neoliberalism. Many scholars have insightfully shown that projects of the self often enact state ideologies through a process of governmentality, whereby subjects are governed through a distance by entertainment, discourse, and mores, all of which are imbricated in modern mandates about markets, individualization, and floating currencies.[5] As Nikolas Rose (1993, 283) has quite poetically (and frighteningly) put it: "The forms of power that subject us, the systems of rule that administer us, the types of authority that master us, do not find their principle of coherence in a State, nor do they answer to a logic of oppression or domination." These forms of power are built into the very apparatus of a spectacular selfhood, which emerges as a commodity of value in a global marketplace that stresses the efficiency of privatization, the stability of financial markets, and the decentralization of government.

In many respects, a friendly but renegade and largely antigovernment group of conscientious lawbreakers (like progressive Mormon polygamists) offers the perfect model for neoliberal development, since political ideologies can be masked by religious imperatives. Thus, the turn away from government and toward individuals seems to be motivated by a drive for spiritual purity and social justice. But when these modes of ideology are mediated and dispersed through an international market of television networks, book sellers, and movie houses, and when they are dedicated to self-improvement in the service of heavenly outcomes, their combined messages soon begin to reinforce a market logic of choice politics, individual autonomy, limited government involvement, and heavenly reward—in short, spiritual neoliberalism.[6]

Mormon polygamy stories position themselves as markedly distinct from other big-family forms of mediation for the primary reason that polygamy (unlike simply having a large family) is illegal. Unjustly so, says the polygamist. In the context of this bigotry, financial woes are due not only to the largeness of one's family but also to discriminatory practices that unfairly prohibit Mormon polygamists from living the American Dream. It is at times like these, they argue, that the polygamist must take matters into his own hands, and such agency in a postmillennial moment requires harnessing the mediascape. Writes Joe Darger in *Love Times Three*: "In the past, people like us who have polygamous relationships have zealously guarded their privacy and sought to stay out of the public spotlight due to this lifestyle's criminal status. We have stayed silent despite widespread misperceptions, mistreatment, and intolerance. To speak up is to risk persecution, prosecution, and, because of discrimination, economic hardship. We have carried the fragile hope that our silence will allow us to avoid unfair treatment. As a family, we have come to see that as unproductive and naïve" (Darger et al. 2012, vii).

Productivity and sophistication mandate that progressive and forward-thinking polygamists enter the court of public opinion in order to change understanding. Progressive polygamy stories thus have justice as their impetus, and the argument contends that understanding will breed fairness. Or, put another way, progressive polygamists are open about their explicit political and religious ideology, and, in being so honest about their objective, they expect to effect meaningful social change. Says Kody Brown when his family comes out of hiding at the start of Season 2: "The fundamentalist Mormon community and the polygamists have become secretive, in such a way as to threaten the rest of America even if it's in their own minds. And so to be transparent, I believe, makes us more safe to them. We're hoping that other fundamentalist Mormon polygamists will follow our example and open their lives up, and eventually we can become an open community rather than a closed community." There is a similar hope for redemption through publicness on *Big Love*. The outing of the fictional Henricksons happens diegetically on a much smaller stage than the worldwide reality television platform chosen by the Browns, but the messages are quite similar. With the Utah capitol building behind him, three microphones before him, and cameras flashing all around him, Bill's acceptance speech after winning the election for state senator is also the moment of irrevocability for himself and his three wives. "I am Bill Henrickson . . . and I believe in the principle of plural marriage." His wives are dressed monochromatically, Barb all in red, Nicki all in white, and Margene all in blue, while Bill—in a red-and-white-striped tie to mimic the star-spangled banner, stands to their side. All of them unsmiling and clasping hands. The entire tableau stands as both symbol for and metonym of America, its plurality on full display, its obligation for tolerance in full demand (figure 3.1).

Indeed, narratives about progressive polygamy overtly press on a logic of American inclusivity to motivate and justify the narratives they mediate. "We're not your typical American family, but we're an American family nonetheless," says Bill from the podium. Kody Brown's fourth wife, Robyn, laments the lack of tolerance that makes it necessary for her and her family to flee Utah for the safer environs of Las Vegas: "This is not the America

FIG. 3.1 Modern Mormon polygamy as both symbol for and metonym of American plurality and modernity.

that I learned about in school." Says Connie Cawley, star of several mediated texts about polygamy including a *Nightline* (Vega 2013) special, Lisa Ling's (2011) investigation, and a reality show called *Polygamy USA*: "This is our version of life, liberty, and the pursuit of happiness. If everyone else in the United States is entitled to that, so are we."

Clearly, in this formulation, representation and visibility serve political ends, and the logic in these stories indicates that American democracy promises all citizens acceptance. Further, the narratives press on a rather remarkable idea that what is known and liked cannot be discriminated against. It's a formula for social change that has important precedents, as, for instance, Harriet Beecher Stowe's use of sentimental fiction to dismantle slavery in *Uncle Tom's Cabin* (1852) or Elizabeth Gaskell's sympathetic portrayals of a fallen woman to rehumanize those who are abandoned and made destitute by circumstances and society in *Ruth* (1853). But this to-know-me-is-to-love-me approach assumes that all visibility brings intimacy, and intimacy, in turn, always and invariably yields affection and fair treatment. As teleological partners along a scale of acceptance, the logic indicates that visibility, intimacy, and affect are always good, positive, and salutary. In this respect, texts like *Big Love* and *Sister Wives* are very little indebted to the generic conventions of sentimental fiction; instead, they are more firmly situated in the parlance of contemporary celebrity, where mediation fosters a feeling of to-be-knownness between fan and star, a closeness that both mimics and departs from the functions of intimacy.

As does modern celebrity, the structures of polygamy create a public curiosity that carries value on the open market. Oddity creates interest, and interest creates customers. The Browns, for instance, have parlayed their struggle for justice into a financial windfall, all while storylines on the reality show itself depict them struggling to make ends meet. Since its premiere in 2010, the Browns have not only capitalized through the show, they have written a best-selling memoir, *Becoming Sister Wives*, started a business called My Sisterwife's Closet, and established a media presence through Facebook, Twitter, and Instagram, all incorporated under Kody Brown Family Entertainment, LLC (established March 30, 2010). The website Celebrity Net Worth posits Kody's value at $300,000, a figure perhaps not in the stratosphere for a celebrity but certainly far above the net worth of the average family that the Browns position themselves as being ("Kody Brown Net Worth" 2015).

Much like A-list celebrities advertising their latest movie, the Browns have hit the talk show circuit, appearing on *The Ellen DeGeneres Show*, *George Lopez*, *Good Morning America*, and the *Oprah Winfrey Show*, to name a few. At this point, all things Brown underscore a philosophy critical to American conservative cultures: everything can be put to use. But in this case, it is not growing food in a summer garden or canning that food for the winter that functions as the marker of resourceful savvy, it is marshaling the powers of the mediascape to sell products, both tangible (jewelry, soaps, handmade clothes) and intangible (personality, charisma, entertainment). Indeed, the Browns have shown remarkable business acumen in using their reality celebrity to the benefit of their entrepreneurial success. Using the logic of new-age aspiration—follow your bliss; do what you love and the money will follow—they characterize their businesses as a form of sister-led financial family adventure (figure 3.2). Similarly, following her legal divorce from Kody (so that he could legally adopt Robyn's children), Meri Brown joined MLM clothing company LuLaRoe, famous for their "buttery soft" leggings and founded by a mainstream Mormon mother of eight. While Meri's Facebook page tries to keep family issues separate, her Instagram account blends marketing and family. In turn, the Browns' own form of mediated

FIG. 3.2 My Sisterwife's Closet (https://mysisterwifescloset.com/), website image, with the following copy: "We have always had a dream to develop and design products that the everyday woman could use and then add our own personal fun and flair to those ideas! My Sisterwife's Closet is our little adventure to see if our dreams can come true and we are working together as a family to make it happen! We are developing new ideas and new pieces everyday. We are excited to introduce the first four products! It is a line of jewelry that we have all had a hand in bringing to reality. We hope you will look through our 'closets' and find something that you can't live without!"

Mormonism has included wife Christine wearing LuLaRoe leggings on the show and daughter Madison posing in LuLaRoe for her maternity photos in *People*. The composite solidifies the bond between celebrity prophets and MLM profits.

A parallel family, the Dargers, operates in a very similar fashion. While they do not have their own reality series, they did share a vacation to Southern California with the Browns on one episode of *Sister Wives* (in which Kody's wives swooned over Joe Darger's manly management skills. *He really knows how to run a family!*). The Dargers starred in a one-off special, *My Three Wives*, that aired on TLC in 2012. They seemed to be set for a show of their own, with the network even advertising upcoming episodes, when everything was canceled for undisclosed reasons. Like the Browns, the Dargers have made use of major media outlets, such as *Dr. Drew* and *Dr. Phil*, and they are the featured family of *The Mormon Moment* (2011), a documentary produced by Australian Broadcasting Company and Journeyman Pictures about a typical American family that is anything but normal. "Disowned by their church," intones the Australian-accented voice of *The Mormon Moment*, "and yet they've inspired the popular and enduring notion of what it is to be Mormon." While claiming that they seek visibility for social justice reasons, the Dargers have also parlayed their moment in the public eye into a financial wellspring of support as aided by the cross-platforming of latter-day screens. Visit their social media sites, called either TheDargerFamily or *Love Times Three*, and in addition to updates about the family's well-being (including sonogram pictures in November 2013 for Joe and second wife Vicki's in-utero baby girl), you will find a link to the Polygamy Store (polygamystore.com), where customers can buy the Dargers' book for $14.95, as well as products such as Orange Cream Lip Balm and Solstice Healing Salve, which are "handcrafted with care with enough love to share." The website, a cooperative venture between the Dargers and "others from the Fundamentalist Mormon culture" promises high-quality merchandise, created by God-loving people. The advertising copy on the website reads: "The work ethic of plural families and the attention to detail, quality and creativity come through in the products we offer." Lip balms, salves, baby hats and booties, professional website design, skirts, hand-crocheted dolls—these are the physical products the Polygamy Store sells.

But housed as it is within the Darger family's website and Facebook page, the Polygamy Store equally advertises a modern polygamy brand, dedicated to promoting a set of practices and knowledges about modern living that is predicated on an American right to plurality. "How are major decisions made in the family?" writes one poster to the family blog in the FAQ tab of the website. Responds the family, "For small issues we all have the ability to use our brains and make decisions. When it comes to big decisions that affect everyone ... we all discuss it and come to an agreement before moving forward." It's representative democracy in its purest form, at least as written here, but paired as it is with goods for sale, it is also citizenship defined by and through consumerism. As such, the Dargers seem to indicate that it is possible to eradicate social discrimination through discriminating consumer choices. "In this kind of country we should all be free," says Joe to Dr. Drew, freedom here simultaneously meaning identity choice and/as consumer choice (Pinsky 2012).

LGBT:FLDS

Some have asked whether polygamy is viable in our modern culture. Our answer? Yes, absolutely. Ours is an example of a family created by consenting adults for whom this lifestyle works. At its core, this is a love story about people who came together to create a family that would support, nurture, and sustain each member.

Every day, people make bonds and blend relationships in ways that are defining what it means to be a "family." Our particular definition is nothing new, however; polygamy is the most widespread family structure in the world, permissible in more cultures than any other. In choosing plural marriage, we have found purpose that goes beyond ourselves, sometimes in ways we never could have imagined as we built a family built on the most traditional of values: faith, love, loyalty, and unconditional acceptance.—The Dargers, *Love Times Three*

Brady Williams said the increasing social and legal acceptance of gay marriage has helped society open up toward plural marriage. Didn't take long for liberals and the elite media to move on to the next step in obliterating the social institution of marriage, did it.—lmlaughlin, internet commenter on Brady McCombs, "'My Five Wives' TLC's Newest Polygamous Family Favors Buddhism"

As I've noted, to underscore the ordinariness of modern polygamy, narratives establish their bona fides by linking to the normative mainstream. What might be more surprising, then, is that these narratives make equal if not greater links to peoples and places often considered non-normative, or, at least, those who are positioned as marginalized, alienated, or non-hegemonic. Typically, these bids for common cause include assertions that oppressed groups are like one another simply due to the fact of their oppression. On *Sister Wives*, for example, this notion of equal-opportunity oppression takes many forms, perhaps none more telling than when the Browns go shopping for new furniture in Las Vegas and meet an African American salesman who, on camera, refuses to judge the practices of polygamy because of the discrimination he has faced as a black man.[7] On *Big Love*, a particularly memorable demonstration of equal-opportunity oppression takes place when third wife Margene accuses the representative of a non-specified Native American tribe, Jerry Flute (played by Latino Robert Beltran), of being a bigot because he does not want to link the reservation to polygamists through a business venture. Jerry takes offense, and Bill tries to reconcile on the grounds of similitude, spiritualism, prosperity, and appeals to authenticity. "We have too much in common to let this fall apart. Your people were forced onto reservations. In a way, my people were too. We're both trying to improve the lot of those we love and maintain a sacred life in the midst of a culture that's forgotten what's holy. . . . Let's mend and prosper at the same time. . . . I'm not Vegas. I'm not glitzy. I'm just a regular guy trying to support my family." The scene ends with them shaking hands. In *The Lonely Polygamist*, these links to outsiders are more commonly made with a sardonic twist. Udall positions the polygamist and a brothel owner as synonymous figures joined by their equal trafficking in women through a sexual economy that rewards men for women's heterosexual sex acts. As his character Ted Leo, owner of a Nevada whorehouse, bluntly puts it, "Fucking for money, fucking for salvation, not a whole lot of difference" (Udall 2011, 496).

While oppression of any sort seems to bind modern polygamists to other marginalized peoples and thus to those in need of equal protection under the law, it is the metaphor of the queer closet that is mobilized most often in bids for recognition and respect. Judith Stacey has noted that *Big Love* often adopted the "idiom of the closet to describe their family circumstances," drawing "analogies between social stigma and discrimination against polygamous and gay families" (2011, 116). As a model for emancipation from unfair oppression and crippling secrecy, the closet apparently serves as a fluid portal for social justice. All of these texts about modern Mormon polygamy depict a white excessively heterosexual patriarch laying claim to a politics of emancipation in order to assert his rights to live his exceptional lifestyle as an American citizen and everyman. The Browns, for example, explicitly embrace the discourses of choice politics and queer cultures to fight for their right to come out of the closet (figure 3.3). Indeed, the Browns lay claim to human rights discourses clearly initiated through gay pride initiatives for queer and transgender justice. "I'm tired of hiding who I am," Kody tells the camera in direct address. "I'm tired of being discriminated against for my lifestyle." Their journey, he notes, is about coming out of the closet and living the American Dream. The appropriation of the language of LGBT+ politics seemingly allows polygamous families the same sort of rights to personhood as those afforded to anyone else who claims a lifestyle as a way of describing a life, particularly gay and lesbian people. Jane Bennion argues that "campaigns to decriminalize and legalize polygamy" are often "promoted in conjunction with right-to-marry crusades of gays and lesbians" (2012, xvii). This sort of reaching across the aisle was certainly in evidence in 2012 and 2013 when the Browns were indicted in Utah on charges of bigamy. Their attorney, Jonathan Turley, drew on templates to support gay marriage as a precedent for fairness with respect to modern polygamy. "We are not

FIG. 3.3 Queer solidarities, established through the celebrity website TMZ and emblazoned with the gay pride banner.

demanding the recognition of polygamous marriage," he wrote in a blog statement (Turley 2011). "We are only challenging the right of the state to prosecute people for their private relations and demanding equal treatment with other citizens in living their lives according to their own beliefs." At the January 2013 Salt Lake City trial for bigamy (which the Browns did not attend but Valerie and Vicki Darger did), Valerie suggested that polygamists were less interested in the right to legally marry. They simply wanted to be left alone: "The thing that's different about what we're asking for is the right to exist and the right to be left alone. We're not seeking marriage licenses, and so, as far as legal marriage goes, it doesn't really pertain" ("Reality TV Show Polygamist" 2013). Turley reiterated this claim: "We're asking for what [U.S. Supreme Court] Justice Brandeis called the most important constitutional right, the right to be left alone" ("Reality TV Show Polygamist" 2013).

We might argue this was modern polygamy's great Greta Garbo moment, if it were not for the fact that the request to be left alone came through the mediated auspices of reality television, celebrity tabloids, and social media, as augmented by an array of accessories from the celebrity website TMZ to the nation's paper of record, the *New York Times*. The demands for privacy and protection were resoundingly and incessantly made across an intermedial continuum that would not leave us alone. Further, the very mechanism these polygamous families chose for their stance on social justice entangled them in an integrated celebrity system, where financial currency, cultural capital, and Q scores (the measurement of the popularity of a brand or celebrity) coalesce to determine value and to perpetuate their public platform. In other words, they could have no sustained political voice if they did not also have sustained positive ratings.

But perhaps these mediated strategies designed to shape popular opinion are necessary critical counterpoints given the range and volatility of mediated scare tactics used to denigrate the end-of-decency scenarios polygamy supposedly augers. The mediascape abounds with fear-based screeds that link same-sex marriage and polygamy to not only the dissolution of conventional marriage but to a series of impurities that include miscegenation, incest, and assimilation. As one example, *The Manning Report*, an overtly Christian news and commentary program airing on the ATLAH Media Network with radio podcasts available on CRUSADE Channel Radio, Skybird Radio, and the Moral Nation Radio Network, aired a trifecta of slippery-slope concerns (gay polygamy and open borders). A caller to the program from Utah urged the African American host, Dr. James David Manning, to speak out against same-sex marriage, since its approval, he argued, would give an automatic green light to polygamy, and this, in turn, to the unregulated importation of illegal aliens, a category that quickly became conflated with Mexican nationals. Remarkably, what most seemed to concern Manning was that gay and polygamous peoples could and would pretend their orientation in order to perpetuate an attack on American racial purity. The line of reasoning would be laughable if it weren't so widely believed. Type "modern polygamy gay rights" into a video search engine, for instance, and you will feast upon a smorgasbord of fear, including major media and political figures like Glenn Beck and Kentucky senator Rand Paul claiming that gay marriage easily leads to polygamy and bestiality. But the mediascape also abounds with amateur video bloggers, like David Pakman (2013), eager to expose the "absurd, amateurish, and juvenile slippery slope arguments" created around these social issues. Modern Mormon polygamists, then, are not only fighting for their rights for intelligibility, they are joining the democratic conversation, making their claim for inclusivity and plurality.

When asked, modern FLDS polygamists typically voice support for gay people and same-sex marriage. The *Sister Wives* stars, for instance, support gay people and gay marriage, though their pronouncements of such often read as the teaser headline that advertises a new season of their reality show or the publication of their book. In this case, celebrity-based websites like TMZ or E! end up occupying the position of social rights gadflies. For instance, E! showcased Kody's declaration: "I married four women and I love them. I chose this out of love and out of faith. . . . Let individuals define their love and their marriage. I don't want the government doing that." Asked if their beliefs extend to gay couples, Kody said, "Let individuals define their marriage and let individuals choose who they love" (Malkin 2012). The piece ended with a reminder of the kickoff for Season 3 of *Sister Wives* and an admonition for further retail commitments: "The Browns' new memoir, *Becoming Sister Wives: The Story of an Unconventional Marriage*, is on sale now." The Browns had an opportunity to put their social justice money where their mouth is in 2017 when daughter Mariah, in great anxiety, informed the family that she is gay. As of this writing, they are all coping—as long as Mariah remains celibate.

It's fairly easy to reveal the commercial underbelly of these kinds of moments, so I don't really want to pursue that line of critique. Instead, I want to pause to be sympathetic to the idea that FLDS polygamists may well offer a progressive stance on tolerance and modern living. While the connection between Mormons (LDS and FLDS) and gay pride might seem somewhat audacious (particularly given the mainstream church's effort to defeat California's Proposition 8), if you squint your eyes just right, modern polygamists and LGBT+ folks do share experience due to the weight of harboring a secret life that hews closely to one's sense of identity. For instance, Robyn Brown speaks of the relief she feels in coming out through the auspices of their reality television show: being public means she no longer needs to be mindful of gestures, comments, and behaviors that tip off people to her identity as a polygamist.

I believe a case could well be made for the way polygamists experience biases that parallel other forms of social oppression. For instance, gay, lesbian, and transgender peoples and polygamists often undergo an intensification of vulnerability in spaces where official documentation is needed, say at border crossings, in airports, at hospitals, and so on. A telling moment of this sort came on *Sister Wives* when third wife Christine gave birth to the family's thirteenth child, Truely. Already the mother of five children, all of whom she birthed at home, Christine elected to have Truely in the hospital due to her age (thirty-seven) and the fact that she had experienced a serious miscarriage a year earlier. Janelle informs the home viewer that largely because of fears of the father being arrested, "In our culture, home birth is a common thing." More striking in this scene than the fear of possible outing, however, is the degree to which Christine takes to the hospital environment, finding birthing drugs to be amazing. Immediately after the birth (before Truely even starts crying), Christine exclaims, "Okay, I'm all for the epidural!" "That was so easy. That was so easy. *That* was amazingly easy." The nurse jokes with Kody: "You'll have all the wives in here to have epidurals." And he seems to be joking back: "Yeah, yeah. Can you dull those needles on purpose?" His reasons for disapproving the pain-relieving drugs aren't made clear on screen, but his position seems to be grounded in the double denunciation of his wife's newfound (and seemingly erotic) pleasure in giving birth and in the contradiction of a tradition of home birth that hospitals and pain medications represent. Literary scholar Mary Poovey has made a remarkable case for the Victorian advent of chloroform as altering the experience of childbirth from pain to one more potentially of pleasure. She argues chlorform effectively converted fetus to phallus, and women who cried out often did so in ways that appeared to the medical men observing them as moans of sexual pleasure (Poovey 1988, 50). In this case, Christine's vaginal/sexual pleasure from anything or anyone other than Kody and her enthusiastic rallying for more drugs challenges certainties about tradition and primacy. In so doing, this moment is incredibly telling about the heteronormative and even patriarchal values that structure both affective and actual labor.[8]

So modern Mormon polygamy may be gay friendly, but is it queer? Before answering that question, it is important to establish that queer theory as a political and intellectual system often overlaps with gay and lesbian studies, but it is not synonymous with it. Queering requires a blurring of categories, a refutation of the binaries of heterosexual/homosexual that leads to a state more polymorphous ideologically and ontologically. Queer theory must possess, says historian of sexuality David Halperin, a "radical potential" that reinvents "its capacity to startle, to surprise, to help us think what has not yet been thought" (2003, 343). This radical potential, says television scholar Samuel Chambers, means that queer theory need not only or always be about sex, "since its resistance to and subversion of the category of the normal has wide-reaching effects" (2009, 17). Indeed, Chambers points directly to *Big Love* as an example of a text made queer not because its protagonist Bill engages in three different ongoing sexual relationships but because the Henricksons "subvert the sanguinuptial model: their queerness emerges not merely through representation of marginalized or deviant family, but through an illustration of the conflict and contestation between their family practices and heteronormativity. It is precisely the agonism here that makes their family queer" (2009, 188).

Chambers augments this reading of the Henricksons as queer through a lengthy and very convincing discussion on the politics of passing. The Henricksons, he argues, are not able to "come out" because the only "out polygamists" are fundamentalist (compound) polygamists—a thoroughly stigmatized and denigrated group not merely marginalized in respect to the norm but thoroughly displaced to the margins of society" (2009, 194). Indeed, argues Chambers, "polygamy has the advantage among queer forms of family of being so taboo as to be both unexpected and un-looked-for" (194). Polygamy, argues Chambers, is not even a presence interpellated into the closet. To paraphrase a line from feminist theory, modern polygamy has no there there—no identity to attach to and make intelligible one's coming out. This point is comedically made in an amateur video posted to YouTube in which an improv group, Is This Thing On?, acts out two sister wives recruiting a third in an otherwise normal suburban neighborhood (Stanulis 2013). The recruit's inability to understand the relationship between the beatifically happy women attenuates the humor of the sketch. "Are you sisters? Are you partners?" she asks. "Wellllll," the sister wives drawl, smiling and holding hands, "we're best friends. Let's just leave it at that for now." It's only when the women reference a single husband that they create a category in which the terms for their own being become intelligible.

Chambers helpfully illustrates that the polygamy the Henricksons represent is so obscure it is queered. Their queerness is accentuated because there is no out space to emerge into. And yet, Chambers's argument is quite specific to *Big Love* as a text standing on its own and primarily relevant to and in conversation with the time period in which it was aired (2006–11). I would argue by Chambers's own logic that modern Mormon polygamy stories, existing as they do within a field of other similar stories, unqueer the queerness of themselves precisely because their presence creates a new epistemology of the closet that contains itself within it. In other words, the just-like-us appeal of mediated polygamous families, the broader network of visible and telegenic portrayals evinced by progressive polygamists (both fictional and actual), and the composite currency of polygamy as celebrity brand all work together to reinforce familiarity and recognition, thus obscuring the degree that they might startle, surprise, or help us think what has not yet been thought.

The temporal fluidity of contemporary television heightens this fact all the more. In a postnetwork age when television products are syndicated, sold as finite texts in DVD form, or downloadable for streaming through Netflix, Amazon, and iTunes, it becomes increasingly difficult to argue for the idea that texts stand in isolation to one another. Indeed, a single television show like *Big Love* is not only in conversation with other television fare such as *Sister Wives* or *My Five Wives*, it is part of a larger discursive network of ideas and identities. (If you doubt this, try buying the *Big Love* boxed set on Amazon and see what other like-minded products are recommended.) So my goal is not to chide Chambers for failing to note a broader field of representation about polygamy that he could not have foreseen when he published his book in 2009 but to argue that this complicated story about the closet, what it means to come out of it, and the very positions of in and out are all informed and reshaped by our very processes of storytelling. Call it the Heisenberg Theory of Mediation, where the tool for measuring modifies what is being recorded. In this case, any epistemology of the closet as it pertains to modern polygamy is very much bound up in and shaped by the mediated contexts that both announce its contours and obscure its position as marginal.

There is one further detail to consider with very specific relation to LGBT+ and queer politics. Although the people in modern polygamy stories often describe themselves as gay friendly, they use the language of gay pride without endorsing the realities of same-sex-desiring lives or of a non-normative erotics. Using the logic of homonormativity, for example, Brown fourth wife Robyn asserts, "We're normal, and we're just a family." First wife Meri agrees, adding a bit of a queer-kinship spin: "And who says where the line is drawn of who you can love?" Meri does, however, draw a line about how you can love, noting that each of the wives has separate sexual relations and relationships with Kody. "It's just how it is. We don't go weird." Joe Darger echoes this claim for decidedly unqueer sexual practices when asked about the sexual contract between him and his wives. When appearing on *Dr. Drew*, the good doctor quizzes the Dargers in the language of value-neutral therapy speak: "Is there one communal sleeping center?" They collectively cringe in response. "We have our own master bedrooms, and Joe visits us separately," says one wife, emphatically. In *The Mormon Moment*, Joe reads from a script: "There is absolutely no kinkiness."[9]

Modern polygamy stories thus rely on the language of LGBT+ social justice to reinforce a resolutely nonqueer social hegemony, constructing their lives and sexual relations in ways that ring bells of recognition for middle-class, white heteronormativity. *We don't go weird.* Many of these stories tie themselves in knots in order to suggest a version of parallel monogamy at work in the progressive polygamist's family, where fully functioning nuclear families live near one another and are linked through a common male. The efforts to establish these normative grooves are both overtly and covertly uttered. So, in addition to the cringes and shudders when viewers ask about sex or insinuate some fluid arrangement or sexual desire in a plural family, the video-cinematic-textual code establishes blocks and separations between houses, bedrooms, and vaginas, sometimes through a wife's story being contained within one chapter or subheading (as in the memoirs) and other times by the structural separations established by sets or circumstances. On *Big Love*, for instance, Bill must walk out the back door of one house, through a shared yard, and then into the separate home of one of his other wives. In Seasons 3 through 5, Kody Brown actually drives from home to home, often leaving his belt or his socks behind. Golden Richards lumbers from wife to wife in an old pickup, going back and forth between Old House and Big House and a new duplex his most recent wife shares with her daughter.

Focusing on ordinary events (the opening of *The Lonely Polygamist*, for instance, contains an exquisite and gut-wrenching twenty-page description of Golden needing to pee—really badly—and finding no bathroom empty in his overcrowded house), these introductions to polygamous households tacitly reinforce that the men in question basically live in multiple fairly conventional heteronormative nuclear families, joined together by proximity, choice, and convenience, a fact demonstrated over and over again by how often speakers reference the idea that consenting adults have the freedom to act as they see fit. The nuclear families' separate-but-together motif is reinforced textually when each child is referenced in relation to his or her mother or by screen shots depicting family portraits of a father and each respective wife and kids. Rather than the communal living arrangements that characterize the polygamists we know, where young girls are married to old men and teenage boys are expelled from the fold so as not to compete with their fathers and where mothers indiscriminately care for each other's children, progressive polygamy stories make the case for a separate-but-together suburban form of living, where wives dress in fashionable clothes, dads drive Lexus sports cars or SUVs, and parents worry about their children, want their teenagers to go to college, and squabble with one another in mostly loving ways. They're living the American Dream, right down to the big houses, pastel walls, bright lights, iPhones, and leather couches.

In structure and substance, then, modern polygamy stories are fables about resolutely middle-class and heteronormative values. They basically say gay and lesbian folks are fine as long as they don't do any gay stuff. This stance is reinforced by other mediated fare, as for instance lurid versions of FLDS polygamy that conflate plural marriage with cultism. In one episode of *Deadly Devotion* called "Mormon Murders" (2013), for instance, an orphaned teenage girl is taken in by a Mormon cult that practices increasingly "perverse" sex rituals on and with her. These rituals begin with a teenager's sexualized display for a seventy-year-old patriarch and her eventual symbolic marriage and rape by him. But the show reserves its greatest alarm for the woman-woman eroticism she is forced to engage in for the prophet's benefit and titillation. Women who have sex with women are here presented as not only perverse but a greater wrong done to a teenager than rape or kidnapping.

Strong-Minded Sister Wives and Postfeminist Patriarchs

While Bill tells you about his money problems, Emily looks at him, concern on her face, maybe even a little pity. Now, wait a second here, you think. Pity for Bill? If you understand polygamy correctly, shouldn't all the pity be reserved for the wives? They are the ones who are oppressed, subjugated, and forced into positions of servitude, right?—Udall, "The Lonely Polygamist"

"What's the biggest misunderstanding that people have when they talk to you guys?" Jeff Probst asks the Brown family on *The Jeff Probst Show* (2012). Kody begins to speak, but Christine interrupts. "They think that we are weak-willed women. Until we open our mouths, and then they're like [in Valley Girl intonation] 'Oh, I get it now!'" Janelle adds, "Also, they think that Kody has this great life and, honestly, he's in the doghouse almost all the time with somebody." Kody chuckles about always having a frustrated wife, rolling his eyes in that "women, can't live with 'em . . ." kind of way. Robyn notes in sort of exaggerated hilarity that they gang up on Kody. If he steps out of line with one of the sister wives, the others send him nagging texts to urge Kody to "get in there and fix it." Probst jokes, "Now I'm feeling sorry for Kody!" The audience laughs.

In this chapter I've suggested that progressive polygamists want us to think differently about the lives and lifestyles they lead. They are not like the iconoclastic old-fashioned people you've seen and heard about. Instead, they are hip, technologically savvy, pressed for time, eager to please, doing the best they can, just like us. Polygamy as an ancient system is supposed to be great for a man, who calls all the shots and can have as many wives as he pleases. Conversely, polygamy is considered hard, inhumane even,

FIG. 3.4 Robyn, incredulous that she has just told the world things are just fine when Kody isn't there.

for women and children, who are subject to the edicts and desires of the prophets who rule their loves and lives. By contrast, according to these narratives, women under modern polygamy do better than anyone else, precisely because having more women around lessens the amount of time they have to be accountable to a husband and heightens their autonomy, independence, and self-nurturing. "All of the security of marriage and all of the freedom of being single" (Udall 1998). On yet another visit to a talk show, the Brown sister wives told *The Real* hosts that life with a quarter of a husband may well be better than life with 100 percent of him. Says Robyn, "A lot of women get really weird, like how do you share your husband? I have a lot of free time to myself. I really love it. [She covers her mouth with manicured hands, in an "Uh oh, did I really just say that?" gesture; figure 3.4.] I mean, I love Kody ... but without him I can do whatever I want. I'm very independent" ("'The Real' Speaks with 'Sister Wives'" 2017). As Arthur Hammon, an FLDS polygamist and Centennial Park, Arizona, elder, bragged to ABC's *Nightline*: "I know of no greater freedom for a woman than living in a responsible, caring, polygamous home" (Vega 2013).

Polygamy as a salutary and loving space for women: that truly is rethinking the polygamists we think we know. If anything in this chapter, I've demonstrated how insistently and consistently mediated texts push on a logic of choice, mutual respect, progressivism, and social tolerance as the defining characteristics of plural families as well as the necessary ingredients for modern subject status. These are also, I might add, some of the critical elements that define feminism, and in this final section I want to spend some time thinking more carefully about the various possibilities for women within modern polygamy. Many would argue that Mormon feminism is a contradiction in terms, fundamentalist Mormon feminism even more so. The key idea I want to investigate in this context is what we might make of the idea of FLDS feminism in a broader mediascape already more than dismissive of feminist politics and peoples.

Judith Stacey tells us in her invigorating investigation of love, family, and marriage that "most critics have associated polygamy with male domination and sexual promiscuity and portrayed it as abusive to women" (2011, 110). She thus contends that a "paternalist patina of feminist sentiments" often mingles with a "racially tinged rationale for criminalizing polygamy as an un-American activity" (110). Yet mediated fare about modern Mormon polygamy offers the rather audacious possibility that this model of marital and family relations might be so woman friendly that it can eschew the politics of feminism altogether and exist in a celebratory postfeminist paradigm. Indeed, modern polygamy allows a woman to solve the work/life dilemma since it gives a working mother backup on the home front—other women invested in a working woman's children, who will gladly offer child care and nurturance without requiring payment. By these accounts, modern polygamy is also so differently situated in relation to masculinist power relations that it might be postpatriarchal. We are, after all, talking about a group of people who espouse tolerance for gay and lesbian peoples, claim bonds of kinship with other minoritized groups, and who believe in a live-and-let-live ideology of radical tolerance. Mormon ethnographer Janet Bennion concedes, for instance, that she entered her field research on FLDS polygamy "with a deep-seated belief in feminine empowerment and a contempt for abusive male dominance. But what I failed to realize was that fundamentalist women offered a new breed of feminism that made perfect sense to them within a rigid patriarchal context" (Bennion 1998, xi). This is the case, Bennion contends, because believing outsiders, those who do not uphold the orthodoxy of their faiths but still claim membership and common cause with the primary mandates of the faith, often "redesign codes within the doctrine," essentially changing the center from its edges (xv).

When the protagonists of progressive polygamy tell the story themselves, one of the dominant themes they provide is women's positive and empowered relationship to one another, even and especially when working through their emotional conflicts. When outsiders tell this story, often in exposé form, they typically highlight the injustices of modern polygamy for the women who are caught within it, either through coercion or brainwashing. Consider, for instance, an interview Cecilia Vega (2013) had with a resident of Centennial Park on *Nightline*. Asks Vega of a young woman, Rosemarie, "Do you feel like you have any say in this [choosing your husband within polygamy] as a person?" "Oh yeah, absolutely," says Rosemarie. "This is my choice. I chose to, basically, give myself over to Heavenly Father to basically give me to whomever he chooses." Rosemarie's response—that she exercises choice by choosing to giving it over to a higher power—flies in the face of how we understand agency as a set of behaviors governed by free will and motivated by self-determination. *Nightline* seems to air Rosemarie's statements about choice as a way of offering commentary on how little influence she actually exercises in her own practices of polygamy.

But Rosemarie's viewpoint in many ways highlights the hegemonies of choice that feminist analyses have worked to expose in a range of contested sites, such as beauty pageants, plastic surgery, or even sex work. If a woman resides within a beauty culture that punishes her for failing to invest the time, money, and effort to be lovely, can we really say she has exercised free choice when she works hard to write a conventional form of beauty on her face and body? Yes and no. She has indeed chosen it. But she makes this choice within a field of relations that expects, even mandates, her decision. Choice happens, then, in a broader context where what one chooses is to some degree preprogrammed into a menu of options. As a member of generational long-standing in the Centennial Park FLDS community, Rosemarie's claim of empowerment through choice seems enigmatic, and so do those claims of the Darger wives, the Brown wives, and any number of subjects interviewed by *20/20* and Lisa Ling or appearing on the National Geographic Channel (in *Polygamy USA*). Tellingly, while several patriarchs in these mediated tales (Kody, Brady, Golden) were raised in the mainstream LDS Church or even in the Gentile world, a very small handful of women in these stories have ever lived outside of the structures of polygamy. Perhaps feeling more obligation for filling in motive and backstory, Udall tells us in *The Lonely Polygamist* that Golden's first wife, Beverly, was once a stripper and escaped to polygamy as a way to flee sex work. Janelle, Kody's second wife, is more circumspect in her rationale for transitioning from LDS to FLDS, saying, "There was something in the doctrines that intrigued me" (Brown et al. 2012, 38). Barb (formerly LDS) and Margene (formerly without affiliation) on *Big Love* choose Bill, and he, in turn, feels the testimony for the principle of plural marriage. Standing by your man means also standing by his ideology. So the great enigma of modern polygamy for women made clear on an intermedial range of programming is that divine guidance can lead both to radical freedom and to the willingness to subject oneself to authoritarian governance.

This is particularly the case, as in both LDS and FLDS communities, when connections to the divine are perceived as being the sole domain of the man. *Big Love* made much of this tension in its final season when Barb, always a voice for independence, felt herself called to a priesthood unattainable within either a mainstream or fundamentalist Mormon structure. Even the newly developed Church of Bill, in which her husband is the primary prophet, cannot bend itself to accepting the possibility of her divine role until Bill lies shot and bleeding to death in the final minutes of the series finale, a conflict I discuss more in chapter 5. *Big Love*'s feminist creators and writers have spoken about building the tension of the narrative in a way that purposefully heightened the feminist fissures at the heart of the faith, ultimately killing Bill so that the women could find solidarity outside of his presence. As some sort of divine blessing, they create a scene that depicts Bill seeing the figure of Emma Smith, Joseph Smith's legal wife, smiling at him across a field of Mormon ancestors, seemingly to reinforce that his new choice to anoint women to priestly roles is a wise one. Yet Emma is a puzzling choice to offer a feminist blessing on a church organized around the principle of plural marriage, given that she was both deeply discomfited by plural marriage and strongly committed to priestly authority (so, basically, a monogamist nonfeminist). Mormonism does have strong women figures to reference, but like modern polygamists, they have faced their own recognition and persecution issues, and so perhaps Emma is the best that *Big Love* can offer as a symbol to reinforce women's love and participatory culture as manifest within and through the principle.

As on *Big Love*, across these stories about modern polygamy, women's relationship to one another is consistently held up as one of the major upsides of modern polygamy. Narratives reinforce the voice held by women, the opinions they assert, their power within the family, and their ability to structure familial priorities, including decisions about pregnancy. Indeed, each of the women plays central roles in securing and vetting (or vetoing) new wives and family decisions, thus putting the emphasis on the closeness of the feminized domestic unit and the power that is a consequence of fused intimacies. On both the primary text of *Sister Wives* and in ensuing interviews, for instance, much has been made of the fact that first wife Meri met and bonded with fourth wife Robyn before Kody did, only later encouraging Kody to dance with Robyn at a party and then later to court her as a new wife. In their memoir, Meri writes that she and Kody were both "bitten by the love bug" as it concerned Robyn (Brown et al. 2012, 72). Kody jokes on *Sister Wives* that Meri is the bait to attract new wives, while comedian George Lopez calls her Kody's "wing man" (*Lopez Tonight* 2011).

Ironically, given that I am using Eve Sedgwick's *Epistemology of the Closet* as the inspiration for my title, Meri's role in relation to the other wives actually offers a reversal of Eve Sedgwick's theory of triangulation, where women are used as devices to further intimacies between men. In the representation provided by this reality TV text, Kody is merely the mechanism that allows Meri greater access to and familiarity with Robyn. As Ellen DeGeneres said amid audience giggles on her show, "Why would they even want the man?"

Indeed, the idealized representation of women within plural marriage could well be taken as a twenty-first-century version of what Carroll Smith-Rosenberg (1986) labels the female world of love and ritual in the American nineteenth century, when women were allowed, and even encouraged, to participate in forms of affection and physical intimacy that coded as sisterly rather than lesbian. What constitutes lesbian identity within the sisterly solidarities of feminism has offered a rich discussion for feminist scholars, and I don't really want to rehearse those arguments here except to note that the gender politics of these mediated stories steer far more toward emancipatory possibilities than they do toward patriarchal hierarchies. I even consider it a sign of progressive gender development that comediennes and talk show hosts (and out lesbians) like Rosie O'Donnell and Ellen DeGeneres would joke about becoming Kody's fifth wife, all the while clearly being intrigued by, if not specifically attracted to, the women in the family unit.

Modern polygamy stories hail not only the political mandates of feminism but the seeming emancipatory possibilities of postfeminism. Melissa Miles McCarter (2010) presciently notes in a blog post, for instance, that *Sister Wives* is "made possible by feminism but clearly reflects a postfeminist perspective," in that it suggests a position of being beyond the political mandates of female equality that feminism espouses. Using Diane Negra as a guide to postfeminism, McCarter identifies three postfeminist principles: having it all, emancipation through consumerism, and fetishized but limited female desire—all of which are highly operative in the show (McCarter neglects to mention Negra's [2008] discussion of the postfeminism cult of motherhood, and certainly *Sister Wives* glorifies motherhood as the most important and real work a woman can do). McCarter notes that the sister wife scheme allows each woman access to the "feminist dream" of "having it all," since the role of wife is essentially split between four women. In this age of work/life dilemmas, the fixative offered by plural families seems more than appealing, as does the sororal solidarity.

On *Sister Wives*, Robyn Brown has characterized her relationship with her sister wives as a nonstop "girl party!" and this effusion, in combination with the market appeal of their brand, raises a banner of postfeminism, where women's empowerment is often construed as the dividend of conventional choices to live as wives and mothers, in specific contrast to second-wave feminist mandates for work-place equality. The narrative logic suggests that these sister wives experience far greater equality in their relationships and affection with one another than in the sisterhood-is-powerful credo feminism upholds. Indeed, writing for the feminist website Jezebel, Dodai Stewart (2011) mocked the Brown wives for their expressed fear of feminists: "On last night's episode of *Sister Wives*, the Browns visited Tufts University, where they'd been invited to be part of a discussion about their religion and lifestyle. When asked if they were nervous or scared. Christine said she was 'imagining an audience full of *feminists*.' OH NO OH MY GOD ANYTHING BUT THAT. She continued: 'They'll look at us and think that we live a suppressed, oppressed lifestyle.' Well . . . yeah. Honestly, these women seem intelligent and communicative and happy. But their religion—invented in the 1820s—is a tool of oppression." Looks like Christine had reason to worry. To be fair, this particular *Jezebel* post didn't rule the day in its judgments on either the Browns or polygamy. Indeed, the column sponsored a very intelligent set of reader responses about personal choice and the meanings of feminism, including several resounding critiques of Stewart's unjust dismissiveness of the Browns' code of beliefs and of Mormonism more broadly.

When questioned about why they do not feel the sting of hypocrisy since the faith does not allow brother husbands, the wives of modern polygamy laugh and respond, "Would you really want that? Men are a lot of work. I need my *me* time." At the same time, however, on *Sister Wives* when Kody and Meri go to Mexico to celebrate their twentieth wedding anniversary, Meri puts this question to Kody in a much more pressing manner. Meri wants him to acknowledge that she feels jealous. Meri: "If I were to be giving attention to another guy, how would it make you feel?" Kody: "Obviously, it's just not something I'm comfortable with imagining. The vulgarity of the idea of you with two husbands or another lover, sickens me. It seems wrong to God and nature. I understand this seems somewhat hypocritical, but I don't know how to get around it. With me answering this question, there's no way I can win. I feel like I'm admitting that what I'm doing is completely and totally unfair. I feel like if I address that emotion, it's an unhealthy place to go." Kody later called this interaction one of his most embarrassing screen moments caught by the TLC cameras.

Modern polygamy stories are structured much like a soap opera, in which feminine storylines about relationships and emotional conflict carry the bulk of the narratological interest. The masculinized presence is thus primarily important to the narrative for the degree to which he accentuates interest in these areas. On the reality shows *Sister Wives* or *My Three Wives*, cameras briefly capture participants when they run errands, go out for dinner, leave for vacation, or even head to the mall, but they are resolutely fascinated with moments of parallel domestic and affective tension—Brady in the privacy of his room with wife one, then two, then three, then four, then five, as they talk about money problems or desires for more children or body image and jealousy issues. On *Sister Wives*, cameras have never lingered on Kody (or Janelle, the other masculinized breadwinner) at work. We only know Janelle is a career woman, and Kody works in sales. In later episodes and largely due to their reality celebrity and TLC paychecks, what each of the Browns does for remunerative work has become less tangible, and so even when strategizing about business opportunities, the narrative focus is on interpersonal dynamics between the family. Indeed, just as in the case of other famous large families on TLC, such as the Duggars (*19 Kids and Counting*) or the Gosselins (*Jon and Kate Plus Eight*), the show itself constitutes the very work of image production and entertainment, members of the family thus functioning in double-coded roles—as befits modernity—as persons and characters, players in an ensemble acting troupe as well as members of a plural family.

And this leads us to the beset and often woebegone patriarch, who frequently functions in these stories as a focal point of pity and bathos. To say that the goofy Kody is unthreatening is a bit of an understatement. He himself agrees he is more like a surfer dude, say Shaggy on *Scooby Doo* or Jeff Spicoli from *Fast Times at Ridgemont High*, than a priestly alpha male, all dripping with gravitas. As presented in TLC's diegesis, he's not exactly a thundering authority figure. And neither is his brother in reality television Brady Williams, whose affectations regularly position him as a male cheerleader before an otherwise uninspired crowd of wives and children, dubious at his enthusiasm. A good deal of the narrative arc of *The Lonely Polygamist* features Golden, beset by a piece of gum that has nestled into his copious amounts of copper-colored pubic hair. As focalized through one of his sons,

Rusty, Golden was "a Sasquatch, who smelled of Ben-Gay and stumbled around blinking like he didn't know where he was" (Udall 2011, 297). On *Big Love*, Bill asserts a certain kind of worldly power as a successful businessman and state senator (as well as a former lost boy with a mean right hook), but Bill is endlessly mocked by his father, his mother, his wives, his children, and the universe itself that won't quite play ball with him.

Men in modern polygamy stories don't come off well—collectively, they are a group of guys with a lot to learn. "The next generation of men is on a mission," says Hammon to *Nightline* (Vega 2013), "learning how to be good husbands. Modern polygamist husbands." Udall reinforces these points in his expository piece on modern polygamy: "It used to be that Bill didn't really know how to deal with family problems, the jealousy among wives, the conflicts among children of different mothers, the competition for his attention, so he mostly tried to ignore it all" (Udall 1998). But what ties these trying-to-cope men both to American everyman stories and to the complexity of modern living itself is the fact that they are educable. They can learn, change, adjust, and if they do it right, they regain the privileges of masculinity and earn their prize as Gods. "Now he realizes," writes Udall, "that he is not merely the head of the family but also a judge, a counselor, a referee, an arbiter of justice. It's as if he were the prime minister of a small, unstable country, mediating disputes, keeping his eye on trouble spots, putting down rebellions from within" (Udall 1998).

The subtext of these stories indicates that success with the complex demands of modern polygamy proves that a husband and father is man enough, able to take on the chin the punches that modern living gives and rise with a smile on his face. Nurse Joanne tells Lisa Ling (2011) that she grew up in a plural family in Centennial Park, but though she still lives in a majority polygamous community she adheres to a monogamous life because her Catholic husband isn't up for the marital demands of FLDS. Most men couldn't do what Kody does, raves Robyn. "The majority of men in our faith have two wives. Fewer have three wives, and hardly any have four. It's just too challenging" (Brown et al. 2012, 73).

This putative title to real man status seems lost on a larger blogosphere that pulls no punches in its critique of male polygamists. "Much as i'm loathe to admit this," writes grumpygirl, a respondent to Stewart's (2011) *Jezebel* post, "these women seem happy (except meri, meri is never really happy). more to the point, they seem to have made this their choice and nobody appears oppressed (no matter what the original edict says). kody, however, seems like a total loser. the women are better off having 1/4 of him than all of him." Sassitron agrees: "It's a show about four very cool women and the potato-head they all married. They'd be better off if they just started an all-lady commune and kicked Kody out." "Totally!" responds AstridColeslaw. "If I lived in a society/culture that was pretty patriarchal and I had to choose between a douchebag and a fraction of a douchebag, I would absolutely choose the latter provided my wives were awesome. I think it really is the sisterwives that make or break this sort of arrangement."

The postfeminist polygamous man deals with added performance anxieties in both love and sex. "Forget the financial stress of having thirty-five mouths to feed and living on the wrong side of the law and having trouble finding the bathroom in the middle of the night," writes Udall, "it's this love thing that would have to be the ultimate complication of Bill's life. Regular guys can't seem to love even one woman without twisting themselves into knots, always wondering if they're saying the right things, being the kind of man they should be. So how could he ever hope to simultaneously give four different women the love they require? Is Bill's heart—along with everything else—oversized as well?" (Udall 1998). In many ways and somewhat astoundingly, modern polygamy stories offer the quintessential portrait of radical postfeminist manhood—where women have joined together to make their lives easier and the sole man is relegated to a position of itinerant helpmeet, never fully knowing in which house all of his belongings might be found or in which womb his seed might have been implanted. But they also offer a complicated telos of masculinity, in which fallibility lends credibility as a marker of the American everyman and where redemption-through-domestic-management is part of his gendered narrative. In contending with the demands of strong-minded women and enormous families (to the power of three and four and five), these men reify codes of modern masculinity that valorize leadership, boundary crossing, and flexible problem solving.[10]

The Polygamist Guide to Modern Living

While the ebbs and flows of either monogamous or polygamous marital life might follow similar tidal rhythms, these mediated texts make clear that modern polygamy is unlike any other practice of domesticity, in that it exponentially heightens the stresses of modern living. As if multiple houses and households, scores of children, strained finances, and police prosecution aren't enough to increase the stress level, in any given moment these families also contend with a broad array of challenges, both interpersonal and logistic. In one episode of *Sister Wives*, for instance, third wife Christine is a week overdue with her sixth child, soon-to-be fourth wife Robyn's wedding is in eight weeks, and first wife Meri's twentieth anniversary is coming up and needs to be marked in a special way. Is it any wonder, then, that when Kody goes to the hospital with Christine for the birth of their baby, he uses the opportunity to multitask by inquiring about fertility options for Meri, who has birthed only one child. Indeed, I would argue that in terms of the representation offered by *Sister Wives* and other progressive Mormon polygamy stories, it is not the appearance, commitment to tolerance, or lifestyle practices of the Browns or the Williamses or the Henricksons or the Richards that mark them as modern so much as the temporal complexity of their lives that brands them very specifically as a model of mediated American (and Mormon) selfhood, grounded in the frontier logic of steely determination and beset by the fast pace of productivity in late capitalism.

Progressive polygamists claim a position of sameness with the rest of America. In so doing, they establish an epistemological dilemma within the binding logic of binary thinking that serves as the scaffolding for a self/other relation between the "polygamists we know" and normal folks, whatever normal might be taken to mean. Even while these statements assume a homogeneity in "the rest of America" that simply isn't present, for modern Mormon polygamists to be "just like us" and thus able to stand in for any given husband in any given (presumably heterosexual) American family, their contrastive Other cannot be a fringe group often considered a cult (if bookstore shelving policies are any indication). So, Kody and Bill and Golden cannot be a prototype for difference and a prototype for everyman at the same time, except within the juxtapositional logic of both celebrity and Americanness.

Indeed, the conjoined desire for both distinction and democratic belonging nicely illustrates the contradiction that lies at the very heart of both celebrity—in which stars are praised for being simultaneously exceptional and ordinary—and American ideological character. The unique/alike axis takes on new dynamics in relation to Mormonism, which, since its founding in 1830, has traded on the value of a democratic and egalitarian message. As Paul Gutjahr notes, "The theme of equality appears constantly through the *Book of Mormon*. . . . Joseph [Smith] built his church upon a firm conviction that all men were created equal, and both men and women flocked to his teaching because it promised that everyone, not just the rich and educated, could enjoy a more intimate relationship with God" (2012, 41). Fittingly, this makes Mormonism a quintessentially American faith.

Yet Mormonism has often found its identity in marked separation from and superiority to mainstream American culture and people. Marvin Hill has argued that since its beginnings in the nineteenth century, Mormonism has been marked by its "quest for refuge" from what Armand L. Mauss describes as a "bewildering religious and political pluralism of the America of Andrew Jackson and Alexis de Tocqueville" (1994, 24). "Since then," writes Mauss, "the Mormons, like many other questing people of history, have struggled to find the optimum balance between sectarian refuge and worldly participation" (24). As Mauss observes, the more that Mormons (both LDS and FLDS) turn to mainstream American culture for acceptance, the more they refute the very terms that have conventionally established what Mormonism might mean, in this case isolation, separation, and, indeed, persecution. So it is not so much the physical barriers of the Rocky Mountains or the Great Salt Lake that create the terms for Mormon exceptionalism; their difference is written into the DNA of the religion itself. To be Mormon is not to be mainstream. All of which leads Mauss, a Mormon himself, to a very important question: "Just how 'American' can a Mormon be without appearing to be like all other Americans (and without undermining the identity that he or she presumably shares with the world's three million non-American Mormons)?" (1994, 25).

This may be true for SLC Mormonism, but modern Mormon polygamy (which is typically FLDS) needs sameness in order to be a stakeholder in the American project. Indeed, sameness, averageness, and the ordinary are primary commercial appeals of the modern polygamy brand. Gallery Books advertises *Becoming Sister Wives* (Brown et al. 2012), for example, by making much of the family's bid to be just like us: "In many ways, the Browns are like any other middle-American family. They eat, play, and pray together, squabble and hug, striving to raise happy, well-adjusted children while keeping their relationship loving and strong. The difference is, there are five adults in the openly polygamous Brown marriage—Kody and his four wives—who among them have seventeen children."

So intent are these texts on striking an American everyman pose that they often neglect to detail the very thing that makes these families like 83 percent of Americans—religion. Certainly, religious beliefs make an appearance in dialogue about religious choices, moments of prayer, or even in scenes depicting a mother chiding her daughter for wearing a short skirt to church, but those beliefs are in every case referenced without being fully explained. In the first episode of *Sister Wives*, for instance, Kody explains to the viewer in voice-over that he and his family are Fundamentalist Latter-day

Saints, a sect that splintered from the mainstream Mormon religion at the end of the nineteenth century, largely due to the FLDS's continued belief in the spiritual calling of plural marriage. As I've noted, the Browns are actually Apostolic United Brethren, which doesn't consider itself a church at all and holds basic doctrinal differences from both the FLDS and LDS communities. But these differences are never alluded to or mapped out, so viewers are left with the vague palliative that Kody's choices are divinely ordained and religiously fostered, even as the specificity of his beliefs is not addressed. On screen, Kody is confused and troubled because, he says, he never became a polygamist out of any disrespect for the law, yet the religious conviction that seemingly grounds the family's constitution and organization is so unspecified as to be unconvincing.

Indeed, as I've suggested, the family is far more likely to make a bid for their lifestyle based on the rationale of liberal tolerance, with very little acknowledgment of the legalities bound up in the practices of polygamy or the events in nineteenth-century American history, including the polygamy wars between Mormons and the U.S. government, that pitted LDS plural marriage against a conflicting discourse of ethnic and racial diversity, tempered by a (hetero)normativity that marks American practices, laws, and beliefs. The logic of modern Mormon polygamy is not just that plural families have a right and obligation to be public, but that the ideology of Americanness guarantees this right and demands that it be exercised. Ultimately, the appeal for visibility finds validation in an ethos of egalitarianism considered to be American. "This is my civil disobedience," says Joe Darger. More to the point, the Mormon Church and American popular media present these families as both average and anomalous, familiarizing viewers to an ideology of Americanness through consumerism and image management.

In spite of this call for social justice, the combined narratives of progressive polygamy seem much more concerned with the details of how a family of twenty-two pays all of its bills, how it manages eight teenagers, and how it apportions the time, attention, and tenderness of one man across multiple wives and two score children. This normalcy is meant to do the work of idea management, functioning as the silver bullet that stops the werewolf of oppression in its tracks. Yet the more famous these families become, the more recognizable their family brand, the less able they are to be avatars of either normalcy or exceptionalism.

In this, these narratives create representative figures who in their extremes both model the hectic pace of modern living and offer a version of excess so far outside of the lives of most viewers that there is a comfortable detachment in the voyeuristic gaze. Even as the represented family dynamics both reinforce and resist the very normalcy the texts seek to establish, the logic indicates that it is impossible to demonize the Browns, Henricksons, or Richards since by all accounts the heteronormative nuclear family they are (times four) means that we must surely relate to them—if we are, as interpellated, sympathetic to heteronormative nuclear families. So, importantly, though these stories hail the viewer/reader through a discourse of liberal tolerance, choice politics, and emancipatory rhetoric about not judging others for their lifestyle practices, these texts are themselves quite judgmental, not through the overt gestures of bigotry but through more subtle strategies that make common cause with outliers only to demonize their practices. Progressive polygamy stories play by and reinforce a set of codes that rely on the stability of the very structures they seem to be challenging. In the end, we must ask, are these stories progressive? I can only answer by saying there could be no *Sister Wives* or *Big Love* or *The Lonely Polygamist* without feminism, queer theory, and gay pride, but equally, there could be no modern polygamy without patriarchy and hegemony.

4. Polygamy USA

VISIBILITY, CHARISMATIC EVIL, AND GENDER PROGRESSIVISM

There are probably a lot of you who don't get why there's such a knee-jerk revulsion toward polygamy in the modern world. After all, if anyone can marry whom they choose, what's wrong with a bunch of women choosing to marry the same dude, or vice-versa? The problem is that, in the real world, it hasn't worked out that way. You'll notice you never hear about one woman marrying four guys—in polygamist cultures it's all about males collecting lots of wives, usually in a way that gives the females very little say in the matter.

—Anonymous, "5 Things I Learned as a Mormon Polygamist Wife"

When I'd awoken that morning, I was a fourteen-year-old girl hoping for the miracle of divine intervention; my prayers, however, had gone unanswered. With no other choice, I'd submitted to the will of our prophet and had married my nineteen-year-old first cousin. As a member of the Fundamentalist Church of Latter Day Saints (FLDS), I'd been raised to believe that marriages were arranged through a revelation from God, and that these revelations were delivered through our prophet, who was the Lord's mouthpiece on earth. As a faithful follower, I'd embraced this principle and believed in it wholeheartedly, never imagining that at fourteen, a revelation would be made about me.

—Elissa Wall, *Stolen Innocence*

In chapter 3, I discuss media that stake out a claim for what modern plural families themselves term progressive polygamy. Progressive polygamists look "just like us": they live in the suburbs, wear jewelry, makeup, and stylish clothes, work in nine-to-five jobs or own their own businesses, hope to send their kids to college, encourage free speech in their families, and use celebrity and visibility as a means of achieving social justice. They stake out a place in the world rather than apart from it. These sorts of narratives depict polygamy as a forward-looking alternative family arrangement predicated on love and free choice and, as such, the quintessence of flexibility, individualism, and egalitarianism.

While progressive polygamy stories like *Big Love* and *Sister Wives* operate under a code of faith-based polygamy that functions as a benevolent democratic order of caring and consent, the mediascape is equally filled with sinister and queer versions of polygamy. In these iterations of more patriarchal fundamentalist Mormon plural marriages, the morality terms are stark: mediated Mormonism preaches that polygamy is rife with charismatic and abusive patriarchs, who are the epitome of wickedness and excess. Their victims, both male and female, are called brainwashed, the women and girls often depicted as cowering and submissive and the boys and men complicit henchmen in the prophet's nefarious abuses of power.[1]

In *Gaga Feminism*, J. Jack Halberstam lays out the rather startling claim that "American audiences can more easily accommodate narratives of Mormon polygamy than they can conceive of a continuum of artificial-reproduction narratives that include pregnant men and lesbian mums" (2012, 52). And while Halberstam may certainly be right that pregnant men and lesbian mothers are their own media hornet's nest in U.S. television and film culture (*The Kids Are All Right* [2010] and *Junior* [1994] notwithstanding), we should be careful about accepting too quickly a claim of easy accommodation when it comes to Mormon polygamy stories. For indeed, as I argue in this chapter, while fundamentalist polygamy stories might look easily palatable, the sheer number and seemingly incessant repetition of these narratives suggest that there is something in the fascinations they offer and fears they encourage that a larger culture struggles to metabolize.

As I argue throughout this book, Mormonism (in both its mainstream and fundamentalist forms) functions as a historical and contemporary symbolic portal into conversations about belief, meaning, identity, and values, as coalesced around gender and sexuality. Plural marriage in the modern moment tells us something very specific about gender norms and identity, as well as their complex embedded relationship to media. This chapter thus evaluates the cultural work performed by mediated patriarchal polygamy, a work that often includes using the devices of "polygamy-visibility" to instill both the knowledge and the vocabulary necessary to recognize and talk about abuse, exploitation, manipulation, and coercion. To see these dynamics in operation, I turn to narratives of victimization and rescue in two reality shows, *Escaping Polygamy* and *Escaping the Prophet*, and then reflect on the scare rhetoric that surrounds the FLDS polygamist Warren Jeffs.[2] I conclude the chapter by considering the original, and simultaneously most obscure and most famous, American polygamists Joseph Smith and Brigham Young. Throughout, I demonstrate how gender justice resides in the eye of the evil hurricane of mediated patriarchal polygamy, largely through the discursive critiques and counternarratives it inspires.

Polygamy-Visibility

Because bigamy is an illegal and socially unacceptable practice in the United States, most adherents of polygamy live their lives in secret, hidden behind heavy drapes and cloistered within closed communities, many of which are located in remote and sparsely populated areas of the Western United States, such as the stark canyon lands of southern Utah and northern Arizona. As with their mainstream Mormon forebears who sought refuge in the arid Salt Lake Basin, geographical seclusion offers a thin assurance of protection. Yet, prior to 1998, the FLDS base of operations was in Salt Lake City, home of the mainstream LDS Church and a bustling metropolis in its own right. The FLDS were thus hidden in plain sight. As Elissa Wall puts it in her memoir *Stolen Innocence*, "What helped families like ours stay under the radar in Salt Lake was the fact that our numbers were few and we were all scattered throughout the Salt Lake Valley. At the time [1990s], there were about ninety FLDS families residing in the area, and if we had all lived together in the same location our way of life may have drawn more attention and brought repercussion from the state government" (Wall and Pulitzer 2012, 11). In advance of the new millennium, the Prophet Rulon Jeffs told his followers the world would end. When it didn't, Uncle Rulon called for the end of the world again in 2002 prior to the Salt Lake City Olympics. To prepare for Armageddon, the FLDS were instructed that they must leave their houses and belongings behind, often sometimes literally fleeing in the night. They converged on Short Creek, the polygamous border town that is one part Hilldale, Utah, and the other part Colorado City, Arizona.

Given that staying under the radar has been a critical survival strategy for the FLDS, it is remarkable that the mediascape is so saturated with stories of polygamy, particularly in news programs, documentaries, and reality television shows that invite FLDS people to allow cameras, reporters, and producers into their compounds. It is not just these genres of the real that are fascinated with polygamy, however. Media are capacious in their reach—from vanity press memoirs to Penguin-produced novels, from reality television programming to independent documentaries, from blogs to Twitter to Facebook and back again to print. In the past ten years, viewers might partake of a veritable feast of this more patriarchal strain of polygamy-focused programming available on mainstream television and internet streaming platforms such as Hulu, Netflix, Amazon, and network websites. These include made-for-TV movies such as *The 19th Wife* (Lifetime, 2010) and *Outlaw Prophet: Warren Jeffs* (Lifetime, 2014); feature films and documentaries such as *Sons of Perdition* (2010), *Follow the Prophet* (2009), *Banking on Heaven* (2005), and *Prophet's Prey* (2015); and other reality television fare such as *Polygamy USA* (National Geographic Channel, 2013–), *Breaking the Faith* (TLC, 2013), *Escaping Polygamy* (Lifetime, 2014–), and *Escaping the Prophet* (TLC, 2013). Print media are also filled with patriarchal polygamy stories, particularly those that detail escape. We might thus say that patriarchal polygamy is conspicuous to the point of overdetermination, and the aggregated effect of polygamy-visibility has been to make the terms of exploitation and abuse discernible categories.

A few examples evidence this claim. Rebecca Musser, who escaped from the FLDS compound in 2004, played a pivotal role in bringing down its abusive leader, Warren Jeffs. In addition to her memoir, she now travels the country as a celebrity human rights activist, particularly through her Red Flags Program, which "teaches people to recognize and avoid manipulation" (Musser 2014). These messages are predicated on the lessons she learned within Mormon fundamentalism, but her exhortations are addressed to a much broader audience. Her objective is to teach vulnerable subjects how to recognize, name, and avoid their own victimization. As I discuss in chapter 5, Elizabeth Smart—famously abducted in 2002 by a man who considered himself a latter-day prophet—similarly works today as a motivational speaker, activist, and ABC News correspondent, educating people about the need for vigilance in relation to sexual violence. For both the ex-fundamentalist Mormon Musser and the present mainstream Mormon Smart, the broader cultures of Mormonism provide the backdrop that make their social justice initiatives resonate for others.

A telling series of passages in the independent documentary *Prophet's Prey* equally demonstrates how representation of the FLDS renders the outlines of abuse visible. Several scenes in the documentary feature local law enforcement officers and reporters in remote areas of Colorado, South Dakota, and Texas, all stunned and outraged when the FLDS bought major tracts of land and set up ancillary encampments near their towns. It was largely the media-attention-trailing antipolygamy crusader Flora Jessop that alerted the town to the presence of polygamists in their midst. "Who is Flora Jessop and why is she coming to Eldorado?" asked the small-town newspaper the *Eldorado Success*. Television news outlets from San Antonio flew their traffic helicopters over the newly emerging compounds, taking aerial photographs that revealed a "secret construction project." Local station WOAI confirmed that a "polygamy cult run by Warren Jeffs" was moving to Texas, raising fears about sexual predators who act in anti-American ways, an invasion from within. Other news accounts likened Jeffs and his followers to the American Taliban.[3]

Now, obviously, sexual violation is not a crime of national otherness; incest, rape, and other forms of sexual assault can be fully domestic violations. But these xenophobic, and one might argue Islamophobic, fears illustrate that Mormonism, particularly fundamentalist Mormonism, is often put in the position of symbolic foreigner, dangerously opposed to democratic norms of consent and due process. In many respects, reactions to these fears have helped forge American identity. As Nancy Cott argues in *Public Vows*, the Mormon threat in the antebellum period was a direct cause for a new coalescing of the value of monogamy as the "law of social life" (2002, 105). In 1856, Abraham Lincoln called slavery and polygamy the "twin relics of barbarism." Twenty-first-century media coalescing around Warren Jeffs make clear the unimaginable—one of Lincoln's barbaric relics is alive and well and moving across America's sparsely populated heartland. Given that the FLDS considers people of color to be cursed and so do not target them for conversion, the fear implicit in these concerns is obviously racialized as a kind of white panic: White people beware! Polygamists are coming for you! Media surveillance is thus discursively positioned as a racialized protective defense against the anti-Americanness of this most American of religions.

Freedom of religion and self-sovereignty are American credos, but if polygamy stands as the antithesis of American ideals, it is largely due to the fact that consent is the putative rule of law in this land of the free and home of the brave. The power dynamics of polygamy operate through what is often branded brainwashing, thus dissolving the American right to choose one's faith. In the fixation on mind control, obedience, and a chattel system that "pass[es] out young women like candy" (Musser and Cook 2014, 23), the large archive of mediated patriarchal polygamy fosters a broader conversation on the values of individualism, free choice, and liberty. In so doing, these texts call into question the tipping point between religious extremism and cultism, between personal conscience and groupthink, between freedom and confinement, between enlightenment and false consciousness, between gender privilege and gender discrimination. *Prophet's Prey* again makes these terms clear, using the voice of FLDS prophet Warren Jeffs to insist that his followers "keep sweet," which is to say that they eschew personal emotional responses or intellectual critiques and instead follow obediently in all things (Berg 2015). Says Jeffs in voice-over: "You can tell right now if you are passing the test. If you are keeping sweet no matter what, you are a person ready to give up your own will and just obey the priesthood over you." Foregoing personal liberties in the name of an all-powerful leader is a most un-American idea. It is precisely because the polygamous patriarch robs his subjects of their democratic function, which is to say the exercise of free will and personal sovereignty, that he is so easily vilified in these mediated accounts.

Sisterhood Is Powerful

A tip leads Andrea and Shanell to a young mother inside the cult who wants to make an escape with her daughter, but after the girls arrange the rescue mission, they unfortunately learn the effects brainwashing can have on a family.—"Best Bets on TV" on *Escaping Polygamy*

"Flora," he said, "I want to thank you. If you didn't keep kickin' the crap out of everybody involved in this, we wouldn't be sitting here [in court for Warren Jeffs's trial]!"

I had to laugh at that. It was true. I kept pushing and pushing, annoying the hell out of everyone. I just didn't want Warren to get away with this anymore.—Flora Jessop and Paul Brown, *Church of Lies*

Given its emphasis on male privilege, conservative gender codes, implicit whiteness, and systemic corruption, the Fundamentalist Church of Jesus Christ of Latter-day Saints might not be the place most people would go first to discover progressivism of any sort, much less that related to feminism and queer empowerment. Considering that the primary tenet on which the FLDS Church stakes its heavenly claim is patriarchal polygyny—or the marriage of one man to several women and their living together in an extended exclusively heterosexual family relation where the man (or more precisely an alpha male prophet and an oligarchy of subordinated male elites) exerts supreme authority over women, girls, and boys—gender justice is all the more elusive. Indeed, in all of its many portrayals, polygamy stands as the height of patriarchal abuse, its male leader covering the baseness of his twin needs for sex and power by the callow appropriation of God's voice and the willful exploitation of his followers' fears. Those trapped in fundamentalist polygamy are white and Western, the diegetic ideographies of Western mountainscapes and the desert's blinding light—the glow of Mormon country—reinforcing the all-Americanness of those brainwashed by fundamentalist cults. Flora Jessop doesn't mince words: "No sympathy for the devil" (Jessop and Brown 2010, 255).

People held within the Church of Lies, as Jessop terms the FLDS, must be persuaded to leave, sometimes forcibly so. Escape is both literal and figurative. There are no fences confining believers inside most compounds—they might come and go—but there is a strong emotional hold on compound residents, emphasized by a generalized feeling of dread and resignation. Reduced education and an extremely inward-looking cohesive culture make it further difficult for compound residents to flee, as do the lifelong instructions they have received that the outside world is evil and intent on harming God's chosen, the FLDS. The heavy emotional affect of fear and dread is often perpetuated in mediated accounts by images of lurking compound police, called the God Squad, who patrol the grounds in their dark-windowed SUVs, surveilling in the name of the prophet. Surveillance is not a weak metaphor in this context but a very real and highly technological business. In the documentary *Prophet's Prey*, the sect's former security officer (now excommunicated) speaks of keeping track of the FLDS flock through an elaborate system of pressure-sensitive mats, concealed cameras, and electronically rigged doors that can measure comings and goings. Save for cell phones, worldly media are banned in the FLDS culture; yet the compound is a highly mediated space.[4]

In both sociological and mediated depictions, fundamentalist persons speak of feeling like ontological misfits, so different from the Gentile and mainstream Mormon world that there is nowhere that they might go, no outside to which they might flee. Yet these narratives are about escape, and so flee they must. Leaving consequently requires not only the reassurance but the assistance of others—helpers on the inside, safe houses on the outside—a whole coterie of underground networks devoted to a version of justice that can challenge the patriarchal dividends of hegemony and oppression. Patriarchal polygamy stories are thus made to function as an objective correlative, in that they are both the thing itself and a symbolic referent removed from the object that performs a separate, but distinct, cultural work.

Janet Bennion's ethnographic work among fundamentalist polygamist women has set forth the rather bold argument that plural marriage can be not only good for women but empowering for them as well. In *Women of Principle* she records the experiences of mainstream Mormon female converts to the Apostolic United Brethren order of Utah, finding that many women were attracted to polygamy because of the socioeconomic and social support it offers (Bennion 1998). Plural marriage allows these women to replace a rather difficult life in the mainstream Mormon Church, where their status as divorcees, single mothers, widows, and unmarriageables limits access to good men and the economic and spiritual affirmation that comes from a community of worship. In *Polygamy in Primetime*, Bennion (2012) finds that some fundamentalist Mormon women experience more individual satisfaction within the dynamics of a polygamous family than they could in conventional LDS marriages. This result may be a greater commentary on the perils of marriage and the restricting gender norms of the mainstream Mormon Church than on the benefits of polygamy, but I leave that to my reader to decide.

In terms of the insistent amalgamation of mediated polygamy tales presently available to media consumers, I would agree that polygamy fosters feminism. But not, as Bennion argues, because it offers women a place of (limited) hope, (promised) status, and (deferred) value within an otherwise male-dominated order. Indeed, countless popular accounts of fundamentalist polygamy depict it as evil, corrupt, and systemically abusive and disempowering to women and other subordinated peoples (like children and/or marginalized men). But here I want to be clear: Bennion and I are approaching this topic from very different scholarly angles—she is an ethnographer, often an auto-ethnographer, working with people to learn from their stories; I am a media and gender scholar interested in the investments and distortions those stories elucidate. As I have mentioned throughout this book— but it bears repeating—I am not so much interested in the FLDS as history or sociology. Rather, I'm taken with LDS and FLDS Mormonism as a recognizable image and an intelligible concept, and thus as both a meme and an analytic. Clear to me is that in their depiction of male excess, these stories often function as self-making devices for women.

While there are many fictionalized accounts of abusive prophetic patriarchs, these figures of evil and excess are typically so one-dimensional that they become predictable and largely indistinguishable. As such, it is not the ego-driven cardboard cutout leader but those traumatized by his autocratic power that have stories to tell and interiorities to share. Indeed, polygamy could well be called a sensational platform that gives its victims a story worth selling, a foothold in a competitive media market eager to showcase compelling lives of extremes. Rather than making this claim as an indictment on the "if it bleeds, it leads" and commercial nature of infotainment or the lowest-common-denominator critique of reality television, I see the complex modalities of media as offering an array of possibilities for silenced and abused women and men to find that most feminist of treasures: voice. As Ruth, one of the subjects of *Escaping the Prophet*, remembers, one thing got her through the abuse: the promise to herself, "I'm gonna write my story, and I'm going to tell my story, and someday there's going to be people who care."

Given this, I want to focus in this section on the feminist politics at the heart of two reality television shows dedicated to liberating women and children from the harms of patriarchal polygamy, *Escaping the Prophet* (TLC), which, as I have mentioned, features Flora Jessop as the heroine who frees those trapped without a voice in Warren Jeffs's Colorado City, and *Escaping Polygamy* (Lifetime), a program that, in its own self-description, "focuses on the dramatic work of three sisters who escaped from the polygamous cult known as the Kingston clan as young women and now help other young men, women and children escape, preferring to face hell than spend another day inside" (figures 4.1 and 4.2; Crawford 2009, 2014).

In terms of setup, the shows are remarkably similar. Both fall within the generic label of reality television with embedded fictional diegetic features, a function that often makes fans extremely angry on posting boards, since the blending of real and re-created events blurs the veracity of documentary for them. This very critique—that truth isn't factual as presented on reality television polygamy programs—has led others to credit negative blog posts as the work of the FLDS, since, bloggers argue, fundamentalists are incapable of thinking in more flexible terms about the nature of truth. In either case, what is striking for my purposes is how much these epistemological fissures between fundamentalist beliefs and mainstream representations are so fully on display for the lurker like me.

Both *Escaping the Prophet* and *Escaping Polygamy* feature a female heroine (or heroic triumvirate) forged in the fires of personal suffering and abuse, which in turn functions as a compelling claim to ethical responsibility. The women have fled to an outside from which they can and must help others escape to freedom. Taken together, both shows evince a strong feminist ethos of care that suggests one pays for freedom through activism on behalf of those who are still captive. It's a version of feminism that reinforces the heroic and oversimplified rescue narrative, where the positions of victims and saviors are clear and motivations for rescue are unsullied.

Both shows also detail the specifics of FLDS abuses. For those in Colorado City, these include marking a woman's body through antiquated dress

FIGS. 4.1–4.2 *Escaping the Prophet* and *Escaping Polygamy*.

and never-cut hair (so that she might wash her husband's feet with her long tresses in the afterlife), the Joy Book (a catalog of eligible, young, single teenage girls), marriage typically against one's will to much older men and/or blood relatives, the mandate to keep sweet, and an arbitrary rule culture that, under Warren Jeffs, increasingly included such things as not wearing red, not allowing children to play with toys or to own bikes or pets, not fraternizing with the outside world, and not allowing sexual congress between husbands and wives (only a small cadre of fifteen men were permitted to sire children). Indeed, it is precisely due to Jeffs's unwavering control over his followers' behavior and beliefs that the news show *20/20* considered the FLDS "highly dangerous" (Rorbach 2012). The Salt Lake City Kingston Group, the polygamous sect in the crosshairs of *Escaping Polygamy*, seems progressive by contrast. People within the order do not live in isolated compounds but are fully integrated into larger urban spaces, primarily across the Mountain West, in cities such as Salt Lake City, Utah. As in the mainstream church, codes of modesty are important, but women are not forced to wear the prairie dresses and holy hair that mark members of the FLDS community. As Jessica, one of the heroines of *Escaping Polygamy*, notes, "We blend in and look like everyone else," camouflaged by normalcy.

Like their split-apart fundamentalist cousins, the Kingston group has a strict top-down code of conduct that limits education for children, forces early marriage, expects multiple children, and considers wives to be the property of husbands. For each sect, mediated Mormonism suggests personhood is at grave risk. "I'm a Person, and I Deserve More," reads the headline on *Broadly*, a news blog engaged with women's rights that exactly gets at the heart of polygamy-visibility and its cry for gendered social justice (Oswaks 2016).

Yet differences between the programs are starkly illustrative of limitations for feminism within television culture. The women of *Escaping Polygamy* are all in their early twenties, with doelike eyes and bright futures ahead of them. Their sisterhood is a literal circumstance of bloodline and genetics, the math of one man, fourteen wives, and hundreds of children, more than the women can easily calculate. The structuring logic of the show is defused in form, working to downplay stridency or even expertise on the part of the trio. As one example, explanatory intertitles emerge on the screen when the audience needs background or history, rather than the women themselves providing necessary context. This editing decision offsets their authority, vesting it in the structure of the show rather than in them. They are nice girls, not know-it-alls.

Another device of the show that undercuts the women's authority has to do with the identity of the victims. While polygamy creates an extended network of blood relations, the women of *Escaping Polygamy* claim a personal and familial relation to the captive needing saving in any given week—my sister, my cousin, my mother. The name of the program notwithstanding, these editorial choices reinforce a notion that the sisters of *Escaping Polygamy* are working to eradicate a circumstance, not a system. They are depicted as reluctant revolutionaries, committed not to toppling the institution of polygamy itself but to freeing their sisters and cousins still caught behind the invisible walls. Theirs is a temporary call to arms that will be over once their sisters have chosen freedom.[5]

As in most circumstances where deep family and religious socialization confront personal values, "choice" is a debatable term. For instance, one of the key members of the *Escaping Polygamy* team, Jessica, works hard in Season 1 to free her sister, Rachel, from the Kingston group. By Season 2, Rachel is having second thoughts, as she entertains the possibility of going back to the order. Both sides use emotional coercion. The order promises Rachel that she might marry the man she loves; Jessica tells Rachel how much she had hoped Rachel would be a model for Jessica's children, who have now grown to love her and will greatly miss her if she goes back to the order. I'm not saying here that either side's strategy is nefarious or necessarily unfairly manipulative, but both complicate a notion of choice that suggests an agent might freely evaluate options and agentively make decisions. John Donne told us long ago, "No man is an island," and in the complicated familial terrain of fundamentalist polygamy where bloodlines and sister bonds overlap by the dozen, free choice is more of a convenient fiction than a reality.

As I've noted, Flora Jessop also pushes on the same ethical issues of free choice, since her premise is that people within polygamy have been brainwashed and can therefore not be counted on to think clearly for themselves.[6] In this, *Escaping the Prophet* positions the forty-nine-year-old Flora Jessop as a kick-ass feminist savior—willing to knock down doors, fight legal systems, and eradicate a system that is "twisted and rotten." Jessop is joined by her aunt and Brandon Jeffs, who also fled the compound in his teens, but both play secondary helper roles to Jessop's revolutionary presence. This is clearly Flora Jessop's show—shot after shot reinforces the authority of her point of view by continual scenes of her stern-faced plotting on the telephone or sitting behind the wheel of her SUV as she outmaneuvers the God Squad. Her guiding descriptions in voice-over narration provide explanations to the viewer about the history and codes of belief that unite the FLDS.

She is an unquestioned authority, the guiding force of the moral imperative staged by a reality show. Dramatic flashbacks she narrates of her own experience reenact the sexual abuse and domination she experienced at the hands of her father and other adult males within the FLDS compound, abuse made salient through dramatizations of her own story. A muffled conversation with Brandon renders systemic oppression with startling clarity, a line I only caught because their mumbled expression was given subtitles: "Who hasn't been raped up there?" Flora says to Brandon as they chat in the kitchen, sexual violation here a horrifying everyday reality.

Since fleeing the FLDS clutches herself, Flora Jessop has been a media darling.[7] Six months after her escape, she appeared on *60 Minutes* and has continued to use media in her war against the prophet. She is outspoken on exposing the evils, the corruptions, and the systemic abuses of polygamy, and she has marshaled the full extent of her story to target the FLDS. In addition to the reality show, Jessop has demonstrated remarkable media savvy, through her published memoir *Church of Lies* (Jessop and Brown 2010) and an active social media presence on Facebook, Twitter, and the Child Protection Project website. Indeed, the project's URL is emblazoned across the back of Jessop's SUV, which serves as a mobile command post and extraction vehicle on *Escaping the Prophet*.

In 2005, the *Arizona Republic* described her role in an extraction of two girls from the FLDS in terms suited to a media folk hero (think Dirty Harry): "Flora Jessop roared into Hurricane, Utah, at the wheel of a white Suburban wearing tight blue jeans, boots and a studded black leather jacket, a 9 mm pistol strapped to her hip, another pistol in her hand and three television reporters in tow" (Crawford 2009). The feature continues: "When Flora swept in the house with the television crew, Fawn thought she looked like superwoman. Flora said if they left with her, there would be no turning back. She would do whatever she could to protect them, starting with the television cameras. If authorities tried to send them back to Colorado City, the world would be watching." Jessop herself reinforces this Dirty Harry trope of vigilante justice: "If you are hurting children, expect to be my target. Because you're going to be in my sights. And I'm coming after you next."

As illustrated by these descriptions and frequent shots of Jessop surveilling the landscape from the front seat of her SUV or scanning the desert landscape with the aid of her enormous binoculars, she uses visibility as a weapon and publicity as a form of justice (figure 4.3). In these vignettes, Jessop both directs looking and is the subject (rather than the object) of the

FIG. 4.3 Flora Jessop surveilling for threats.

mediated gaze. As much as the men she fights, Jessop herself signifies as a charismatic object of attention, a celebrity figure. This, in turn, has led to the largest critique against Jessop: she demands the same degree of obedience to her will and fealty to her commands as the forces she fights, and she's doing it not for the sake of the women and children she frees but for the benefit of her own publicity-hungry ego. Given this criticism, the reality show she heads makes perfect sense, for it allows her to be both political revolutionary and glorified egomaniac in one. And really, what's wrong with that? Why not use celebrity to effect change? What thus makes less sense is the fact that *Escaping the Prophet* was canceled by TLC in 2015, after only six episodes. The reasons for cancellation have not been made public and are thus are not entirely clear, since the ratings were healthy, and we do not seem to have reached an ebb in a public fascination with polygamy and its many complications (as of this writing in 2019, *Sister Wives* and *Escaping Polygamy* are in ongoing production).

I use the case of the mighty Flora Jessop to consider a different possibility—that it was not only the FLDS but a larger media culture that found Jessop too big for her too-tight britches. The authoritative, politicized, and in-your-face defiance that Jessop evinces does not fit well in a telegenic culture that prefers its polygamists to be friendly and its crusaders to be cute. If the sisters of *Escaping Polygamy* are twenty-year-old (and fecund) freedom fighters with husbands and children, Jessop is depicted in terms that reinforce her age—

as ornery, wrinkled, wizened, and old-fashioned: the second-wave feminist put out to pasture. In a larger culture uncomfortable with feminist stridency, particularly when manifested by older women who demand to be in charge and hold a referendum for change, it's no wonder that Flora Jessop has had to move on to a new mediated format. But cancellation notwithstanding, her will to endure lives on.

So you may be wondering, given this reading, how I can argue that mediated Mormonism opens a window to feminist-friendly discourses if these examples are not always so feminist friendly? These shows, which rely on the notion of abusive patriarchal figures and their heroic counters, reinforce the analytical and cultural heft that feminism as a system both recognizes and understands. Issues of voice, visibility, desire, seeing and being seen, power and fighting the power—these are all well-traveled roads in feminist theory. In turn, discursive reactions to mediated Mormon polygamy necessarily draw on the vocabulary of feminism to talk about and for social justice. Even if these programs' representational codes can be complicated or contradictory in their understandings of feminism, they keep the idiom of feminism and progressive gender politics front and center.

Warren Jeffs: Patriarch, Prophet, Pedophile

What is it about this man that would allow him to so completely dominate the lives of thousands of people? He didn't have the appearance of a maniacal prophet, didn't sound like one either. His droning voice and gangly appearance were more likely to bring to mind a nerdy middle-school teacher than an all-powerful tyrant.... Not one of his personal traits could be considered remotely charismatic. He is, nevertheless, a man who exudes an almost mystical power over his more than ten thousand FLDS followers, most of whom would do literally anything he commanded them.—Sam Brower, *Prophet's Prey*

Given this discussion on the role of feminist agents of rescue and their complicated gendered implications with respect to visibility, empowerment, and free will, what happens if we move from mediated accounts of the crusaders who fight polygamy to equally mediated depictions of the perpetrators who sustain it? In the contemporary context, there is no polygamous prophet more notorious than Warren Jeffs, leader of the FLDS. In many respects, Jeffs has given a face to patriarchal polygamy, and he is often the reason more progressive polygamists cite for needing to change the brand of polygamy by suggesting it can be loving rather than abusive. As I discuss throughout this book, several incidents have put Mormonism on the many composite screens of the twenty-first century. Of them all, it is arguably Warren Steed Jeffs who has most galvanized attention and continues to serve as the personification of fundamentalist polygamist culture, in turn fostering his own wave of mediated Mormonism.

Scores of books and films discuss Warren Jeffs and his megalomania, so I won't belabor those biographical and historical details here except to offer an abbreviated story: after the death of his father, Rulon Jeffs, in 2002, Warren became, some argue through self-appointing rather than divine anointing, the president/prophet and absolute leader of the FLDS, a group that traces its bloodline and divine authority back to church founder Joseph Smith and before him to Jesus. Following in the footsteps of his patriarch father, who reportedly had seventy-five wives and sixty-five children, Warren amassed between seventy and eighty-seven wives and roughly sixty children by the time of his arrest in 2006.[8] That arrest played on the front lines of international media outlets, heightened by Jeffs's status as a fugitive. Between May and August 2006, Jeffs was coupled with Osama bin Laden as the top two targets on the FBI's ten most wanted list: in 2008, while he was behind bars, federal agents invaded Jeffs's Yearning for Zion (YFZ) compound in Eldorado, Texas, an event that brought the world's media to the gates of Jeffs's dusty compound. As of this writing, Jeffs is serving a sentence of life plus twenty years for two counts of sexual assault of underage girls, but he continues to govern the FLDS flock from prison through taped sermons and revelatory transmissions that he communicates through visitors to him at the penitentiary.

While Uncle Warren ruled his followers with absolute authority, that unbending and often irrational grip was in many ways his undoing. In an already restrictive culture, he removed many of the joys of FLDS life, including community socials, music, toys, pets, and all forms of media. He also got greedy, taking most of his father's former wives for his own, which violates church rules, and eagerly marrying younger and younger girls, who were more tractable and could be "worked with" ("Court Releases" 2011). Jeffs also raped young children (reportedly between the ages of five and seven), including his nephews Clayne, Brent, and Brandon Jeffs, among countless others. The unquestioned obedience that is often part of the polygamous life offers limitless opportunities for prophets to prey on the weak, since children do as they are told, and evidence of sex crimes often goes unnoticed in large families. To this point, Brent Jeffs writes in *Lost Boy* that after Warren Jeffs raped him the first time (when Brent was five years old), "My feelings of shame were confirmed when no one even noticed there was anything wrong with me. I just went home after class and changed my clothes. In the chaos of my household, the squeaky wheels got the oil. If you weren't complaining or causing trouble, you weren't very visible.... It was the only way such a large family could function. The physical evidence of Warren's crimes left in my soiled and bloodstained underwear simply disappeared into our massive laundry pile" (Jeffs and Szalavitz 2009, 68).

In the mediation that addresses both mainstream and fundamentalist Mormonism, a common theme of obedience and submission underscores the wrongs perpetrated by adult men. This position of absolute obedience to a single man presents a true dilemma within mediated Mormonism, since one of the major F/LDS principles is, and always has been, free will. Just as Joseph Smith established the "One True Church" by retreating to a grove of trees, asking God for direction, and then creating that church himself, members now are asked to feel their proof of the church's validity. The significance of testimony underscores an epistemology of affect: *I know what is real because I feel what is real.* Unlike old-world religions that demand a leap of faith into a void outside the self, the American Mormon tradition vests authority in individual affective confidence. If you do not feel a personal testimony, the logic goes, you will forfeit this opportunity for earthly happiness and eternal salvation. As is probably obvious, this is also assuredly an epistemology of emotional coercion. Personal conviction, a feeling of belief, is critical, but as countless memoirs suggest, young Mormons (both mainstream and fundamentalist) are carefully taught to discipline their interiorities—from thoughts, to desires, to feelings—so that they conform to church mandates, including the unwavering authority of the father/prophet figure who galvanizes the faith as a personal guarantor of divinity. To doubt the father is to undermine one's own salvation as well as that of others. In Season 2 of *Escaping Polygamy*, for instance, the sisters work on behalf of Rachel Jeffs, daughter of Warren Jeffs. Rachel explains that she was sexually abused by Jeffs as a young girl, and he and others pressured her to keep silent so as not to cause a faith crisis in the community that would undo people's testimony. In the mainstream church, Martha Beck (2006) speaks of a similar pressure about her father's abuse of her and the cultural demands for silence in the mainstream church. Indeed, according to web searches, Beck's siblings still will not speak to her following her accounts of incest in her memoir (Lythgoe 2005).

It probably comes as no surprise that sex is critical to the power matrix asserted by the prophet within fundamentalist polygamy. In these stories and by all news accounts, Warren Jeffs considers sexual activity to be his divine right, even while denying sexual expression to the majority of his followers. Brent Jeffs recalls that adolescents within the FLDS community were warned to have no contact with one another.

> Basically Warren's version of sex education: you should want death rather than sex outside marriage or a "wrong" marriage that wasn't arranged by him or his father. He kept on about this, always emphasizing obedience and not questioning the leaders. Every Bible story became a tale of how the obedient were blessed and the disobedient were cursed, no matter how much twisting it took to make the story fit the moral. Even thinking about a girl was a "great sin"—and God had killed people for it, he preached, giving what he said were biblical and *Book of Mormon* examples. (Jeffs and Szalavitz 2009, 102)

In turn, Jeffs determined that many of the male patriarchs in the community were unworthy largely because they did not support him without question. He banished these apostates and redistributed the remaining wives and children to other, more loyal men in the community, in effect restricting sexual relations to a small cadre of fifteen male loyalists.

In the FLDS temple built at the now notorious Yearning for Zion Ranch near Eldorado, Texas, many on social media speculated that the white platform bed found during the government's 2008 raid on the compound was intended for the purpose of spectacularized sex—in other words, a stage where Jeffs would have had ritualized sex with new brides, many of them underage girls, while adults watched from chairs positioned around the room (see figure 4.4; West 2008). Writing for the *San Antonio Express-News*, Karisa King reports, "In the thousands of pages of what he termed his 'priesthood records,'" Jeffs described the specs for the bed's construction: "It was to be made from hardwood, sturdy so it wouldn't rattle, long enough to support Jeffs' frame and equipped with padded sides that could be pulled up to hold him in place 'as the Lord does His work with me. It will be covered with a sheet, but it will have a plastic cover to protect the mattress from what will happen on it.'" The bed was obscured within a table and sat on wheels, so that it could be rolled away, in Jeffs's words, "so that it can be taken apart and stored in a closet where no one can see it. When I need it, I will pull it out and set it up" (King 2016).

In Jeffs's criminal trial, jurors heard audiotapes recorded at these "heavenly sessions." Covering the case, Britain's *Daily Mail* noted that jurors wept

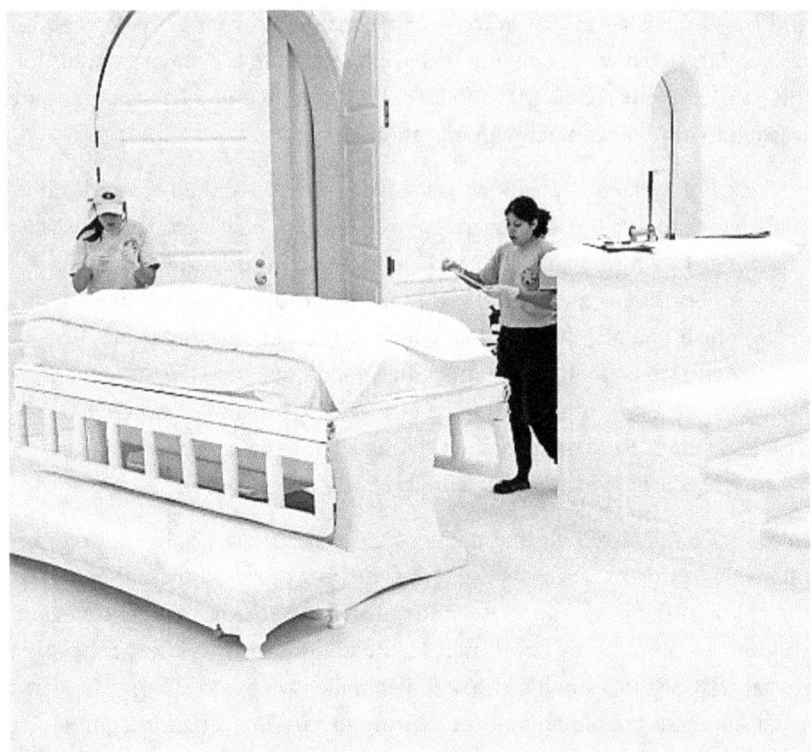

FIG. 4.4 FBI agents cataloguing evidence, in this case the Temple Bed at the YFZ Ranch (http://www.childbrides.org/sex_DM_Warrens_rape_bed_at_YFZ.html).

as the court heard "twisted tapes of sexual instructions Warren Jeffs gave brides," including threats that "God would 'reject them'" if they refused sex with him as their new husband. Writes the *Daily Mail*, "Softly telling five girls to 'set aside all your inhibitions,' the convicted pedophile was heard giving the young girls detailed pointers during a graphic ten-minute tape played for the Texas jury. The audiotape from 2004 was played before another, made within hours of the first, in which prosecutors say Jeffs can be heard having sex with all the girls at the same time. In one tape, he is heard telling the girls they 'need to be excited'" (Bentley and Quigley 2011). Mainstream U.S. news sources, including CNN, also quoted from the tapes: "You have to know how to be excited sexually," Jeffs said. "The Lord has intended that my ladies, all of my ladies be trained" ("Court Releases" 2011).

The audiotapes are excruciatingly painful to hear: a soft-spoken man in his fifties instructing teenage girls in how to pleasure him sexually and demanding that they express erotic response as a sign of heavenly obedience. Jeffs starts with an invocation: "Oh Lord, our God, in heaven, join us in a circle of prayer." He then instructs them, "All the ladies back away." He begins breathing heavily, his ardor increasing. Speaking to one girl in particular, twelve-year-old Merianne, he prays, "We bless you of the Lord at this young age." Breathing harder, he says in a whisper, "That feels good." His breath speeds. "How do you feel, Merianne?" Her voice so small it is barely discernible, the sound of a frightened child responds: "It feels good. Thank you." Warren finishes. "In the name of Jesus Christ, Amen."

It's hard to write this scene out. It's even harder to listen to it, Merianne's voice so small and timid. My earbuds put her voice so deep inside my head that my teeth hurt. The reason to commit these details to the page, though, is because they demonstrate without question that Jeffs used sexual coercion to forward his authority as prophet. These scenes also indicate how fully the voice of Warren Jeffs has created the persona of the prophet, sound here functioning as an aural pedagogy on the banality of evil that is critical to mediated Mormonism. For my purposes, these disturbing moments in which an audience might hear the details of a man having sex with children offers a telling portrait of perversity in the twenty-first-century. Yet it is not just pedophilia that so disturbs about Warren Jeffs, although this, by itself, is certainly enough. It is group sex with teenagers, it is coercion in the name of faith, it is spectacularized sexuality, it is the naive consent of the girls and the willful denial of their parents who may have been watching their daughters be raped, it is demanding the girls respond as sexual agents who feel pleasure. And it is recording these atrocities, transforming them into media that, in turn, are easily accessible as downloadable sound files.

Prophet's Prey is particularly mindful about foregrounding Jeffs's voice as synonymous with his evil. In an interview with the documentary's director, Amy Berg, *Vanity Fair* positions Jeffs's voice as the soundtrack of fundamentalist evil. "Stitched throughout the film is the voice of Jeffs himself, delivering sermons in his creepy, low-energy lisp" (Hogan 2015). Because the tapes were used as evidentiary materials against Jeffs, they are also a part of the legal record, accessible for free as court documents. Berg perceives the audiotapes' legal function as part of their mediated necessity: "I like to take the position that, if a jury sees it, the audience will see it" (Hogan 2015).

Brent Jeffs describes his uncle's voice as containing a

> peculiar hypnotic quality . . . calming, almost narcotic. . . . He spoke quietly, in a low tone, so if you wanted to take in his actual words, you

had to pay close attention. He kept a lulling kind of rhythm that was hard to avoid being entrained to, with an almost maternal quality, like he was trying to soothe a baby to sleep, like a relaxation tape. . . . It kind of washed over you and crept round your defenses, speaking to the unconscious parts of your brain. It got to you, even when you didn't realize you were hearing what he was saying. (Jeffs and Szalavitz 2009, 61)

As described, the adult Jeffs's voice negotiates the relationship between hearing, listening, and self-understanding. I would argue, in turn, that sound works to blur the positions of inside and outside, intimate and formal, exteriority and interiority that are so fully manifest in the sensationalized media connected to Warren Jeffs.

Note again Brent Jeffs's description of Warren Jeff's voice. It is "hypnotic" and "almost narcotic," "lulling" and "maternal," "like a relaxation tape" that works on the "unconscious." It forces the listener to attend more fully, to silence the self in relation to a more powerful other, even as what defines the self is obliterated in the hearing. In this, Jeffs's voice conveys an affective urgency that is coercive and corroding, but it is also compelling, charismatic. His voice evidences a different kind of investment on the part of his followers: the desire to blot out the often chaotic noise of worldly things, of rapidly changing and divergent social, moral, and political conditions, so that his voice might be the only voice. If Warren Jeffs's aural hold on his followers worked as a narcotic to the unconscious, the structure and mandate of Mormonism more broadly is an intoxicant similarly reassuring and addictive.

Authoritative patriarchy is here not a premodern iteration; it does not reach to a place of the past or try to engage with a religious tradition that refuses time, as one might argue other religions are perceived as doing. Instead, this religion is a reaction to the challenges of modern living, fully cognizant of and reliant on complex morality and frenetic temporality. Much like progressive polygamy in the Kody Brown family, for whom plural marriage solves the increasing dilemmas of modern living, the structures of FLDS polygamy under Jeffs are very much reactive to, and dependent upon, the chaos of modern problems. For those inside the FLDS, Jeffs's voice might unify; for those outside the FLDS, Jeffs's voice is ominous. As Jeffs's voice is increasingly spliced into the soundtracks of movies, documentaries, news, television shows, and even court evidence, it becomes inseparable from the sound of danger. In this Jeffs serves as a recognizable warning, his prophet-visibility making clear when danger is nigh.

Given that the overall objective of this chapter is to highlight the manner in which visibility helps create the cultural work performed by mediated fundamentalist polygamy—specifically through sexualized power relations fed by celebrity and an authoritative patriarchal masculinity—it is worth thinking more about Warren Jeffs's ungainly body, in every description opposed to what one might consider to be hegemonically appealing or powerful. Brent Jeffs again offers the description that makes these matters clear. He describes his uncle as "a scrawny, delicate child, tending to fade into the background among his more boisterous sisters and brothers. He had no athletic talent, and soon came to prefer music, books, and art. He was socially awkward and shy. Tall and thin as a beanpole, as a young man he looked like the archetypal pencil-necked geek: dull brown hair, thick square glasses, a goofy, distracted face, and a clumsy gait" (Jeffs and Szalavitz 2009, 63). No big man on campus is he. Instead, Warren is feminized, learning his "mother's tricks" and her "manipulative ways," drawn to aesthetics rather than athletics (63). Warren's unbounded sexual appetites are depicted as lasciviousness enacted on the juvenile bodies of boys and the early pubescent bodies of girls. He is a predator, both devious and deceptive.

Given the factual details captured by these "heavenly sessions" audiotapes, the consequent reenactment in the only feature-length fictional portrayal of Jeffs, *Outlaw Prophet: Warren Jeffs* (2014), is tame by comparison. The heavenly sessions between Jeffs and his young brides do not include audiences, recording devices, elevated beds, ceremonial folderol, or accomplices. We do not know the age of his sex partners. Indeed, in the advertising still for the made-for-television film (see figure 4.5), there is only one fully clothed man and three young women who appear to be in their twenties, making the heavenly sessions here far less lurid than in real life. Within the diegesis of the film, the depictions are quite a lot more graphic. As Jeffs, actor Tony Goldwyn appears in a PG-13 version of nakedness, often in boxers or unclothed, his more private areas referenced but unseen (see figure 4.6). The most graphic scene in this made-for-TV movie depicts an unclothed Jeffs, in the dark bedroom he shares with his first wife, rather than on the elevated bright platforms of the YFZ temple. With five of his young, very white wives gathered around him, Jeffs sits naked on a bed, shadows doing the work of indicating not only the materiality of the penis but the symbolic power of the phallus. Yet, even with the body of the actor carefully obscured, I must say,

FIG. 4.5 French advertising still, *Outlaw Prophet: Warren Jeffs* (2014).

it is still shocking to see a naked adult man instructing young women in how to pleasure him, particularly on the Lifetime network. Watching these scenes is incredibly difficult, for they enact the processes of intimidation in extraordinary detail. "Ladies, you need to concentrate on the bond of oneness," says Goldwyn in his whispered voice meant to represent Jeffs. One girl is reluctant, and Jeffs immediately hones in on her. The others, trying to be obedient, gather around her lovingly, but then begin to hold her down while Warren rapes her. The girl's face shows confusion, then fear, then pain. It is excruciating to watch, only partially because of how the scene captures the dynamics of failed consent and forced consummation.

While it is harrowing to view these scenes, it is also disconcerting to see Goldwyn in this role as the ungainly Jeffs, described by his nephew as "6′4″, gawky, scrawny, and awkward—his neck is too skinny for his head and his

FIG. 4.6 Goldwyn as Jeffs, enacting the "heavenly sessions" of sexual coaching to his young wives. Screen grab, *Outlaw Prophet*.

glasses are too big for his face" (Jeffs and Szalavitz 2009, 1–2). Jeffs's scrawny body, his countenance, his wispy voice all raise questions about how he might convince more than ten thousand followers of his absolute divine authority and charismatic appeal. By contrast, Goldwyn, who played President Fitzgerald Grant on Shonda Rhimes's popular ABC hit *Scandal*, is known as much for his six-pack abs (put to full scopophilic display on *Scandal*) as for his Hollywood pedigree as grandson of Samuel Goldwyn of MGM Studios. He has a distinctive cocky walk that is halfway lope and halfway strut, and a head full of wavy chestnut hair that seems to drive his fans mad with desire.

In turn, Goldwyn's celebrity as a sexy leading man lends *Outlaw Prophet* its own Shonda-land eroticized allure. Many viewers watched the premiere of *Outlaw Prophet* in viewing parties as appointment TV, earning ratings that made it the second-most-watched show on June 28, 2014, second to NASCAR (M&M_Vlogs 2014). Its continual re-airing and worldwide syndication have furthered the spread of *Outlaw Prophet*, often through the appeal of the Tony Goldwyn brand. And much like *Scandal*, which staked part of its claim to history-making prominence on the social media chatter its actors and fans (called Gladiators) fostered during broadcasts, both Goldwyn and Rebecca Musser (one of the real-life women who escaped the FLDS and later helped to convict Jeffs) live tweeted during the first airing of the movie. For good measure, Kerry Washington, who plays Olivia Pope, *Scandal*'s lead character and

Polygamy USA   185

Goldwyn's love interest, also tweeted along with the premiere, adding another level of celebrity appeal. In turn, the Twitter feeds for Goldwyn, Musser, Washington, and *Outlaw Prophet* all reinforce the actor's sexy good looks, his acting talents, and how "messed up" and "disturbing" Jeffs's narrative is.

To be sure, I do not believe audiences confused Goldwyn with Jeffs—they seem quite aware of the performance feat involved in playing him, and tweets on the *Outlaw Prophet* feed show fans, many with screen names that express *Scandal*-related meaning like Olitz or Fitzlover, complimenting the actor for his talent. My point, rather, is that the terms of representation so fully reinforce an almost contradictory logic whereby the actor's body cements the attractiveness of Jeffs as a charismatic leader with a powerful and insistent sex drive, even as it separates the actor's body from the prophet's. "Michelle FO918" writes, "My mom is now hysterical at the 'sex teaching' scene. She is in love with the way that TG is sitting on the bed." Likewise, "Dirty Sock" posted, "Fitz always gotta have all these womenfolk to love him" and "The Daily Gawk" describes *Outlaw Prophet* as a "sexy makeover" for Warren Jeffs.

Indeed, coverage of *Outlaw Prophet* very much worked to blur the sexually alluring bodies of Goldwyn, his *Scandal* character Fitz, and Jeffs, the actor's movie-star body and his character's persona of a sexy president reinforcing the shared properties of eroticism that bind the two stories of male authority—president and prophet. In their plugging of the movie, *Entertainment Tonight*'s segment on the film is called "From President to Prophet." ET starts with a sex scene between Fitz (Tony Goldwyn) and Olivia (Kerry Washington) on *Scandal*, only to move seconds later to the above-described rape scene in *Outlaw Prophet*, calling the made-for-TV movie "extremely graphic" and a "real-life sex scandal" (O'Dell 2014). The problem here should be rather obvious—rape is not an expression of sexuality; it is an abuse of power through violent sex. In this case, the limited registers of representation flatten the difference between these sex acts depicted on screen, marking them as two points on a continuum rather than as deeply incommensurate actions.

Whether or not we perceive Warren Jeffs as the kind of charismatic person to lead a cultlike religion, lifting his story to a field of mediated visibility relies on the telegenic biases of mainstream television that cannot, without difficulty, imagine a leading man who is not also sexually desirable in conventional terms.[9] Playing the awkwardly embodied Warren Jeffs thus problematizes the folds and overlaps of embodied authority, sexual power, and bullying intimidation, Goldwyn's muscular form and "sexy walk" mak-

FIG. 4.7 Warren Jeffs.

ing Jeffs's charismatic hold on his followers somehow understandable, even natural (see figures 4.7 and 4.8).

In sum, while this fictional portrayal of Warren Jeffs in *Outlaw Prophet* positions Jeffs as its protagonist, a man made notorious and who believed himself to be bigger than bin Laden, it defaults to a portrayal of the power-crazed and pedophilic prophet that is one-dimensional and fairly common in what we might call an archive of mediated polygamy and patriarchal abuse. I do not necessarily fault the film or its producers for this—it's hard to humanize a man like Jeffs, responsible for so much abuse and intimidation. Indeed, it is precisely this difficulty that helps reinforce my claim that the figures at the center of these fiction and nonfiction tellings about the charismatic celebrity are themselves little more than a backdrop to a different form of emergent hero figure. Within these portrayals, it is the women and subordinated men who defy him in order to flee to a modern world where their voices might overpower his that emerge as the subjects of celebration. In this, representations of abuse, victimization, and brainwashed

FIG. 4.8 Putting a pretty face on polygamy: Tony Goldwyn as Warren Jeffs.

groupthink ultimately serve to make the perpetrator uninteresting except for the way the prophet and his brotherhood of patriarchal leaders function as a backdrop for the calling-into-being of feminist conscience, resistance, and social justice.

Polygamists OG: Brothers Joseph and Brigham

As I note, the FLDS and LDS religions sprouted from a common seed, sharing the same prophets until the splits that occurred in 1890 and 1904 when what is now the mainstream church disavowed plural marriage. The mutual prophetic heritage is not just a historical matter but a representational one as well, since references to the original Mormon polygamists and prophets, Joseph Smith and Brigham Young, riddle these contemporary imaginings of patriarchal power and the charismatic prophet. Look to the background of most documentary and nonfiction television representations of patriarchal

FIG. 4.9 Fusing narratives: *Outlaw Prophet: Warren Jeffs* and the Annunciation of Joseph Smith, bound together through polygamy and desires for underage brides.

polygamy, for instance, and you are sure to see the framed visages of Joseph Smith and Brigham Young looming behind the action playing out at the front of the screen. In *Church of Lies*, Flora Jessop literalizes these connections by including the images of Smith and Young in the section containing family photos, visual evidence here reinforcing her rights to patriarchal critique (Jessop and Brown 2010).

Indeed, as troubling as the incest, pedophilia, and rape I've discussed in this chapter are, they are telling for their equation of fundamentalist polygamous perversions with mainstream Mormonism through the figure of its founder, Joseph Smith. If we briefly return to *Outlaw Prophet*, we see a scene with a mural behind three of Jeffs's naked young sister wives (see figure 4.9), a rendering of Smith, featured in iconic pose as he receives the spirit of the Angel Moroni in his own queer ecstasy. This not-so-veiled reference to the Mormon origination story follows a well-worn pattern. The mimetic properties of what defines the prophet do not arise from a vacuum: they are referential to entrenched visual and aural codes that solidify the meanings of the all-American prophet, even as they critique those terms. In this respect, while the mainstream church has worked hard to distance itself from its polygamist past, media keep the past always present. We can see the truth of this contention in many places, but another telling illustration occurred on the TLC reality show *90 Day Fiancé*, when a young mainstream Mormon boy from Idaho brings a Russian girl back from his mission so that

Polygamy USA   189

they might marry. At their wedding, her Russian parents ask if the family is polygamous. His LDS family is shocked at the question, but the audience is in on the joke. Media here function as a pedagogical reminder of a history that is not always spoken but also isn't forgotten.

The founding fathers of both Mormonism and polygamy in the USA—Joseph Smith and Brigham Young—thus remain part of a living history, told and retold through other persons and stories in the present moment. But the prophets are fully present in their own skins as well, usually as the good cop/bad cop of Mormon history. While in their own day both Smith and Young were deeply flawed and highly controversial figures whose audacity brought the wrath of angry mobs, state troops, and, ultimately, the federal government, in the long whitewash of history, Joseph Smith has emerged as the good, jovial, and charismatic first prophet, and Brigham Young is often cast as the less-compelling organizational genius of the church. Basically, Smith upholds the charismatic center, the holy force of reckoning that brought the church into being. By contrast, Young is more phlegmatic: Brigham is plain where Joseph was handsome, parsimonious where Joseph was generous, practical and plotting where Joseph was whimsical and impulsive. In her nineteenth-century denunciation of Mormon polygamy, former Mormon Fanny Stenhouse speaks of a "contagious rapture" that occurred among believers in response to Smith. By contrast, she says that Young "discouraged" the exercise of these charismatic gifts, to be "excited to frenzy" (Stenhouse 1875, 38, 39). Stenhouse claims that Young possessed a "narrow soul," incapable of looking beyond anything but his own small frame of reference.

While she concedes that Young held great fame in midcentury America, Stenhouse denounces his legitimate right to this stature, saying he had "obtained a place in the recognition of the world, to which by nature or by grace he had not the shadow of a claim." Instead, she characterizes him as having the "mind of the wildest savage who prowled among the cliffs and canyons of the Rocky Mountains." "He probably is one of the greatest cowards in existence, both morally and physically" (Stenhouse 1875, 238, 240). Her most damning critique? Stenhouse accuses Young of a debased morality due to his practice of blood atonement (what she calls the "ditty of assassination"), the enforcement of polygamy, the sustenance of the Adam/God doctrine, and robbing Christ of his birthright by putting him on equal ground with humans (245).[10] Ann Eliza Young (1876), Brigham Young's nineteenth (or thereabouts) wife, was equally condemning in her published memoirs and one-woman stage performances. She calls him a man of "selfish cupidity and egotistical vanity" (123), who cannot tolerate criticism and "sneaks, and skulks, and cowardly hides behind any one he can find who is broad enough to shield him" (123). He is a "grasping lecherous, heartless tyrant" (160), a murderer with "moral rottenness to the very core" (315). "His avarice is so inordinate that no amount of suffering stands in the way of his self-enrichment" (317). He is an entitled despot who has created a "reign of terror" (131), and in this sin, he commits the distinctly American crime of acting like royalty.

Brigham Young's heartlessness is particularly reinforced in relation to two historical travesties: the handcart disaster of 1856 and the Mountain Meadows Massacre of 1857. In the former, the prophet spoke of a vision urging converts to come to Zion immediately. Mormon faithful walked the thousand miles from Iowa to Salt Lake, pushing and pulling their belongings—and often their sick and fragile family members—on rickety handcarts. Scores died along the way, but Young never relented in his demand that the faithful keep coming. By media accounts, he did little to help. Also in 1857, the Mountain Meadows Massacre is named for a mass killing in southern Utah. An expedition traveling from Arkansas to California was surrounded by the Utah Territorial Militia, many of them Mormons dressed as Paiutes to make their abuses seem the work of Native Americans rather than white men, in turn reinforcing the racial appropriation that is behind so much of settler colonialism. Young's involvement was highly suspected but never proved, and both *Tell It All* and *Wife No. 19* speak in harshly condemnatory terms of Brigham Young's culpability with respect to the lives lost in these travesties.

Now clearly, memoirs of this sort have an agenda, in that their representations are meant to undermine the institution of polygamy that both Stenhouse and Young considered to be corrosive to womanhood, which is to say to the nineteenth-century prevailing social code of monogamous heteronormativity. Yet this sort of reactive nineteenth-century media set the template for how both Joseph Smith and Brigham Young continue to be read today: Joseph as laughing and loving, Brigham as devious and dour. It is telling, given these differences, that Brigham Young was first anointed Smith's successor after giving a speech some weeks following Smith's death. Suddenly bathed in a column of light that blinded all present, Young seemed to the assembled crowd to take on the appearance and sound of Joseph Smith—one seeming to speak through the other. By contrast, in mediated accounts such as *Avenging Angel*, *September Dawn*, and *Brigham Young*, Young emerges in the model made salient through memoir, as a commanding, if often heartless, leader who will sacrifice all for power.

It is largely due to this more benign rendition of Smith that his relation to polygamy has been hotly contested. During his life, he disavowed his own participation in plural marriage. In a 2014 move for transparency—believing that a little bit of truth is better than a whole lot of spin—the mainstream church released a statement through its website Mormon.org, acknowledging that Joseph Smith both practiced polygamy and had several young wives, probably ten of whom were only barely into their teens ("Plural Marriage in Kirtland and Nauvoo" 2014.). These are statements that decades earlier had been excommunicable offenses. Yet, as *Outlaw Prophet* and an increasingly active blogosphere make clear, the polygamy that Joseph Smith started in the nineteenth century will always be something that modern-day Mormons must address, in both the idea of who they are and in actual practice, since so many present-day Mormons are descended from polygamist ancestors and because polygamy as an institution is very much an open possibility in the LDS afterlife.

The power dynamics at the heart of polygamy constitute the very DNA of Mormon belief, and really of orthodox culture, in which the truth of God can only be known through the words of man, and one man in particular holds unwavering power. For both mainstream and fundamentalist versions of the faith, the male leader of the church is considered to be its absolute authority figure and the exclusive receiver of divine revelations from God. Obedience becomes the primary, and in some respects only, way for those under the prophet to show their belief in God. In the words of the mainstream church: once the prophet speaks, the thinking is done. In the words of Warren Jeffs: "Obey the prophet when he speaks, and you'll be blessed. Disobey him, and it is death" (Knoll 2009b). Those who do not obey are threatened with banishment from family and loved ones, both now and in an eternity of outer darkness. Within the fundamentalist faith, the disobedient can also be punished and/or compelled to prove their faith through blood atonement. Oddly, however, this draconian demand for obedience has yielded depictions so grandiose and over the top that they often speak through the idiom of queerness and camp culture, particularly as related to that first all-American prophet, Joseph.

More Famous Than Jesus: Joseph Smith as Audacious Celebrity and Queer Figure of Excess

There is a charismatic appeal to audacity. The man of renown often raises the twin banners of the visionary and the egoist by breaking preconceived notions about decorum and decency. It's not by accident that these are also the qualities of a certain kind of narcissistic hegemonic masculinity that assumes its own right to rule, reinforces hierarchical power relations, boasts of its heterosexual prowess, and continually seeks affirmation of its own authority. The great man is a highly gendered construct that reinforces masculinist codes of singularity and exceptionalism—and though a woman and certain subordinated males can certainly aspire to and achieve these heights, the category of the great man itself carries the markings of an alpha heteromasculinity that tilts toward the bold, the daring, the fearless, and the audacious. Yet I would submit that hegemonic masculinity itself is an elaborate stage-crafted artifice, filled with bravado, theatricality, and quite a good bit of homoeroticism, the style codes that mark a queer camp sensibility that self-consciously toys with its own hyperbole. Indeed, I'd outright label hegemonic masculinity camp were it not persuaded by its own performance—so camp, minus the self-aware irony, perhaps.

As I've noted, Joseph founded his church in 1830 in Palmyra, New York, a small town on the edge of the Erie Canal, not far from Seneca Falls where a different kind of political action would soon take place for women with the 1848 Declaration of Sentiments. In the 1820s and '30s the entire country was awash in a fevered emotional moment when a mass of people turned to religion and religious extremes to counter social ills and affective malaise. The mid-nineteenth century reinforced a doomsday scenario that preached the end of the world was nigh, and this, in turn, opened the door to a religious fervor that fostered fantastic leaders (celebrity) and bred unswerving devotion (fans). As one demonstration of this religio-celebrity culture, in the 1850s, the Congregationalist preacher Henry Ward Beecher (of the renowned Beecher clan) was "the most famous man in America," preaching twice a day to audiences of five thousand or more. Historian Debby Applegate notes Beecher's "spectacular sermons at Plymouth Church in Brooklyn Heights had made him New York's number one tourist attraction, so wildly popular that the ferries from Manhattan to Brooklyn were dubbed 'Beecher Boats'" (2006, back cover).

Beecher allows me to emphasize an important point: it was a crowded moment on the religion/celebrity stage, where any Tom, Dick, or Harry had to fight against the charismatic powers of Joseph and Henry to assume the glories of fame and adulation, and only the rare woman need even presume such grandiosity. Indeed, one could argue Joseph Smith played the politics of commemoration impeccably: by the time of Beecher's ascendancy in the 1850s, Joseph Smith had already outdone Beecher's fame. Smith had emerged as a martyr (killed by an angry anti-Mormon mob in 1844), transcending—might I even say, resurrecting—from body to idea and fusing his own overlarge personality with God's. Now that's audacious. And a bit campy.

I admit that it is more than sacrilege in certain circles to think of Joseph Smith, founding prophet and fallen martyr, as a camp celebrity figure. His memory is revered by legions of Saints worldwide as the earnest, God-inspired founder of the One True Church. Often mimetically linked with Jesus, Joseph Smith stands as the righteous man of honor, who brought God's truth to American soils. Joseph was an unusual prophet, in that his human weaknesses and appetites were so fully manifest in his celebrity bearing. Unlike the prophets of biblical times, Joseph was a robust man of the moment. Writes Irving Wallace, "Combining the delicate and handsome features of a matinee idol with the physique of an athlete, he wrestled, gambled, swore ('like a pirate', the governor of Illinois would observe), drank and whored" (1962, 35). Mormonism, in its twentieth-century commitments to conservatism and its nineteenth-century roots in polygamy, is ever the fascinating touchstone for these registers of sexuality, faith, regulation, and rules.

Given all of this, it might be counterintuitive that if one reverts to that most contemporary form of scholarship, Google, little of this background is revealed. Typing the three words "Joseph" "Smith" "celebrity" into a search engine yields a fairly lackluster array of possibilities: famous people named Joseph, a website on a split-apart faction of Mormonism called Strangism or the Strangites that emerged after Smith's death in 1844, Joseph Smith's zodiac sign, a church-authorized history of Joseph Smith that calls him a "humble man"—and a list of famous Mormons, including "Hey Girl" Ryan Gosling, who was raised LDS but no longer considers himself Mormon.

Some of this absence may well be because the mainstream LDS Church is both resolute and savvy in its telling of its own story and the policing of search algorithms. The mainstream church's website describes its founding prophet's story as a young boy, who asked God's help in knowing which church to worship. As they explain it, "When Joseph asked which church he should join, the Savior told him to join none of the churches then in existence because they were teaching incorrect doctrines. Through this experience and many others that followed, the Lord chose Joseph to be His prophet and to restore the gospel of Jesus Christ and His Church to the earth" ("Joseph Smith" 2016). A most unusual moment made perfectly reasonable. Rather than seeing Joseph Smith as a pious fraud or divine charlatan as do many of his biographers and historians of the period, the mainstream church insists on Smith's unwavering veracity because the entire embedded structure of faith requires a buy-in to the truth of Joseph's vision. In their words, "The truthfulness of The Church of Jesus Christ of Latter-day Saints rests on the truthfulness of the First Vision and the other revelations the Lord gave to the Prophet Joseph. In the Doctrine and Covenants we learn, Joseph Smith, the Prophet and Seer of the Lord, has done more, save Jesus only, for the salvation of men in this world, than any other man that ever lived in it" (Maynes 2017).

But let us not be overly persuaded by a telling of history that presumes Joseph Smith's meekness, kindness, and all-around humbleness simply because he began a church whose mainstream members are now marked by many of these adjectives. Joseph Smith was a man of presence and audacity, marked by "religious genius" (Bloom 1992, 80), even in a nineteenth-century context dominated by big personalities. Indeed, Bloom argues that Smith possessed charismatic appeal "to a degree unsurpassed in American history" (98). In his own time, Joseph Smith did not just look like a matinee idol, he lived a life of immense celebrity that, in our present moment, is rivaled only by entertainment celebrities. Joseph was a figure of charisma and controversy, a personality that generated strong and polarizing reactions. His church—largely due to its rumors of non-normative sexual behaviors but also because of its capacity to thrive under separate sovereignty (indeed, it had its own standing army)—generated strong fascination and fear.

Joseph Smith and the towns he created—first in Ohio, then in Arkansas, then in Illinois—became celebrities of untold fascination. Alex Beam (2014) notes in *American Crucifixion* that there were "four landing slips in Nauvoo, and in the summer as many as ten boats a week stopped by, often filled with tourists and day-trippers eager to catch a glimpse of the exotic Mormons." R. Lawrence Moore similarly reports, "Mormon communities were three-star sights in European guidebooks to North America" (1987, 26). In *Manifest Destinations*, J. Philip Gruen writes that by 1900 Western tourists visited Salt Lake City in great numbers—"150,000–200,000 per year"—in order "to experience what they perceived as a deviant population on native soil.... This alone set [Mormons] apart from most tourists, and as historian Patricia Limerick has argued, cast them as exotic and 'other' in the popular imagination" (Gruen 2014; see also Seppi 2015). As Moore rightly summarizes, "Although Mormons were publicly despised and ridiculed, visitors to the United States sought them out as if they provided vital clues to the nature of the American people," perhaps to the American people themselves (Moore 1987, 26). Indeed, Kurt Andersen considers Smith a "quintessentially American figure," whose "extreme audacity—his mind-boggling *balls*—is the American character ad absurdum. America was created by people resistant to reality checks and convinced they had special access to the truth, a place founded to enact grand fantasies," argues Andersen. "No Joseph Smiths emerged elsewhere in the modern world" (2017, 72).

Though dead at age thirty-eight, Joseph drew the most important of American and European personages to himself and later to his proxy, Brigham Young, in Salt Lake City. Mark Twain, P. T. Barnum, Stephen Douglas, Horace Greeley, Richard Burton—all trekked to either Nauvoo or Salt Lake for the Mormon experience. Josiah Quincy, the mayor of Boston, with his cousin Charles Francis Adams (son of President John Quincy Adams) visited Smith in Illinois in 1844 when Smith was himself running for president. Quincy described Smith as "a man of commanding appearance, clad in the costume of a journeyman carpenter.... He was a hearty, athletic fellow, with blue eyes standing prominently out upon his light complexion, a long nose, and a retreating forehead. He wore striped pantaloons, a linen jacket, which had not lately seen the washtub, and a beard of some three days' growth" (Quincy 1883).

In his biography of Ann Eliza Young, Wallace refers to this meeting of early American celebrities—Smith, Adams, and Quincy. "During their conversations Quincy frankly told Smith that he possessed too much power. Smith was not abashed. He replied, 'In your hands or that of any other person so much power would, no doubt, be dangerous. I am the only man in the world whom it would be safe to trust with it. Remember, "I am a prophet!"'" To which Quincy added for his readers: "The last fine words were spoken in a rich, comical aside, as if in hearty recognition of the ridiculous sound they might have in the ears of a Gentile" (Wallace 1962, 36). Smith, who had appointed himself mayor of Nauvoo, general of the Nauvoo legion, and, by some accounts, king of the world once the apocalypse occurred, was fond of surveying his troops while clad in a uniform "made according to the latest pattern." Beam writes, "Joseph favored a cerulean officer's tailcoat, dripping with weighty gold braid and epaulettes, topped off with a black cockade chapeau that was adorned with a black ostrich feather. As accouterments, he wore black leather riding boots, white gloves, a gold campaign sash, and a four-foot-long, leather-handled, forged cavalry saber" (2014, 56–57).

In a more contemporary context, Jane Barnes (one of the producers of the PBS documentary *The Mormons* and author of *Falling in Love with Joseph Smith*) considers Joseph a "pure product of America," grounded in contradiction and hyperbole, a charismatic celebrity presence as iconic and irreverent as Huck Finn and Tom Sawyer, as poetic as D. H. Lawrence and Walt Whitman, and with more sheer aliveness in him than Jesus Christ (Barnes

2012). She writes, "Not to confuse Jesus with Joseph, just to compare their biographical trajectories for a moment: Christ's life has been so swarmed with commentary, the *feel* of religion has all but been squeezed out of it for me. Joseph's life still simmers in the vital, chaotic, wondrous aftermath of his big bang encounter with God. The facts about Joseph are still being unearthed; and as messy as Joseph continues to be, he's still in on the *mysterium tremendum*" (Barnes 2012, 61–62, emphasis in original). Clearly, Barnes doesn't overstate the case when she calls her book *Falling in Love with Joseph Smith*.

Joseph Smith's bravado admitted no equal: "I have more to boast of than ever any man had. I am the only man that has ever been able to keep a whole church together since the days of Adam.... Neither Paul, John, Peter, nor Jesus ever did it. I boast that no man ever did such work as I. The followers of Jesus ran away from Him; but the Latter-day Saints never ran away from me yet" (Smith 1920, 6:408–9). His over-the-top regard for himself made him a diva of the nineteenth century. Indeed, Alex Doty (2007) notes that "divas are frequently portrayed as both victims and villains" since they can be "figures of worship as well as of ridicule for their attempts to confront, transcend, or carve a new space within the patriarchal dominant culture." They create what Doty calls "category trouble" by refusing to stay in their proper culturally assigned roles in order to "live life on their own terms, making them important figures for other groups at the margins of the dominant culture." Doty's version of the diva positions her as resolutely counter-hegemonic, always working to undermine dominant culture in the service of marginal identities, always gendered feminine. By contrast, the figure, fortitude, and ongoing camp personality of Joseph Smith allows for what I consider to be a more frightening possibility: the political work of the diva might well be marshaled through hegemonic white hetero-masculinity, the audacity of difference working to naturalize the codes of patriarchal power relations found in the polygamous prophet.

Conclusion: The Logic of Open Secrets

While in Canada, I was introduced to Uncle Jason's brother Winston Blackmore, the bishop of our FLDS community there. He was a jovial yet callous man, a product of his environments and his beliefs. I laughed at some of his jokes but cringed at how harshly he treated his wives. Even at the pulpit, he would couch unkind remarks in humor. "Like Brigham Young, I don't like whiny women! Just like him, I tell 'em, 'Leave! I'll replace you in an instant with another wife, and she will serve me the way a woman should serve her Priesthood Head.'"—Rebecca Musser, *The Witness Wore Red*

"Inside Bountiful: Polygamy Investigation," is an episode of *16×9*, a news magazine television program on the Canadian network Global that aired in October 2011 and is in perpetual readiness for international viewing and reviewing on Youtube (16x9onglobal 2012).[11] Amid the legal backdrop of the Canadian Supreme Court's deliberations about the relative legalities of polygamy, *16×9* promised an exposé of "Canada's most famous polygamist," Winston Blackmore, who had, at the time of the show's taping, fifteen wives and 130 children.[12] All of Blackmore's family practiced a version of the Jeffs-inspired FLDS faith that espoused polygamy as one of its primary tenets. In the program, Blackmore notes that his tally of wives had been considerably higher at some indeterminate point in the past—twenty-four by his reckoning. And though we are not told what happened to these women—the program notes in vague terms that they "left"—it is a sign of this polygamist patriarch's relative gender progressivism that wives and children might come and go as they choose from his compound in this bucolic valley, situated less than an hour from the U.S. border with Idaho.

In the program's hands, Canada's rather notorious polygamist comes off as a non-prepossessing granddad kind of fellow, who jokes with community members, doesn't mind if his children date or choose to live outside of the plural marriage commitment, and repeatedly encourages the interviewer, Carolyn Jarvis, to ask her questions of his wives and children rather than of him. Jarvis herself seems somewhat stunned that none of the things she expected to find in Bountiful are there. "We were warned to expect 'no trespassing' signs," she tells the viewer in voice-over narration, "women who would hide their kids in bushes at our arrival. Much to our surprise, there was none of that." Jarvis claims she couldn't even detect the pioneer-style clothing associated with the FLDS plural marriage lifestyle—at least not in the extended family over which Blackmore is the patriarch. Occasionally, the camera glances off to the fields, to the other parts of Bountiful not run by Blackmore. Haunting the edges of the frame are those very silent and secretive figures in long hair and longer pastel dresses that Jarvis expected—these are the FLDS folk who still follow the other Mormon patriarch, Warren Jeffs.

In Blackmore's compound, the camera comes back and holds intently on the scuffed and battered white high heels worn by one sister wife as she works intently in the kitchen, her shoes clearly meant to indicate that this is not your father's polygamy (see figure 4.10). Over the images of these white shoes, Jarvis narrates the separate-spheres labor of polygamy. She is fascinated by the sheer effort involved in feeding so many people. "The biggest meal of the week feeds anywhere from two to three hundred people," says

FIG. 4.10 White pumps: the semiotics of gendered personhood.

Jarvis in voice-over. "The sister wives take turn staging this production.... The preparation begins the night before. By daybreak, the baking begins. Homemade rolls, by the hundreds." The screen is filled with images of slicing, chopping, boiling, setting tables, all in fast motion as if to accentuate the pace of women's work. Thirty-two hundred pounds of tomatoes arrive that have to be canned. "It will take two 12-hour days and all the girls pitching in to finish," says Jarvis. "The one thing you won't find in this kitchen is a man. The odd boy wanders in and quickly wanders out.... This is a community based on gender roles. To find the men, you have to go to the mill."

The camera and Jarvis quickly do just that—heading off to the mill where men labor for money, rather than nourishment. As one might expect, the switch to a mill necessitates the background sounds of power saws and heavy machinery, the aural signifiers here punctuating the work of masculinity with a soundtrack fit for the industrial revolution. But rather than following them so quickly to the spaces of male industry, I want to stay with the sister wives, in the kitchen and home spaces, amid the domestic hurry and flurry that is their labor.

Indeed, the trope of those white high-heeled pumps fascinates me too. For in their impracticality, they represent the very semiotics of women's leisure within modernity, even as (oxymoronically) the woman wearing them is, herself, at work. The shoes seem out of place, beckoning to a world of dancing or fancy lunches, not to the backbreaking labor of incessant food preparation. In the gendered economy of labor that is the FLDS, there will be no rest for this woman, no moment when she might put those fancy shoes to fuller spectacular display. Hers is a life of labor, both the work of domesticity and the literal labor of childbirth. Yet she wears those impractical shoes anyway—I assume as a gesture of individualism, defiance, beauty. Or perhaps she wears them as a self-conscious awareness of being on camera. To engage with the mediated logics of patriarchal polygamy is precisely to tangle with this paradox as attached to the obligations of obedience and the promises of salvation: perpetual servitude is the only way that one might be free in the afterlife, but that afterlife has continuity with a mortal frame in which women serve men and birth children.

Many media accounts of patriarchal polygamy tease viewers with the secrets they will reveal; yet, as this chapter has demonstrated, patriarchal polygamy is an open secret in media culture.[13] The prophet and his not-always-willing followers create a combined meme that is far from clandestine. Indeed, the patriarchal polygamist is a recognizable trope, made legible through his very celebrity as a figure to be despised. The alpha of Joseph and the omega of Warren thus bracket patriarchal polygamy as a key fixation for a culture working through the meanings of justice, fanaticism, intolerance, personal choice, and sexual regulation. On this screen a woman claims her voice to speak an impassioned truth—not as a satisfied, obedient, and silent victim within polygamy, but as an angry, wronged, and inspired warrior intent on demanding a justice for others that she herself was denied, wearing white high heels while she speaks truth to power.

5. Gender Trouble in Happy Valley

CHOICE, HAPPY AFFECT,
AND MORMON FEMINIST HOUSEWIVES

I had a very interesting opportunity to teach one of my nieces a very valuable lesson last night. . . . As I sat with [her] allowing her to tell me all about her life, experiences, friends, and what's important to her, she made a comment that struck a nerve with me. She was telling me of a young girl (my niece is in the 5th grade) that is choosing to "Go Out" with a boy. She was telling me in not so many words that she was better because she was choosing to not "date" because she's not old enough. She then made a very revealing comment. She said, "This girl probably won't get very far in life because of the choices she's making." I about jumped out of my skin. It reminded me of the way so many of my family members treated me over the years. As I finished letting her tell me about this girl, I said a silent prayer asking the Lord to help me teach my niece a very valuable lesson. We should never judge anyone.

As she finished I said, "Sweetie, do you think Aunt Jilly is a good person?" She said, "Yes," then I said, "Do you think I've gotten very far in life?" (Knowing that this little angel thinks the world of her Aunt Jill). She said, "Well, yeah." I then took a beautiful opportunity to teach her something. I shared with her that I stopped going to church when I was 14 years old. Her mouth about hit the floor. I told her that I didn't believe in the church, I swore, I hung out with bad people, and I even dated boys before I was 16. She was stunned. Then I asked her this, "Do you think Aunt Jilly turned out okay?" You could see her little brain turning. She said, "Yeah you did." I said, "Do you think that this little girl might turn out okay too? She's doing the same things that Aunt Jill did, and you just said that I turned out okay." She said, "Yeah Aunt Jill. She might." Then I took the opportunity to teach her how very wrong it is to judge another person. Not only that, I taught her that judging someone can often keep them away [from the church] longer, but if we will show them love like the Savior, they might come back.

—Jilly Strasburg, "Judgement Is of the Devil," from *The Mormon Housewife*

As I discuss throughout this book, happiness as affect and as visual signifier is critical to the broader ideology and implications of mediated Mormonism. Indeed, aspirational cheerfulness—at times, coercively so—is very much in evidence in the above posting from *The Mormon Housewife* blog. Riddled as it is with sentiments of positive advice giving, sunny affectation, and encouraging lifestyle modeling, undercurrents of damnation eddy just below the surface. In this particular entry, a young Mormon woman (age twenty-eight) counsels her preteen niece on the matter of social relationships, cautioning the girl to veer away from judgment and, in so doing, to avoid the devil. It seems somewhat churlish to point out that in chiding her niece about judging others, Jilly participates in her own form of judgmental and potentially damning behavior. What I want to focus on, then, is the way this Mormon housewife's "very important message" is less about judgment and more about the need to develop one's capacities for personal choice as a governing apparatus for spiritual aspirationalism.

By abstaining from active participation in judgment culture, the argument goes, this young girl will also develop the possibility of moving herself and others closer to a heavenly goal. In this context, both self-reflexivity and personal choice work as agents that may lead to salvation. Conversely, however, poor self-reflection and bad choices lead directly to Satan. To "get very far in life" is thus not only coded in the double valences of heaven and earth, since the upward mobility referenced by Aunt Jill connotes both earthly riches and celestial paradises, it is also marinated in the spiritual neoliberal juices of redemptive (and condemnatory) individual choice. In this case, spiritual neoliberalism is made all the more piquant through mediation, since it is not an interaction between aunt and niece that we witness in this exchange but the telling of that interaction, as disseminated through and amplified by the internet colossus.

For this Mormon housewife blogger, choice about normative gender roles for girls and romantic intimacy (to "go out") and their implied extensions and variations—to abstain from going out, to commit to modesty and virginity, to buy into the sexual-moral mythos of both the mainstream Mormon Church and a larger politically right way of positioning and restricting girls' sexuality—are, by themselves, not enough. A young girl must cultivate her powers of self-reflection, to see herself from the outside and work to make others happy by comporting herself in a way that will not cause discomfort or harm. She must always be pleasant and seemingly kind to the outside world, at least to those within her faith system. In doing so, she must internalize the critical gaze of others and guard herself from being offensive to those around her—femininity at its most perversely toxic.

I discuss this term "toxic femininity" in far greater detail in the next section, so here I will bookmark my use with a condensed definition: toxic femininity takes the mandate of a usually white, mostly middle-class, relentlessly heterosexual, and typically politically conservative norm of gender for girls and women and insists on the internalization of these mandates to such a degree that it immolates the self. The workings of toxic femininity within F/LDS cultures follow the routes of most hegemonic systems, which is to say this form of gender instruction is anything but particular or specific. It is both overt and invisible; it is everywhere and nowhere; it seemingly doesn't exist and yet is extremely influential. While individualism and personhood are prized, particularly in the mainstream church, patriarchal authority governs the hierarchy of access to spiritual power and thus to social organization. And because F/LDS cosmogony dictates that righteous men (and only men) might inherit their own heavenly kingdoms and rule as a God, personhood-into-Godhood is a prized objective for men, while being a helper to male priesthood holders is the sine qua non for women.

Awareness of this gendered two-class system floods the writings of Mormon women. Novelist and memoirist Judith Freeman reflects, for instance, on an emerging consciousness of her second-class status: "From a young age I realized that men would always have powers unavailable to me and thus I would always be beholden to them, required to obey their dictates as bearers of the holy priesthood, and thus I would forever exist in a somewhat lower realm" (Freeman 2016, loc. 976). Former FLDS member Elissa Wall offers a similar reflection: "It should have dawned on me that many aspects of the religion were based on revoking the rights of women. If a girl speaks her mind, get her married. Once she's married, get her pregnant. Once she has children, she's in for life—it's almost impossible for any FLDS woman to take her children if she leaves, and no mother wants to leave her children behind" (Wall and Pulitzer 2012, 235).

Throughout this book, I have written much about voice as a defining characteristic of feminist and queer empowerment, a trait that is readily manifest through such media as FLDS polygamy stories, including Wall's, where formerly victimized subjects describe their experiences of consciousness raising, of learning to speak, shout, and scream in defiance of patriarchal mandates that demand their silence and submission. In this chapter, I reflect on feminist identification in relation to affect and choice, specifically the sort of feminine persona espoused by Aunt Jilly in *The Mormon Housewife*. Cultivated femininity requires careful honing and shaping. For many bloggers and memoirists, it is called simply being a good Mormon girl. The notion of choice is, of course, central to progressive gender movements, particularly the pro-choice arm of feminism and the Act Up activism of many LGBT+ political movements. Progressive gender politics demand that individuals have the right to sovereignty over their bodies, desires, and modes of expression.

Somewhat ironically for a religion stressing absolute obedience, personal choice is also critical to Mormonism. Fueled by a belief in individual authority as reinforced by American democratic values, Mormonism (in both mainstream and fundamentalist forms) highly values conscience, personal truth, feelings of individual conviction or testimony, and going against the grain of worldly trends as part of its ethos for being—free agency. Mormonism also, however, governs through a patriarchal hierarchy. In women's writings, this theme of the harsh demand for an unerring submission to male authority and the difficulty in meeting the high bar of perfectionism is a raging river that etches out the gendered canyon lands of mediated Mormonism.

In fundamentalist parlance, the demand for obedience often requires total physical, emotional, and sexual compliance with the prophet; in a mainstream context, while obedience to church authority is highly valued, enacting the codes of submission is often more internalized and socially maintained. Edicts from the LDS such as the Proclamation on the Family make the Mormon mandate for conventional gender ideology clear with statements featured on lds.org like, "By divine design, fathers are to preside over their families in love and righteousness and are responsible to provide the necessities of life and protection for their families. Mothers are primarily responsible for the nurture of their children" ("The Family" 1995). But the policing of these "solemn responsibilities," particularly for women, often devolves to the realms of social criticism and private shame.

In both LDS and FLDS contexts, earthly behaviors, beliefs, and desires accrue value toward a heavenly balance sheet: if one lives the gospel and obeys all church rules, a life of glory in celestial heaven awaits—one hopes. This paradise is made all the more appealing by the reassurance that a righteous man or woman can be sealed for all eternity to an eternal companion and children, the forever families of the afterlife an insurance policy against the dark anxiety of floating alone in perpetuity in the isolation of outer darkness.[1] In this, mediated Mormonism doubles down on the meritocracy promised by the American Dream, but it does so by taking advantage of the fear inherent in these ideologies of self-making: if you fail, it's your own damn fault.

I engage in this consideration of choice, happiness, perfectionism, and gender by thinking quite specifically about women, female and woman-identified embodiment, and femininity in mediated stories about F/LDS culture and lives. Gender, of course, is not a synonym for women, and femininity is not the sole domain of biological or women-identified persons. It is, in turn, extremely important to resist the conflation of masculinity with men or as naturally and exclusively issuing from the male body. In the popular context, however, sex and gender are in almost every case understood and referenced as fused, so male equals masculine and female equals feminine. In mediated Mormonism this is also the case. Given this, I work to balance the gender-fluid objectives of scholarship with the gender-as-sex worldview of my subjects and textual examples, all as set within the mediation that catapults these ideas into the public sphere.

Indeed, while men are also implicated in the complex gender codes of Mormonism, the privilege of patriarchal authority (not surprisingly) gives natal men greater flexibility, status, personhood, and guarantees for the outcome of the Godhead.[2] Gendered dynamics are made all the more complicated in the F/LDS insistence on heteronormative desire and cis-gender identity. As I discuss more thoroughly in chapter 6 on queer politics, neither the mainstream nor fundamentalist churches recognize LGBT+ individuals or partnerships as viable unions eligible for personal exultation, celestial marriage, or family sealings. In the context of this chapter's discussion on women, lesbian and transgender women might as well be invisible, and, indeed, they are frequently excommunicated from the LDS church or expelled from the FLDS branches, making their absence virtually assured.

Yet the democratizing impulse of twenty-first-century media formats gives voice and presence to these persons. These include Marnie Freeman's (2014) *To the One: You Don't Get to Be Mormon and Lesbian, Even If You Were Born Both*; Alex Cooper's (2016) *Saving Alex: When I Was Fifteen I Told My Mormon Parents I Was Gay, and That's When My Nightmare Began*; Sue-Ann Post's (2005) *The Confession of an Unrepentant Lesbian Ex-Mormon*; Katherine Jean Denton's (2015) *Breaking Free: Gay Mormon Guilt Free*; Cindi Jones's (2011) *Squirrel Cage*; documentaries such as *Believer* (2018), produced by the rock band Imagine Dragons and starring the band's frontman Dan Reynolds, who was also the film's executive director; Pinterest sites such as Lesbian Mormon Poetry; independent documentaries such as *Transmormon* (2014); and YouTube channels or podcasts featuring the stories of transitioning Mormons.[3] These are but a small sampling of the insistent mediation that establishes the existence of queer difference in a tabula rasa of hegemonic sameness. This queer residue adheres to Mormonism even when, as in most cases, it is expressed from outside of Mormonism's center, post-excommunication. I examine Mormonism's negotiations with queer lives, identities, and desires at greater length in the next chapter.

In this chapter I go to the heart of toxic femininity by working through the mediation that surrounds the category of Mormon womanhood, in its pressures to be perfect, its affective imperative for happiness, and its mandate for obedience and social homogeneity. I look at these social practices amid Mormon women's struggles for agency and personhood, as circulated through a broad range of media including published memoirs, blog posts, YouTube videos, and news events. Indeed, within the vapors of toxic femininity and the restrictive measures manifest through strong codes of modesty and sexual purity, one of the more surprising social consequences of the restrictive gender codes of Happy Valley is that Mormonism fosters an exceptionally robust strain of political feminism.

Toxic Femininity and the Compulsory Logics of the Glow

Sometimes in Mormonism we go a little overboard on the striving for perfection stuff. There are lots of cultural rules (and gospel rules) that we feel guilty over because we aren't following like we think we "should" (or maybe the way other people think we "should"). "Should" is a pretty heavy burden to be carrying around all the time.

I'm not saying that everyone should (see—there it is) stop trying to do their best in whatever areas feel important to them. I'm suggesting that continuously holding ourselves to impossible standards is a recipe for mental health distress.—Alliegator, "When Striving for Perfection Just Makes Us Feel Bad about Ourselves," in *Feminist Mormon Housewives*

Let's begin with a fuller discussion of toxic femininity, a state of being that works against itself, in that it denies full personhood to those who are women and women-identified. In this, toxic femininity is not a synonym for femme (as in the femme fatale or the lesbian femme) or even heterofemininity. To be femme is an outward manifestation of style and demeanor. It is often (but not always) deliberate, values driven, and reinforcing of an ego state. By contrast, toxic femininity is corrosive, internalized, and shame filled. Toxic femininity is based on core beliefs that are not always cognitive but are always insistent: I'm not worthy. I don't deserve good things. I shouldn't bother people. Love and acceptance are conditional on my compliance. Toxic femininity works in negating imperatives: Don't take up too much space. Don't ask too many questions. Don't challenge orthodoxy. Don't upset others with your needs or concerns. Don't be unpleasant. Relying on a logic of compulsory heteronormativity, toxic femininity positions a girl or woman's value as first and foremost heterosexual. Her worth is thus conferred through male desire and secondary to male needs. It undermines her right to sexual expression and pleasure and makes her a device for achieving the goals of men and boys. In all of these ways, toxic femininity reinforces its own unworthiness by suggesting there is no a priori female self that merits priority, protection, or empowerment.

I want to be very clear about my discussion here. Toxic femininity is a prescriptive code, not a descriptive reality. It stands for an idea, and for some even an ideal, of gender, and thus I do not mean to indicate that any woman, Mormon or otherwise, is herself toxic or that femininity is in all cases contaminated. Instead, I hope to show that these forms of gender ideals function as impossible-to-achieve imperatives. And here I hasten to add that while Mormonism (both mainstream and fundamentalist) neither created nor solely perpetuates toxic femininity, the many screens sustaining mediated Mormonism witness toxic femininity's workings with remarkable clarity.

Described as "America's sweetheart" (Cooper 2018), entertainer and generational Mormon Marie Osmond offers a ready resource for seeing many of the characteristics of toxic femininity at work, sometimes reinforced and other times repudiated. In Osmond's memoir *Behind the Smile*, which details her long-term struggle with postpartum depression after the birth of her seventh child, she writes: "Sunk deep in depression, I found when I tried to throw myself a lifeline that I didn't have a self or even a life I could identify as my own" (Osmond, Wilkie, and Moore 2001, 15).[4] Why? Because, according to Osmond, "Women are caretakers by nature. We know how to fix things. I didn't need help. . . . I was the one who gave help" (15). Her job as entertainer, mother, and wife was exclusively other-oriented, she explains. Her function was "making everyone [else] happy" (25). She had no capacity to even discern her own needs, she confesses. "What defined me as an individual?" Osmond wonders. Her value had always been determined by others. "I had gone from a little girl who was her mother's helper to a businesswoman who took care of her coworkers, to a wife who took care of her husband, to a mother who took care of her children" (195). And though she was and is an international celebrity, Osmond acknowledges feeling like a hapless failure. "I had always felt the need to please, to fit in, to succeed, so I set aside my need and desire to explore on my own, fearing that I would fall short, make an irreversible mistake, or embarrass myself and my family" (213).

For some, Marie Osmond—with her wide smile, upbeat personality, and showbiz panache—personifies both Mormonism and a certain kind of hyperfemme glamour, what Judith Freeman calls "the Marie Osmond look" (2016, loc. 3687). For others, such as memoirist and scholar Joanna Brooks, Marie Osmond set the template for how to embody Mormon womanhood with style, grace, and celestial certitude. Brooks writes in *The Book of Mormon Girl* about turning twelve and being given *Marie Osmond's Guide to Beauty, Health and Style*: "She was, after all, someone I could really trust. A Mormon girl, for starters—and better yet, a rare kind of Mormon girl, just like me, with dark hair and a twinkle of definite ambition in her eye.... Who else could give me up-to-date but faith-tested insider information on 'turning 12 clothing separates into 3 dozen outfits,' 'ten hair do's and don'ts,' 'complexion routines for four kinds of skin,' and my 'three makeup personalities'" (Brooks 2012, 47–48). Much as I describe the workings of self-management in chapter 1, adhering to Marie Osmond's beauty principles constituted a time-managed exercise in personal governance and self-control. Brooks writes of following Osmond's "repertoire of routines essential to [her] personal transformation" (50), including self-scrutiny of skin type, aspired acquisition of "cosmetic, applicators and other beauty tools" (51), and the adoption of "Marie's 62-minute... early morning routine," which consisted of seventeen "numbered and precisely timed steps" (55) from calisthenics, to moisturizing the eyes, to hair styling, to breakfast. But Brooks also perceived, at least in hindsight, how Osmond's careful regime served as a religious system in itself for the indoctrination of a spiritualized toxic femininity:

> You and me, Marie, wrestling the dark energies of childhood depressions and nascent eating disorders. You and me, with visions of self-harm, dark impulses we could only describe as religious. These wars with our own bodies, how did we understand them but as a battle against the traitorous flesh that stood between us and our holiest inner selves, that stood between us and God?
>
> What to do with our bodies? If they were not instruments of priesthood power, and not yet instruments of eternal procreation, what was our purpose? It was you, Marie, who gave me the doctrine of the wardrobe grid, the seven quick and healthy breakfast plans, three makeup personalities, the sanctifying discipline of daily reducing exercises, the promise that I could have as much diet gelatin, chicken bullion, or vinegar-dressed salad as I wanted and still keep my diet virtue....

> Marie, your precisely numbered regimens gave me great comfort. Especially the idea that with a little practice, I could change, I could convert those long columns of personal minuses into a perfect string of plusses. (64)

For Brooks, and one might argue also for Osmond, the gospel of personal body management and gendered beautification provided a necessary function for the early adolescent girl, neither (and never) the bearer of priesthood power nor prepared for the years of continuous pregnancy that is the destiny of many Mormon women—indeed, Osmond reminisces in her memoir about motherhood, *The Key Is Love*, that her own mother, Olive Osmond, bore nine children and endured/experienced/enjoyed "twenty-five consecutive years of teenage children" and "twenty-two consecutive years of changing diapers" (Osmond and Wilkie 2013, 15).

Brooks also indicates that the major unexpressed function of these sanctified beauty rituals is to contribute to a woman's erasure by removing the flaws and distractions of the flesh, so that she might serve as an object of space, a window, a shimmering absence that allows for a greater divine (and male) presence: "I too wanted to be pure and clear, an open door, a spotless window. I wanted the love of God to shine brightly through me like a perfect frame, no bitten nails, or blemishes, or extra pounds, flyaway hairs, or personal character minuses to bar the view of His eternal brightness. What, after all, was the point of the small but burdensome body I freighted about in these middling years, when already I knew, I knew, that beyond this life was a place of total understanding, and already I hungered to evaporate into it" (2012, 63). We would be wise to remember Naomi Wolf's prescient observation about these sorts of evaporative fantasies with respect to weight loss and beauty regimes: "A cultural fixation on female thinness is not an obsession about female beauty, but an obsession about female obedience" (2001, 187). In this case, the Book of Mormon Girl desires an obedience so pure that, in her words, "I too might disappear" (Brooks 2012, 65).

In chapter 2, I discuss the trope of the Mormon Glow at some length, indicating its historic ties to Americanness and racialization, as well as its continuing presence as an epistemology of light that teaches to be bright and white is to be righteous and to be dark and dull is to be a sinner. In the context of this discussion on toxic femininity, the properties of the glow take on added meaning, for here the glow asks of women a form of self-immolation. It is the female Saint's absolute management of the body, the perfect obedience of her will, her unending commitment to perfectionism and cheerfulness that yields the prized goal—not of personhood but of dissolution into light.

These, of course, are not new ideas as they relate to female embodiment, norms of beautification, or to Western religious systems: the achievement of spiritual union between the female body and the transcendent god is often sexualized with tropes of light. Gendered acculturation for women and girls has likewise long stipulated erasure, smallness, being and becoming diminutive. In many religions, spiritual annunciation requires the absolute control and subordination of the body. The history of anorexia nervosa cannot be told, for instance, absent the backdrop provided by fasting nuns of the twelfth century, whose emaciation and paper-thin luminescent skin seemed to prove their closeness to the divine (see Vandereycken and van Deth 1994). As with so much else, Mormonism transports these features of the ancient spiritualized world not only into the lived experience of the modern but through the very devices and technologies of modernity. Indeed, if we take both self-help culture and self-improvement strategies to be technologies of identity in a postindustrial frame, as scholars such as Micki McGee (2005) and Anthony Giddens (1991) argue, then the incessant shaping, scrutinizing, and obsession with the body that Brooks describes through Osmond perfectly epitomizes the modern subject.

Further, if we consider the glow to be a prominent feature of not only a light-as-right epistemology but also of the imperative markers of feminized value, then Mormonism provides another vivid screen on which to witness its operation. As a colloquial referent, the glow is almost exclusively tied to women's experiences of what are considered to be the three major rites of passage in the heteronormative frame: when she falls in love, when she marries, and when she is pregnant, typically with her first child. In this, the glow is temporally bound; it marks the moment out of time, the nonquotidian, when something special and supposedly singular occurs. We often hear of glowing brides and luminous expectant mothers; we rarely hear of women who glow due to the personal accomplishments of a degree earned or a raise secured. For that matter, rearing children does not carry associations of the glow. Instead, in the words of Marie Osmond, the period of motherhood is the time when women need an especially good "under-eye concealer stick" with "incredible camouflaging capabilities," particularly when parenting infants and teenagers, since parental sleep deprivation is rampant during these stages of a child's life (Osmond and Wilkie 2013, 11).

In the broader aura that is hegemonic femininity, the glow is not only temporally bound; it is for the young: the dew of youth. Yet, across media,

FIG. 5.1 Bobbi Brown cosmetics ad, direct email, January 2017.

women of all ages and races are hailed to "develop your glow," to "awaken the glow" and to let the glow be the solution for the problem you didn't know you had (but certainly, you felt that something was not quite right). The glow, and other light-filled words indicating luminosity such as "sparkle," "brilliance," "brightness," and "shine," constitute a normative birthright—something immanent to a woman that can only be experienced through her active commitments for resuscitation and, typically, her continual purchase of just the right face cream, exfoliant, aesthetic procedure, diet, workout regimen. Rather than the glow being time-bound, natural, and only on offer for one or two years during the teens and twenties, the glow here functions as an elusive, critical, and enduring requirement of the worthy female self, available for those willing to work hard enough to achieve it. Indeed, there are even pedagogies in the contemporary mediascape on how to manage one's glow and prevent oneself from "glow-verload," an idealized state in which the glow is hyperarticulated (see figure 5.1). Even when the glow securely articulates itself, then, it is management that is most at the heart of these imperatives. The trick of these meritocratic claims and pedagogies for success? No amount of care or work is, or ever will be, sufficient for achieving and managing the glow in its consummate fullness.

As it pertains to LDS women, the glow reinforces a broader ideology of reflective beauty where the righteous Mormon woman visually signifies her adherence to the body/beauty-as-good motif. The properties of the glow fuse into an amalgam of attraction and attractiveness, where conventional forms of feminine beauty serve as evidence of righteous living and as lures for those who desire the rewards of sanctified living. Emily Pearson writes of her responsibility to "sparkle for the Lord" as part of her experience as a member of the Young Ambassadors, an LDS singing and dancing troupe. "It was our job to sing, dance, and above all else, smile as we shared the gospel of Jesus Christ through our Broadway Musical Review and Sunday night firesides" (Pearson 2012, loc. 2589). It was not lost on Pearson that her physical attractiveness was critical to the success of the appeal she offered audiences, particularly when her wardrobe notes included (in bold letters): "Emily P: WEAR PADDED BRA WITH EVERYTHING. THANKS. YOUR CLOTHES WILL LOOK BETTER." Pearson ruminates: "May as well have read: 'SISTER PEARSON: WE HAVE GOT TO GET YOU SOME TITS.' Heaven forbid my small breasts should ruin the entire show and keep hundreds, perhaps thousands, from feeling the love of Jesus Christ" (loc. 2626). Pearson's function in the Young Ambassadors was to serve as a bright object—a dazzling, glittering, sequined, "personification of all that was good, and pure, and joyful in the Mormon Church" (loc. 2652). Yet the brightness brings a dark side. "We sparkled so brightly," she recalls, "that no one would ever have been able to see into the shadows where, among the fifteen of us, there were a staggering number trying desperately to hide their homosexuality, eating disorders, cat fights and love triangles. We even had one future polygamist" (loc. 2652). Here we see a different aspect of the glow—it not only attracts the gaze but it blocks it, or at least obscures the process of seeing to such a degree that the gazer is blinded by its light.

In chapter 2, I argue that the Mormon Glow is often referenced as a particularly effective and irresistible tool in the arsenal of erotic attractiveness that Mormon girls use to draw their eternal companion and thus ensure their personal plan of happiness. "So, you're in love with a Mormon girl," writes Gale Boyd (2014) on *Mormon Hub*, congratulating her interpellated male, heterosexual, and Gentile reader. "You've been attracted to a girl who is glowing for all the right reasons, which means you chose her not because she was wearing black and red skin-tight jeggings from Frederick's of Hollywood. Aha! That's a clue you might be leaning toward the light yourself." The Mormon girl's gravitational pull is potent, writes Boyd: "The Mormon girl has the light of Christ shining through her, and you were drawn in." And the "lucky" fellow pulled into her orbit should anticipate not only the light of her beauty. He should know that he "will be expected to give the gospel a chance." Her glow is thus assurance of not only her own eternal progression but of the church's as well.

Radiating Mormon girls cannot help their luminescent attractiveness; their glow is simply a by-product (rather than a calculated effect) of pure living. Writes one LDS woman (unnamed) about living in Israel: "I can tell you that both the citizens of Israel and the Palestinian merchants in Jerusalem's Old City could identify a Mormon on sight, just by the 'Mormon glow' that studies have shown is palpable and identifiable by Mormons and non" ("Those Beautiful Mormon Girls" 2013).[5] While the writer attributes the glow to all Saints, she notes that this aura is particularly resonant for "those beautiful Mormon girls." In a series of examples, two are particularly telling:

> On the Fourth of July, the Jerusalem Center faculty and students joined Marines and U.S. Embassy staff for a picnic at a large park in downtown Jerusalem. The lunch was great, and a softball game ensued. Everyone was having a lot of fun, but the students had other commitments and had to abandon the game a little before its natural end. As the girls walked together across the diamond and up the hill to the buses, the Marines stood frozen in place, gazing after them, longingly, for a very long time. It seemed to me that they stood there even after the girls were out of sight. What was it that had made such an impression? All the girls were modestly dressed and clean-cut.
>
> A Sunday at the beach was even more interesting. The beach near Tel Aviv was managed by a nearby kibbutz and closed on Sundays. The kibbutz had reserved it during the closure for the BYU students to enjoy a day at the Mediterranean seaside. Again, the girls were dressed in modest swimsuits in [sic] a day when many European beach-goers wore nearly nothing. Two bus-loads of Israeli soldiers arrived in the spacious and empty parking lot so that the soldiers could buy lunch from the kiosk on the beach. In full uniform they filed from the parking lot to the kiosk, but a few stragglers made their way to the seaside. As one approached, he caught sight of the Mormon girls arrayed on the sand, at least 60 of them, glowing. Gradually, he eased from a slow walk to a little run and then raised his arms in the air to signify a rejoicing soul, and he began a slow spin. He looked like a dancer from Fiddler on the Roof. He looked like he had found heaven on earth. ("Those Beautiful Mormon Girls" 2013)

I leave it to my reader to determine if linking kibbutzniks, Israeli solidiers, and *Fiddler on the Roof* evidences a poverty of imagination that cannot see outside of reductive ethnic stereotypes. More importantly for my purposes is the way the glow is positioned as a reflective property immanent to Mormonism that exudes in a palpable, eroticized, and feminized manner, transfixing the soldier and the Jewish man (whom Mormons consider to be a Gentile) in a spiritualized scopophilia. The writer of this post notes that she sees "this kind of resolute, secure morality everywhere ... in Mormondom. Mormon girls know who they are. They are educated, talented, and beautiful inside and out" ("Those Beautiful Mormon Girls" 2013). The spiritualized allure—this composite of good choices and righteous living that makes itself visible on the bodies and faces of glowing teenage (and nubile) girls—here also functions as a sweetly provocative proselytizing tool for the mainstream Mormon Church.

As comments such as these clearly evidence, the glow is here understood to shine more brightly on and through girls who know themselves and "choose the right" (CTR)—the aura conveniently making itself legible through conventional signifiers of beauty. Choice is not only important in this formulation, it is critical to the glow. Indeed, CTR is a central component of the ethos of modesty and sexual chastity that binds all of Mormonism together, as I discuss later in this chapter. For now, I want to stay on this idea of the glowing Mormon girl as objectified lure.

Perhaps nothing makes this claim more salient than a discussion on a mail-order bride web forum called Happier Abroad that evaluates the pros and cons of F/LDS Mormon women as potential wives. Writes Winston (2013), "I just got back from traveling through Southern Utah and was impressed by how wholesome and friendly people there were. ... And the girls had this wholesome innocent look that is rare in America today. I think it's due to a combination of their Mormon religion which emphasizes a clean, pure, moralistic lifestyle, an inner glow in them that is divine, and the unparalleled beauty of the nature in Utah." Winston asks the hive mind if a Mormon girl would make a good prospective spouse, a question that generates seventy-two responses. In a viral village that can often generate thousands of reactions, seventy-two sounds modest, but it's helpful to be reminded of the niche within a niche that a question about Mormon women as wife material on a site dedicated to shopping for international brides otherwise connotes. Indeed, amid embedded images of available and, one presumes, desirable women, male-identifying responders sort out the dilemma of the Mormon woman: she seems perfect and glowing, but she is a demanding princess. She is uninterested in sex except for children. She will only marry a fellow Mormon. She will get fat, presumably the aftereffects of birthing many children as well as from all of the baked goods consumed in lieu of alcohol or tobacco.

Interestingly, for my purposes, these respondents (who identify as heterosexual men, both Mormon and non) denigrate Mormon women for being feminists, their glow functioning as a currency that has purchased them entitlement. Winston's first respondent, Bladed 11, notes in rather misogynist terms, "The only difference between them and other feminists is they are less whoreish but will likely still cheat on you if they can get a better deal. Most of them are snobby too. They are pure evil" (Winston 2013). Another responder, Tre, carries the conflation of Mormon women and feminism to a similarly woman-phobic conclusion:

> They absolutely do [have unrealistic expectations], they have their heads in the clouds. I grew up LDS and TRIED to date LDS women. They know they have plenty of options and they are nearly ALWAYS the "dumpers." These guys come off of those 2-year missions and have absolutely no idea how to deal with women around their age. They don't even know how to talk to girls anymore as they are 2-years without ANY practice. They are awkward and then get walked over. At the same time, young LDS women will ONLY date you if you are a returned Missionary or planning to go on a mission. Don't expect them to wait 2 years for you to get back though. Even if young men DO get married . . . guess who most often wears the pants in the relationship? Make no mistake, LDS women are FEMINIST. (Winston 2013)

None of the responders on this discussion board define what they mean by the term "feminist," but it is clear that Mormon women are like many AW (American women), in that they hold expectations for their partners and demand that their needs be considered. In this, we can see a rather surprising turn on the trope that suggests women in orthodox religions more generally and F/LDS women more specifically willingly participate in a patriarchal agenda, which calls for women's perpetual secondary role. As these respondents make clear, female needs of any sort code as feminist, a trait too threatening to be attractive, even amid the wholesome, glowing good looks that so powerfully pull unsuspecting male converts into their orbit.

Molly Mormons: "If You're Not Happy, You're Failing"

It was in Mrs. Torrey's class that we were told what to do if we ever felt as if we might get sick while listening to a concert. This really only applied to girls, she said. Don't try to leave in the middle of the music, she advised, disrupting other people in their seats, but instead just very quickly grab your handbag and empty the contents on your lap and throw up in your purse.
—Judith Freeman, *The Latter Days*

The expectation for feminized perfection of body and behavior both overlaps with and departs from the stereotype of the Molly Mormon (or MoMo), an idealized and largely mocked extreme of gender conformity within mainstream Mormonism.[6] The MoMo enacts the gender script of Mormon womanhood with scrupulous perfection: she is attractive, chaste until marriage, composed. Her house is spotless; her children well behaved. She always has a smile on her face. Her life revolves around marriage, family, and the church. She never disagrees with her priesthood husband, and she supports the church's social and political views without question. She is a helper and a giver, cheerful, resourceful, never a burden. As Nicole Hardy describes her, the MoMo goes against her own personal convictions in order to "be polite," sitting quietly in her church pew so that she might "pretend all [she] needed was a drink of water" (2013, 103). She would barf in her handbag to prevent someone else from being disturbed.

The ideography of Happy Valley—its simultaneous existence as a geographic location and an affective ideal—announces a specific concern, particularly for women: the unending pressure to be domestically passionate, logistically unflappable, and blissfully happy in all circumstances. These expectations create a life that for many feels like an emotional straitjacket of not-enoughness. In *Confessions of a Molly Mormon*, for example, Elona K. Shelley lays out the gendered aspirationalism that is part of the Molly creed:

> She was everything I aspired to. She was organized, efficient, and always in control. Not only was she an attentive and charming wife, she was also the mother of several immaculately groomed, brilliantly creative, and perfectly behaved children. . . .
>
> Her home was spotless yet comfortable. She sewed all of her family's clothing and promptly took care of any mending that needed to be done. Each week she made delicious whole wheat bread, often dropping off a loaf to someone who needed a little extra love or encouragement. She canned hundreds of jars of homegrown fruits and vegetables each summer and generously shared the bounties of her

flourishing garden. She served three delicious, carefully balanced meals every day, and of course she made full use of her ample food storage, which she rotated regularly. . . .

Without fail, Molly got up early each morning, studying the scriptures for at least thirty minutes before going out for an invigorating five-mile run. She magnified her church callings, volunteered at her children's school, worked on family history, and attended the temple every week. She also babysat for her neighbors so they, too, could go to the temple. No matter how much she had to do, she was always calm and pleasant. I could go on listing the virtues of this amazing woman, but I'm sure you already get the picture. Suffice it to say, Molly was absolutely everything I thought I should be. (2013, 3–4)

Shelley writes of her struggles to achieve the qualities of "inspiring Mollies," facing defeat at every step. "I couldn't seem to discipline myself enough to conquer even one of the many weaknesses plaguing my life *today*. Furthermore, in spite of my constant nagging—oops, I mean 'loving persuasion'—I couldn't get my husband and children to do everything I thought they were supposed to be doing, either" (4). The potential consequences of Shelley's lack of self-discipline (as she calls it) were enormous. "Regardless of my frantic attempts to prepare our family for that marvelous, celestial eventuality, it appeared that none of us were celestial material" (4). Shelley responded to the pressure through technologies of self-management: "I made endless lists of goals to avert the tragedy [of the separation of her family in the afterlife]. Whether I wrote them on paper or carried them around in my head, the lists were always there to remind me that I was completely and utterly failing. While my Molly Mormon obsession continued to thrive, the crushing weight of perfectionism left my guilt-ridden spirit struggling for survival" (6). The "chasm" between her "lofty ideals" and her everyday reality put her in a "losing battle with depression" (5).

Many have speculated that these pressures for female perfection are precisely why Utah, which is 62 percent LDS, leads the nation in antidepressant use, with women being prescribed SSRIs such as Prozac, Paxil, and Zoloft at twice the rate they are prescribed for men. While it cannot be proved that Utah's majority Mormon culture is the direct cause of the high rate of prescription drug use, the correlation is compelling. The relentless demand for optimistic cheerfulness in both men and women has, according to mediated reflections in blogs, documentaries, and memoirs, created a culture of denial and despondency in church members, who often paper over their bad feelings for the sake of obedience and perfectionism.[7] These tendencies are particularly acute for women, who bear the brunt of sustaining the nurturing happy homemaker image as a stay-at-home mother and nurturer of a priesthood husband and many children. Dr. Curtis Canning, president of the Utah Psychiatric Association, speculated to the *LA Times*: "In Mormondom, there is a social expectation—particularly among the females—to put on a mask, say 'Yes' to everything that comes at her and hide the misery and pain. I call it the 'Mother of Zion' syndrome. You are supposed to be perfect because Mrs. Smith across the street can do it and she has three more kids than you and her hair is always in place. I think the cultural issue is very real. There is the expectation that you should be happy, and if you're not happy, you're failing" (Cart 2002). This is Betty Friedan's (1964) "problem with no name" in a different key, though equally tied to the middle-class, white, heterosexual women who are the focus of *The Feminine Mystique*. Here we see that malaise and depression haunt the visage of the idealized Mormon woman.

How to deal with Molly Mormon and the Mother of Zion syndrome? Kill her. The MoMo is a dangerous fiction, writes Lisa Ray Turner:

> If we are too anxious and overwhelmed, our relationships with each other suffer. Sisterhood fizzles in such a volatile pressure-cooker. Our friendships become counterfeit. Healthy, give-and-take connections are not possible if we always wear our Sunday faces, afraid our real selves are unacceptable. Sisterhood will elude our grasp if we continue to pursue the fictitious Molly Mormon prototype. We will never be as spiritual, knowledgeable, or kind as this mythical creature—just as horses will never be unicorns. The Typical Mormon Woman, much like the unicorn, is one-dimensional. Happily, Real Mormon Women are not. We are blessed with unique gifts and strengths, as well as idiosyncrasies and weaknesses. Thank goodness! Diversity enriches and deepens our bonds. Sisterhood happens when we permit each other to be human. (Turner 1993)

For Turner, staging a requiem for the Typical Mormon Woman (paralleling Virginia Woolf's admonition to kill the Angel in the House) actually allows for the Real Mormon Woman to flourish.

But let's be clear: the Real Mormon Woman is an equally idealized trope. The more realistic Mormon woman must still make good on the exhaustive list of tasks assigned to her under Mormonism (childbearing, child rearing, domestic management including freshly baked bread and the preparation of years of stored preserves, church relief society, journaling, genealogy projects, daily prayer and scripture devotions, monthly fasts, visits to the homebound, Relief Society, family home evening, temple rituals, journaling, etc.), and she still must safeguard the worthiness of her husband and children for the highest of Mormon heavens, and she still must be cheerful. The LDS prescriptive codes for eternal advancement, in which earthly deeds directly build into heavenly rewards, make every feature of living not only important but critical to eventual residence in a celestial paradise. In this regard, the Molly Mormon stereotype functions as an ideological release valve, allowing more flawed versions of Mormon womanhood to hold hegemonic sway since they can be perceived as less extreme and more attainable by contrast. The Real Mormon Woman might engage with these imperatives somehow relieved by the perfectionism creed exerted by the Molly Mormon. It seems the very epitome of a Pyrrhic victory.

So even if the good Mormon girl has made peace with the cartoonish perfectionism of the Molly Mormon, she must still contend with the threat—implied and overt—that her failure to behave according to conventional gender scripts will result in hellish outcomes, for the girl herself, for her later womanhood, and for the unborn spirits that rely on her compliance to enter the mortal frame. Indeed, without the Mormon girl's buy-in to the pact of childbearing and family nurturing, the eternal progression of Mormonism's promises are dead before they can ever begin. As the epigraph that opens this chapter attests, the good Mormon girl must therefore be scrupulous, self-aware, and conscientious, working to subvert her baser and more selfish instincts in the service of the larger, divine good.

One of these baser instincts is resisting the rightness of the church and its fathers, since those who question will experience what Laura Roper Andreasen, the granddaughter of a church apostle, describes as "the shame attached to not being faithful" (Dehlin 2015b). On the topic of critical thinking, Heidi Bernahard-Bubb illustrates her own experience: "I wanted to keep being a good girl, one who didn't stay up late thinking about scary questions, so I never told anyone about the nights I stayed up, my seven-year-old self plagued with anxiety over where God came from. If God had created me, who had created God? I didn't know why, but asking felt like it would break my whole world apart. . . . I wanted to keep being a good girl, one who didn't stay up late thinking about scary questions, so I stuffed my first crisis of faith down deep" (2016, loc. 784). Emily Pearson reinforces this idea of doubting as a dangerous form of resistance in a chapter tellingly titled "Doormat of the Damned," saying simply and ominously, "It was dangerous to question the church and the brethren" (2012, loc. 3667).

Though I did not grow up Mormon, I had my own experience with toxic femininity and the sin of critical thinking in a scene I detail in the afterword: As a teenager, I entered a heated debate on the nature of the Mormon Godhead with a patriarchal authority in the LDS Church. Though I probably scored a number of intellectual points in our tussle, I felt far from victorious. Indeed, I felt shame and a tinge of personal inadequacy, believing I had acted wrongly by behaving boldly. The subtext of the exchange was clear: do not be difficult; do not be too smart; do not challenge men, particularly those in authority. It's why I still feel myself shaken in inexplicable ways when I push back against my father or the dean of my college, as if I have done something unseemly. And in February 2017, after I posted a politicized call to arms urging people to send postcards to the White House, two of the LDS friends on my Facebook feed unfriended me on the grounds that I was unfriendly. *"You have always been a lovely person. But if you don't have anything nice to say, you shouldn't say anything at all."* I will admit that their public disapproval bothered me. The angel is so hard to kill. And while this form of prescriptive pleasantry is not by any means exclusive to the Mormon Church, I do have a new appreciation for the particularly virulent form of gender instruction that girls and women within both the mainstream and fundamentalist churches experience.

Indeed, the relentless teleology of eternal progression, what Naomi Watkins calls the "Plan A" life, keeps firmly in place not only the domestic proficiency and affective cheerfulness of the Molly Mormon but also the appearance of the glowing Mormon girl. "At church, I learned what to expect from a Plan A life: meet a returned missionary, date, fall in love, get married, have a basketball team of babies, and live happily ever after. To make Plan A happen, I needed to be sweet and kind. I needed to cook and sew. I needed to be pretty (Watkins 2016, loc. 1710). Much as in mainstream culture, "I need to be pretty" tends to be the basso continuo sounding insistently below these messages of Mormon womanhood. In this logic of spiritual neoliberalism, prettiness thus serves as an earthly down payment on a heavenly paradise.

Given the young ages (typically eighteen to twenty-four) at which most Mormon women begin the heteronormative work of attracting a husband, the equally young age at which they start bearing children, the high number of children they are expected to birth (and thus the degree that multiple pregnancies alter a woman's adult body), and the larger connection to the glow as goodness, it's hardly any wonder that Utah boasts more plastic surgeons per capita than any other state in the Union. That unique fact and Utah's high consumption of beauty-enhancing products, such as facial cosmetics and hair dye, caused *Forbes* to crown Salt Lake "America's vainest city" (Ruiz 2012). Writing for *Deseret News*, the Utah-based Mormon-owned newspaper, Marjorie Cortez took faux issue with *Forbes*'s use of the word "vain," suggesting that it wasn't vanity but insecurity that propelled Salt Lake City to the top of the charts. "As people in a small American city, we want very much for the world to take us seriously. We want very much to put our best foot forward. But not until it has been waxed, tanned, manicured, the unsightly veins removed and the extra fat purged through liposuction. Come to think of it, we may very well be vain" (Cortez 2007).

The major roads and highways going in and out of Salt Lake City are sprinkled liberally with ads for cosmetic surgery: billboards promising women a gift of perfect breasts for the benefit and satisfaction of their men or guaranteeing women that they might become an object of desire, even to themselves (see figures 5.2 and 5.3). The predominance of these ads is so strong that it has prompted beauty blog writer Emily Woodruff (2017) to note, "Utah's Mormons can't get tattoos, piercings or even drink green tea, but appear to be getting plastic surgery in droves. What gives?" Her conclusions are that the high level of homogeneity and like-mindedness in Happy Valley combined with the culture of perfectionism and conventional norms of femininity for women (wide eyes, perky breasts, youthful glowing skin, and straight white teeth) make plastic surgery culture normative. Woodruff quotes Amy Smith, a thirty-three-year-old Mormon and mother of two who has had both breast augmentation and liposuction. Smith presently lives in Utah but formerly resided in Los Angeles: "There is this weird thing in Utah. In Los Angeles, people accept you for who you are and being different is valued, but here it's very 'keeping up with the Joneses.' You have to try to be perfect, everyone is kind of cookie-cutter and everyone looks the same. I think that the [popularity of] plastic surgery has to do with the image of being perfect. That's very big in Mormon culture. If you're different, you're kind of ostracized" (Woodruff 2017).

Even given the ever-presentness of these literal billboards for personal enhancement, feminist resistance percolates. Writes Nicole Bullock (2013), "Utah's freeways are littered with billboards . . . which tell women they are not beautiful enough until they choose plastic surgery." Bullock finds this message offensive. She also takes issue with the frequent lessons on chastity and modesty Mormon girls are often subjected to as part of their weekly religious indoctrination. Mormon women are often, in Bullock's words, "given lectures full of propaganda about why their dress and appearance will be the downfall of men," men who will be led astray by a hint of lace or cleavage. Bullock argues

FIG. 5.2 Billboard advertising plastic surgery, I-95, Utah.

FIG. 5.3 Billboard along Interstate 15, which runs through the Mormon corridor of Utah.

FIG. 5.4 The blame-the-victim mentality of modesty culture.

(meme included, see figure 5.4) that it is "much easier to ask women to dress like shapeless, sexless adolescents than to expect men to think and act like decent human beings," a feminist sentiment of particular resonance.[8]

I want to be clear: I am not opposed to plastic surgery. Indeed, I see it as a particularly effective and often agentive tool for achieving one's goals within a culture of ideals that makes success for women otherwise elusive. Say what you will about the moral complexities of plastic surgery, but as a technology of self-change designed to earn women greater points within a rigged system of beauty culture, it gets the job done. So I do not mean to vilify Happy Valley for its high reliance on plastic surgery and other forms of cosmetic rejuvenation that are often practiced within it but to indicate the way that a happy Mormon affect and pretty appearance effectively function as microcosms of a larger American culture that is committed to appearance as the visual manifestation of ideals of meritocracy (effort earns rewards), image-as-currency, and beauty-as-goodness. The glow here puts a spotlight on the spectacular pleasure and anxiety of being looked at and suggests that modifying the body to maximize the glow is one way to survive the surveillance of the gaze.

These questions about gazing and the gaze raise old debates within feminist theory. The notion that women are rightfully the objects of the gaze and men are the gazers (in John Berger's words, "Men act and women appear" [1990, 47]) reinforces a norm of masculinized agency and feminized passivity that feminism as a system of thinking and consortium for political change has long sought to critique and undermine—with great success, I might add. Yet we err if we believe that the mandates of toxic femininity as they assert themselves through bodily markers have been completely eradicated. Even in the midst of new modalities of power and possibility for women and new horizons for gender inclusion and LGBT+ diversity, toxic femininity continues as a hegemonic system that influences the intersubjective experience of woman-centered selfhood.

It is not so much that toxic femininity and the glow are common in Happy Valley or that plastic surgery might do much to heighten one's currency in a dysfunctional system of value where beauty for women is a stand-in for goodness and worth. Instead, my argument is that Mormon women often exemplify a set of gender ideals long considered a thing of the past, ideals and even norms that are still active, pervasive, and pernicious in twenty-first-century Western hegemonic culture. In a political moment in which many strains of toxic femininity are still present—even while popular postfeminist discourses argue for their disappearance—mediated Mormonism offers a potent set of strategies for how to detect and resist them. Think of it like this: if toxic femininity is, metaphorically speaking, a resurgent old-world disease long thought defeated, like polio or smallpox, mediated Mormonism provides a petri dish allowing for the careful observation and study of the illness. As C. L. Hanson observes, "Sure, it's not just Mormonism—girls also get these sorts of negative messages about their own value and importance from the culture at large. But Mormon culture shouts at them with a megaphone" (Hanson 2016, loc. 3932). In this amplified dynamic, mediated Mormonism offers a composite screen that renders generally opaque gender dynamics more discernible. Indeed, it may well be precisely because Mormon-centered and produced media so blatantly stage the inculcation, internalization, and resistance of these gender codes that it holds such an intense fascination for a broader public.

Through its many screens, mediated Mormonism allows viewers to play voyeur to a set of gender prescriptions that seem restrictive, regressive, and even anachronistic—yet it also implicates the reader, the viewer, the spectator in a gendered world that may feel uncomfortably familiar and contemporary. Like the ambient glow from a thousand television screens, mediated Mormonism spreads a diffused light that makes visible a network of gendered objectives that have implications far outside F/LDS cultures. Nowhere is that relevance clearer than in the way Mormonism is made to do a larger cultural work around the meanings and implications of sexuality for girls and women, a point I discuss in the next two sections.

Elizabeth Smart: "Just Be Happy"

I want people to know that "these things" [rape, being sold into slavery, abuse] happen, but it doesn't have to define your life. You can move forward and you can be happy.—Elizabeth Smart quoted in Alan Duke, "Elizabeth Smart: 'I Couldn't Be Happier'"

Perhaps no Mormon girl has captured the twenty-first-century collective consciousness quite like Elizabeth Smart, who was abducted from her home in Sandy, Utah, on June 5, 2002, at the age of fourteen by Brian David Mitchell, who considered himself a fundamentalist polygamist prophet in search of a new wife. Given that the long history of Mormonism not only allows for but deifies self-nomination to prophet status, Mitchell's belief in his own power is not so incredible. Yet the national and international discourses attached to Smart's abduction and rescue play on fears of fanaticism, extremism, and the bizarre underworlds of the cultish. As I discuss in chapter 4, polygamous or fundamentalist Latter-day Saints adhere to a titillating rendition of religious extremism that often positions them as an American Taliban, fueled by unswerving devotion to a set of values perceived to be vastly outside of the American middle stream.

Elizabeth Smart struck a particular chord, as a young, white, innocent, and virginal girl, kidnapped from her bedroom in the dark of night, and forced to endure nine months of captivity and daily rape before she was freed. The abduction, which occurred less than six months after Salt Lake City's shimmering presence on the global stage as host to the 2002 Winter Olympics, reminded the world of Mormonism and its darker polygamist history. When Smart was rescued in March 2003, the world breathed a sigh of relief that the happy, golden, blonde-haired girl was now reunited and returned to her family idyll. But how does the perfect Mormon family—and the budding Molly Mormon at its center—carry on and "be happy" after abduction, rape, rumor, and an "increasingly invasive" media? (Nelson 2012).[9] In this case, by willing herself to happiness, by not dwelling on her trauma, by trusting God to demand restitution and recommitting herself not only to be unphased by her experience but to be happy in relation to it.

Near the end of her memoir, *My Story*, Smart recalls a moment when her mother pulled her away from her jubilantly celebrating family:

> "This is important," [Lois Smart] started. . . .
>
> "Elizabeth, what this man has done is terrible. There aren't any words that are strong enough to describe how wicked and evil he is! He has taken nine months of your life that you will never get back again. But the best punishment you could ever give him is to be happy. To move forward with your life. To do exactly what you want. Because, yes, this will probably go to trial and some kind of sentencing will be given to him and that wicked woman [Mitchell's other wife, Wanda Barzee]. But even if that's true, you may never feel like justice has been served or that true restitution has been made. . . .
>
> "You be happy, Elizabeth. Just be happy. If you go and feel sorry for yourself, or if you dwell on what has happened, if you hold on to your pain, that is allowing him to steal more of your life away. So don't you do that! Don't you let him! There is no way he deserves that. Not one more second of your life. You keep every second for yourself. You keep them and be happy. God will take care of the rest." (Smart and Stewart 2014, 285–86)[10]

Smart calls her mother's words "the best advice that anyone has ever given me" and credits the plea for resistance with changing her life from that point forward (Smart and Stewart 2014, 285). We can well understand why, since Lois Smart freed her daughter from a potential future of self-recrimination and bitter indignation. But her mother's sentiments also robbed Elizabeth Smart of the expression of negative feelings. While the admonition to be happy is in some way a license for a better life, it is also an implication that sexual trauma is too dark to be aired. To spend time dwelling on her experience is to fill the world with the darkness of her pain; it is also to mitigate the justice God will exact. *Let go and let God.*

For her part, Smart converted the media attention her abduction and rescue garnered to her own advantage, parlaying her celebrity as a national figure of female suffering into a public platform as pundit and crusader on behalf of children. Popular media went along with her. In October 2003, her parents published *Bringing Home Elizabeth* with the major publishing house Doubleday; in November 2003, NBC premiered *The Elizabeth Smart Story*, a fictionalized made-for-TV telling of Elizabeth's story (now available on DVD). Smart also hit the talk show circuit, from Oprah Winfrey and Meredith Viera to Anderson Cooper and Larry King. Tabloids, National Public Radio, and papers such as the *New York Times* and *Boston Globe* sought out her story. In April 2006, Smart's uncle, Tom Smart, coauthored *In Plain Sight*, a retelling of the legal dimension of Smart's case; in 2011, Elizabeth Smart became a guest commentator with ABC News, primarily commenting on missing children cases. In 2013 she published *My Story*, a memoir of her experience. In 2017, A&E aired *Elizabeth Smart: Autobiography*, a two-part retelling of her abduction and abuse, and *I Am Elizabeth Smart*, a fictionalized re-creation of her story. In 2018 and as evidence that Smart's abduction still puts her (and Mormonism) in the national Zeitgeist, *USA Today* selected Smart's new publication, *Where There's Hope*, for its national book conversation (the book is a reflection on resiliency, featuring her own experience as well as twelve other stories of adversity and resilience in the lives of public figures, many of whom are LDS). This bounty of media certainly follows the Mormon affective credo of turning lemons into lemonade, though one wonders if writing a memoir, becoming a national activist, speaking frequently on the college lecture circuit, and serving as a spokesperson for abducted children and on-air commentator for ABC News counts as inappropriately dwelling on her experience. The outcome of that question is between Elizabeth Smart and Happy Valley. Even so, I do find myself pondering when she was allowed to howl with rage and pain because she was kidnapped, raped, and tortured.

As a cultural meme, Elizabeth Smart has been made to serve a semiotic role as the very epitome of innocent victim, who triumphs over adversity by refusing to engage with it and later is rewarded with happiness and the restoration of the marriage plot. *People* magazine, arguably the U.S.'s most prominent and trustworthy tabloid, offers strong evidence. *People* put Elizabeth on its cover six times (see figures 5.5–5.9).[11] There have been no features or cover considerations of Elizabeth since 2012. Apparently, marriage and motherhood assure us that Elizabeth is normal again, her story now simply a happy woman's life that does not need featuring in the pages of *People*, so often committed to profiling celebrities and hard-luck stories.

In these articles, Smart's innocence and victimization are heightened by her abduction while sleeping, spirited away in her pajamas, so she can't be repurposed through blame-the-victim rhetoric that would discount the tragedy of her kidnapping by claiming she was in the wrong place at the wrong time or wearing provocative clothing. Her victimization is sealed by the brutal daily rapes and mental harassment she endured. She writes, "Before, I was just your average Mormon girl. And since everything I've gone through, there's been a lot of learning and growing. I've learned to listen and not jump to conclusions. I'm not sorry this happened to me anymore, because it made

FIGS. 5.5–5.9 *People* magazine's archive of Elizabeth Smart's pain and triumph: "Their Untold Story," November 3, 2003; "My Untold Story," June 23, 2008; "Her Fight for Justice," October 19, 2009; "Elizabeth Smart Engaged!," February 2012; "Elizabeth Smart's Dream Wedding!," March 2012.

FIG. 5.6

FIG. 5.7

FIG. 5.8

FIG. 5.9

me grow up. It is important to remember that just because something bad happens to you, it doesn't mean you are bad. You are still entitled to every possible happiness in life" ("Kidnap Victim Elizabeth Smart" 2006).

More broadly, the national rhetoric about Elizabeth Smart suggests that she might now only choose happiness precisely because she did not choose kidnap and rape, here the logic of choice relying on a trauma narrative that can be exploited but in the case of Elizabeth Smart will never be affectively expressed. Indeed, in a similar representational mode, Smart's celebrity also puts her in a passive role. As she writes, "I never asked for or wanted this platform, but it is what it is, so I'm determined to use it to help others" (2018, xii). Unlike Warren Jeffs's victims, we need never fear that she will show rage or indignation, that she will make hearing her story too difficult for the listener, that she will be anything but the good Mormon girl. Indeed, she is eerily cheerful and even funny as she recounts her experiences, even while, as in the A&E biography special, her mother's howls of pain provide the emotional backdrop to her story.

In sum, the symbolic association of Elizabeth Smart as a figure of redemptive happiness very much requires this other story of sexual harm for its anchor. Her story has ascended to national morality tale precisely because Smart chose to get over it. Blogger Carol Shaw Johnston (2008) praises Smart for her ability to "rise above" the kidnapping:

> What impressed me most about Elizabeth Smart is that she has refused to be a "victim." The first night she was home after her abduction, she insisted on sleeping in her own bed—the bed from which she had been abducted nine months earlier. She proved to others—and herself—that she would still be there in the morning. Many people would let that horrific experience scar them for life. They might move to get away from the bad memories and associations. Instead, Elizabeth has learned from it and resolved to make her life better. She has taken charge of her own life and has refused to let that experience define who she is. She is a brave and impressive young woman.

Based on a survey of Johnston's publicly available social media, she appears to be Christian but not Mormon. So the point is not that Mormons recognize Elizabeth's commitments to emotional self-regulation but that these qualities—to refuse to become a victim, to resolve to make her life better, to "refuse to let that experience define who she is"—are broadly recognizable within U.S. culture and articulate affective behaviors considered worthy of praise and admiration.

The Mormon economy of emotion here speaks to and makes legible a very specific nationally valued affect. Indeed, it may well be because the long story of Mormonism is itself so grounded in suffering—through nineteenth-century pogroms and hate crimes, dispossession and imprisonment, murder and war—that the faith now so fully is allowed to stand in for a temperament of happiness through an ethos of optimism and not-talking-about-it-ness. The Latter-day Saints are often referred to as the American Jews, largely because of the suffering and oppression they have experienced. But Judaism is very much dedicated to a world ethos of never forgetting atrocities and pogroms such as the Holocaust. *There is power in saying its name.* Mormonism, by contrast, articulates a different code of suffering—historical pain can be remembered and used as the impetus for celebrations (as in the annual Pioneer Day celebration), but individual, ongoing, and contemporary trauma is to be willed away. In this, Elizabeth Smart chooses the right, not just in how her choices underscore a mind-over-matter approach to violations of basic human decency, but in how her very function as a cultural meme—the Mormon virgin who was grievously wronged but doesn't hold a grudge—reinforces how we understand and talk about both sexuality and sexual assault.

The obsequious demands of toxic femininity require placing oneself in a diminished role in relation to a more powerful partner, who uses physical, sexual, financial, emotional, or psychological actions or threats of actions to gain or maintain power over another person. As I note, this trained subservience makes it difficult to put up barriers to harassment, incest, and rape. As Marie Osmond describes her own experience of childhood sexual abuse, she felt she had "no right to personal boundaries" (Osmond, Wilkie, and Moore 2001, 20).[12] In more general terms, Osmond had learned the double negative, not to say no, "because I [didn't] want to seem uncaring. In my mind, taking care of myself by saying no to a request [meant] that someone else might have to go without" (97). Here Osmond epitomizes the good girl, who works to suppress her own needs so that others might have theirs met first.

When safety verges into and overlaps with desire and sexualized violence, these codes of the good girl become all the more problematic, since they are both internalized and systematized. The Mormon flagship university, BYU, for example, has a long-standing code of conduct that forbids students from engaging in sexual activities. One consequence that has stemmed from the school's honor code has been a greater reticence for women about reporting sexual assault, since these women are frequently brought up on honor code violations related to modesty. It was only in 2016 that BYU began to consider shelter provisions that would protect students who report sexual assault from also being investigated for honor code violations (Brown 2016). In a similar way, Bonnie Ricks (2012) reflects in *The Mormon Woman . . . Goddess or Second Class Citizen?* that the enormous pressures for perfectionism put on LDS women make any potential flaw a major moral failure. If a woman is raped, the mandate for sexual purity erases her personal worth. Ricks relates a personal anecdote from an ex-Mormon: "She told me that her father refused to have anything to do with her after she was raped. The perpetrator was never caught. But her father was furious with her that she had fought to live and succeeded! He said she should have let the man kill her, because she was of no use now that she 'had sinned and lost her virginity.' This line of thinking is almost identical to Sharia law, under which a woman can be given the death penalty for surviving a rape" (2012, loc. 1970). It's not by accident that Mormons are here explicitly linked with Muslims, the notion of godly law unjustly taking precedent over national legislation. More perplexingly, the unbending commitment to sexual chastity and affective pleasantness effectively works to rob the assault victim of his or her personhood.[13]

FIG. 5.10 Rebecca Musser's Creed: *Red Flags for Girls*.

I am my own best friend.

I watch out for myself. I protect myself in the way I think, the things I do, and the people I choose in my life. I think healthy thoughts and choose healthy actions that are right for me and bring the best outcomes for my life. I stand up for myself and I forgive myself. I wish success for myself physically, relationally, spiritually, and financially.

I recognize that every choice has results and consequences. I choose wisely.

I am honest about my behavior and the behavior of others. I have clear and healthy boundaries in all of my relationships. I interact with empathy and I am conscious about my rights and the rights of others.

I ask for what I need and want in healthy ways. When situations or relationships are difficult or uncomfortable, I seek guidance from those I trust. I keep myself safe in every way and I am a voice for others when they are not safe. I am true to my feelings and my dreams. I give myself permission to grow, permission to make mistakes, and permission to succeed. My life has infinite value and purpose.

With respect to modern values of consent and choice, then, female worthiness and sexual purity are made to be the discursive doulas that birth personhood in the modern moment. The willingness of Mormon women to reference, even if not always to discuss, their experiences of childhood sexual abuse, sexual repression, and sexual knowledge gives voice and intelligibility to the connections between gender socialization, personhood, and freedom. Here the public interest in Mormon sex lives fulfills a broader feminist objective of giving women voice and the rights of resistance. For example, Rebecca Musser—once famous for being the witness who wore red to testify against FLDS prophet Warren Jeffs—now is a public advocate for human rights. In addition to her memoir about fleeing FLDS polygamy, Musser (2014) has produced a DVD called *Red Flags for Girls*, designed to teach girls and women how to fight toxic femininity at its root (see figure 5.10).

Important for this discussion, the Red Flags Creed asks girls to be mindful about self-protection, personal boundaries, personal worth, and individual choice. Adherents are asked to pledge, "I recognize that every choice has results and consequences. I choose wisely." Even in its efforts to free women and girls from emotional manipulation, however, the Red Flags Creed sounds the tones of a spiritual neoliberalism, which suggest that those who do not "choose wisely" make themselves vulnerable to abuse. If a girl violates the creed's rules for self-protection, she is to blame for her own victimization. The creed also echoes an ethos of self-determination that is critical to the American project. Musser declares, "Choose to be free!" Much as we saw in the case of Elizabeth Smart, woman-centered liberation here is positioned as the triumph of mind over matter. Yet Musser concedes, "If a girl didn't even *know* she had a choice, she had no choice" (2014, 226). Choice and consent here unfold as puzzles rather than platitudes. Freedom and a happy life depend on free choice, except that "free" is a term with no stable referent, since a culture of sociality and emotional coercion eliminates choices before they can ever manifest.

It is because of these ambiguities around what counts as brainwashing and mind control that the powers of desire play such a large epistemological function. For many Mormons who have had a crisis of conscience and decided to leave either the fundamentalist or mainstream churches, it has often been the restrictive culture around sexuality that has caused the final rupture into knowing. This is particularly true for those whose sexuality is out of sync with the F/LDS Church's edict on heterosexual identity. In *To the One*, for instance, Marnie Freeman writes of her emerging awareness of being a woman-loving woman in the context of a mainstream LDS culture that equated lesbianism with the gravest of sins. "If you were to be hung on a cross," said her bishop when she sought guidance, "you would belong between a murderer and a pedophile" (Freeman 2014, 45). Like so many other memoirists, Freeman poignantly details her efforts to toe the Mormon line, continually pledging and repledging to the heteronormative code of eternal progression. Each failure left her feeling more and more worthless. Choosing her self required leaving a system that could not accommodate her personhood. "I sobbed through the night about the Mormon life I had to leave behind," she recalls, "the people, my family, the clear lines, the caring community, the safety, the pre-set path. I had worked so hard to keep it together, but now I understood it was an impossible undertaking. Hope of being Mormon and gay moved out of my heart, and a haunting emptiness moved in. You don't get to be a Mormon and a lesbian, even if you were born being both" (122).

While the F/LDS churches do explicitly forbid homosexuality, violation of sexuality mandates is not exclusively an LGBT+ concern. In *Confessions of a Latter-day Virgin*, for instance, Nicole Hardy offers what can only be understood as a feminist cri de coeur. She writes that girls were insistently told, "'there is no role in life more essential and more eternal than that of motherhood'" (2013, 34). While Hardy said she was willing to believe this edict, she also didn't feel its truth. She wanted to be a writer. Desiring to break out of the stereotype of the Mormon woman who is obedient and enthusiastic about mothering, Hardy also speaks of craving intimacy, affection, and love.

> How condescending to be told that the time before marriage is a time of "preparing" or "creative waiting." To be reminded that nothing I have done is good enough, nor will it be, to grant me access to the highest level of exaltation. To be told that my life has consisted of a series of placeholders.
>
> How can [people] understand how frustrating it is: on the one hand, to *want* marriage—because it's the vehicle to love, sex, and intimacy—and on the other to know that the word "wife" is defined so narrowly in our community that it can't fit me. There is not room for what I feel, what I'm drawn to, what I'm good at. My leaders tell me what my gifts are, and they're wrong. They tell me what my nature is, and they're wrong. They tell me what my purpose is, and I feel nothing. (2013, 159)

Hardy remained in the church until her midthirties, working to reconcile her need for a rewarding professional and personal life with the church's mandate for married motherhood. The "tortured strain of self-denial," as Carlene Bauer (2013) termed it in a review for the *New York Times*, coupled with the increasingly unlikely possibility that Hardy could find an LDS man who was "wickedly funny, politically liberal, brighter than the average bear and uncommitted to 1950s gender roles" (not to mention a man who in his thirties was not already sealed to another woman) became too heavy a burden for her to bear. Ultimately, she found more soul-sustaining joy outside the church than within it.

Ordain Women: Feminist Throwdowns

I believe that many Mormon women—even those who have chosen very traditional roles and don't ask many questions—have an uneasy feeling that when women's minds and hearts and voices are peripheral and not central, everyone loses. Women have no power in our church, no voice and zero authority. No wonder there's so much depression among my Mormon sisters.—Carol Lynn Pearson, *The Ghost of Eternal Polygamy*

The good Mormon girl said, "I am fine." . . . For too long we have been seduced into walking a path that did not lead us to ourselves. For far too long we have said yes when we wanted to say no. And for far too long we have said no when we desperately wanted to say yes. . . . I am growing beyond my own conditioning, breaking set with what was breaking me.—Terry Tempest Williams, *When Women Were Birds*

On the HBO series *Big Love*, the tensions and passions of plural marriage play out in gloriously long-form serialization, as Bill Henrickson and his three wives, Barb, Nicki, and Margene, negotiate living independent fundamentalist polygamy in a modern enclave, the Salt Lake City suburb of Sandy. While much about this show is relevant to my overall conversation on mediated Mormonism, it is first wife Barb's personal and spiritual journey that I want to focus on as a concluding meditation in this chapter. We are meant to understand that prior to the show's diegetic open, Barb had been raised in a conventional LDS household, the mainstream church's teachings and practices dear to her heart. As a teenager, Barb falls in love with Bill, a lost boy who had been forcibly ejected from a fundamentalist compound run by the prophet Roman Grant. Barb and Bill's union represents a triumph of LDS over FLDS, of new world versus old. But when Barb faces a cancer scare and is unable to have more children than the three she has already borne, Bill receives a prophetic message from God commanding him to practice plural marriage, which, in turn, requires breaking from the Saints and, ultimately, forming his own church, the New Assembly of Mormon Pioneers.

The show begins in medias res, with Barb and Bill already united with Nicki and her two sons (by Bill), and babysitter Margene soon to become the third sister wife. Barb's faith journey from mainstream Mormon to fundamentalist maverick is told in ways both compelling and sympathetic: she craves the assurances her childhood church provided for her; she misses the forever family promised to her through church covenants. But more, in the brave new world with Bill, their extended family, and his new church, Barb yearns for feminist selfhood. Throughout the series's five years, she travels many roads toward her own self-identity, including higher education, alternative religious practices, and potentially breaking from the family and going it alone. Ultimately, she settles on priesthood authority as a way to be both true to her religious calling and respectful of her need for full selfhood. For his part, Bill is perplexed by Barb's demands and adamant that he cannot allow her priesthood standing. Fighting in their bedroom, Bill asks in frustration, "What would the priesthood give you that you don't already have?" Barb is both incredulous and upset as she answers: "The power to grant blessings, to comfort through the laying on of hands, a powerful *direct* connection to Heavenly Father and the generations of prophets of those who came before, to be saved and to be able to save others and to lead them into the Celestial Kingdom on my own." In short, she wants everything.

Barb is guided in her quest for priesthood by an academic feminist Mormon studies character in the show named Renee Clayton, who tells Barb over tea—the semiotic marker of both her ex-Mormon and present-lesbian status—"You know, it was the practice of polygamy that emancipated Mormon women from the many constraints of Victorian family life. They were the first feminists."[14] Barb demurs: "Well, I don't think of myself as a feminist." Puzzled, the professor responds, "You feel you have a calling for the priesthood though?" Barb responds enthusiastically, "Yes, I do!" She wants to be Bill's equal and reasons that if he can create a new church, he can just as easily agree to new rules that vest her with power. Although her character might deny it, the show's logic is unequivocal: Barb's desire, indeed her demand, for equal access to God is a feminist throwdown, a request that in the new imagining of the relation between the earthly and the divine, plurality might prevail. Priesthood also allows women to be more self-reliant with respect to their own salvation. Indeed, present F/LDS cosmogony dictates that women are allowed into the Celestial Kingdom only as wives to worthy priesthood holders and only when those men awaken their wives from their postdeath slumbers, calling them forward to paradise. Women are never admitted to the highest of heavens on their own terms. The threat of angering or insulting one's husband and thus imperiling salvation serves as an effective cudgel compelling obedience and silence for many F/LDS women. But Barb refuses silence—instead telling Bill that if he cannot respect her need for equal priesthood standing, she cannot attend his church.

Barb's conscientious journey and desire for equal access to not only a Heavenly Father but also a Heavenly Mother very much voices concerns felt by many others within mediated Mormonism. Although the insular nature of the FLDS church makes it difficult to discern where gendered divisions arise, it is possible to see feminist resistance in the outrage expressed on such shows as *Escaping the Prophet* and *Escaping Polygamy*, two reality programs I discuss at much greater length in chapter 4. Barb's longing for priesthood authority can also be readily seen in the tensions exemplified by the Ordain Women campaign. Founded in 2013 (two years after *Big Love*'s finale) by Kate Kelley, a Washington, DC, human rights attorney, Ordain Women describes itself as an organization dedicated to working for "equality and the ordination of Mormon women to the priesthood" ("Mission Statement"

Gender Trouble in Happy Valley 237

2014). They describe their mission thus: "Based on the principle of thoughtful, faith-affirming strategic action, Ordain Women aspires to create a space for Mormon women to articulate issues of gender inequality they may be hesitant to raise alone. As a group we intend to put ourselves in the public eye and call attention to the need for the ordination of Mormon women to the priesthood. We sincerely ask our leaders to take this matter to the Lord in prayer" ("Mission Statement" 2014). Ordain Women's website is painstaking in laying out its reasons for being and its mandate for change:

> Despite their gifts, talents, and aspirations, women are excluded from almost all positions of clerical, fiscal, ritual, and decision-making authority.
>
> While women perform significant service in the Church's auxiliaries, such as the Primary, Relief Society, Sunday School, and Young Women's organizations, their contributions are always mediated and under the direction of male priesthood leaders. According to the Church's Gospel Principles manual, "Men use priesthood authority to preside in the Church.... Women who hold positions in the Church ... work under the direction of the priesthood." As such, Mormon women have many delegated responsibilities but lack the authority to define and oversee those responsibilities.
>
> This lack of female authority does not stop at the church doors. The Church's Proclamation on the Family declares that men preside over their wives and families, thus preserving an antiquated and unequal model in both the domestic and ecclesiastical realms. ("Frequently Asked Questions" 2015)

Ordain Women was and continues to be very savvy about the use of media in enacting political justice. The campaign deliberately cultivates public, and pointedly non-Mormon, attention to its cause for gender equality. To help faithful LDS adherents visualize a female priesthood practice, the campaign created a series of photographs of women healing the sick. Many images specifically merge nineteenth-century and twenty-first-century dress to make a bigger point about Joseph Smith's early openness to women as priesthood holders and leaders within the Mormon Church (see figure 5.11). Perhaps not surprisingly, Kelly, as the leader and founder of Ordain Women, caused great consternation to the leaders of the mainstream church. In May 2014, she was placed on informal probation, which serves as an official sanction and serious warning. Kelly was told to remove what were perceived to be incendiary materials from the organization's website. *And yet, she persisted.* In

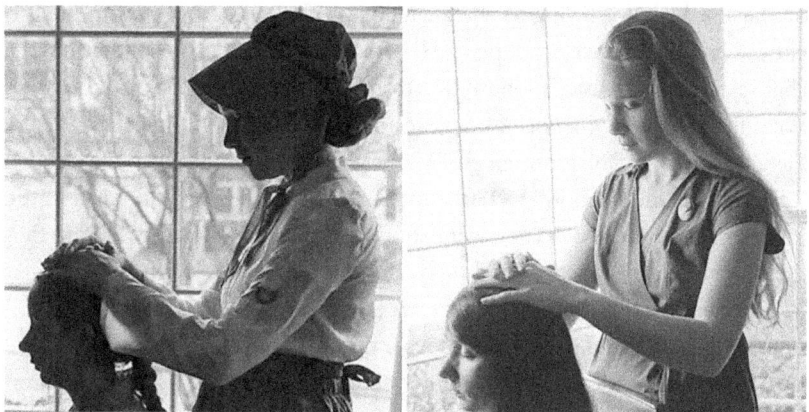

FIG. 5.11 Healing of the sick: women performing priesthood blessings (Stack 2015a).

June 2014, Kelly was called to a membership tribunal, called a court of love, and formally excommunicated for apostasy.[15]

The stunned reaction to her excommunication was felt worldwide. In the U.S., outlets such as NBC, CBS, CNN, National Public Radio, and the *New York Times* clamored to tell the story of a Mormon Church dangerously behind the gender curve. Her letter of excommunication, with its scolding tone, was excerpted by NBC: "The difficulty, Sister Kelly, is not that you say you have questions or even that you believe that women should receive the priesthood. The problem is that you have persisted in an aggressive effort to persuade other Church members to your point of view and that your course of action has threatened to erode the faith of others. You are entitled to your views, but you are not entitled to promote them and proselyte others to them while remaining in full fellowship in the Church" ("Mormon Women's Group Founder" 2014). Kelly's crime was not of belief but of publicity. Her conscience dictated that to choose the right was to defy the church. Openly. She told NBC in response to her excommunication, "It's not that I won't abandon my cause. I can't. The church that has excommunicated me has taught me to live with integrity. They're asking me to go to church every Sunday and pretend I don't think there are problems with gender equality." She told the *New York Times*, "I am not an apostate, unless every single person who has questions to ask out loud is an apostate. I am a faithful, active Mormon woman who has never spoken anything against the leaders of the church, and that's not my definition of an apostate" (Goodstein 2014).

For the most part, public reaction supported Kelly. While the comment sections on various media sites such as YouTube skewed toward the misogynist or chastised her for trying to change a church that was clearly committed to patriarchal governance, most people (particularly those outside of the church) championed Kelly as a modern warrior fighting an anachronistic system. Writing for the *Huffington Post* a year after Kelly's excommunication, Peggy Fletcher Stack (2015b) commented, "Many Mormon feminists also experienced Kelly's excommunication as a harsh slap felt around the world, not just to the activist, but to them all. They were shocked, horrified and discouraged that their carefully constructed building blocks of progressive LDS history seemed to have been toppled with a single blow." Stack illustrates that Kelly's dismissal struck many Mormon women at a deep emotional level. But Kelly's experience and excommunication have also strengthened the resolve that many Mormon women feel to eliminate their secondary status, politicizing those who now proudly embrace the politics of feminism and further feeding the mediascape so fascinated by gender and Mormonism.

Exiting Happy Valley

This chapter has covered a good deal of ground: the prescriptive gender codes of the mythic Happy Valley, the idealistic trope of the Molly Mormon, the compulsory heteronormative logic of the glow, the commitment to body and beauty regulation, toxic femininity and modesty culture, and politicized feminism. The governing stereotype of the F/LDS woman claims she is a selfless, smiling, long-suffering giver, committed to the patriarchal authority of husband and church. Her most political act is to (try to) wear pants to church on Sundays. And this stereotype clearly carries some truth. But what I hope this chapter makes equally evident is the degree to which the truth of Mormon womanhood disallows the complexity of personhood, experience, and feeling that is very much a part of the lives of actual women within Mormonism—also part of the narrative grist that fuels the larger mill of mediated Mormonism.

Indeed, largely because the idea of women's absolute submissiveness to men strikes a larger culture as both archaic and unjust, these mediated stories about Mormon women coming to terms with the gendered expectations of their church joins a cultural discussion infused by a common theme of gender justice. It is by and through these contested conversations on the meanings of justice, fair play, self-regulation, free choice, and rights of individuals that a larger culture debates with itself the definitional and gendered boundaries of democracy, egalitarianism, and personhood.

6. "Pray (and Obey) the Gay Away"

CONSCIENCE AND THE QUEER POLITICS OF DESIRE

While my family and I would prefer to be left alone by LDS church leadership at this time, I would much rather face excommunication than disavow my moral convictions.
—John Dehlin, "Disciplinary Council," *Mormon Stories*

Simply asking questions has never constituted apostasy. Apostasy is repeatedly acting in clear, open, and deliberate public opposition to the Church or its faithful leaders, or persisting, after receiving counsel, in teaching false doctrine.
—Kathryn Joyce, "The Coming Crackdown on Mormon Liberals"

It's the eleventh commandment. The most important one to the brethren. Thou shalt not commit publicity.
—Martha Beck, *Leaving the Saints*

In chapter 5, I discussed women's rights and the feminist movement in relation to mediated Mormonism, seeking to establish how cultural production about both mainstream and fundamentalist communities negotiate doctrinal demands for perfectionism and obedience in the context of self-making and social justice. In this chapter, I stay with the theme of progressive politics, subjectivity, and gender, turning ever so slightly to the mediated Mormon stories that put queer life and politics in the spotlight. As the epigraphs that start this chapter indicate, there is something very particular about the public announcement of one's individual conscience that stands as central both to self-making and to Mormonism itself. Self-improvement and personal moral conviction are critical to the Mormon project, and so is publicly sharing one's belief, or testimony, in personal statements. For True Believing Mormons (TBMS), this personal truth is often about the One True Church. For those who have left or been excommunicated, or X'd, from the church, personal truth often morphs into exposing the wrongs of an authoritarian system. Whether one stands within or outside the faith, conscience and shared narrative carry forth as sustaining values.

As it concerns personal truth-made-public stories, this chapter centers very specifically on queer identities and desires. Mormonism maintains that heterosexuality is God's plan. This maxim also applies to transgender identity, since in F/LDS doctrine the "perversions of desire" are often cemented to the challenges of sexed and gendered identity. Since the conventional LDS thinking holds that God would never hardwire same-sex desire or gender dysmorphia into his otherwise perfect creations, those expressing such feelings are perceived as having chosen non-normativity or of having been duped by Satanic forces. This attitude puts most (though not all) Mormons in league with other conservative religions that expect sinners to pray the gay away.

Given that being out and proud is so much a factor of modern LGBT+ initiatives, the central tension at the heart of these F/LDS stories about LGBT+ lives hinges on a basic dilemma: if self-worth, life-after-death salvation, and familial connection are contingent on a truth ethic whereby one's personal conviction supports the church's structure, then how does a Saint manage if self and system are in conflict? In this chapter, I thus examine a range of mediated texts that place Mormonism and queer practices in tension with one another. As I will elaborate more fully, by "queer practices" I mean not only those marked by same-sex desire, but those clustered under the banner of sexuality and sexed identity that establish tight regulation of the body and its desires as the sine qua non of Mormon belief. Indeed, it is the perceived economy of F/LDS sexuality that marks mediated Mormonism as simultaneously prudish and lascivious, thus reinforcing F/LDS identity as not only peculiar but also queer (see figures 6.1 and 6.2).

The meme of Mormonism signifies a series of interchangeable sexual oddities, which explicitly link suppressed sexuality to other forms of non-normative intimacy, expressly Mormon polygamy. This trope also aligns the sexual "perversions" of queer love and polygamy. In both the novel and film version of *Latter Days*, for example, a scene depicts the protagonist Aaron's disciplinary council, or court of love, for potential excommunication due to kissing another man. The church authority, who is also Aaron's father, states: "This isn't easy for me, Aaron. But in light of your abnormal and

FIGS. 6.1–6.2 From prudish to lascivious: the representational extremes of Mormon sexuality.

abominable state, and your refusal to see that you've been duped into some hogwash alternative lifestyle, I wish my shame was enough for the both of us—not to mention the shame you've brought to our church, our family, our ancestors..."

Aaron interrupts. "Our ancestors?" he adds incredulously. "Dad, your grandfather had at least a half-dozen wives, and the same goes for every single person in this room. I'd say we were the original definition of 'alternative lifestyle.' But now that we've conveniently erased that episode from our theology, that gives our church the right to define normal for everybody else? Do you see what a contradiction that is?" (Fabris and Cox 2004, 186). Polygamy and same-sex desire are here lumped together as queer bedfellows, any form of non-normative sex and sexuality coming to represent all forms of alternative. In this, we see the truth of Peter Coviello's (2014) claim that normativity entails a specific way of living in relation to race, to gender, to sex. Thus to reside outside of normativity is always a racialized and queer experience.

The Siren's Song of Self-Improvement: Work, Pray, Smile

Given the idea that individuals hold the key to their own salvation and that perfect obedience to the codes fostered by the faith (even more than faith itself) yields eternal rewards, Mormonism contends that suffering Saints can work their way straight by engaging in prayer, fasting, obedience, temple ordinances, and tithing. Those who are not saved by and through these rituals are not working hard enough. If obedience to such mandates offers salvation, disobedience yields eternal punishment or banishment to an endless darkness adrift from affective connection and familial belonging. In this rubber-meets-the-road philosophy, sin is not about feeling but about action, and the moral mandate indicates there are distinct and meaningful differences between affect and behavior. This template in turn requires that individuals deploy exacting self-monitoring and behavior/emotion modification technologies in order to curb wayward desire into acceptable (in)action. As such, the prescriptive code of the faith creates what Foucault has termed the "docile body," or one that might be "subjected, used, transformed, and improved" (1991, 136). In this case, those bodies also follow a Foucauldian model of panoptic surveillance, in which individuals willingly subject themselves to a culture of surveillance organized around compulsory norms. The joking way to put this about the church is plainly evident in

Meghan McCain and Michael Ian Black's reflections on Salt Lake City and its mostly LDS population: "Mormons have a lot of rules. No caffeine, no alcohol, no premarital sex, have lots of babies once you do get married, work hard, be self-sufficient. These are all pretty good rules, and maybe if you are able to live by them you can be happy. Of course, people are still people and a common joke about Mormons is, 'How do you keep a Mormon from drinking all your beer? Invite another Mormon'" (2012, 63).

The less funny way to understand this totalitarian code of personal and social surveillance, however, is plainly demonstrated in the tactics of the Strengthening Church Members Committee (SCMC). The SCMC is a body composed of members of the general authority, or ecclesiastical leaders often called the Brethren. The charge of the SCMC is to serve as a repository for church members to report concerns about other members' perceived violations of church codes. In an age before social media, the SCMC worked through stealth, gathering gossip and other forms of damning testimony, often clandestinely. In the present climate, the SCMC often lurks on members' Facebook pages, blogs, Twitter feeds, and other social media platforms.

This combination of surveillance and self-monitoring is a technology of regulation remarkably in tandem with the modern project of selfhood. For instance, Joseph P. Forgas, Roy F. Baumeister, and Dianne M. Tice characterize "the ability to control our actions" as not only the "quintessential characteristic of human beings" but also a specific feature of modern mass societies in which "most of the people we encounter are strangers, personal anonymity is widespread, and mobility is high" (2009, 1, 4). The authors propose a form of dispersed knowing, or what we might also refer to as a mediated intimacy, as a primary reason for "more sophisticated self-regulatory processes" (4). These processes can take many forms, largely authorized through a secular metric of measurement and calculation—such as the rise of psychology, the quantification of the body through weight loss and other forms of corporeal modification, or the calculus of social relationships and self-actualization through self-reflexivity. Management of the self is not only big business, it is important and painstaking work and a high-stakes affair. Write Forgas, Baumeister, and Tice: "Most major social and personal problems that afflict people in modern, Western cultures have some degree of self-regulation failure as a core part of the problem. Inadequate or misguided self-regulation is involved in drug and alcohol addiction, eating disorders, obesity, crime and violence, prejudice and stereotyping, cigarette smoking, underachievement at school and work, unwanted pregnancy, sexually transmitted diseases, debt, failure to save money, gambling, domestic abuse, and many more. The solving of many social problems thus assumes that individuals are capable and willing to self-regulate" (5).

By contrast, the authors contend, self-regulation yields the "positive value" of "health, happiness, and optimal human functioning. The ability to self-regulate, and in particular, to regulate affective states, also lies at the core of blossoming research on emotional intelligence phenomena" (Forgas, Baumeister, and Tice 2009, 5).[1] These capacities for control of the mind, emotions, and body yield highly prized outcomes: "getting better grades, avoiding trouble and pathology, having better relationships with others, doing better at sports, and a host of other benefits" (5). At some level, the authors might be guilty of slightly overstating the case a bit to solidify the contribution of their volume. Indeed, I might modify these psychologists' claims to argue that it is not a failure of self-regulation so much as the perceived failure of such that gives the notion of self-control such cachet. But by and large, Forgas, Baumeister, and Tice give voice to a governing Zeitgeist of secular modernity: the well-regulated self is the key to wellness, happiness, and success. Perception is key in this regard, since the notion of self-regulation provides a revised godly assurance—the promise of everlasting peace if one can simply get the self under control.

Given what is at stake in these major agonistics, it is no wonder that a larger world is fascinated by stories that center Mormons and their complex relation to self, control, and sexuality. The viewing public looks at Mormonism in fascination, with equal parts shock (at its demands for strict personal regulation, its iron-clenched jaw behind the milky-white smile, its historical commitments to polygamy, its banning of black people until God changed his mind in 1978, its intolerance of homosexuality) and amazement (at its worldwide growth in membership and its believers' work ethic, its high degree of financial success, its ceaseless happiness, and its stable families). Here is a people who sing the siren's song of self-improvement through an American affective entitlement of optimism, confidence, and exuberance. Here is a people for whom meritocracy is not a myth—hard work might still pay off in dividends both material and spiritual. But here is also a people, we are told by mediated accounts, who believe in their faith so unbendingly that they will cast out their own brothers and sisters if those people fail to believe (and act) as mandated. There is a broader public sense that the Janus face of Mormonism is both appealing and not to be trusted. In turn, mediation by and about Mormons serves as an educational tool for a discursive public culture devoted to debating the meanings of fairness. Nowhere is this more evident than in conversations about LGBT+ peoples within the church, people who have been taught that their same-sex desires or transsexual fixations are the lures of Satan, and they might still choose righteousness and live the promises of eternity if they only work hard enough to be straight.[2] Indeed, the notion of hard work is critical here, since, as I discuss further in this chapter, the Mormon work ethic puts its paler Protestant cousin to shame. Indeed, Bloom contends that in its resistance of Protestantism, Mormons are "perhaps the most work-addicted culture in religious history" (1992, 103). But first, let us think more about sexuality, self-regulation, and emotion, and their combined relation to both Mormonism and the modern subject.

Conscientious Objectors: Sexuality and Self

Michel Foucault and many other sexuality scholars have made clear that the calibrated and discursive sexualized self is very much the modern self, and it is not just sexual desire but talking about desire and understanding desire as the foundation of identity that constitutes the foundation of modern norms of identity (see Foucault 1978). While Foucault famously argued in *The History of Sexuality: An Introduction* that same-sex desire offers the crux of modern sexology, other scholars have more recently made a similar argument about heterosexuality. In *The Invention of Heterosexuality*, for example, Jonathan Ned Katz (2005) argues that heterosexuality has often been positioned as an assumptive universal, and gender scholars must subject its construction to critical scrutiny in order to interrogate its hegemonic content and contours. Kim Phillips and Barry Reay argue in a similar vein in *Sex before Sexuality* that "the power of heterosexuality resides in a strange combination of ubiquity and invisibility" (2011, 40), and their book offers an important challenge to gender and sexuality scholars to take up heterosexuality as a constructed category of identity, since power and desire (over and above behavior) have so often marked the emergence of heterosexuality as a category. Heterosexuality thus functions, as does whiteness, to reinforce its own privilege and operation through absence. Indeed, Richard Dyer (1997) contends in *White* that whiteness and homophobia are insidious bedfellows (and I use that sexy word deliberately).

These debates are all the more complex when we consider that the T under the LGBT+ umbrella does not, by itself, reference a sexual orientation, whereas lesbian, gay, and bisexual all mark sexual desire as consonant with identity. I want to allow for this distinction but follow a larger trend in the field of gender studies that positions these identity locations as necessarily intertwined, largely because all who reside within the broad identity label of LGBT+ contend with similar forms of oppression and related, though not identical, social punishments that include banishment, shame, and seclusion.³ In this, then, I join other scholars, such as David Valentine (2007) and Susan Stryker (2017), who consider transgender identity an indispensable contribution to the contemporary discourses on sexuality.

As such, we might say that a fraught sexuality in all of its many forms emerges as a category of invention and fascination in the modern moment.⁴ For these reasons, I use the broad rubrics of sexuality and sexual identities, regardless of their particular orientation/s, as an analytic for thinking through modes of normativity and regulation in relation to gender and mediated Mormonism. But I also very specifically hone in on non-normative, gender nonconforming, and queer practices as a way of locating these conversations about sexuality and normativity.

There is no shortage of sexuality stories in the Mormon mediascape. These tales of Saints and sexual identity reveal complicated narratives about desire and selfhood that cut across and through the labels of sexual orientation. Whether the focus is on latter-day virgins trying valiantly to find their Mr. (Mormon) Right while staying pure along the way, semi-celibate gay and straight, sane and manic missionaries recruiting (or seducing) in the name of the church, same-sex-desiring husbands in heterosexual marriages, LGBT+ youth who are also F/LDS, transgender teens and adults committed to finding the true self Heavenly Father created, or polygamous patriarchs who run the sexual-desire gamut from virile to vile to Viagra addicted, mediated Mormonism is fully saturated by this notion of the sexualized self as the quintessential modern subject.

The mainstream LDS Church puts strong bodily injunctions on its members in the form of overt rules and more tacit (but equally coercive) codes of conduct, related to the broad gamut of expressions through which a soul might be wayward. These regulations very specifically include curbing sexual expression, but they also extend into the bodily habitus of dress, food, beverage, and stimulant consumption (no hot beverages, no alcohol, no caffeine, no cigarettes), and the strict management of media, money, and time. Mormonism as a mediated meme is fully aware of these mandates for bodily regulation, and so often to speak the word "Mormon" is also to import a wide set of expectations (some admiring, others amused) about disciplining the body and its desires.

Mormonism's emphasis on behavior suggests that Saints are allowed to feel prohibited desire; they just can't act on it. According to this logic, Mormons are technically allowed to believe themselves attracted to others of the same sex (a seemingly temporary condition of defiance or delusion), but they aren't allowed to be gay, lesbian, or bisexual (a permanent position of orientation and identity). Neither are they permitted to proclaim publicly their homosexuality. Similarly, while transgender Mormons might not be excommunicated for cross-dressing or hormone use (perceived as temporary and private), they will almost certainly be X'd for transition surgeries (perceived as permanent and harder to keep secret) (Petrey 2015). The eleventh commandment that Mormons shall not commit publicity thus reinforces an epistemology of the closet whereby non-normative desires and bodies must stay shrouded in shame and darkness.[5]

The appeal of normative continuity is strong. The 2014 independent documentary *Transmormon* features a poignant scene in which Ed Hayward, father of the subject's protagonist Eri, says,

> We believe that the church leaders are receiving revelation that helps them to be able to better serve in the callings we are receiving in the priesthood. We have the Proclamation of the Word on the Family, which states clearly that a marriage is between a man and a woman. In my opinion, Eri is a woman, so I don't see a problem with that. And I'm hoping that the leaders of the church are going to see it that way. And that she will be able to get married. She won't be able to have children, but she can hopefully adopt children.

The comments on the YouTube posting for *Transmormon* are noteworthy for the degree they praise Eri's father for his acceptance and love of his daughter. Writes "Jimmy Lindberg": "That dad deserves an award for his awesomeness." Of course, this being YouTube, the post has generated a good amount of trolling that is hateful and extremely transphobic. But the overall celebration of Eri and appreciation of Ed allows for a remarkable takeaway whereby conservative Mormonism as juxtaposed against LGBT+ lives might be used as the motivating reason for mediation, and mediation of this type might, in turn, foster transgender acceptance.

Postdocumentary interviews with Eri, for instance, note that she is still on the outs with the church, but now the reprimanding letters she receives from her bishop are because she and her boyfriend are "living in sin." Eri told the *Daily Beast* with a laugh, "I was having to deal with all these things that were trans related . . . now it's related to being a regular skank making bad choices kind of things" (Shire 2014). Here Eri shares a joke with a non-Mormon world about the restrictive, even prudish, policies of a church that can overlook her transition but cannot forgive the sin of living together outside wedlock. As a fully realized self, Eri is heralded as a triumphant gender warrior, in contrast to the restrictive regime that worked to suppress her true personhood. Eri's true self and personal conviction—two elements so critical to Mormonism—thus emerge in specific counter to the religion.

Keep Sweet: Mediated Mormonism's Economy of Emotions

Mormonism puts a high premium on rules and regulations that establish normativity and perpetuate its own hegemony, through the self-discipline of emotions, sexual desire, and pleasure. Indeed, the Mormon flagship university BYU runs a public-access website through its library called *The Encyclopedia of Mormonism*. Included within this encyclopedia are roughly three hundred explanations, edicts, and expectations, many of which include the regulation of the body through the governance of sexuality. Under "Dating and Courtship," the entry reinforces Mormon norms of separation from a broader Gentile culture largely through a governing code of commitment and premarital celibacy. It states:

> It is expected that LDS youth will not begin dating until the age of sixteen. Serious, steady dating and marriage-oriented courtship are expected to be delayed longer, perhaps until after a mission for males and after completing high school for females. A chaste courtship is expected to lead to a temple marriage, in which a couple make binding commitments to each other for all time and eternity.
>
> Two doctrinally based principles guide the dating and courtship of LDS youth: first, because of the religious significance of marriage, virtually everyone who can is expected to marry; second, because of the spiritual and social importance of chastity, sexual relations must wait until after marriage. (Miller and Goddard 2017)

The entry on sex education clearly notes the critical role that control of emotions and the body plays in the governing codes of chastity that stand over both mainstream and fundamentalist Mormonism: "Parents are counseled to help their adolescent and older children understand the need to stay in control of their emotions and behaviors relative to physical desire and to teach them how to make personal decisions about sexual behavior based on moral awareness, with the realization that virtue and moral cleanliness lead to strength of character, peace of mind, lifelong happiness, and a fulness of love. LDS scriptures counsel, 'See that ye bridle all your passions, that ye may be filled with love' (Alma 38:12)" (Hutchison 1992).

In parallel, the FLDS injunction to keep sweet refers both to adolescent girls retaining their sexual purity and to the expectation that everyone (man, woman, boy, girl) regulate emotions in the face of crisis, catastrophe, and stress—Britain's "keep calm and carry on" aphorism in an American key, suffused with sexualized meaning. According to FLDS 101, a blog devoted to the doctrine and covenants of the Fundamentalist Latter-day Saints Church, Warren Jeffs has taken the

> phrase [keep sweet] a step further, making it into a commandment, a mantra to keep your feelings under control.... "To be loyal to Heavenly Father, to truly love Him and obey Him, you must keep sweet no matter what. If your feelings can be disturbed and you simply need more of the spirit of God to have and earn more of that sweet spirit, you must pay the price. The price is sacrifice. Set aside any feeling or thought that disturbs the spirit of God." (WSJ 1/28/2003) "Keeping sweet means saying your prayers and obeying the priesthood over you" (WSJ 3/6/96). (Knoll 2009a)

As I note in chapter 4, Jeffs is probably the poster child for bad polygamy due to his reckless abuses, ranging from rape to pedophilia to sex trafficking. But in the mediated spheres of political opinion, it is often this insistence on keeping sweet that lifts Jeffs from a figure of derision to one of evil, because to suppress the emotions means also suppressing one's inner conscience. This repression obliterates the tie to selfhood that is the lifeline of free agency and democratic citizenry.

The FLDS commandment to keep sweet has very much to do with the mainstream LDS ambition of "perfect obedience" and to "fast, pray, read the Scriptures, and never give in to your feelings" (Freeman 2014, 11) that speak both to a gendered tension between autonomy of the self and obedience to authority resonating through mediated stories about Mormons, sexuality, and the regulation of desire. As former Mormon and present "fabulous gay man" Steven Fales (2006) writes, "The Church taught us from a very early age to deny the pain and smile anyway."

It is not a coincidence that a key number in *The Book of Mormon* musical is called "Turn It Off!" Clark Johnsen, himself an original cast member of the Broadway production of the musical and a man who left the faith because it could not support his same-sex orientation, chuckles, "That number is just so crazy accurate.... The one thing... a Mormon wouldn't say, 'Oh, I just turn off my feelings.' But you know, the concept is 'I'm having improper thoughts so instead I will hum my favorite hymn.' I don't think a Mormon would say 'I'm going to turn it off,' but it's exactly what we do" (Dehlin 2015a). Of course, the broader hilarity of this campy number stems from a kind of sweet incredulousness attached to the fact that the impeccably conscientious Mormon missionaries depicted in the musical are as consumed with guilt over their desire for a donut as they are over their lust for other men. As well, the bright-sequined pink vests the missionaries don for a high-energy tap dance finale solidifies the camp aesthetic the overall lyrics pretend to suppress.

"A Mormon Just Believes": Not-Knowingness Made Known

Whether large or small, serious or silly, mediated Mormonism makes clear that the F/LDS economy of emotions requires a form of belief bred through an absolute obedience that is often fostered through lack of thinking critically, or what I am calling here not-knowingness. Noted fashion photographer Brian Shumway tells of his own struggles with his Mormon upbringing in *Time*: "Most people may not know or realize, but Mormonism, if lived as it's supposed to be lived, is an orthodox religion. As an orthodox religion, anything that waivers from the orthodoxy set by Mormon authorities isn't tolerated" (McClelland 2011). Shumway remembers at age sixteen beginning to read the works of philosophers such as Friedrich Nietzsche, Jean-Paul Sartre, and Erich Fromm, thinkers who gave voice to his own sense of doubt. "Eventually," Shumway reflects, "it became obvious I was going down another path and I had to 'come out' to my family" (McClelland 2011). It isn't obvious, however, if to "come out" for Shumway meant revealing himself as a nonbeliever, a gay man, or both.

In *The Mormon People*, historian Matthew Bowman traces a historical movement starting in 1953 during which the church worked to underscore not-knowingness as a desired mode of being. To wit: Bowman notes that education at Brigham Young University and the Church Educational System began "eliminating outside influence in favor of faculty trained in education rather than in religion" (2012, 206). In turn, argues Bowman, this pedagogical refocus reinforced a broader exhortation among the LDS faithful "to live the moral code of their faith rather than to encourage intellectual inquiry" (207). In other words, good Mormons don't ask too many questions; a Mormon just believes. Rather than only being a tool for compartmentalization, however, not-knowingness restricts information in a world overflowing with it. Not-knowingness requires an active effort, worthy of the suffering of Mormon pioneers, to police the mind into a state of obedient belief. One does not ask questions; one does not break the rules. The will creates the willingness. In not-knowingness there exists a powerful refusal to see or acknowledge what is already known, a refusal that ricochets across the screens of mediated Mormonism. As a consequence, many stories of those who grew up in the faith depict the very painful tearing away of the veils of not-knowingness in the name of personal conscience. Similarly, memoirs often talk of the shame of thinking in critical ways about God, the church, the rules.

For many ex-Mormons who tell their stories in published form and circulate them through vanity presses, blogs, amateur video, and even major publishing houses, breaking from the church and its totalitarian mandate for perfect obedience is like escaping an abusive father hell-bent on his own authority. Consider, for instance, the advertising copy for Emily Pearson's (2012) memoir, *Dancing with Crazy*:

> [This] is the true story of her personal derailment, both horrifically and humorously demonstrating what happens when mindless obedience to religious authority supersedes plain old common sense. As a young Mormon girl Emily gave up her own personal power, relinquished the ability to think for herself and allowed herself to blow with a wind that carried her from studying scriptures in the Sunday School classes of correctly clothed, righteous descendants of Mormon pioneers, to studying porn on San Francisco's Castro Street with her gay father and half naked drag queens, to drowning in depression in a stinky apartment in Hollywood, to puking in the toilet of a courting polygamist, to marrying her very own gay man in a Mormon Temple. After nearly losing her mind several times over, Emily disentangled herself from toxic and narcissistic personalities, walked away from a crippling religion and finally learned to think, act and live for herself.

While it may seem contradictory to position the self as the antidote to toxic systemic narcissism, the advertising copy here reinforces a theme found throughout Pearson's memoir: sacrificing personal need creates powerlessness and silence. Pearson calls on the gumption of her preteen self: "I desperately needed that fearless girl to pound on the door of whoever was holding [my light, my courage, my soul] hostage" (2012, loc. 7896). She felt invisible and voiceless because of the incessant demand for her obedience. Hers is a feminist outrage.

By and large, Mormon not-knowingess resonates in the larger mediascape as both sinister and frightening. But sometimes it is played for laughs. Sings the lead Elder Price in *The Book of Mormon*'s major ballad, so enthusiastically earnest and high energy that it reads as farce, "I believe! I am a Mormon, and a Mormon just believes." If there are stumbles along the way in the quest for a goodness that borders on perfection, the stalwart Saint doubles down on devotion, praying harder, fasting more often, increasing devotions of time, becoming ever more invested in the workings of the church as a means of achieving perfection and thus feeling accepted by that church.

The Mormon iteration of the demand to will oneself straight is slightly different than the "pray the gay away" gospels of conservative faith groups, in that the larger culture of LDS perfectionism and exceptionalism reinforces a simultaneous feeling of inadequacy and superiority among the majority of Mormon peoples (regardless of sex or orientation). As I discussed in chapter 5, the concentrated conversation of Mormon mommy blogs hints at feeling overwhelmed and unable to meet high expectations for constant happiness and overall domestic superiority—all while F/LDS Mormons are encouraged to perceive themselves as chosen and special. *We should feel sorry for the Gentile.* Many Mormon missionaries speak of their cocksure assurance that their time in the missionary field will be a holy crusade of Truth against worldly values. Matt Stone and Trey Parker, the creators of *The Book of Mormon* musical, get it right when they have their egocentric missionary characters enthusiastically vow, "I will do something that blows God's fricking mind!" But even for men, living up to high Mormon expectations is no easy task. As Steven Fales sardonically states in *Confessions of a Mormon Boy*, his one-man play about growing up gay and LDS, when he was married to a woman (Emily Pearson), "Being perfect is exhausting." But being gay and perfect is an oxymoron or, as Fales terms it, an "oxy Mormon" that, within the tautology of church doctrine, might be ameliorated only through more work. "God made no man a pervert," Fales reminds his audience in the mimicked voice of authority. "Remember, homosexuality can be cured. You may totally recover from its tentacles. Don't be selfish, lazy, and weak. How can you know you cannot change until your knees are sore from praying and your knuckles bloody from knocking on the Lord's door for help?" (Fales 2003, 44).[6]

Ancestral Mormons, such as Fales, labor under a further psychological hurdle: the knowledge that the church's nineteenth-century pioneers faced dire circumstances—persecution, starvation, privation—without complaint, without giving up. These first Saints literally walked across North America, forming what is now referred to as the Mormon Trail, all enduring great suffering and adversity, many of them dying along the way. As Fales writes, "Our hardships [as contemporary Mormons] were nothing like what the early Mormon pioneers had to endure: house burnings, tar and featherings, sweating and freezing across the plains, crickets! Grit was in our genes" (2003, 45). The hardships experienced by those first Mormons have set the bar high for the ensuing generations of Saints whose adversity, the thinking goes, can never be as bad as that already bested by their ancestors. The good Mormon thus works hard with an internalized sense of greater suffering that has come before her. If she does not achieve the desired outcome, the only solution is to work yet harder.

Conscientious objection, personal testimony, and exacting effort all factor in a *Mormon Stories* podcast from 2006 that features a two-part interview with Buckley Jeppson, a lifelong ancestral, or what is sometimes referred to as DNA, Mormon, who realized after he had been married to a woman for nearly two decades that he was gay. Jeppson's nineteenth-century Mormon ancestors were from England on one side and Scandinavia on the other, giving him the Mayflower bloodline of the first Saints, who were converted in their homelands and conveyed to Joseph's Zion in Nauvoo, Illinois, and later Salt Lake City, Utah. As a multigenerational Mormon, Jeppson's public life as a gay man required not only severing himself from a faith system he believed in but cutting himself from all familial ties, past, present, and future. His story of coming to sexual consciousness reinforces the notion of a cultivated not-knowingness that fosters mandates for emotional control and sexual naïveté. In Jeppson's words:

> I didn't know when I first got married that I was gay. I guess I'm at that age where it didn't even occur to me that such a thing was an option. . . . The only gay person I knew in high school was this strange young man who wore makeup, and I thought that was very peculiar. . . .
> As a youth growing up in the church, any feelings you have for anybody (male or female), you don't talk about them much. So I didn't. I just assumed the older I got, that everybody has these trials and feelings they have to go through, and if I worked hard enough and excelled and studied and prayed and fasted and all of those things, I would get over it, just like everyone else around me had gone through it and gotten over it. (Dehlin 2006a)

Jeppson speaks of a "don't talk, don't feel" culture, where a pervasive logic of silence, or not-knowingness, seems to keep all forms of "deviance" perpetually off the radar. Similarly, Mormon poet and playwright Carol Lynn

Pearson writes about her sheltered homogeneous LDS life in *Goodbye, I Love You*, her own memoir about coming to terms with a gay husband: "We didn't know there was any such thing as homosexuals. We hardly knew there was such a thing as Democrats. We'd heard of blacks, but many of us had never seen one in person. I attended BYU high school, a laboratory school run by the university. As a takeoff on a television show of the day we nicknamed ourselves Purity Playhouse. Attending school at Purity Playhouse in the confines of Happy Valley made for a lot of insulation" (1986, 28).

Not-knowingness works as a prescriptive epistemology for the fabled True Believing Mormon. Coming into consciousness largely involves emerging through the sheltering veil of obligatory affect and action that is part of not-knowingness. Emily Pearson's memoir again offers a poignant rendition of not-knowingness in her combined relation between the paternal presence of her father (Gerald Pearson) and the patriarchal authority of her church. She writes, "In Gerald's kitchen I learned to sit quietly, not think, and nod. I had to. I alone had been issued a special invitation into his world. My mom didn't get to be there, my brothers and sister didn't get to be there. Only me. It was just Gerald and me, and I would do whatever I had to do to keep it that way. So I erased myself. I became a blank movie screen upon which he could project anything and everything he wanted. A small price to pay for feeling loved the way he had once loved me" (Pearson 2012, loc. 773).

Emily perceives this erasure as parallel to the tacit agreement she has made with the church: "The other place I learned to sit quietly, not think and nod, was at church. I was never overtly taught to not think, but I was taught to have unwavering faith and unquestioning devotion to the Lord and the leaders of His kingdom here on earth" (Pearson 2012, loc. 773). "It became clear to me that if I didn't do everything perfectly, keep every commandment and agree with everything said over the pulpit, then Heavenly Father could stop loving me just as easily as Gerald might" (loc. 782). It is precisely in relation to one's personal truth, or testimony, that these tacit forms of coercion rise up most strongly. Emily notes,

> [I] learned to recognize and trust the burning "confirmation" feeling in my chest. When my heart raced and I felt excited, or when I was filled with warmth, joy and peace, I knew it was The Spirit of God, through the Holy Ghost, speaking to me. And I was told I could trust that feeling—unless, of course, what I received through personal revelation went against the decrees of those in authority over me which,

to me, was everyone in line from my Sunday School teacher right up to the prophet himself. If that was the case I was taught to get back on my knees until I had received the right answer. Until I had the right feeling. So, I guess more accurately, I learned to submit my will to what I was told by others was God's will for me. (loc. 779–807)

Personal choice, in this regard, functions as an individual guessing game for which the rules are established by a loved authority one must, and indeed wants to, please and obey. Personal testimony reinforces the truth of that dynamic.

These operations are not, of course, limited to the Mormon Church—they constitute the very workings of hegemony that scholars have long critiqued. As illustrated here, the terms of oppression become desirable, indeed pleasurable, to the oppressed, even while the terms of that oppression largely operate without detection. "I learned to submit my will to what I was told by others was God's will for me." In Emily Pearson's case as for so many others, she notes that her own personal testimony isn't fully to be trusted, the technologies of choice subject to the toxic sway of hegemony. In their complex interweaving of knowing and not-knowing, these tales within mediated Mormonism thus provide a very precise latter-day screen on which to view the usually invisible technologies of hegemony. Indeed, in the broader mediascape I would argue that it is the juxtaposition between these two strong impressions—clean-cut sparkle-smiled happy goodness and strong-willed draconian disciplinarians—that secure a broader fascination with Mormons and Mormonism. But it may well be the governing culture of not-knowingness that most fascinates and frightens a population that is riveted by stories about the Saints.

"The Mormon Sex Thing"

In a 2017 special for TLC's reality program *Sister Wives*, the Browns (Kody and his four wives, Meri, Janelle, Christine, and Robyn) gather to watch video footage culled since the program began in 2010 organized around the thoughts and experiences of third wife Christine. Going back to an early episode, Meri notes that a wife's individual relationship with Kody is very much influenced by the larger marital ecosystem. "When he's ornery with another one, he gets weird with me. And I don't want that. So it's very important for him to have a good relationship, and the sexual nature of it is definitely a part of that good relationship." A very pregnant Christine chimes in, referring to sex, "And we know that that's required in each relationship, so some people think, 'How do you feel when he's off with another woman, sleeping with her and you know they're having sex?'" Christine rolls her eyes and gestures into the air: "Well, gosh darn it, they better!" Watching the footage seven years later, Christine yells out, "So painful!" Laughing and a bit truculent, Kody explains the family's pain is due to the fact that producers ran and reran Christine's statements about sex as a "teaser for our show" as it was just debuting. Says Kody, "We're polygamists coming out of the closet, freaking out about the fact that we were coming out. And our church leaders had a fit, rightfully so, because [in a high voice] *we're discussing sex!* Which is kind of the rule, we don't ever do that. It just got so dang ugly, right out of the starting blocks." Says Meri, "That conversation was a conversation I never wanted to have, in public."

As it concerns the public interest in the sex lives of polygamists or in their reticence with respect to it, the Browns aren't alone. Indeed, as I discuss at greater length in both chapters 3 and 4, mediated Mormon polygamy stories have long held a front-page fascination for U.S. and international viewers, who are intrigued by the complicated sexual dynamics at the heart of what could otherwise be considered serial monogamy lived in a simultaneous temporal frame. I would go so far as to venture that no public tell-all about polygamy exists without some speaking about that which is not to be spoken—sex. Indeed, sex is such a forbidden topic within mediated Mormonism that the word itself is sometimes not intelligible. Rebecca Musser notes with particular respect to the FBI raid on Warren Jeffs's Yearning for Zion Compound, FLDS cultures speak a different language when it comes not only to sex but also to consent. For instance, when government agents questioned teenagers who were either pregnant or young mothers, the women consistently denied ever having had sex at all. The FBI considered this willful deceit, and began to treat the women as hostile informants. Musser realized that the women had probably never heard the word "sex" and certainly never used it. She writes, "We had to repeatedly remind hundreds of different investigators and workers to use the term 'marital relations' instead of 'sex,' as well as explaining Warren's peculiar indoctrination so they could understand our people better, without judgment" (Musser and Cook 2014, 273).

While the Browns represent a more open version of fundamentalist practice, and mainstream LDS culture is yet another level removed from more extreme versions of the faith, the injunction on sex talk is a binding thread that runs throughout the broad quilt of Mormonism. Mediated Mormonism makes much of this tension between what can be discussed and what cannot, sounding the string of erotic suppression with insistence and agility. Mormonism is a culture very much predicated on puritanical commitments to regulation of the appetites and preservation of the virginal body. As I've noted, for both men and women, sexual relations and heavy foreplay are forbidden outside of heterosexual marriage, as are other forms of nonprocreative sex such as masturbation. This, however, does not prevent F/LDS adherents from devising clever work-arounds (at least in media representation)—sexual activity that doesn't count as sex. For instance, the Amazon series *Alpha House*, otherwise a political comedy about four Republican senators who share a single house in Washington, DC, made much of Mormon soaking, an alternative sex practice engaged in by two LDS characters on the show. Soaking basically allows for penis-vagina penetration but absolutely no friction. Insertion is OK; pumping will send you to hell. A web search suggests this practice is not something concocted by the show. Similarly, as I mention in the introduction, Jodi Arias spoke of oral and anal sex between herself and her boyfriend, Travis Alexander, whom she later murdered. While both were Mormon and pledged to chastity outside of marriage, they reasoned that the nonprocreative nature of their sex practice removed it from the category of sexual sin.

At very young ages, F/LDS children are sex segregated from one another, encouraged to idealize the opposite sex and to search for an eternal companion, but admonished to refrain from any form of intimate touch, sexual experimentation, heavy petting, or passionate kissing. Adherents to the mainstream faith are encouraged to wear CTR (Choose the Right) rings from as young as age four as a reminder of the necessity for making good daily choices that might eventually yield heavenly rewards. While other personal effects—like necklaces, key chains, zipper pulls, tie clips, and oil vials—are available through online retailers such as CTR Ring Shop, it is the CTR ring that predominates, the signet an ever-present reminder of the significance of choice.

Choosing the right encompasses a set of choices bigger than sexual activity, yet it is clear from the CTR mode of public address that the most important choices individuals make correlate to sexual temptations. In January 2017, for instance, CTR Ring Shop offered a free gift that perfectly emblematizes the fusion between latter-day screens, gendered morality, and choice: a green crest emblazoned with CTR, to be used as computer wallpaper. Writes the company:

> We are aware of the blessings that information and technology can be in our lives in our modern day.... We are also aware of the tremendous risk that individuals and families take by having computers and the internet in our homes. Pornography, chat rooms, and anti-Mormon literature are easily accessible and can destroy the soul.... In an effort to make 2017 a great year full of spiritual progression and faith-building experiences, we want to do what we can to help resist temptation. CTR Ring Shop has teamed up with Elvtech, a Utah web design company and created a FREE, eye-catching CTR wallpaper background for your computer! We believe that having CTR on our fingers and our computers will help us choose the right. ("We Have a Free Gift for You . . ." 2015)

As this free gift demonstrates, constant on-screen reminders are meant to provide a perpetual internalized mandate to choose the right, which is to say to avoid "pornography, chat rooms, and anti-Mormon literature"—forms of polymorphous perversity here rather deliciously conflated with media.

Similarly, Emily Pearson writes that as soon as teenagers hit puberty, "they, in turn, are bombarded with endless lessons and lectures on the Law of Chastity. We were expected to grow up never touching the opposite sex, or ourselves, in 'inappropriate ways.'" She continues, "Until we got married in the temple, we were to do everything we could to keep ourselves morally clean. Sex or 'anything like unto it,' before or outside of marriage, was simply not an option and was the 'gravest of sins, second only to murder'" (2012, loc. 1224). As with many conservative faith-based groups, compulsory purity is part of the moral instruction, doled out in weekly sessions. Writes Pearson of these chastity lessons, "If we had sex before marriage we were a squeezed out orange rind, or a chewed up piece of gum, or a squished Twinkie, or a board hammered full of nails. The boys' class had these lessons too. One was even rumored to involve a destroyed banana, stressing the vital importance of refraining from 'self-abuse. And not stoking their little factories.' Some were even told not to look at their naked bodies too long after getting out of the shower or to tie their hands to the bedposts, if necessary, to keep from masturbating" (loc. 1225).

Other writers also reinforce Pearson's descriptions. In *Breaking Free*, Katherine Jean Denton reminisces, "Sex is forbidden in the Mormon Church before marriage and, I hear, not very exciting after marriage either because of the sex guidelines and rules governing temple recommends (special permission required to enter the temple). We were taught that the main purpose—the only purpose—of sex was to have children and replenish the earth" (2015, loc. 156). Joanna Brooks (2012, 102) similarly reflects, "So important it was to keep our virtue about us that our church leaders reserved entire weeknight meetings to offer us strict how-to instructions" (or, in this case, how-not-to instructions). Brooks paints a picture of Standards Nights, during which early pubescent girls wore their "Sunday dresses," while leaders covered tables in the church classrooms with lace tablecloths, lights dimmed, "a vase of white long-stemmed roses before us" (2012, 102). The girls were asked to take a rose and "smell its fragrance, feel the soft petals" (103). They each did so, passing the flower from person to person. By the time the rose had traveled through the teenage hands of each of the girls, "it was a different creature: its tight inner bud pried open, petals missing, others crimped and browning" (103). The object lesson, states Brooks, wasn't hard to understand. The virginal unhandled rose was much more desirable than its brown and bruised counterpart.[7]

For FLDS girls-into-women, the indoctrination is even more extreme. Girls are told to avert their eyes even when changing their younger brothers' diapers. They are not to touch boys, who can be expelled from the community for offenses such as holding hands. The obligations of the fertile female body—to bring as many spirit children into mortal bodies as possible—begin sooner, creating a binaried zone between not-knowing and sexual action. Writes Elissa Wall, who was married at age fourteen, "No matter the age of either party, a couple would spend their entire lives pre marriage with no romantic or sexual contact with anyone. After the union, there was a drastic change, just as I had experienced. Suddenly, within as little as a few hours, a child would go from having absolutely no sexual understanding, experience, or basis of discussion to being told that it was time to lie down and make a baby" (Wall and Pulitzer 2012, 587).

Because of the high premium put on priesthood authority and female obedience as coupled with an overall culture of reticence and repression with respect to sexuality, mediated Mormonism clearly illustrates that the insistent politics of purity can also create a toxic breeding ground for sexual assault. The angel makes the good girl exceedingly vulnerable to exploitation and abuse. Toxic femininity puts those who experience it at greater risk for relationship violence—and here it is important to be reminded that toxic femininity is about a gendered state of being that any sexed body might experience, so it is not so much a man/woman dynamic as a dominant/submissive paradigm.

Given this, Mya Grey's secret memoir *Mormon Girl to Sex Slave* depicts a dynamic that maps onto a broader F/LDS culture with remarkable ease. "Very early on, probably from birth," writes Grey, "young Mormon girls are taught, or more accurately brainwashed into being submissive to men" (2013, loc. 158). While Mormon men must also follow an exacting set of rules, Grey argues—in line with many other memoirists—the submissive dynamic is more demanding for women. "The woman's job is to submit and obey her husband at all times and in all things. The females aren't capable of thinking for themselves and making large decisions" (loc. 161). Without irony, Grey notes that her childhood lived in Mormonism made her uniquely suited to the role of submissive in a BDSM (bondage domination sadism masochism) master/slave relationship. "It's funny now that I think about it. From the time I was born and even today, I live and have lived my life by strict rules and guidelines. The ones from when I was Mormon, and now the ones my Master has given me to live by . . . I wonder if having been born and raised living with all these rules and being accustomed to being told what I can and can't do, has helped shaped me into a better slave" (loc. 173, 175). Although Grey speaks of being a sex slave as a choice she has made, and I have no desire to undermine BDSM as a legitimate sexual subculture, it is clear that we are meant to answer "yes" to her questions. Mormonism trained her nicely for subservience, sexual and otherwise.

Indeed, Grey uses the word "brainwashed" to suggest she was incapable of making an autonomous choice within her Mormon upbringing. Whether we agree that Grey's use of brainwashed is warranted or not, a larger culture considers it unfair to hamper free choice and individual consent through psychologically and emotionally coercive practices. It's un-American to use propaganda to influence people and otherwise deny them the capacity for rational choice. In other words, brainwashing is cheating. Mediated Mormonism's insistent reminders of the tight rules that psychologically bind the faithful in turn create a resonant discussion articulating freedom, justice, and Americanness as concepts that require the capacity for free choice. While Mormon scriptures underscore the importance of what is termed free agency, or the "ability and privilege . . . to choose and act for ourselves," mediated Mormonism equally makes clear that one common travesty of church membership is the withholding of the conditions that allow free agency to express itself ("Agency" 2018).

SSA the Gay Away: My Husband's Not Gay

Reality television offers an excellent domain for analyzing one such story about Mormonism, sexuality, and self-knowledge. On January 11, 2015, the reality network TLC announced a one-hour TV special called *My Husband's Not Gay* that would profile the lives of men in the mainstream LDS Church contending with same-sex attraction (SSA). While freely acknowledging their sexual attraction to other men, the subjects of this docu-reality program (and broader sociological phenomenon) marry women and father children with them. In so doing, these men abide by a central mainstream and fundamentalist mandate that heterosexual marriage and the propagation of children are mandatory prerequisites for entrance into the Celestial Kingdom. As a state of being and a descriptor of sexual desire, SSA has considerable saliency, primarily for those in conservative religious cultures that consider homosexual behavior immoral. The church website's entry on SSA articulates a similar ideology, with just a touch of characteristic Mormon friendliness: "The Church's doctrinal position is clear: Sexual activity should only occur between a man and a woman who are married. However, that should never be used as justification for unkindness" ("Same-Sex Attraction" 2016).

As is the way with much on reality TV, the pointed profile of men who desire men but don't act on it in the name of religion provided the kind of controversial narrative grist that draws attention. The announcement of the special drew fire from popular journalism, including *Rolling Stone* and *The Atlantic*, while the mainstream Mormon Church praised the couples featured on the show as "true to their religious convictions," a theme picked up and broadcast internationally through Britain's *Daily Mail* online and other global news sites ("Mormon Church Applauds" 2015). Progressive advocacy groups such as GLAAD charged the show with setting a dangerous precedent for the advocacy of antigay conversion therapy, something the mainstream LDS Church had been advocating and supporting with various degrees of transparency for at least thirty years.[8] Change.org circulated a petition that drew over 130,000 signatures, demanding the cancellation of the program (Sanders 2017). While Hotsnakes Media, the production company behind the one-hour special, had taped enough footage to build an entire series, TLC has of this writing in 2019 declined to air more than the initial program. This may be due more to market share than to politics, however. The lead-in show for *My Husband's Not Gay* was more Mormon fare, *Sister Wives*, which, as I've noted, follows the polygamous Brown family. *My Husband's Not Gay* drew roughly 24 percent fewer viewers (1 million as opposed to 1.4 million) than *Sister Wives*, ranking the special sixty-ninth among its competitors in cable offerings. *Sister Wives* averages between 1.5 and 2.7 million viewers, according to TLC, so the discrepancy between the two shows was quite marked for network officials ("Sister Wives" 2017). Indeed, *My Husband's Not Gay*'s relatively weak ratings led Hal Boedecker (2015) of the *Orlando Sentinel* to quip, "Your husband may not be gay, but he's not that interesting, either."

I'd beg to differ on that point. Not only is the program and the phenomenon that it is designed to showcase/exploit interesting, the dialogue it sparked through both mainstream and new media sites (including major news outlets such as ABC, NBC, and FOX and social media mechanisms such as YouTube, Facebook, and Twitter) makes visible the complex nexus of identity, choice, and desire that are critical to my discussion on the gender politics of mediated Mormonism. Indeed, the mediated conversation functions as a flashpoint for other discussions around the nature of gender justice in a modern moment. To understand why, it's important to know more about the program.

My Husband's Not Gay profiles a series of white, middle-class Mormon couples living in Salt Lake City who, according to a title broadly displayed in white letters across a black screen, "live their lives a little . . . differently." In these families, the men are openly attracted to other men while being married to women and having children with those women (fertility through what my friend Judith Wenger calls "the direct deposit method," which is to say through heterosexual intercourse rather than through reproductive technologies or other assistance devices like turkey basters). The men and their wives use diagnostic terms to describe their sexuality. "I experience SSA (same-sex attraction)," says Jeff. This, we are quickly meant to understand by the title and the men's ensuing comments, differs greatly from being gay, not for lifestyle or political reasons necessarily but strictly in terms of behavior. Because they admit, both privately and publicly, their same-sex desire but do not act on it, these men claim the description SSA, not the identity gay. In this respect, the men of *My Husband's Not Gay* share residency in an increasingly recognized sexual subculture, in which, much like MSM (men who have sex with men) or those on the DL (down low) in which heterosexual men have sex with other men but nonetheless consider themselves straight, the label "gay" does not work as an adequate descriptor of sexual practice, desire, and/or identity.

While other faith groups have injunctions against homosexuality and thus could likely offer their own cast of closeted same-sex-attracted men married to women, the Mormon element here is critical for several reasons. Notes one of the subjects of the show, Curtis, "When it comes to our faith and our belief, what matters is how we act." As we have seen, these mainstream Mormons live in a world where outward action trumps interior emotion. Rather than feeling that one has sinned if he has contemplated sinful behavior, these men give free rein to their desires, even taking their wives along occasionally to rate good-looking men, whom they all call "eye candy." Indeed, the men do not hide their desire for other men, joking among themselves of a four-point danger scale that ranges from looking, to staring, to needing restraint. According to the logic of the program, this openness with other SSA men and with their wives creates the terms for happiness, healthiness, and, somewhat ironically, increased intimacy with women, both sexually and emotionally. It's a logic that posits both emotional and heterosexual intimacy as the consequence of conversation-sustained honesty over body-determined orientation. Mind over matter; if you don't mind, it doesn't matter.

Further, as with many conservative religions, sexuality is approved as a means toward procreation, not pleasure. Toward this end, the church has become somewhat notorious for its summer youth retreats where troubled teen boys are sent to curb their masturbatory tendencies. An anti-addiction video released in 2015 by BYU-Idaho went viral for its über-serious comparison of those who are addicted to pornography and/or who masturbate as "spiritually wounded on the battlefield of the great war," followed by a 100-second intradiegetic narrative featuring a wounded soldier on what appears to be a World War I battlefield. In a scene that is a bit of a dream sequence focalized through a porn addict's consciousness, the soldier/addict chooses his last moment of injury and pain to masturbate, while his battalion looks on in embarrassment and discomfort (Secular Talk 2014).[9] The purpose of these hilariously unsubtle documentaries and extended PSAs is to foment social pressure around the topic of errant sexuality. Friends don't let friends jack off, apparently, and thus the lost soldier must not be left behind on the battleground of self-pleasure.

It makes sense, given these injunctions, that pornography (both gay and not) is so central to the Mormon mediascape. Bodies distinctly marked as Mormon are central to the broader network of internet porn that fetishizes garments (Mormon underwear) and secret temple endowment ceremonies as the setup for eroticized viewing. It is difficult to determine the demographics of pornography consumption, but LeGrand Wolf (not his real name), founder of the gay porn site MormonBoyz, speculates that the "audience ranges from ex-Mormons who are living out their own past desires to current Mormons who feel super guilty about 'sinning' to folks who are barely familiar with the Mormon church but sure enjoy watching the tainting of innocence that happens with and without those fancy underpants" (Aran 2015). The companion site MormonGirlz eroticizes the life of LDS and FLDS women—sisters and sister wives in full sexualized fantasy mode. Yet Mormons as memes are not only the subjects of pornography, they are often its consumers. The dirty little secret of LDS living is that pornography is considered by church leaders to be a public health crisis, particularly in Utah, where search histories show a predominance of people wanting to see scenes of pornography, threesomes, and anal sex. Internet technology has only heightened the brethren's concerns. Writes Sarah K. Burris (2016), "Anyone with a smartphone can excuse themselves to the men's room for a self-satisfying afternoon delight. Leaders in the LDS church are paralyzed in the face of First Amendment law and the ease of privacy. All a Mormon masturbator must shoulder is his or her own guilt, and the church plays up the shaming to the extreme."

The mainstream LDS Church compels adherence to its marriage-as-salvation scheme by indicating that those who defy its rules will be excommunicated and thus blocked from a shared eternity with family members—present, past, and future. For many Mormons who claim multigenerational membership within the church, Mormonism functions not just as a faith system but as an ethnicity, making it impossible from the point of view of those who live it to defy its principles, since doing so would mean alienation from family, both historically and in futurity. The church and its teaching, then, begin to operate as inalienable from the self. As Jeff Bennion, one of the subjects on *My Husband's Not Gay*, told ABC's *Nightline* (2015), "My sexuality is not a choice, I agree with that; my faith isn't a choice either. This is a deep, deep part of me that's very important to me. So my challenge is to reconcile this, and I feel that I've been able to do that." Jeff and all of the men on the show—and in the broader LDS SSA network—contend that they in no way mean for their stories to be imperatives for the way that all same-sex-desiring people should live. Some of them have tried reparative therapy, and all of them are against it. Sounding the neoliberal creed of individualism and the American ethos of rights to free expression, the subjects of this show claim their realties as male-desiring men married to women is a personal choice based on the needs to balance conscience and creed.

At one level, *My Husband's Not Gay* could thus be perceived as presenting a realistic work-around for a very specific group of people. The show could be understood as a way to reconcile dogmatic restriction with personal truth, were it not on television and remediated through news outlets and social media—and if it seriously addressed homophobia rather than papering it over with a smile and a can-do attitude. Indeed, I would argue that the amplification provided by mediation and remediation—through these various latter-day screens—alters the very notion of individual choice, particularly in this context where conservative groups have so often sought to find a holy grail of behavior modification that might pray the gay away.

It is not only this program's relation to conversion therapy that tears at the heart of *My Husband's Not Gay*; gender justice is also at its core. Writing for *The Atlantic* the morning after the program's airing, for instance, Emma Green (2015) noted that the show had started a controversy that "reveals a lot about cultural tensions in America." Not only does the premise of the show position a "woman's identity [as] less important than her husband's—she's defining herself in terms of his sexuality," writes Green. "If she has to explain that her husband's not gay, she's already admitted that his attraction to her is less than self-evident." As feminist-friendly as Green's critique might have been, it also positioned a "self-evident" economy of desire as the hallmark of heterosexual female self-worth, suggesting that a woman shouldn't be defined by her husband's sexual drives (yes!), but also bemoaning the sadness of the poor woman in a mixed-orientation marriage, who knows she is not the one her husband ogles on the basketball court. This in turn repositions a woman's self-worth as being the object of her husband's desire, putting Green right back into the very critique she lobs at the program. But Green is not alone in this regard. Indeed, in a roundtable discussion on the YouTube channel RoyalzFamily, a panel of African American young people who discuss issues related to the LGBT+ community, panelists insightfully discussed the ethics of *My Husband's Not Gay* but agreed that any woman willing to enter into marriage with a man open about his sexual desires for another man was lacking in self-esteem.

By contrast and rather remarkably, all of the subjects featured on *My Husband's Not Gay* and the overall logic of the text position the wives as agentive, knowledgeable, and the epitome of satisfied, although nowhere is there a sense that SSA might as easily apply to women as to men. As another important measure of agency and self-satisfaction, none of the wives are depicted as working outside of the home or otherwise explode the frame of domestic contentment. The husbands are depicted as playful, caring, and loyal, if somewhat naive, as in a moment when Jeff excitedly pitches the idea of going on a men-only camping trip, only to be rebuked by his wife's eye rolling and reminders for caution in the face of temptation. While scenes such as these suggest there is more tension around the mixed-orientation pairing than the couples or the show acknowledge, moments of tension also reinforce avenues for recognition of a normal state of relations between spouses in a logic that all couples have differences to negotiate.

Indeed, I believe that public reaction and criticism have largely been trying to work through this issue of how one understands the normal and the normative and, through this, how one negotiates a relation between obligation and choice, between natural and learned, and between affected and authentic. Many critics of the show are torn by the semantic distinction these men make between gay and SSA, feeling that to claim oneself same-sex attracted but not gay is to be unaccepting of one's truth.[10] Reactions indicate a critical mass of people committed to notions of what it means to inhabit an authentic sexuality to such a degree that critics of the show cannot allow for the ways that mediated accounts such as these further a heterosexual agenda that is anything but normative.

Much as with polyamory, kink, or modern FLDS polygamy, these couples contend that love, families, and sexual economies are about choices and consent. If you are honest and clear about the rules, they say, then unconventional arrangements are not only permissible but pleasurable. Indeed, the logic goes that due to the high level of cognitive rationality and discursive clarity needed to make an unusual intimate relation work, non-normative unions are superior to outmoded relationships.

Overall, then, *My Husband's Not Gay* takes a distinctive page out of a modern sexuality handbook, which is to say it allows for self-determination and thus flexibility in how one might create and adopt identity labels, choosing to alter codes governing humans as sexual beings rather than capitulating to traditional binaries, particularly those imposed by the Mormon Church. And though the men and women of *My Husband's Not Gay* refute a tie to gayness, the discursive public culture that has arisen in response to this show clearly opens a dialogue intent on negotiating the meanings of queer-friendly gender justice. In this regard, even the most conservative and/or closeted of behaviors can give rise to a discursive public culture where queerness is not only central to the conversation but highly valued as critical to the meanings of the self.

Joseph and His Forty Wives

Learn to do as you are told.... If you are told by your leader to do a thing, do it. *None of your business whether it is right or wrong.*—Heber C. Kimball, "Faith and Works"

I bring this chapter on the mediated discourses surrounding F/LDS conscience, queer identity, and sexuality to a close by revisiting the sexual economy of the church's beginning. One of the primary topics about which the mainstream church has asked its members to engage in not-knowingness is polygyny, the marriage of one man to several wives. Within F/LDS culture, the practice is more commonly called polygamy, plural marriage, or simply "the principle." I discuss the long and complicated intertwined history of polygamy in LDS and FLDS communities in much greater detail in chapters 3 and 4. But here I want to think more about the open secret of Joseph Smith's involvement in, indeed, his particular innovation of, non-normative marriage in an American and Christian frame.

While Smith drew precedent for the principle of plural marriage from Old Testament accounts of Solomon and David, his nineteenth-century revitalization of the practice in the American heartlands marked the early church as both exotic and, to many, threatening. For many years, Joseph was quiet about the principle, practicing it clandestinely himself and urging his small oligarchic circle of leaders to do the same. It was not until 1843 that he received a revelation from God mandating that plural marriage was a heavenly edict and no man might pass to celestial paradise absent multiple wives (and their combined children). "For behold, I reveal unto you a new and an everlasting covenant; and if ye abide not that covenant, then are ye damned; for no one can reject this covenant and be permitted to enter into my glory" (*Doctrine and Covenants* 2018, 132.4). For good measure, Revelation 132 also threatened Emma Smith, Joseph's legal wife, with divine retribution should she fail to support plural marriage. She had resisted earlier attempts to canonize polygamy, threatening Joseph that what was good for the gander was good for the goose, and she would take plural husbands. God's prophetic words to Joseph clearly barred her the option of polyandry. It's worth noting that this same prophecy dissolved the legitimacy of marriages performed by the state or within other faith systems, requiring that all Saints had to be sealed in marriage through temple ceremonies and conveniently exonerating early practitioners of polygamy from charges of adultery if they took otherwise-married women as plural wives. Though fairly recent in historical terms, the hazy workings of disremembering have watercolored away most contemporary Mormons' awareness of their church's polygamous past. The rise of mediated FLDS polygamy—in the form of *Big Love* or *Sister Wives* or other television fare—simply serves as another opportunity for not-knowingness, since TBMS argue these forms of popular culture depict the ideas of wayward apostates, not of true believers.

But, as I have noted, in 2014 social media forced the church's hand about Joseph's polygamous activities, compelling an admission 124 years in the making when the mainstream Mormon Church acknowledged through its website that church founder and prophet Joseph Smith had indeed married up to forty women, ten of whom were teenagers and eleven of the forty already married to other men. While the church had never denied its nineteenth-century polygamist roots, it had also not advertised these connections, preferring to let the faithful and the inquiring public assume that plural marriage rose up with Brigham Young and died out in the 1890s. Indeed, Joseph Smith himself publicly denounced plural marriage and denied his involvement in the practice, writing into the church's *Doctrine and Covenants*, "Inasmuch as this church of Christ has been reproached with the crime of fornication, and polygamy; we declare that we believe that one man should have one wife; and one woman, but one husband, except in the case of death, when either is at liberty to marry again" (2018, 101.4).

Though any student of history or reader of a particular set of LDS-inspired novels, like for instance Orson Scott Card's romantic fictionalization in *Saints*, would have immediately known of Joseph's many wives, more than one Mormon scholar has been excommunicated from the church for publicly refuting Smith's claims to monogamy.[11] Indeed, given the persecution that early Mormons endured and the fact that Mormon cosmogony requires marriage and the propagation of children in order to pass into the highest of its three heavens, polygamy makes sense as a religious and political system. But Joseph Smith's code of sexual relations with plural partners has been hard for the church to manage, particularly since, in a twentieth- and twenty-first-century context, having sex with twenty-one of his wives was fraught with social taboos about pedophilia and polyamory. Many within the church have called Joseph's girls and women "spiritual wives," indicating that Joseph acted benevolently and asexually to secure their eternal fate. Perhaps the more explosive admission on the part of the church, then, was the concession of a strong "possibility of sexual relations" ("Plural Marriage in Kirtland and Nauvoo" 2014) between Joseph and his (underage or already married) wives, lending a perverse spin to this resolutely heterosexual faith. I might add that the dispersed spermatic network between Joseph and his wives was something already fully experienced by a number of generational Mormon families, many of whom could trace their lineage back to the church's founders but could not decisively determine if their patriarch were a great-great-grandmother's legal husband or the prophet Joseph. For example, the blog *Feminist Mormon Housewives* has an ongoing series called

"Remembering the Forgotten Wives of Joseph Smith," in which commentators write of their own indeterminate bloodlines.

What is perhaps most surprising about the shocking announcement in 2014, then, is that so many people were actually surprised by the news of Joseph and his forty wives. Notes fifth-generation Saint Leslie O. Peterson, when church leaders broke the news, "At first, I was angry. Why the heck have I not known this? These women have become like ghosts in our history, and we don't teach or talk about their lives" (Dobner 2015). She had been taught about Joseph's legal wife, Emma, but no others. And while Peterson was less bothered by the disremembering of Joseph's practice of polygamy, she was troubled by the consequent forgetting of his forty wives. Peterson's response: paint the women into being through a series of watercolor portraits titled *The Forgotten Wives of Joseph Smith* (figure 6.3). Her act generated international attention, from the *New York Times* to the *Huffington Post*. "I just felt the need to get these women out of the closet and let people hear about them and celebrate them," said Peterson (Dobner 2015).

As we have seen throughout this book, Peterson is not the only person who invokes the closet metaphor when it comes to things Mormon, and though I resist the use of the idiom of the closet in my discussion about progressive polygamy in chapter 3, here the metaphor seems apt. Peterson does not accept the non-normative erotics in Joseph's closet, but she does work to dismantle not-knowingness by pointing to the shame and darkness that attend to suppression. Her portraits lend the women character, depth, backstories. Fourteen-year-old Helen Mar Kimball is depicted in pigtails, with tears running down her cheeks. Emma Smith grounds the collection from its center, her dark hair in a long bob like a modern-day Sylvia Plath. Each woman is unsmiling, with red (even lipsticked) mouths. They all make direct eye contact, erasing the distance between their world and ours. *They will not be forgotten—again.*

Yet even in this new moment of openness in which the Church is now willing to acknowledge what it has heretofore denied, what constitutes transparency is negotiable precisely because this history-making admission is extremely hard to find. While media outlets like CNN and NPR reported on the news, the essay itself, named with the decidedly untitillating title, "Plural Marriage in Kirtland and Nauvoo," cannot be found on the church's website through obvious search terms like "plural marriage," "polygamy," or "Joseph Smith wives" (to arrive at the article through LDS.org, one must input the full title or URL from the home page; a search through the frequently asked questions link does not connect to the essay). An editor for the blog *Mormon*

FIG. 6.3 *The Forgotten Wives of Joseph Smith.* Courtesy of Leslie Peterson.

Think observed that the essay was not included in the table of contents for Gospel Topics, which also addresses controversial social issues related to the church such as the ordination of women and the church's historical refusal to grant black men leadership roles. Wondering why the church might make this announcement and then block its availability, the author of the post contends, "The Church doesn't really want all of its members to read the essays. The Church appears to only want members that already know about these issues to read these essays" ("Plural Marriage in Kirtland and Nauvoo—Response to LDS.org" 2015).

Here we see a moment when knowledge is ostensibly made available to people who inquire, but an undergirding obedience culture has already suppressed open discussion and active inquiry. The hegemonic system asks believers to tacitly agree to a condition of not-knowingness, whereby subjects don't realize what they already know. This situation is made all the more tenuous due to the church's history of arduously guarding information; the church has excommunicated several dozen people for allegations it now openly acknowledges. Not only did early church members like Smith and Young publicly deny polygamy even as they privately lived it, the practice of polygamy functioned as an epistemological rite of passage that marked believers as distinct from Gentiles. Just as to spill the blood of the innocent in the logic of blood atonement might not be murder, to know and profess not-knowingness was a token of identity, not falsehood.

Conclusion: Latter-day Screens

Even while the church has gone public about some previously highly protected elements of its past, it has also worked to demonize media, discrediting it as a viable source of learning and information for its members.

> Satan uses media to deceive you by making what is wrong and evil look normal, humorous, or exciting. He tries to mislead you into thinking that breaking God's commandments is acceptable and has no negative consequences for you or others. Do not attend, view, or participate in anything that is vulgar, immoral, violent, or pornographic in any way. Do not participate in anything that presents immorality or violence as acceptable. Have the courage to walk out of a movie, change your music, or turn off a computer, television, or mobile device if what you see or hear drives away the Spirit. ("Entertainment and Media" 2018)

Seemingly, the delicious irony of this warning about the dangers of media being located on and spread through the church's own public relations campaign is lost on the brethren.

Yet for those who recognize themselves as both LDS and LGBT+, media offer a path to the light. One major consequence of the church's seeming (if not actual) new tolerance of LGBT+ Mormons is that it has taken place amid a larger cultural move toward queer visibility. Support groups have sprouted and begun to grow rapidly in the post-Stonewall United States and the fertile soils of the internet. Mormon LGBT+ youth, adults, and allies now have the growing resources of *Sunstone*, a liberal-leaning magazine that supports the idea of many Mormonisms. Progressive Mormons also have Affirmation, a website and social organizing consortium dedicated to encouraging spirituality and empowering LGBT+/SSA Mormons so that they might "make valuable contributions within and outside of the Church" ("Who We Are" 2015). And while parents whose children are gay may still turn to conversion and extreme behavior modification therapies, many more are joining groups such as Mama Dragons, composed of Mormon mothers on Facebook who are united on behalf of understanding and acceptance for their gay children.

New media and old media alike are thus giving voice to the experiences of LGBT+ Saints, making visible the labor of self-governance and the agony of self-recognition. Marnie Freeman writes in her poignant account of growing up both Mormon and lesbian:

> I clung to a guarantee a leader in the church from Salt Lake City had made to our youth group. . . . "If you attend early morning seminary, and fast and pray, I *guarantee* you will grow up and be married in the temple, every single one of you." I believed his promise included me . . . so I worked even harder, but my feelings for girls remained. I assured myself it couldn't be true. I was Marnie Freeman. I loved God. I obeyed the rules of God and the church. I was an obedient child, who took good care of my brothers and sisters, and I was a loyal friend. How could God let me be a homosexual? He wouldn't. I would pray and obey it away. (Freeman 2014, 26)

Freeman's memoir joins that of many other LDS LGBT+ people, who have chosen to go public with their orientation and identity, in defiance of their church's mandate for silence. As Freeman describes her plight, it was either obedience to self or suicide. She chose the former, though not without considerable anguish and serious suicidal ideation. She, like many others, was later X'd by the church not for her homosexuality per se, but for her refusal to live a closeted celibate life. Just as the camera-loving reality TV Kody Brown family speaks of going public as a matter of principle and equal rights, Freeman broadcasts her public voice as a free woman, choosing fealty to self in defiance of a system that tells her never to stop trying to obey.

But, in the flowing streams of hegemony, honoring one's personal moral convictions is not such an easy task. Even as LDS dogma encourages members to cultivate the self and make principled decisions based on conscience, that same belief system undermines the very terms under which autonomy might be established. Being good, doing right, standing in the light of one's personal truth—all are filtered through a larger church authority that has predetermined the meanings of these positions and mandated obedience. As Johnsen notes about one's affective interiority: "As a Mormon, it's really hard to trust your emotions because your emotions have been so manipulated by what you *should* be feeling" (Dehlin 2015a). Johnsen suggests that the LDS faithful are "used to being guided by people who have answers.... The path is clear; the path is straight." And for those like Johnsen who realize the path is anything but straight, the culture of Mormonism creates a "violent atmosphere" of intolerance and communal loathing, all sheathed behind a bright smile of purported friendliness (Dehlin 2015a). Says Fales, "I found it [his court of love] fantastical and barbaric.... Mormons excommunicate you with a smile!" (Edwards-Stout 2012).

It is some measure of the threat that twenty-first-century media poses that the church must continually reposition itself and its history across a multiplicity of latter-day screens. In the cluster of platforms that broadcast these stories about sexuality, sexed identity, and the Saints, we also encounter a brave new world of social media, post-network cable, vanity publishing, and blockbusters, working collectively to change the very meanings of publicity and information gatekeeping. So here's the irony: in using media's many platforms to openly defy Mormonism and honor their personal convictions, Freeman, Johnsen, Jones, Pearson, Fales, Jeppson, and a host of brave others actually enact Mormonism's most sacred codes: work hard and suffer, obey one's conscience, share one's truth. They trump Mormonism's mandate by out-Mormoning the church through a gospel of the self. Talk about oxy-Mormonic.

CONCLUSION

Afterthoughts and Latter Days

In a speech in 1993, [Boyd K. Packer, then an elder in the LDS Church and later the president of the Quorum of the Twelve Apostles,] warned that three groups—feminists, homosexuals and intellectuals—posed the greatest threat to the church. In 2010, he condemned same-sex attraction as unnatural and immoral, making him a prominent target of gay rights advocates in Utah and elsewhere....

Mr. Packer also warned against "the disease of profanity," "bad music," and substances that "interfere with the delicate feelings of spiritual communication," namely coffee, tobacco, liquor and drugs....

Mr. Packer will be remembered "for an unyielding resistance to the secular, social world, especially as that world evolved during his lifetime," Armand L. Mauss, a Mormon scholar and retired professor of sociology and religious studies at Washington State University, told The Associated Press.

—David Stout, "Boyd K. Packer, Advocate of Conservative Mormonism, Dies at 90"

Why end this book with an obituary for one of the mainstream Mormon Church's highest leaders? Am I suggesting that Mormonism is dead—or should be? Is this obituary a nostalgic retelling, a strategic denunciation, or some kind of clever metaphor about the nature of the Mormon Church? None of the above. Instead, it offers a ready portal into the book itself, illustrating the way that gender, sexuality, and media play critical roles in relation to the idea of Mormonism. I hope that the consideration of religion, identity, and mediation I offer in this book has plausibly made the case for how Mormonism reveals something quite intriguing about gender, sexuality, and modern identity as projected upon and dispersed throughout our latter-day screens.

In this book, I invoke many terms—spiritual neoliberalism, the Mormon Glow, not-knowingness, Mormonism as a meme and analytic, toxic femininity—to make an argument that mediated Mormonism fosters a discursive culture that hews more toward the queer left than the heteronormative right. As I acknowledge in the introduction, my claim is less about actual Mormons in the world and whatever their political, racial, and sexual sensibilities might be than about an idea of Mormons fostered across every conceivable sort of screen, from the Cineplex to the iPhone. But just as working in genres of the real—like reality television or celebrity studies—obligates the scholar to engage with people and ideas as simultaneously natural and created, as living, breathing people and as fictional characters, this project has required that I consider both the practices and belief principles of the F/LDS church as well as the many mediated stories that populate the mediascape.

Boyd Packer and his denunciations of the enemies of the church—"feminists, homosexuals, and intellectuals"—demonstrate the conservative mind-set that leads this religion. Yet Packer's war on liberals and liberalism has become a meme in itself, quoted and requoted, bandied about in the public sphere of social media, published memoir, and, as my epigraph indicates, the nation's paper of record. As I say none too tongue-in-cheek in this book, feminists, gay people, and intellectuals are a highly educated and literate group to piss off, and much of the primary source material that constitutes the latter-day screens of mediated Mormonism use Packer and others like him as evidence of the shocking inhumanities that orthodoxy espouses. While certainly not all Mormons in the world are conservative or close-minded—and indeed, there is a thriving liberal, pro-feminist, pro-intellectual, and pro-LGBT+ agenda among some members of the mainstream church—the broader register of representation uses the idea of Mormonism to illustrate the wrongs of a larger system. To comment on the conservative right, the liberal left need only import the Mormon.

I have offered many examples of this phenomenon throughout the book, but one particularly interesting illustration comes from spring 2017, on a television show otherwise having nothing at all to do with Mormons, Shonda Rhimes's *The Catch* ("The Bad Girl"). Much like other Shondaland material, such as *Scandal* and *How to Get Away with Murder*, *The Catch* follows the eroticized world of the workplace, this time that of a professional detective,

Alice, and her secret love, a professional grifter, Ben. Ben is a member of the Kensington Firm, a fictional London mob run by a brother and sister team, whose murdering and lying ethos is underscored by their polymorphous perversity. Both enjoy sex and a lot of it, and both brother and sister are openly bisexual in their ardor.

All of this sets the scene for what would otherwise be a throwaway moment on the primetime show. Brother Rhys sits on a couch in his posh hotel room, in a white robe, reading a book, a smirk of satisfaction on his face. Beside him sits a woman also in a robe, whom he has just bedded. We know from previous episodes that Rhys has a penchant for sexual role-play with partners in uniform. From the bedroom emerges an African American woman dressed as an EMT, buttoning her shirt and smiling seductively. And then, out of the same bedroom come two young white men in black pants, white short-sleeved dress shirts, and black ties, grinning as they button their pants. The men approach the couch, one kissing the woman and the other kissing Rhys. "Thanks for the book, boys!" says Rhys as he nonchalantly tosses it over his shoulder, the book's blue cover with gold lettering barely legible for a millisecond as a mockup of the Book of Mormon (see figures C.1–C.3).

"What did I just see?" I ask myself, incredulous, wondering if I have been thinking and writing about Mormonism for so long that I have superimposed something on the screen that was not there. Were the two men emerging from a polyamorous orgy really supposed to be Mormon missionaries? After repeated reviewing, I could not dispute the fact that such was the message of the brief clip. This is a scene in total lasting about forty-five seconds, and so details are sparse. We don't know if the EMT and the missionaries are playing a part or if they are supposed to be recruits to Rhys's erotic desires. But in either case, the larger point is securely made: the public understanding of what missionaries look like and what they stand for (virginal, conservative, religious, peripatetic, young, white, sexy) underscores their perfect use as foils to provide a rapid shorthand about Rhys and his sizeable sexual desires. Here the function of the Mormon missionary as meme offers a quick indication about a character. Proving Rhys's erotic fluidity in the eight seconds the two missionaries are on screen is dependent on the polysemic associations connected to the Mormon missionary and leveraged through the cultural work that Mormonism as a meme performs.

In a more fundamentalist register, the same kind of shorthand is at play. The internet series *Transparent*, for instance, includes an off-the-cuff remark about a diminutive female character in a dominant/submissive lesbian rela-

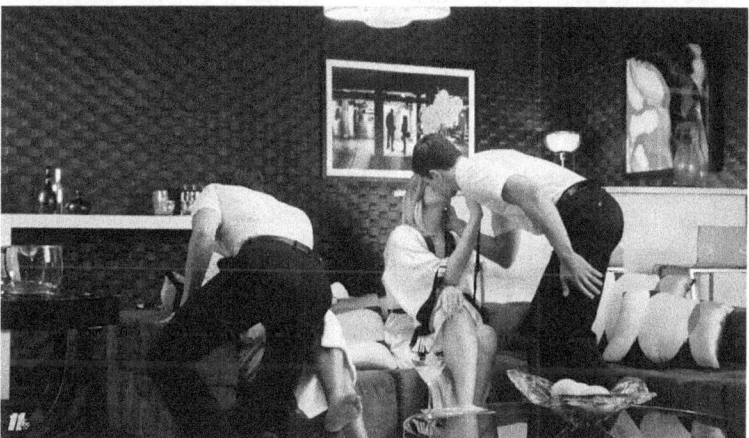

FIGS. C.1–C.3 ABC's *The Catch* and eight seconds of Mormons as meme.

tionship. In this brief scene to establish characterological depth, a woman is depicted as the wide-eyed and manipulated castoff of a Mormon polygamy sect, clearly the sexual economy of polygamous fundamentalism standing as a gateway to other forms of non-normative sexuality.

As I have noted, often to talk of and about Mormonism is also to talk about sexed and gendered identity. And this linking of Mormons with sex has been true from the religion's founding. One might wonder, in this age of overt sexuality and open discussions of desire, why we might still be fascinated by what Mormons represent. Are we still in such need of objective correlatives that allow us to talk about sex without speaking its name? Perhaps. Clearly, sexuality—or pluralized sexuality and the regulation of both desire and jealousy—is very much at the heart of stories about FLDS polygamy. In turn, the chaste economy of sexuality that attaches to mainstream Mormonism carries its own fascinations. It is a religion committed to resistance of the secular through exacting self-discipline and ethical devotion. It creates a peculiar people who operate in the very heart of the mainstream world.

Indeed, Mormonism provides a glimpse of an old-world organization on the brink of its own evolution. Many forms of media would serve to illustrate this claim, but one memoir in particular indicates the attraction of a church born in the new world whose living prophets might be seen and touched. The same book also indicates the pain of apostasy as well as the sadness and anger of being betrayed by a system that promises, well, everything in this world and the world to come after life is ended. In *Tell It All: The Story of a Life's Experience in Mormonism. An Autobiography*, Fanny Stenhouse (1875) speaks of the phenomenon of conversion that gripped much of Britain in the mid-nineteenth century. Suffering under poor working conditions and stultifying class structures, the British working classes, particularly in the Midlands, Northlands, and Wales as well as Irish peoples in the Republic of Ireland, were drawn to Mormonism for its message of hope and assurances of individual agency and the glories of contemporary prophecy. Mormonism blew a fresh breath, the breezes of the new world, into the dusty registers of millennia-old Christianity, offering a religion for the end of times rich in the powers of the contemporary. Writes Stenhouse of her own conversion, "I was captivated by the picture which [the missionary] drew of the marvelous latter-day work which he affirmed had already begun. The visions of by-gone ages were again vouchsafed to men; angels had visibly descended to earth; God had raised up in a mighty way a Prophet, as of old, to preach the dispensation of the last days; gifts of prophecy, healing, and the working of miracles were now, as in the days of the Apostles, witnesses to the power of God" (1875, 25).

Mormonism does not require that a believer adhere to the words of a prophet voiced two thousand years in the past; instead, it offers democratic citizens a contemporary voice, one authoritative yet adaptable, in the here and now. Further, it promises that male adherents might themselves hold such prophetic powers, both on earth and in the hereafter. Mormonism tantalizingly holds out the possibility that worthy men might inherit their own kingdoms, become Gods of their own planets, surrounded forever by their (multiple) wives and children in perpetual sealed unity. The heavenly rewards of this Celestial Kingdom require massive sacrifice, the foregoing of food and drink in ritual monthly fasts, abstinence from other food and drink on a daily basis, mandatory tithes and financial contributions, perfect obedience to patriarchal leaders. These mandates are difficult to uphold—purposefully so, since their goal is to forge strength through adversity.

Stenhouse speaks to all of these issues and more, and her voice has not been lost to history. Though her memoir has been given various titles and subtitles and may not be on the tip of the tongue of popular discourse culture, her thoughts on the "tyranny of Mormonism" have been consistently available since their first publication in 1874.[1] Similarly, in 1875, when Ann Eliza Young, one of the many wives of the Mormon Church's then second president Brigham Young, divorced him, she published a sensational memoir, *Wife No. 19: The Story of a Life in Bondage, Being a Complete Exposé of Mormonism, and Revealing the Sorrows, Sacrifices and Sufferings of Women in Polygamy*. Largely due to the notoriety that attached to her tale, she was able to earn a living on the public lecture circuit, speaking against polygamy and for women's rights, most of which serves as a backdrop to the twentieth- and twenty-first-century reprints of *Wife No. 19* as well as the novel and television movie reimagining of the story in *The 19th Wife*. For both Stenhouse and Young, Mormonism presents itself as a common foe, allowing for a flourishing of feminist voice and identity as acts of defiance and courage.

Queer and Feminist Frontiers

I leave my reader with one final moment to testify to the way that Mormonism helps shape a collective understanding about social justice, particularly for women and LGBT+ people. In February 2017, Utah politician, LDS elder, and vice chair of the Wasatch County Republican Party James C. Green wrote a letter to the editor criticizing a new legislative equal pay bill designed to rectify gender-based pay gaps in the workforce.[2] He argued that men have traditionally earned more than women as a matter of "simple economics," claiming that "[men] need to make enough to support their families and allow the Mother to remain in the home to raise and nurture the children." Green contended that legally mandating equal pay for women would necessarily mean that men would be paid less, in turn creating a "vicious cycle" that would create more competition for men's jobs, "further downward pressure on the pay for all jobs," and thus more mothers "forced into the workplace. And that is bad for families and thus for all of society."

While these comments are no doubt unsurprising given the mainstream LDS Church's now notorious blocking of the Equal Rights Amendment in the 1970s, Green's words struck readers as particularly backward in 2017. A post on the Reddit site r/exmormon went up a day after Green's letter was published, calling public attention to his comments. "This needs to go viral. I have already put out a couple of feelers to reporters," wrote Fearless Fixer (Bednars_Gay_Son 2017). Reporters clearly were interested. Utah Policy reported the same day that Green's post had attracted so much negative attention that it had "blown up Facebook" (Schott 2017). A few days later, the national outlets were on the story. Indeed, I first learned of it through a push notification on my phone from the *Washington Post*. By then, only four days after the publication of Green's letter in two small-town papers, there had already been such a national hue and cry against Green and his thinking on wage equity that he had both apologized and resigned his position with the GOP. The *Post* noted that "Utah Women's Coalition, which supports SB 210, took to social media with its criticism of Green's comments. 'Are we really having this conversation in 2017?' asked a Facebook post sharing a local story about Green" (Phillips 2017). The Salt Lake City Fox affiliate KSTU published a story online, featuring Green's comments and the ensuing response from Stephanie Pitcher, director of the Utah Women's Coalition. "His suggestion that we just don't pay women equally is unlawful," she said. "It's against the law by both the Fair Labor Standards Act and the Utah anti-discrimination provisions here in Utah law. Utah has one of the widest pay gaps in the nation, so I think it's definitely a positive development that our legislators are looking at these issues and trying to find solutions" (Green 2017).[3]

In featuring this controversy, I do not mean to suggest that Mormonism is behind the times with respect to gender norms and everyone else is progressive. Far from it. Instead, I hope to show how Mormonism so easily lends itself as a cultural screen on which the idea of a religion symbolically negotiates the meanings of gender justice through media. Whether it is on the cover of popular tabloids, through social media, in the ruminations of pop superstars, as part of a published memoir, or somewhere along the dial of extended cable television, mediated Mormonism largely features stories about individual rights, ethical treatment, and subjects who do not hold conventional forms of moral authority, creating a complex modern milieu where old-world solutions do not apply. As it concerns gender, choice, and agency, these latter-day screens forge the path to possibility, fluidity, and progressivism.

EPILOGUE

Mormons on My Mind, or, Everything I Ever Needed to Know about Hegemony I Learned in Mesa, Arizona

The West always paralyzes me a little. When I am away from it I remember only the tang on the tongue. But when I come back [I] always feel a little of the fright I felt when I was a child. I always feel afraid of losing something, and I don't in the least know what it is. It's real enough to make a tightness in my chest even now, and when I was little it was even stronger. I never can entirely let myself go with the current; I always fight it just a little, just as people who can't swim fight it when they are dropped into water.

—Willa Cather, *The Selected Letters*

This book no doubt had its genesis way back in the second grade, when I was a winsome, if a bit homely, seven-year-old with a massive crush on Scott Smith, the cutest boy in my class. Indeed, if you had asked me in 1971, the cutest boy in the entire school. Maybe the world. Scott was a swimmer, and he had super shiny blond hair that wrapped in straight waves around his tanned head, like a golden helmet. Even then, he had a big smile, a square chin, a killer sparkle in his slate-blue eyes, and a teasing manner that made its way to my heart and set it aflutter when we played girls-chase-the-boys on the playground. One day when I actually caught him, I felt the sizzling energy of first love electrify my entire body.

For his part, Scott played hot and cold with my affections. Sometimes he flirted with me and other times he was far more taken with Amy, the flaxen-haired and ringleted new girl in our class, whom I perceived as my primary competition in the battle for Scott's heart. By the third grade—a full year after I had tagged Scott and felt the crackle of romantic ardor—I was even more desperately in love, and Amy was still on the scene like over-chewed gum on my sneakers. But then, the death knell.

In February, my parents informed me and my brothers that we'd be moving to a new house in the same town but a different school district, and given how many miles our desert city contained, I wasn't sure that I'd ever see Scott again, the hot, dry streets stretching like a long highway into oblivion. In desperation, I decided to give him a handmade valentine that laid bare my longing. I'm not sure what I wrote on that frothy concoction or really just what I expected from him once he knew of my feelings, but I do remember working very hard into the night on that valentine, coloring and glueing his card together as I watched a documentary about Abraham Lincoln's assassination (Valentine's Day and Presidents' Day always such odd bedfellows).

This story foretells its own ending, since when Scott opened my declaration of love and devotion, he was first surprised and then mockingly amused and a little confused, no doubt because I had managed to write out my love in an awkward iambic pentameter. My hopes were dashed when, after reading the valentine, he threatened to show my handmade creation to the entire class. Amy, who sat next to him, simpered along with the joke, her ringlets bouncing in time with her smirks. I sat in front of them and felt the sticky tendrils of mortification: shamed, panicked, and exposed. As Scott pushed his metal chair back from the desk—a tinny sound I can still recall with absolute clarity—I seized my opportunity, reached back, grabbed the valentine from his hand, and ripped it into indistinguishable pieces of pink and red confetti—the evidence destroyed. Scott was surprised by my quick and even violent reaction, and he voiced the statement that would define more than one relationship as I came of age in Mesa, Arizona. Looking a bit sad (or so I imagined), Scott said to me with resignation, "It never could have worked anyway, Brenda. You're not a Mormon."

Even at the age of eight, I knew that was a really odd thing for one kid to tell another. Though I had pledged my love in mangled Shakespearean form, my passion knew its limits. I hadn't proposed marriage or a lifetime together, for Pete's sake. And when, a week later, two Mormon missionaries arrived at our house to try—yet again—to convert my family, I felt more freaked out than hopeful that Scott was trying to turn me in order to accept my valentine and ensure our celestial future in eternity (yes, I'm aware of the vampire metaphors).

I only saw Scott in person one time after we moved, three years later when the then first lady, Betty Ford, came to town to dedicate a new civic center, and all of the Girl Scouts, Boy Scouts, and Campfire Girls in town kitted out in motley costumery to show Mrs. Ford our proud patriotic spirit. I was one of the Campfire Girls selected to help raise the flag and then stand in salute as we all said the Pledge of Allegiance. But right as I hooked the flag onto the pole, I caught sight of Scott out of the corner of my eye, and my public patriotism soon gave way to a pounding in my heart and head so palpable that I couldn't even hear the national anthem above my own internal pulse. Squinting into the bright glare of the sun as my eyes traced the flag's ascent into the cerulean blue sky above, I felt this excruciating vulnerability that was equal parts desire and disappointment. Scott seemed more taken with the multiple teams of white-shirted and tie-wearing Mormon missionaries, who were patrolling the celebratory site in search of potential converts. Perhaps Scott had in his mind his own version of desire and dread, as he watched the young missionary he himself would soon become in a few short years, working the crowds in the name of Jesus and Joseph Smith.

Those missionaries in pairs, often on bikes, with their short haircuts, white dress shirts, black neckties, black pants, and laminated name tags with formal names of Elder So-and-So printed on them, were ubiquitous symbols of my childhood. Though I lived in a city that had a large Latter-day Saint population and its own temple, young white Mormon men were still sent to Mesa to try to convert the rest of us. As I discuss in the book, by divine decree (as interpreted through the church's prophets), black men were not called to serve missions until 1978; women were and are eligible to serve missions, but they tend to be rare, and they are still barred from holding priesthood positions in the church. So it really was clean-cut white male teenagers—their still-growing frames, pimpled faces, awkward hands, and bony Adam's apples emerging from inexpensive and too-large suits—who patrolled the streets of my childhood.

Even as a nonmember, the exclusionary privilege that blocked women and people of "African blood" from membership in the LDS Church struck me as colossally unfair, and it was one of the many things that made the culture of Mormonism around me more suspect than desirable. As a junior feminist, I was invested in social justice and equal rights and so was never good conversion material, a knowledge that somehow engendered in me an odd combination of pride and embarrassment. Certainly, Scott knew what he was talking about when he said things would never work between us.

It was pretty hard to walk a neighborhood street in Mesa without seeing missionaries doing their work—we'd meet them coming and going on our way to school or trips to the dusty playgrounds. I always figured the missionary teams in Mesa must have been the borderline boys, those reckless teens who needed to be closer to the master church rather than being cast into the wilds of the Saharas or the streets of Shanghai, where some of my friends from high school were later sent. Doing a mission in Mesa was much like serving in Salt Lake City or Provo—Mormonism was in the earth, the air, the water. We ingested it with our orange creamsicles, limp French fries, and bland macaroni and cheese served in the food court at Kino Junior High. We waded through it in the pools and irrigation canals. We tubed down it on the Salt River in black oily inner tubes that smelled of warm petroleum. Over the years of growing up in Mesa, it became customary to expect a visit from missionaries weekly, either because they stumbled onto our house or because one of our neighbors, or the parents of our friends, or our teachers at school, or my parents' bosses or coworkers sent them over to try again. And again. And again.

It also became customary to turn down, politely refuse, and sometimes outwardly spurn gifts of the Book of Mormon offered by friends at school or my piano teacher or the man who coached one brother's Little League team or the leader of my other brother's Boy Scout troop. One time I was in an eighth-grade algebra class, and the girl in front of me turned around with a huge smile on her face. "Brenda," she said warmly, offering me a beautifully wrapped present, "I want to give you this. And I'd like to invite you to my house next Monday night. Will you take it? Can you come?" No stranger to these sorts of maneuvers, I politely declined. Mondays were Mormon family home evenings, times when families stayed home to commune together, do crafts, play games, engage in Bible and Book of Mormon study and prayer, and eat sweet treats. In truth, I admire that sort of commitment to familial solidarity, but when I was thirteen, being invited to a family home evening was code for a subtle gang conversion. So was being invited to a dance at the stake center or to before-school seminary (religious classes). Yet even though I knew invitations were thinly veiled attempts at conversion, being invited was somehow quite sweet. And alluring. I must have said yes to some of these events, because I distinctly remember standing on the edge of a recreation room at the stake center as Mormon boys asked Mormon girls to dance. Even in the dark, I wore a fluorescent scarlet sign flashing GENTILE (their word for non-Mormons) that made it obvious I was not like them.

In fact, I wasn't even a prime conversion prospect because I was deemed too pushy and opinionated. While I was generally a good girl, sometimes to my own detriment, I had a particular talent for getting into heated religious debates with Mormon kids (and their parents, and their stake leaders, and even visiting Mormon dignitaries). My parents were of the mind that the best way to deal with the proselytizing fever of Mesa was to live and let live in public but to push Presbyterianism with equal fervor at home. The problem with this idea is that Presbyterians as a group are somewhat unextreme. Inheritors of the rational tradition through Calvinism and the Church of Scotland, Presbyterians tend to be orderly and reasonable in all things, and they take great pride in their self-described open-mindedness and rationality, which can often feel stale and emotionally empty. Naturally, then, the right way to deal with Mormons according to Presbyterian doctrine was through reasonable conversation and scholarly debate.

At one point when I was in ninth grade, I actually had a sit-down with a member of the Seventy, the elevated LDS officials who serve as general authorities within the higher orders of the church. Brother Seventy was himself actually close to seventy; I was fourteen. Our conversation mostly centered on the idea that in the LDS cosmogony there are three levels of heaven: celestial, terrestrial, and telestial (much like Dante's Paradise, Purgatory, and Inferno, the celestial level is the highest and most wonderful, the terrestrial a sort of heavenly waiting room, and the telestial no place anyone wants to go). I had also heard what struck me as a weird rumor from my Mormon friends that their dads could inherit their own planet if they made it into the Celestial Kingdom, which required that they marry in the temple and have enough children, tithe regularly to the church, and let themselves be baptized in proxy for the dead. It didn't square for me, even as a young teenager, that a faith allowing for real people on earth to later become Gods could also call themselves Christian under the orthodox view of monotheism that I had been taught. Of course, this was before I began a more studied contemplation of the world's religions and began to realize how deeply complex, and contradictory, most organized faiths can be. And it was long before I gave up on organized religion altogether.

In those talks with Brother Seventy, I was as doctrinaire and unbending as he, pushing my points with equally dogged religious fervor as we both kept circling back to arcane biblical passages to buttress our respective positions. The deck seemed crazily stacked in his favor, and I'm sure nothing I said fazed him. But he did seem oddly unnerved by the fact that I didn't back down. Indeed, in going to verbal holy war with him, I failed to exemplify the perfect obedience and subservience that is expected of girls and women within Mormon culture. Weirdly, his surprise at my intensity eroded my fire. I was ashamed of myself for being so difficult. Though I wasn't a Mormon, I had already internalized its central mandate for girls: be good, be pure, be docile, be obedient. Let men win. Work to deserve their love and approval. Feel guilty when you express yourself. Of course, these values about gendered ways of being simply mirror a larger cultural investment in how good men and women, boys and girls, ought to behave, but this was yet news to me.

I suppose one of the other things that Mormonism taught me is that I would be punished if I did not conform—not literally, of course, but in the figurative expression of judgment and social shunning that is wounding to human relationships but particularly crushing to a teenage heart. One day, you'd have a best friend; the next day the missionaries would visit; the day after, you were eating lunch by yourself. It was a shocking form of cognitive and emotional dissonance, brutal in its expression. Mormons are not, of course, the only group that uses social belonging and exclusion as part of the establishment of its worldview, but in the Mormon world of Mesa, these forms of affective vanishing were common.[1]

Like many who grow up in these kinds of environments, the only way up was out. So when I was eighteen, I left Mesa and the Mormons for Tucson and the University of Arizona. I dealt with Mormons most of my life primarily by not dealing with them—tucking them away into the oddities of childhood. But childhood shapes everything about a life. And the Mormons have very much influenced mine—both directly and indirectly, both when I lived in their midst and now that I might pick and choose my exposure. Due to how thoroughly Mormonism dominated my coming of age, it is now impossible for me to filter out the Saints when I think about my early life. Mormonism, as both religion and culture, was critical to my experience, both because Mormon kids tended to dominate every activity—sports, student council, band, drama, choir, speech, and debate—but also because my childhood was defined by exclusion. If Joanna Brooks can write a story of her life called *The Book of Mormon Girl*, I could just as easily write a memoir called the *The Book of Non-Mormon Girl*, for not-being-a-Mormon-ness saturated every part of my life between the ages of five and eighteen.

Seen and Unseen

Joanna Brooks is a good place to expand this reflection since her memoir takes as a given that Mormons are invisible to mainstream American culture, passing among us as regular folk only detectable to each other. "Invisible as our differences might have been to the non-Mormons we lived among," remembers Brooks,

> we Mormons were never invisible to one another. . . . Even in airports, gas stations, and department stores, we Mormons could spot other Mormons: married people with several children in tow; always modestly dressed, our dresses and shorts to the knees, our shoulders covered, the shadow of the neckline or hemline of our sacred undergarments barely visible through the clothes; our faces soft and pale from the church commitments that kept us indoors most of the weekend; our men clean-shaven and sort of girlish because they were free of vices, and still wearing haircuts short as missionaries'; never a curse word uttered, never a Coke or a coffee or cigarette in hand. Maybe driving a two-toned blue passenger van with bench seats, and always carrying an extra book of scripture: never just the Bible but our Book of Mormon too. (2012, 15–16)

It's not like those codes were such a big secret. Not in the desert city of Mesa, Arizona, anyway. In Mesa, Mormonism held sway, in all of its smiling, persistent, bland everywhereness. And it wasn't just the missionary teams you'd pass on the street or endless copies of the Book of Mormon that were handed out freely; it was the way ordinary everyday events—a kid's birthday party, a play date, a field trip—had to be factored through an elaborate set of church-centric calendars, menu restrictions, and do's and don'ts. No Sunday afternoon events. No before-school meetings. Not if you actually wanted anyone to show up. Mormonism asserted itself in the way that practically any kind of adult clothing you could buy in stores was designed to cover Mormon garments (their holy underwear), and Mormonism showed itself in the way that Mormon kids had so many brothers and sisters that they didn't need friends. Launette Hunt even had an electric drinking fountain in her backyard for all her brothers and sisters!

Indeed, many of the tells that Brooks identifies are as legible to me as they would be to church members. I may not know all of the words to LDS hymns (though now I can find them online, if I'm so inclined), but much of the treasure trove of mediation that fills this book is absolutely familiar to me from my own childhood. The Brown family with arms folded across their stomachs in prayer on *Sister Wives* or Barb, the first wife on HBO's *Big Love*, exclaiming, "Oh my heck!" in frustration. Indeed, I was recently at a family wedding in Chicago, and my son's babysitter (whom we had found through a babysitting app) exclaimed, "Oh my heck!" when my son startled her with a pig mask he had found in the closet of our Airbnb. In discussion later, I asked if she had grown up in Chicago. She said no. She was from Utah. It was only a hop, skip, and a jump from there to her story of growing up LDS and leaving the church—but its distinctive expressions are still a part of her speech when she's off guard.

When I read Martha Beck's (2006) compelling autobiography *Leaving the Saints*, about growing up Mormon in Utah with a father who was a high-ranking LDS official and also a child abuser, I was floored by how much of her experiences with the rigid patriarchies of "The Church" resonated for me—not because I had also experienced abuse but because I had such a deep recognition and familiarity with the people she described, the cadences of their speech, the coercive power of their smiles. The culture of Mormonism that Beck evokes felt like pages ripped from my own personal history, even though I was never Mormon. Yet I internalized and metabolized more than a little bit of Mormon ideology and injunctions as if the righteous life was something in the fluorinated waters pumped through the dusty desert landscapes and the tract housing of Mesa, Arizona. I never smoke or drank or took drugs; I upheld the law of chastity. I didn't swear; I tried hard to be pure and upright. Indeed, I barely drank caffeine until my late twenties, and I didn't have a beer until I was twenty-eight years old and working on a master's degree in Scotland, much to the dismay and shock of my Irish flat mate, who proudly introduced me to the pleasures of a pint. I lived through the cocaine-addled decade of the eighties swathed in a Mormon-made cocoon that kept me away from sex, drugs, and rock and roll. Safe but wrapped in layer upon layer of latter-day bubble wrap.

Of course, some—maybe even most—of my prudish behaviors and limited forms of experimentation are due to the fact that I was a particularly cautious kid with modestly conservative parents, who encouraged me to be thoughtful, sober, and careful in all of my choices and to stay away from cosmetics, fashion, and boys. But even they were baffled by my righteous (often self-righteous) behavior—in fact, at the age of ten, I scolded my mother when we were waiting in line at the grocery store for reading the headline of a tabloid out loud. The magazine announced Elizabeth Taylor's latest divorce. "Will Liz go to hell?" my mother read aloud with a delighted laugh. "Mother!" I said with indignation. "You shouldn't say that word, ever, but particularly not in public." She could have looked at me like I was a space alien, but instead, she appeared startled and ashamed, as she quietly tucked the tabloid back into its metal cage.

In another visit to the grocery store and another run-in with the tabloids, I stared in judgment at a starlet who had conspicuously gone from brunette to blonde, her vanity on full display. "I will never dye my hair," I vowed to myself at the age of eleven, feeling that the color of one's hair served as a necessary and incontestable key to one's integrity and honesty. These memories are a bit laughable to me now, given that I'm divorced, I swear, I read tabloids, and I dye my hair. I even have a subscription to *People* and a standing appointment for highlights, damn it. But in those dawning days of individuation, I had swallowed the pure life hook, line, and sinker, and I was committed to being a good girl in the eyes of my parents, in the eyes of my church, and in the eyes of my very Mormon community.

So, there's a good deal of my own personality that inclined me to invest in the moral razor's edge inculcated by the LDS Church. But my personality also makes of me a sort of sensitive sponge—I cry when other people cry, feel what others feel, pick up on what's around me. Those qualities help in writing cultural analyses, but growing up, they made it very hard to know the boundaries of my own ego. Think of it this way—in those emerging days of teenage consciousness, when one's changing body, relation to self and others, and desires for sexual expression begin to emerge, my sponge-self wordlessly absorbed a strict life of disciplined devotion. My Mormon friends (boys and girls) were being quietly inculcated into a chastity culture. Boys in the Aaronic Priesthood were learning about their "little factories," the storehouse of sperm in the testicles that had to be protected at all costs.[2] Masturbation was a sin, these boys learned, not just because it spilled the seed but because it led to a dangerous form of self-indulgence and self-pleasure that, according to the slippery slope logic, resulted in the perversion of homosexuality. Girls were taught that their virginity was a flower that, if handled too much (or at all), would become crushed and unbeautiful (though apparently not turning them into lesbians). It's no wonder that my friends' strong indoctrination in these codes that demonized sex and sexual expression would trickle into the ether and be absorbed by ever-ready sponges like me, particularly since these codes of chastity were similarly (if not quite so drastically) reinforced by my own faith tradition and gender socialization.

But clearly, I was not the only one confused by (and even suffering from) the cognitive dissonance of it all. Consider Ali Vincent, the first female winner of *The Biggest Loser*. In 2009, Vincent penned a memoir about her weight loss journey. Specific to this story: Vincent was a Mesa Mormon but always felt herself to be unlike the Mormon ideal her community projected. In her words,

> I grew up in Mesa, Arizona, in a community with a strict moral code based on the Church of Jesus Christ of Latter-Day Saints—Mormonism. I can't emphasize enough how important a role the church played in how I felt I was supposed to be and act and what kind of family I thought I was supposed to have. I grew up thinking that you were supposed to have both a mom and dad who raised their kids at home, your mom and dad weren't supposed to drink or smoke, no one was supposed to have sex before marriage, and you were not supposed to associate with anyone who did those things. That's what I learned in Sunday school. (2009, 5–6)

Because Vincent's parents were divorced, her father was Catholic, and her Mormon mother bucked the rules of the church, and because Vincent's weight and own sexual behavior put her outside of the idealized frame of the church, Vincent believed herself a failure. "I wasn't a good Mormon girl" (18). The prescriptive bar is high, and being a Mormon does not ensure that one is a good Mormon. Indeed, part of what I began to metabolize in and through Mesa's Mormon culture was this sense of not-being-enough-ness, of always needing to push more toward self-improvement and success.

Growing up immersed in the Mormon tradition while knowing myself to be outside it accentuated a need to be like Mormons yet to somehow be better than them—like I wanted to beat them at their own game. This compulsion extended to a whole swath of activities that had nothing to do with bodily purity, self-control, or belief and had everything to do with prominence. For me, distinction took the form of achievement, and I drove myself mercilessly to earn As in every class, in every year, on every report card. This kind of pressure did not come without consequences, including teenage insomnia and panic attacks. When I was in high school, my mom came into my room late one night to reassure me that she and my dad would both still love me if I didn't get straight As. As two people committed to moderation in all things, they were startled by my overachieving tendencies. But the fact is, I was competing against my peers, who were primarily a group of Mormon kids coached to lead in every quarter of school life: academics, sports, cheerleading, drama, music, student council. You name it, the Mormons had monopolized every seat of power in the Mesa public schools.

In truth, I held my own OK and I'm not arguing here that losing the lead in the school play or an officer role on the student council was necessarily unfair. They were better than me. My Mormon classmates could rely on a lifetime of communal coaching and familial encouragement that made their success a foregone conclusion. The imperative to grin in big toothy smiles, exert happy energy, be friendly and play nice, move through the world in an endless wholesome kineticism, and refuse to listen to anyone who doesn't agree with you, and yet to do so in a way that effaces vanity or self-aggrandizement, is a ready template for a prescriptive Americanness grounded in optimism and pluck.

If M. E. Thomas, a Mormon lawyer who penned the memoir *Confessions of a Sociopath*, is right, however, this mask of cheerfulness may also be the breeding ground for pathology, since it glorifies the traits of "interpersonal domination, verbal aggression, and excessive self-esteem" that mark psychopathology (2014, 55). It may also breed, as the cheeky Broadway sensation *The Book of Mormon* suggests, a culture of repression and denial—the cute little Mormon trick of just turning it off. I'm not arguing here that Mormonism is inherently pathologized, but I am suggesting that the relentless code of optimistic do-goodism might itself be a bit suspect. Incessant cheerfulness has its costs, the least of which is the culture of judgment that accrues to people who experience doubt, depression, or anxiety. But even so, perhaps these costs are minimal sometimes in relation to the corrosive tax levied by realism, cynicism, and critical awareness. I readily admit that when I was a college freshman bumbling uncertainly into my own future, fearful about my confusion and my lack of direction, I envied the scripted pathways laid out for my Mormon peers. I wanted to know that cool little Mormon trick, how to turn off the chatter of my monkey brain, how to escape the dark clouds of desolation and uncertainty that would often force their way into my life.

It all reminds me a bit of having finally found myself, well on the road to a PhD. I attended a springtime graduation ceremony for a younger friend who earned a bachelor's degree at Yale. Ivy League self-belief and entitlement wafted through the air that day, its heavy scent empowering to the graduates and stifling to me. The Yale grads breathed in the oxygen of taken-forgrantedness that of course you will achieve, do meaningful work, be great, while I struggled for air. That casual sense of specialness and belief in oneself was something I never experienced in Mesa. Indeed, my high school didn't even have vocational counseling or college preparatory advising for girls, aside from a few advanced placement courses and nominal aptitude tests that said I should be a hairdresser or a librarian. Most of the boys were headed to missions and then Brigham Young University in Provo. Most of the girls would either marry a returning missionary or go to BYU to find a husband. Who needed more vocational counseling than that? On one occasion when I was actually asked what I wanted to be when I grew up, I answered, "I want to write art reviews for the New York Times." Honestly, I might as well have said I wanted to grow snakes from my head, such were the stares of incredulity that met my answer. It was with more than a little satisfaction when doing research for this book that I sat in a theater in London's West End watching The Book of Mormon, while scribbling furiously in a notebook and peering eagerly through the binoculars I had hauled to England from the States. "Excuse me," said the woman next to me in a posh accent. "Might I be impertinent and ask if you are reviewing this production for the papers?" In a manner of speaking, yes.

Mesa: West of Everything

It's no secret that I grew up in Mesa, Arizona. This may not strike you, reader, as such a big deal, but for the longest time I refused to admit I was from Mesa, only obliquely answering questions about where I was raised by saying, "A suburb of Phoenix." Even recently in Bloomington, Indiana, where I live and work, I was introduced to someone who, like me, grew up in Arizona. She was raised in Tucson. When I told her I was from Mesa, she said, "Oh, I'm sorry." The connection to Mormonism was clear. "I took a Mormon to lunch once," she said, "just to see what it was all about." Since I left Mesa, it's been a place for forgetting, not for remembering. And much like Willa Cather's ruminations about the West, I approach this home place with a hesitation that borders on paralysis. But recently, I've begun to realize that Mesa tells a distinctive story not only about my own life but also about Americanness that is born and bred in the West.

Situated seventeen miles southwest of Phoenix, Mesa sits prominently in the Mormon Corridor, or what is sometimes referred to as either the Book of Mormon Belt or the Jell-O Belt (Mormons having acquired the dubious distinction of being an extraordinarily high consumer market for Jell-O). Mesa also has more Mormon-bodied people than any other place in the world. More than Salt Lake City. More than Provo. Of course, many other cities and towns have a higher percentage of Mormons, and Utah wins the distinction of having the highest per capita concentration of Mormons in the U.S. (somewhere around 62 percent), but the thriving and quite large desert city of Mesa is surprisingly loaded with LDS folks (about 381,235 of them, according to the 2010 census). Together with their Mormon brothers and sisters (and their sprawling households of children) in the neighboring cities of Gilbert and Chandler, this part of the Phoenix metro area wields an amazing power base of LDS ideas and influence.

My parents first moved to Arizona in the late 1960s when I was about three. We were an Air Force family, and my dad was stationed at Williams Air Force Base about twenty miles outside of Mesa. My mom stayed home with the kids until I was nine. The endless hot air and rainless skies made the desert a perfect place for learning to fly, first helicopters and then refueling tankers. Dad later left the Air Force, but rather than moving back to the Midwest where both of my parents were raised, they stayed in Arizona, moving from the base into town when I was around five. From that age until I left for college, I called Mesa home. These days downtown Mesa has experienced a bit of a revival and now boasts a Square Mile of Unique Style that includes a few museums and shops, but when I was growing up there were no nearby movie theaters or museums or malls (Fiesta Mall—what we used to call Festering Mall—didn't open its doors until I had almost graduated from high school). Indeed, there was precious little to do in the long hot days of summer other than to tan at the local swimming pool (crazily, with baby oil and LP record albums wrapped in foil). Every year we would hear cautionary tales about girls who had fallen asleep while sunbathing, never to awaken due to heat stroke, their blood boiling in the cauldron of their bronzed bodies. But it didn't seem to stop us. In 2014, researchers at MIT and UCLA named Mesa "the most conservative American city," a fact reporter Ethan Epstein (2014) found ironic since "it hardly feels like a city at all."

I don't mean to malign Mesa too much. In many ways it was a good place to grow up, with a top-rated public school system and a wholesomeness about it that surely kept a good many Mesa kids out of trouble. Filled with dusty wide streets charted out in even orderly grids that went on forever, Mesa's expansive boulevards are part of my muscle memory. Indeed, I vividly recall standing at stoplights, waiting in the hot desert sun for the green light to signal that pedestrians might cross the street. Because of the relentless sunshine and heat in the Arizona desert, to wait at a stoplight is an endurance contest, made memorable by the intensity of a heat that bores into the skin. It would take nearly a minute to get from one side to the other, the blacktop shimmering under my feet. I had always thought Mesa's wide streets (and thus long wait for stoplights) were a function of being in the Wild West—leaving room for wagon trains to turn and all that. I discovered in writing this book that those wide streets are due to the fact that the First Mesa Company, the Anglo group of Mormon founding fathers who established the city, based the city plan on Joseph Smith's perfect city.

Crossing Stapley and Brown, I was already treading through Joseph Smith's imagination.

At 133.13 square miles in size and splayed across the top of the Sonoran desert, Mesa epitomizes the meaning of hot suburban sprawl. For a town of its size (roughly the population of Atlanta or Cleveland), the Mesa of my childhood was depressingly empty. All that vast expanse of land meant to me as a kid was that it took hours to get anywhere. Even unimpeded by traffic, we could easily expend two hours driving from one edge of the city to the other. In the summer when temperatures hovered around 110 degrees, those trips were as much about enduring the sun's relentless rays as about actually going anywhere. I carry the markings of those interminably sunny drives on my skin to this day, sun spots emerging with age, brown patches and freckles sprinkled liberally across my face, arms, and back, vestiges of a relationship to the sun before SPFs and warnings of a diminishing ozone layer, the sun's tattoo on my skin that says I grew up west of the Rio Grande and south of the Colorado.

Two things typified the Mesa of the 1970s and 1980s: Mormons and winter visitors or snowbirds, as they were often called. With its mild winters and more-than-mild city life, Mesa was the perfect habitat for both LDS and old folks, and often on the long drive to the one Dairy Queen in town, we'd encounter both of Mesa's major demographics, Mormons (with their large families buckled into Chevy Suburbans) and retirees (with their white heads just topping the steering wheels of their gigantic Cadillacs or LeBarons). Getting to Dairy Queen involved going down Apache Junction Boulevard, which turned into Main Street. The Dairy Queen in those days was a drive-in where you had to eat your ice cream outside. Since the DQ parking lot was positioned directly beside the white Grecian edifice of the towering Mormon Temple, for the longest time I connected the cold refreshing sweetness of soft serve with the white coolness of the temple's stones, an impression that was only intensified by the large reflection pool in the temple gardens. Just thinking of the temple brought a welcome cool relief from the blistering desert sun. But it was also baffling to me as a child to see people—all dressed in white—standing outside the private back doors of the temple, dripping with water. Perhaps, I reasoned, there is a swimming pool in there. Or they have to take showers—in their clothes. It was more than my eight-year-old brain could comprehend that those smiling damp white-clad white people— my piano teacher, Mrs. Mortensen, or my neighbor Mr. Osbourne—were participating in ritual baptisms, offering their bodies as proxies for the dead sometimes up to forty times in a day. Those wet white-wearing folks I saw at the temple's back doors were taking a break from their proxy service, drying out in the desert's bright sunshine.

Because of that temple, which was completed in 1927, the seventh of the presently 141 worldwide temples built by LDS Church, Mesa in many ways serves as both a pilgrimage destination and a religious battle zone. When I lived in Mesa, the temple was this gigantic thing, an unmissable enormous white shimmering edifice in an otherwise unremarkable light-brown expanse where tumbleweeds literally blew across the streets. Unlike the Salt Lake City Temple with its steep gothic spires and glowing golden angel trumpeting the new dawn, the Mesa Temple is square and flat, more like a large white box with columns or the federal Treasury Building. In its mass, the temple took up a full city block and was positioned directly across the street from Pioneer Park where my brothers and I often played on the hot slides and swings, or more often taught each other the curse words etched into the undersides of the park's railroad cars. Surrounded by an armada of palm trees, both freakishly and oddly dwarfed, like a coxcombed jester in the furry fronds of a hulu skirt, the temple rose like an exotic mirage from the desert floor. This surreal impression was only exaggerated at Christmas when the elaborate light display festooned across the palm trees and cactuses on the temple's ground and reflected back to itself in a large still pool made the entire display appear not unlike Disneyland (figure E.1). I say this with admiration more than critique: like most kids in suburbia (and like most Mormons), I had a great fondness for Disney. A trip to "Disney California" was a promise of mystique, magicality, and verve, open to me for the (steep) price of a ticket. Getting into the Mesa Temple, however, cost a fee I could never quite muster, its magical kingdom always outside my experience.

We—the nonbelievers—were not allowed inside the building, only on the temple grounds or in the visitors' center, where an enormous white marble statue of Jesus stands ready to greet those who inquire within. But restricted access is also the case for Mormons, who must first be baptized in the faith (which typically happens at age eight) and then receive a temple recommend before they can go inside. If you are an active LDS member who defies the church—or even appears to go against its teachings—the first act in retaliation or punishment will be to deny you access to attend the marriage sealing ceremonies of your sister or best friend, since these activities occur in the temple. And these ceremonies are themselves highly secretive affairs, in which a man and a woman are fused to one another through all eternity. The logic of sealing is complicated, and I remember doing a lot of permutations in my head as I tried to sort out whether it is at all desirable to be sealed to

FIG. E.1 The Mesa Temple, ready for Christmas.

the same group of people in an endless afterlife. Or what do you do with the circumstances of modern living like divorce? Or whose family do you belong to most? These things become a bit trickier, too, when the ghosts of polygamy are thrown in.

Those who are sealed in the temple learn a special language, a Priesthood handshake (also called the patriarchal grip), and undergo a process called "going through the veil," all of which are meant to equip the couple for their eternal life on the other side. Temples are not places where Mormons go to church but sacred spaces where Mormons do a special kind of ceremonial worship that is hinted about but rarely discussed. This subtext, the other life that only some may know, was a consistent theme in my childhood, and I often felt that there were ghostly specters dashing just outside my line of vision, there for a split second and then gone with no proof of existence—perhaps the faint smell of sulfur.

I have stepped into the private spaces of a Mormon temple twice, once in Mesa, in 1975, and the second time forty years later in Carmel, Indiana, in 2015. It is a common practice for all new and newly renovated Mormon temples to be fully open, so that the public might view the sacred spaces within the building, a privilege available only by appointment. After a period of two to three weeks, the temple is consecrated and made both sacred and secret, so that only Saints who are temple worthy might enter and engage in the secret ceremonies that take place inside. I'd like to say that my experience of being inside the Mesa Temple was all rather awe-inspiring, but what I mostly remember from my eleven-year-old exposure to the inner sanctum were many small rooms and very plush light carpeting, which to me seemed somewhat odd in a holy place of worship. Perhaps I had in mind the elaborate mosaic tiles that line the floors of the world's great Catholic cathedrals, like St. Peter's Basilica in Rome or St. Mark's Basilica in Venice, though I had only seen these places in books at that point in my life, and Catholicism was far more exotic and mysterious to me than these fiercely private Mormons and their exalted church structures. In preparation for this book, I drove ninety minutes north of my college town in Bloomington, Indiana, to a new Mormon temple in the tony Indianapolis suburb of Carmel. The opportunity to gaze, again, on carpets and couches, on the golden rams that hold up the baptismal pool, allowed me to meet my eleven-year-old self through the various rooms of this most holy of holy places. As before, I was struck by how not-cathedralesque the space felt. Indeed, in art and ambience, the temple felt like the equivalent of an elaborate McMansion or a three-star hotel, which in some ways is altogether fitting given that the Marriot hotel chain is owed by a Mormon.

At the Indianapolis Temple, I was struck by two things: how many extremely expensive cars were in the parking lot and how much the smiling volunteer tour guides reinforced the greatest dividend of Mormonism, forever families. It is clear all of the volunteers had been coached to push the concept of family sealings as a central element of Mormonism distinguishing it from other religions. At the end of the tour, I was invited to take a souvenir photo. Standing in line, I watched families with massive quantities of children squeeze into the camera frame before me. One dad, one mom, and eight children. Or ten. Or twelve! When my turn came, I sat down alone in front of the camera, the new temple my backdrop. "Oh my heavens," said the woman taking my picture. "You poor thing! Are you all by yourself?" The picture shows all too clearly my mixed reaction of bemusement and alienation (figure E.2).

In the Mesa of my childhood, the temple was mostly a big building in an otherwise obscure desert city, and it had little draw or appeal to those not doing business within it—except at Easter. In the spring everything changed; or at least, things got a bit more interesting because in the week before Easter every year, the Mesa Mormons would host an elaborate pageant that in-

FIG. E.2 Bemusement and alienation. Photograph courtesy of the author.

volved upward of nine hundred people in its cast and crew. It was a veritable extravaganza of sight and sound. Now remember, Mesa had precious little else to offer in the way of live entertainment or community events. So the Easter pageant was the go-to social event of the year that was rivaled as a place to see and be seen (at least as a teenager) only by cruising Main Street every Saturday night. Nowadays, the organizers of the pageant duly note that its purpose is to "invite the spirit to testify to cast and audience members of the divine mission of Jesus Christ, the promised blessings of the Atonement, and the restoration of the fullness of His Gospel to the earth" ("Code of Conduct" 2013). But in the 1980s and '90s, the pageant was also a veritable religious revival, where believers of every stripe and denomination flocked to convert the picnickers arrayed on blankets, their elbows chapped by the dry brown flakes that pass for grass in the Southwest. The Easter pageant served as a polyglossic religious attraction that pulled religious fervor to it like iron shavings to a magnet. It was on the Mormon temple grounds that I met my first Hare Krishna (bused in from California), and it was before an Easter pageant that I received my first evangelical cartoon booklet from a Phoenix fundamentalist, who told me I was no kind of Christian and would go to hell unless I quickly gave up my seat, renounced my secular ways, and was born again into his church. Their extremism made the mild-mannered Mormon missionary patter that I had grown used to somewhat sweet and adorable. I'll say this for the Mormons—they can be relentless and secretive, but they are invariably nice.³

Said and Unsaid

I grew up non-Mormon in a Mormon world, and given that most of my information came from kids like me, it's not surprising that much of my knowledge about the practices and beliefs of Mormonism was cloudy. There was some talk about special underwear, or garments, but I never really saw them. Did they really wear such long hot scratchy underwear all the time? Even in Arizona's incredibly hot summers? Even when mowing the lawn? Either those wearing these abbreviated long johns took them off before they went to public pools and dressing rooms, or Mormons had their own private swimming areas and gyms, because I never bore witness to garments. But other things were too obvious to be missed—houses filled with children, and yet whole bedrooms reserved as larders, with upward of two years of supplies lying in wait just in case—of what I was not sure . . . the end of times? A run on cereal and canned beans? Nuclear fallout? Given the LDS relation to Armageddon, commercialism, and atomic bomb sites, any of those three options are distinct possibilities.

And then there were sort of in-between levels of knowledge. For instance, in the context of a people pledged to bodily purity through the WOW (Word of Wisdom), which required no drugs, smoking, caffeine, or premarital sex, I would often see kids behind my high school—those called Jack Mormons—who smoked cigarettes and drank Cokes at lunch. Even the quarterback of the football team would attend afternoon classes with bloodshot eyes and a demeanor that suggested pot smoking during school rather than other red-eye-inducing activities, like swimming or being caught in an Arizona dust storm. We were supposedly in a culture of chastity, where young Mormon teens pledged their sexual purity until marriage. Yet when I graduated from high school, I was amazed at the commencement ceremony to see at least a dozen Mormon girls march past me with extended pregnant bellies. Somehow they had all gotten a message that I didn't quite receive: yes, the faith mandated a set of severe behavioral codes and limits, but you didn't really have to follow them all that carefully. Not when you were a teenager. Unless you didn't know this. And so, like me and my cohort of overachieving nonbelieving friends, you followed the rules without being in the club. My friend Daniel, an über-successful, gay lawyer who now lives in San Francisco, still can't swear. The last time I was in the Bay Area, we had a reunion over lunch, and when he stumbled over a crack in the sidewalk, he yelled loudly, "Flip!" I laughed out loud. "Did you really just say 'flip'?" I asked him, teasing. "You're fifty. You can say 'fuck' if you want to." He looked at me in equal parts amusement and shame. "It's those g-d Mormons. They stole the swear from me when we were growing up."

There were other stories never told at all. I did not know about blood atonements or secret handshakes. I didn't know there were special healing ceremonies or bunkers built into the hills of Utah that housed the names of everyone who had been baptized into the church (whether by choice or by proxy). I didn't know that the LDS Church was so antigay that they regularized realignment treatments that included aversion therapies and electroshock therapy. I didn't know that Brigham Young taught LDS believers that black skin was a sign of sin, though it was painfully clear how very white the Mormon world could be. And I didn't know until reading message boards for *Big Love* about MMPs—or multiple mortal probations—essentially the idea of reincarnation from person to person (rather than through animals or plants), that is, that the physicality of the founding prophet Joseph Smith might be fully embodied and emboldened in our own present day. Indeed, although my early experience of Mormonism did not come to me through mediated accounts, it has been media that have provided the context and specificity that allow my memories to make sense to me now.

My childhood friends also never told me that Joseph Smith and the early Mormons practiced and promoted polygamy, or more accurately polygyny, the marriage of two or more women to one man. But then, given how easily even the largest of experiences can be rubbed out through the sands of history, I'm not sure they knew much about their own polygamous roots. Now, even as a child, I had some idea what the "fullness of exaltation" meant in the Mormon lexicon, because I could see evidence of it all around me in Suburbans bursting to overflowing with children. So having a lot of kids was clearly critical to the Mormon mandate. But I didn't realize that the "fullness of exaltation" was a euphemism for what it took to get into the Celestial Kingdom, the highest level of Mormon heaven, where a man (and only a man) can inherit his own world, and he achieves this promotion through the number of wives with whom he is sealed, the number of children he begets, the number of people he baptizes for the dead, and other good works and proper ways of living. Also, because Mormons believe there are a finite number of premortal souls waiting for bodies and once those souls have been assigned bodies the end of times is nigh, the more children one has, the sooner Christ will come again. So, in this context, more children literally brings the end of the world. Although Arizona's Colorado City is home to one of the largest and most notorious FLDS settlements, polygamous patriarchs and their plural wives weren't really on my radar growing up. The Mormons around us in Mesa were primarily jolly, super-straight, friendly folk, who made their own root beer and formed family bands with one mom, one dad, and up to seventeen children. Part of their banter: "Mother's name is Joyce. We ran out of names, so our youngest daughter is Rejoice!" I never suspected the aunts who lived with these large families might actually have been sister wives.

Mormons on My Mind

Mormons are very nice people, sometimes excruciatingly so. They are wholesome, family oriented, and devout, and demographic records indicate that where the concentration of Mormons is the highest, crime rates are the lowest (and pornography consumption the highest). They make good neighbors and decent acquaintances—but only to a point. If you aren't a Mormon, you are always at the top of the list for being turned into one, meaning that missionaries (or their many helpful advisors) watch you moving around your own town like birds of prey eyeing carrion. After a while, you get used to that. What's oddest, and at times most painful, is that try as you might, when you're a non-Mormon growing up in a Mormon world, you never fit, are never fully accepted, can never do things particularly right, and there is always a subtle and wholly unspoken disconnect between what people say and what they do.

In November 2012, I returned to Mesa, to its wide dusty streets and its big open skies, to attend my thirty-year high school reunion and to revisit places rich with personal history, places that I had for most of my life spurned and avoided. Top of the list for that visit was the Mesa Temple. I took both my mother and my almost three-year-old son with me, thinking they would legitimate me somehow, the feminist always suspicious in her resistance to the temporalities of convention and families. My son Jakey was immediately amazed by the thirty-foot white marble statue of Jesus that stands at the entrance to the visitors' center, calling him Cheezus and begging to touch his foot (seriously!) (see figure E.3). After feeling his stone-cold toes, Jakey and my mom strolled outside to gaze into the reflection pool. I poked around inside, noting the gigantic pile of dark blue books stacked to resemble a pyramid in one central room (figure E.4). These were various translations of

FIG. E.3 At the feet of Cheezus. Photograph courtesy of the author.

the Book of Mormon, testifying to the colonializing sweep and international popularity of the faith.

As in most LDS temples, a lovely young woman approached, asking if she could answer questions (and lead me to eternal salvation). I was more friendly to these questions than I have ever been before, which, I'm sure, puzzled her, since my level of openness, curiosity, and pleasantness would have been more conventionally expressed by someone who was already a good Mormon, and thus in the actual temple rather than its visitors' center. I asked her a few questions about herself, her background, and so on. She asked me a doozy in return. Looking puzzled, she scanned my forty-something face as she gestured toward my toddler. "Who is that boy's mother?" When I told her I was, she looked incredulous. "Is he your youngest?" she asked. "He is my only child," I answered. For her, it absolutely did not compute that I could look as I did and be a mother of a two-year-old. A

FIG. E.4 The tower of Babel, Mormon style. Photograph courtesy of the author.

grandmother most assuredly. But a Mormon-friendly forty-eight-year-old mother was an oddity too rare to be believed.

The surreality of it all became even more pronounced when at the reunion event itself, many of my former classmates spoke of children in their thirties, of nineteen-year-old grandsons soon departing for their missions, of having birthed children in duplicate and triplicate. They gushed over my books, told me how smart I was, congratulated me on making something of myself. A former cheerleader, who had never given me the time of day in high school, awarded me a keychain as the prize for being most photogenic. Yet no one took my picture. (So how did they know if I was photogenic or not?) They tsk-tsked about our missing classmate and their fellow Mormon, Tim, who had once been so handsome and full of life, now in the grips of a horrible depression. "He's not himself anymore," they said with bright smiles on their faces. "But you're doing great!" It all made me feel unbearably sad.

Amid all those smiles, I knew I had broken some kind of covenant. I knew it as clearly as I knew that ordering a vodka and cranberry at a social event primarily attended by Mormons would send more than a subtle message. Except that they all thought I was just drinking red juice—my subtle sign of resistance converted to a gesture of sameness. And this is how it goes. Somehow despite yourself, you end up playing a game whose rules most people seem to know but you can't quite make out—like being at a loud party where you aren't fully hearing what people are saying, but you nod in agreement anyway. It creates a cognitive dissonance that isn't quite a recipe for insanity, but it's not too far removed from it either.

The most formative years of my development were marked by this muffled relation to acceptance and authority, desires for belonging, and implicit sense of alienation. I suppose in many respects, that's why I'm now interested in the ambivalent presence of Mormons in mainstream media, since these subterranean currents create powerful eddies about status and identity. In my youth, this separation between being and belonging was profoundly confusing and painful. In the broader culture, Mormonism and the followers of the Church of Jesus Christ of Latter-day Saints are often considered a fringe religion and people. For me, Mormons and their codes of behavior and faith were a dominant force that permeated every major experience of my early life. But the point of this book isn't about me—or really, when you get down to it, about Mormons as people. The point of this book is about identity and ideas and how the two are often fused in ways that illustrate the workings of hegemony, the consolidation of gendered ways of being, and the saturation of media, in this case through the meme and analytic that is Mormonism.

NOTES

PAST AS PROLOGUE

1. In 1852, Brigham Young spoke to the meaning of the Adam/God theory: "When our father Adam came into the garden of Eden, he came into it with a celestial body, and brought Eve, one of his wives, with him. He helped to make and organize this world. He is MICHAEL, the Archangel, the ANCIENT OF DAYS! about whom holy men have written and spoken—He is our FATHER and our GOD, and the only God with whom WE have to do. Every man upon the earth, professing Christians or non-professing, must hear it, and will know it sooner or later" (Young, "Mysteries," April 9, 1852).

2. Throughout this book, I discuss the notion of forever families, or the idea that spouses and family members might be sealed to one another for all eternity. Indeed, "forever family" could well be a trademarked brand of the Church of Jesus Christ of Latter-day Saints, and the concept is often used as one of the primary draws for investigators who are considering conversion. Yet mediated Mormonism plays fast and loose with just what is involved in the forever family, particularly its ties to polygamy. For instance, *Charly* (Weyland 1980) is a hugely famous young adult novel that was made into an equally popular film, *Jack Weyland's Charly* (2002). Both narratives feature a love story between a non-LDS woman with a sexual past, Charly, and a devout, virginal LDS man, Sam. She converts, they marry, and after the birth of their son, she develops cancer and dies. Both novel and film are sad, but both play on the idea of forever families as a salve against the pain of Charly's death. Yet because eternal sealings require temple recommends and these, in turn, require that both partners be "pure," it would not be possible for this particular couple to be married in the temple and thus be sealed into a forever family. They could, however, marry legally, wait a year, and then be sealed, but this interrupts the temporal alacrity of her cancerous end. The movie makes much of the never-ending monogamous love story between Charly and Sam, even ending with words on the screen, "This is NOT the end." In the book, eternal marriage is also critical. However, Charly encourages her husband, Sam,

to find another wife, being sure to pick someone she will like since they will all live together in the afterlife.

3. Ancestry's brands include Ancestry, AncestryDNA, AncestryHealth, Ancestry-ProGenealogists, Archives.com, Family Tree Maker, Find a Grave, Fold3, Newspapers.com, Rootsweb, AncestryAcademy, and AncestryInstitution. Under its subsidiaries, Ancestry.com operates foreign sites that provide access to services and records specific to other countries in the languages of those countries. These include Australia, Canada, China, Japan, Brazil, New Zealand, the United Kingdom, and several other countries in Europe and Asia (covered by Ancestry Information Operations Company). See Ancestry.com on Wikiwand (http://www.wikiwand.com/en/Ancestry.com). As one case in point, my university library just bought an institutional subscription to Ancestry.com for research use.

INTRODUCTION

The quote in the title of this chapter is by Brigham Young, in J. Turner (2012, 301).

1. Kody and Meri Brown legally divorced in 2015, so that Kody might legally marry his fourth wife, Robyn, and thus be eligible to adopt her children from another husband.

2. Utah lost another reality polygamist family in 2018, when the Alldredge family of *Seeking Sister Wife* left for South Dakota, thus increasing the theme of persecuted non-normative families on the run to more welcoming places.

3. In the feature film *Brigham Young* (1940), one of Hollywood's retellings of this exodus, Mormons vacate Nauvoo—much like the Browns—under cover of a single night.

4. Las Vegas—famous as sin city for its legalized prostitution and gambling—is a present-day Mormon stronghold highly populated with both mainstream and fundamentalist peoples. Las Vegas is also a ready symbol for the early church's colonizing fervor. Under Brigham Young's direction, a team of fifty-five missionaries built and occupied a fort in Las Vegas in 1855, becoming the first occupants of European descent to live in the area. Although they abandoned the fort due to the Utah War (1857–58), in which the U.S. government engaged in armed conflict with the settlers of Utah Territory (largely over public polygamy), the National Park Service still calls the Old Mormon Fort "the birthplace of Las Vegas," reinforcing the settler colonialism and white supremacy that effaces the complex history of indigenous peoples such as the Paiutes, who had been living in and near Las Vegas for nearly 1,200 years ("The Old Mormon Fort" 2017). In Season 9, which began airing in January 2019, the Brown family moves to Flagstaff, Arizona. In contrast to the move from Utah to Nevada, this move is depicted not so much as a response to persecution but as a test of Kody's patriarchal authority.

5. In 2016, a three-judge panel of the Tenth Circuit effectively reversed the 2011 ruling, arguing that it was very unlikely the Brown family would have been prosecuted for bigamy absent other charges such as child bigamy, fraud, or abuse.

6. One good place to see such a sliding hermeneutic about Mormons and sexuality is in the 1969 feature-film musical *Paint Your Wagon*. Based on a Broadway musical of the same name, the film took off in a new direction from the Broadway original to offer a more detailed picture of life in a California mining town called No Name City, where bourgeois conventions do not exist. When a polygamist Mormon comes through town with two wives, the miners persuade him to sell one. Elizabeth agrees to be sold, reasoning it can't be worse than her present living experience. She is sold to and then marries Ben, and this relation sets up the possibility that the film might introduce an intriguing subplot, whereby the former Mormon wife might fall in love with yet another man, Pardner, while still wishing to be married to Ben. The reasoning here: she had been a sister wife, why couldn't they be brother husbands? Ben and Pardner think it over and can come up with no reason to decline. For most of the film, Elizabeth, Ben, and Pardner create a home and family together. And though, by the film's end, the polygamous threesome becomes a monogamous twosome, this deviation (and perhaps deviance) allows for a delicious recasting of sexual economies courtesy of the Mormons.

7. A few examples from mediated Mormonism: The Lifetime movie *Outlaw Prophet: Warren Jeffs* contains a scene of Jeffs smiling as he looks into a mirror. "I'm more famous than bin Laden," he intones with satisfaction when they both are on the FBI's ten most-wanted list, a historical truth that occurred in 2006. In the memoir *Breaking Free*, Rachel Jeffs (daughter of Warren) notes the isolation she and others experienced on the FLDS compound, reflecting on the 9/11 terrorist attack: "Years later, when I saw documentaries about bin Laden, the man's ability to brainwash his people to do his bidding reminded me very much of Father" (Jeffs 2017, 167). And scores of media use bin Laden as a reference point for Jeffs, each standing in as a symbol of evil and depravity. Writes the *Los Angeles Times* about the documentary *Prophet's Prey*: "At one point, we see the FBI most-wanted poster that first included Jeffs, his gaunt, deceptively meek-looking mug at No. 2 next to Osama bin Laden. *Prophet's Prey* is a sobering reminder that tyrannical monsters who hide behind religion can be homegrown too" (Abele 2015). More general comparisons between Mormons and Muslims can be found in many media forms, including Scott Carrier's (2011) *Prisoner of Zion: Muslims, Mormons, and Other Misadventures*; Dennis Kirkland's (2008) *Mormons and Muslims: A Case of Matching Fingerprints*; Avraham Azrieli's (2012) *The Mormon Candidate*; and Robert Robinson's (2017) *Muslim Mormon Koran*.

8. For a fictional accounting of Mormons on the front lines of gender-related matters, see Mette Ivie Harrison's (2014, 2016, 2017) Linda Walheim mysteries—*The Bishop's Wife, His Right Hand, For Time and All Eternities*—a series of murder novels that also consider Mormonism's precarious relation to domestic abuse, homosexuality, transgender identity, female authority, and polygamy.

9. Dr. King used this statement about the nature of justice in a baccalaureate sermon given during the commencement exercises at Wesleyan University in 1964. His printed version of the sermon puts the sentence in quotation marks, indicating that he attributed provenance to an earlier source. Its actual first use is not fully known, but

most scholars believe the statement initially appeared in a sermon given by Theodore Parker (1853).

10. "The dangers I speak of come from the gay-lesbian movement, the feminist movement (both of which are relatively new), and the ever-present challenge from the so-called scholars or intellectuals" (Packer 1993). In this book, I use LGBT+ to indicate the broadest extension of identity amassed under the gay pride rainbow: LGBTTQQIA (lesbian, gay, bisexual, transgender, transitioning, queer, questioning, intersex, and ally).

11. Romney's political career and two runs at the U.S. presidency have created their own niche of mediated Mormonism, including a memoir, *No Apology: The Case for American Greatness* (2010), and *Mitt* (Whitely 2014), a feature-length documentary. Mitt Romney's wife, Ann Romney, has also authored *The Romney Family Table: Sharing Home-Cooked Recipes and Favorite Traditions* (2013), the memoir *In This Together: My Story* (2015), and an inspirational self-help book: *Whatever You Choose to Be: 8 Tips for the Road Ahead* (2015).

12. The website Famous Mormons makes this case empirically with respect to the mainstream LDS Church, offering a comprehensive list of famous Mormons (like Mitt Romney) and recognizable Mormon cultural producers (like Stephenie Meyer) that numbers in the thousands and ranges from government to entertainment to sports to business professionals. While the website is a good resource for determining which reality TV participant is LDS, it pointedly does not include Mormon-themed media that are either controversial (such as the many Jodi Arias exposés) or fundamentalist (such as *Sister Wives* or *Big Love*).

13. Indeed, as described by Zoe Chase (2018) in her *This American Life* feature, Flake could well be one of the plucky missionary characters designed by Matt Stone and Trey Parker and starring in *The Book of Mormon* musical: "How do I describe Jeff Flake?" she asks. "Suit and tie, clasped hands, earnestly looking at me on his office couch. I mean, he's a senator. He's deeply earnest to the point where he's kind of dorky. He's a Mormon. He's super disciplined. He often goes to the gym twice a day. He has this way of being more hopeful than it seems like he should."

14. In a similar vein, Jeff Benedict's (2007) *The Mormon Way of Doing Business* argues both tacitly and overtly that the religious and cultural principles of Mormons directly aid their success in the business world. In a survey of nine LDS men who are also CEOs or the founders of major companies like JetBlue or American Express, Benedict contends that the work ethic, devotion to righteousness, discipline, and commitment to equality led these men to "naturally" flourish. Not incidental, according to Benedict, is the fact that each of the men had ancestors who survived the crossing of the American plains in the mid-nineteenth century. Benedict does not include women in his survey, underscoring the hegemonic gender roles that are so much a part of the ethos and mythos of Mormonism.

15. The mainstream LDS Church partnered with the Boy Scouts of America (BSA) in 1903, believing that their common ideals of God, country, and masculinity were in tandem. In 2018, the church formally severed that partnership, after the BSA became instead Scouts BSA (meaning girls and transgender scouts were welcome). The Scouts

also welcomed those who were lesbian and gay, which further led to the church's move for separation.

16. In the mystery novel *The Mormon Candidate*, Avraham Azrieli (2012, 288) puts this same sentiment about the potentiality for change in Mormon doctrine in different words: "We know our fellow Mormons.... All they need is a spark to ignite their righteousness, to set free their suppressed recognition that the Church must change. They will fight to end racism, to end women's abuse and subjugation, to end homophobia, to end the dictatorship from the top, and to end the shameful suppression of the Church's true history.... A revolution! Just like the Arab Spring.... We will instigate a Mormon Spring!"

17. One of the more nuanced academic considerations of this phenomenon is E. Marshall Brooks's *Disenchanted Lives* (2018). Brooks rightly notes that neither belief nor church membership is an on/off switch. He writes, "I quickly found that intellectually renouncing the church's teaching did not mean that they [former Mormons] had successfully rid themselves of the feeling of *being Mormon*. Ex-Mormons continued to inadvertently remember what they longed to forget" (122). As my own memoir in this book attests, this ambivalent relation between knowing and forgetting is also true for non-Mormons raised in Mormon communities.

18. As a point of comparison, there is much similarity between the secret temple ceremonies, or ordinances, of the LDS Church and the equally secret ceremonial rites of the Freemasons. Joseph Smith was himself a member of the Masons, as were four other founding members of the church. And there is great flow between the two secret societies in terms of their iconography, ideology, and structure. I do not, however, devote a good deal of space to investigating these links, since the larger archive of mediated Mormonism seems largely uninterested in these connections. While several books do lay out the relation between Mormons and Masons, that connection and/ or influence has not found its way into the active concerns of twenty-first-century discussants, as, for instance, polygamy has.

19. Another lurid Mormon sex/murder scandal played out in November 2013, when Martin MacNeill was convicted for the 2007 death of his wife, Michele. A *New York Daily News* headline offered the best synopsis of events: "Utah Doctor Martin MacNeill Found Guilty of Murdering His Wife after Coercing Her into Plastic Surgery, Drugging Her and Leaving Her to Die in Tub." Not included in this overview was the role played by his long-term mistress, the fact that his daughters pushed for his conviction, and other mysterious deaths now tracked back to "the Mormon Doctor" ("Utah Doctor Found Guilty" 2013).

20. See William Shunn's (2015) glossary for Mormonism.

21. The adversity experienced by the early settlers—starvation, illness, animal attacks, freezing, death—in turn have created one of the largest truth narratives in the F/LDS self-mythology: our ancestors endured great suffering and were able to survive only through sheer determination and divine intervention. For a direct rendering of the struggles and salvific message of the settlers, see the feature film *17 Miracles* (Christensen 2011).

22. Many serialized television Westerns contain an episode with Mormon themes, including *Wagon Train* (1959–65), *Zane Grey Theater* (1956–61), *Death Valley Days* (1952–70), *The Big Valley* (1965–69), *How the West Was Won* (1976–79), and *Bonanza* (1959–73). Interestingly, when *Bonanza* was rebroadcast in syndication in the 1990s, the rights were owned by Pat Robertson's cable Family Channel, which refused to air two episodes, called "The Pursued," about Mormon polygamists. Not all episodes are fixated on the sexual economies of plural marriage. Most histories of the West contain stories of outlaws, and Mormonism has one of the most notorious: Robert LeRoy Parker, also known as Butch Cassidy, who was raised in a strict Mormon family and struck out on his own to look for fame and adventure, as depicted in the "Drop Out" episode of *Death Valley Days*.

23. In 2017 active LDS member and former bishop Sam Young started a website and petition called Protect LDS Children. Included on the website are several hundred stories detailing the "shame and abuse" and "suicidal thoughts" experienced by LDS children and teens around the topic of sex. The website archives both written and video testimonials of Mormons of all ages, who have been asked explicit, specific, and "vile" questions about the nature of their sexual experience, knowledge, and experimentation, including masturbation. Writes #165, a thirty-year-old woman, after an experience of drinking and having sex at age seventeen: "I've done everything from counseling and therapy to studying shame and shame resilience, [but] I still can hardly bring myself to think it or speak it out loud: I was raped. . . . The bishop—this shy, mousy accountant—took me in to our home office and asked me if I had been drinking. . . . He asked probing questions like how many times we had sex, what I meant by sex ('oral on you, or on him, or actual sex.'). . . . Shame suffocated me. I wanted to disappear" ("See the Stories" 2015). Similarly, former missionary and now ex-Mormon John O'Connor created a parodic Twitter account, @LostMormon, through which he creates highly sexualized commentary about the church's president, Russell M. Nelson, as a form of social protest. Writes reporter Tarpley Hitt (2019), "The LDS Church has been sharply criticized in past years for its practice of 'bishop interviews,' where teenagers are required to be interviewed in detail by adult male faith leaders about their sexual experiences. 'It's OK to acknowledge the extreme sexual abuse by making fun of it,' O'Connor said. 'The church itself is a very sexual church. It's repressive. It creates a lot of pedophiles. It creates a lot of abusive men.'"

1. MORMONISM AS MEME AND ANALYTIC

1. There is a much smaller subset of representation that engages the female Mormon missionary. While more news accounts exist, fictional representation seems to be limited to the Mormon-produced film *The Errand of Angels* (2008) and the erotic novel *Sisters in Sin: A Forbidden Mormon Romance* (Abney 2017).

2. In April 2017, news accounts ran rampant with the tragedy of retired NFL tight end and practicing Mormon Todd Heap, who accidently killed his three-year-old daughter when he hit her with his truck. Similarly, in January 2017 one of my LDS friends from childhood lost his wife and youngest son in a house fire. Although I'm

sure both Heap and my friend received much love and support from their extended communities, the idea that such horrifying incidents would be perceived as the just consequences of unrighteous living is just heartbreaking.

3. "'Bring the whole tithe into the storehouse, that there may be food in my house. Test me in this,' says the LORD Almighty, 'and see if I will not throw open the floodgates of heaven and pour out so much blessing that there will not be room enough to store it.'" Malachi 3:10, New International Version.

4. See also "85: Mormons and Money" (2004). Given that Joseph Smith himself was accused of bank fraud when his Kirtland Savings Society failed in the Panic of 1837 and many of his followers lost all of their savings, one might argue that affinity fraud and Mormonism have long been on speaking terms.

5. It is not only dōTERRA or essential oils that use these appeals, of course, but empowering women as "Dr. Mom" does seem to be the primary rhetorical sales pitch of essential oil companies, particularly those related to LDS concerns. Consider Butterfly Expressions, an essential oil company run by the Westover family, made infamous in Tara Westover's 2018 memoir *Educated*. According to Tara, the Westover family lived off the grid. Deeply religious and LDS, they eschewed formal education and medicine. Instead, Tara's mother treated the family's illnesses with essential oils, a hobby now turned into a multimillion-dollar company. As with dōTERRA, Butterfly Expressions (2018) encourages the use of essential oils for "empowering yourself." The website also offers a link for "Dr. Mom: A complete guide to using essential oils for everything from A-Z."

6. In 1992, Harold Bloom put this idea of the LDS long game into a more nationalist frame: "One gets the impression that the present Mormon leadership is very patient; they believe that much of the future is theirs, particularly in America. We have not yet had a Mormon President of the United States, and perhaps we never will, but our Presidents are increasingly responsive to Mormon sensibilities, rather more than might be expected for a religious movement representing just two percent of our population" (89).

7. Other famous Mormons, both active and former, include Glenn Beck, Aaron Eckhart, Ryan Gosling, Derek Hough, Julianne Hough, Chelsea Handler, Roseanne Barr, Amy Adams, Christina Aguilera, Gladys Knight, Jewel.

8. For more on Mormons and image management, see Chen and Yorgason (1999).

9. Lawrence pointedly excludes the FLDS from his consideration, and there is no doubt the overall popularity statistics on Mormons would have fared far worse had he asked people their impressions related to fundamentalism and polygamy.

10. Similarly taking the pulse of America's regard toward Mormonism, in 2009 Salt Lake leaders hired two big-name advertising agencies, Ogilvy and Mather and Hall and Partners, to discover what Americans think of the LDS Church. Relying on focus groups and surveys, they found that Americans used adjectives about Mormons that were primarily negative: "secretive," "cultish," "sexist," "controlling," "pushy," "antigay."

11. One case in point is MormonLeaks, the Mormon equivalent of Wikileaks. Founded in 2016, MormonLeaks is dedicated to provoking transparency in the otherwise secretive Mormon Church, with the hope of producing "fewer untruths,

less corruption, and less abuse within Mormonism." In particular, MormonLeaks's archives are filled with hidden church pamphlets and policy doctrine on homosexuality, sexual abuse, and chastity laws, but it also engages with materials related to finances and recruitment strategies (https://mormonleaks.io). Indeed, Mormons who experience a faith crisis because of things they discover on the internet are considered members of the "Google Apostasy" (Hitt 2019). Other materials, such as Patrick Q. Mason's *Planted* (2015), work to provide counters to the many questions provoked by the internet around such topics as nineteenth-century Mormonism, race and the priesthood ban, the Mountain Meadows Massacre, or women and feminism.

12. In the U.S., 74 percent of Mormons are Republican or Republican leaning (Passey 2013).

13. Franklin Quest, named for Benjamin Franklin and his quest for personal perfection, and the Covey Leadership Center merged in 1997. Together as FranklinCovey they continue the Mormon-based ideals of personal efficiency, in the words of Jennifer Brostrom, to "spread the good word about time management, appealing at once to the uncertain identity, greed, and superficial morality of the business community" (1997, 117).

14. Mormons are a common unexplained reference and throw-away punch line in contemporary film and television culture. My two favorites: In Season 2 of *The Marvelous Mrs. Maisel* (2017–present), a character urges Midge and Susie to put Utah license plates on their stolen car, saying, "They'll think you're Mormon and leave you alone. I mean, no one talks to Mormons unless they have to." In *The Santa Clarita Diet* (2017), the two lead characters frantically try to dispose of a body the newly zombified wife has half-consumed. They see a car coming and quickly develop a cover story: "OK, we'll say we came across this murder site, and we're just cleaning up." The wife asks through clenched teeth, "Who cleans up murder sites?" The husband responds through a forced smile, "I don't know. We're Mormons." She doesn't like the idea: "Mormons don't clean up murder sites." He responds with authority, "Mormons are helpful." For other seemingly off-handed references, see Peterson and Moore (2014).

2. THE MORMON GLOW

1. Kolob is the planet or star where God is thought to reside. While knowledge of Kolob is understood to be very protected, it is an open secret in mediated Mormonism. For instance, in an interview with *Mormon Stories*, Clark Johnsen, a former LDS member and one of the original cast members of *The Book of Mormon* Broadway musical, spoke of his amazement that Matt Stone and Trey Parker knew about Kolob. Yet any fan of pop music would have had similar access to this information, had they bought and listened to the Osmonds' 1973 LP *The Plan*, which details and provides illustrations of the Mormon cosmogony and is produced by Kolob Studios.

2. For more on Brigham Young's statement on race, see Young (n.d.).

3. As with polygamy, fundamentalist Mormons double down on race, declaring both plural marriage and white skins to be mandates for heavenly admission.

4. In QB, Steve Young (2016) (great-great-great grandson of Brigham Young) credits the health codes of Mormonism for his physical resiliency and capacity to recover quickly from the literal bone crushing of playing football at the national level.

5. Donny's memoir, *Life Is Just What You Make It: My Story So Far* (1999), could well be read as a prototype for American masculinity that must struggle against adversity, in this case his own childhood success, to rise triumphant in a second act of mature manhood.

6. Immediately following the appearance, Protandim ranked first among Google searches in the United States. Visits to LifeVantage.com increased 300 percent, and visits to Protandim.com increased 800 percent.

7. The internet is a remarkable thing. The contract between Osmond and LifeVantage can be found here: "Agreement between LifeVantage Corporation and Donny Osmond Concerts, Inc., Securities and Exchange Commission, September 12, 2011," https://www.sec.gov/Archives/edgar/data/849146/000119312511309812/d241721dex101.htm.

8. This fact is not lost on Osmond himself. In 2006, he appeared with "Weird Al" Yankovic in the parody "White and Nerdy," a music video making fun of the bad dancing, awkward speech, and nebishy uncoolness that both Yankovic and Osmond personify.

3. THE (TELEVISED, POLYGAMOUS) CLOSET

1. For example, the 2018 lead-up to TLC's *Seeking Sister Wife* made a particular note of the three families being profiled and their relation to Mormonism as part of their commitment to living plural marriage.

2. Of course, whenever we are talking about mediation, we need to be mindful of how ideas are shaped and by whom. In the specific context of reality television, positions of producer, consumer, and product are tremendously obscured, if not altogether unintelligible. *Sister Wives* is a mediated text, made by Puddle Monkey Productions and Figure 8 Films, the latter also responsible for such freakish reality fare as *17 Kids and Counting* (now *19 Kids and Counting*), *Salvage Dawgs*, and *Abby & Brittany*, a reality series about conjoined teenage twins. As I have argued in *Makeover TV* and *Reality Gendervision* (Weber 2009, 2014), reality TV is remarkable for its polymorphous perversity. Its featured actors are both professional and amateur, both real people and characters. Its situations are simultaneously factual and fictional, vérité and concocted. Reality TV's mode of production slips the confines of standard conceptions of artistic creation, since there is no single author/director/creator and no coherent artistic product. Indeed, the stories of reality television are told as much through blog posts, Twitter feeds, Facebook pages, Instagram, and tabloids as they are through the diegesis that unfolds each week on the small screen (of television, phone, tablet, and computer). In this respect, we can look to the conglomerate intermedial message to determine the overall logic of shows like *Sister Wives* or *My Five Wives*, but we cannot really ascertain whether this logic is the specific intent of its participants or producers. In the brave new world of twenty-first-century mediation, the author is dead like never before in history.

3. Brooks describes going to birthday parties and ferreting out the noncaffeinated drinks from the Cokes and Pepsis. It is probably worth noting that very few parents I know, either now or back in the day, thought it was a particularly good idea to give a kid a highly caffeinated drink. We only started sneaking Mountain Dews and Cherry Cokes during lunch breaks at high school, and the Mormon kids were as taken with those high-adrenaline quickies as the rest of us.

4. Polygamy also serves a divine end in speeding the number of immortal souls who can claim bodies in the physical realm, thus bringing the return of Christ. Brady Udall puts it this way: "It was Joseph Smith, the prophet and founder of the Mormon Church, who first instituted polygamy. There were various theological justifications for the practice, one of which was rooted in the doctrine of premortal existence—a spirit world where millions of souls await the chance to come to earth and receive a mortal body. Once this finite number is exhausted, once every spirit has a body, Christ will come again and bring with him the Day of Judgment, and who can provide bodies to these waiting spirits better than a man with multiple wives? So what is Bill doing with four wives? Bill is hastening the Second Coming of Christ" (Udall 1998).

5. Michel Foucault's work is, of course, the chief theoretical literature for laying this claim. And many media and cultural studies scholars have extended Foucault's concepts, applying them to media culture. See, in particular, Ouellette and Hay (2008), Barry, Osborne, and Rose (2005), and Couldry (2010).

6. Of course, modern morality fables about the proper care of the self and the right way to live are not limited to the Mormons of *Sister Wives* or *Big Love*, or the Mormon mommy blogs that dispense advice on coupons, child rearing, and leftovers. Nor are these tales only about groups who represent religious extremes, as with the Duggars, the Christian fundamentalist family of *19 Kids and Counting*, or the proliferation of Amish-themed media in television, film, and books. The mediascape is rife with big-family stories that offer parables about managing scarcity in the context of enormous demand, of learning to marshal one's resources to the best possible end, of playing smarter not harder. Progressive Mormon polygamy stories are like these parallel tales in that they help chart a middle through their depiction of extremes. Exposure as entertainment yields significant economic capital for the real families who turn their lives into television shows or memoirs (successful and serialized reality shows such as *Sister Wives* pay their participants upward of $75,000 per adult per episode, and tell-all memoirs can often produce six-figure payoffs).

7. This representation, of course, completely glosses over LDS and FLDS participation in race-biased policies, including disallowing black men from being priesthood holders (overturned by prophecy in 1978). When the Brown family appeared on the talk show *The Real* in 2013, host Loni Love joked, "I wanna know, when you gonna get a black wife. That's a real sister wife" ("'The Real' Speaks with 'Sister Wives'" 2017). Her question was an occasion for hilarity but not answerability, since Kody, his wives, the hosts, and the audience all laughed, but no one held the Browns accountable for answering the question.

8. It's worth remembering that Kody Brown grew up in the mainstream LDS Church, and his distrust of big medicine is not such an unusual one. Still, the larger

logic of birthing as a scene of dampened emotionalism is eerie, almost creepy, on this show, particularly when Robyn is depicted giving birth in her bedroom with nary a peep or tear, the TLC cameras and her father watching.

9. To date, I have never seen a polygamy-themed reality TV program or interview ask about other practices of shared bodily intimacy, such as whether or not the sister wives nurse each others' babies. Somewhat surprisingly, the young-adult novel *Charly* (Weyland 1980), which is hugely popular among mainstream LDS readers, features one woman occasionally nursing another woman's child as a gesture of sharing and good neighborliness.

10. Two examples of cleverness in the context of scarcity can be seen with how modern polygamy contends with the demands of providing shelter to so many bodies. Cecilia Vega (2013) on *Nightline* featured Michael, who copes with his growing family by putting shipping containers in the backyard as self-contained spaces that can be used for working, sleeping, or doing homework. The Foster family lives in a 4,000-foot sandstone cave near Canyonlands National Park. "It has terrific acoustics," the seventy-two-year-old husband told a *New York Times* reporter, Florence Williams (1997). "We'll just keep blasting more apartments as we need them."

4. POLYGAMY USA

1. History is a big place, particularly with regard to polygamy. Often, what is represented as traditional is not that which began in the 1840s with Joseph Smith and Brigham Young but what was consolidated in the 1950s, after repeated federal raids on polygamous families. The long hair and pastel dresses that so many people link to an adherence to nineteenth-century culture were, instead, a deliberate dress code imposed on FLDS peoples by their prophet Leroy S. Johnson in 1955 (after a massive arrest of polygamous men in 1953), a gesture to mark them as separate from more mainstream ways.

2. As if the closeness in titles of these two reality programs is not confusing enough, there is also the TV movie *Escape from Polygamy* (2013).

3. News accounts of the emerging awareness of the FLDS encampment in Texas could be found through the Childbrides website (http://www.childbrides.org/texas.html, accessed November 3, 2016).

4. In the ABC News exposé "Breaking Polygamy: The Secrets of the Sect," Amy Rorbach (2012) promises a look into "a hidden America" made queerer by its restrictions on networked communication: "No Internet, no television, no contact with the outside world." Oprah Winfrey's version offers a look into the secret world of the FLDS of YFZ. Winfrey is equally fascinated by media, but in her case, she remarks that "the people here are surprisingly high-tech: Almost everyone over sixteen has a cell phone, and iPods are everywhere" (Winfrey 2009). Media, and its relative presence or lack, here functions as a necessary feature of these stories, almost as central to the unveiling of secrets as the complex sexual economies of one man and multiple women.

5. I should note that these codes changed somewhat in the transition from Season 1 to 2, when the polygamy rescue squad was put in the service of freeing members of

the FLDS sect. While a special two-part episode allowed for the conventional trope of long hair and dresses and the abuses of Warren Jeffs, it was also exceptional in its depiction. The rest of the season returned to the domain of the Kingston clan and to the extended family of women, girls, and boys in the system needing to be removed, while leaving the system itself intact.

6. Jessop writes in *Church of Lies*, "Condemned to a life of ignorance, brainwashing, and brutality; treated like property; producing as many as sixteen children; dying prematurely, all used up.... I was so damn mad, I decided I would spend the rest of my life saving every last one of them" (Jessop and Brown 2010, 3).

7. Flora Jessop is not alone in being such a highly desirable media presence. Most former FLDS members can expect a keenly interested outside world, eager to offer momentary celebrity. In *Lost Boy*, Brent Jeffs writes about his appearances with Larry King, Anderson Cooper, Greta Van Susteren, Montel Williams, Britain's Channel 4, network morning shows, and all Salt Lake City media.

8. Because of the insular nature of these communities, where neither state law nor bureaucratic medical systems operate, the number of wives and children sealed to Jeffs cannot be absolutely known. Also, the rate of infant death is quite high among secluded fundamentalist polygamous communities, further obscuring the metrics of family size. In one episode of *Polygamy: What Love Is This?* (episode 6.26, August 1, 2013), two former members of the Kingston group speculate that the high rate of early childhood death is likely influenced by inbreeding (forced marriage between half-siblings and first cousins to protect the purity of the bloodline), birth defects, and accidents (due to the fact that much child care is performed by other children) (Hanson 2013).

9. It's interesting to question, by contrast, if Steve Buscemi as Nucky Thompson on *Boardwalk Empire* and James Gandolfini as Tony Soprano on *The Sopranos* evidence the ugly-man-as-leading-man as part of the artistic contribution quality TV makes.

10. In fairness, these are doctrines of the early church promoted by Young but not created by him.

11. In *Under the Banner of Heaven*, Jon Krakauer describes Bountiful and Colorado City as "inextricably linked. Bountiful is home to some seven hundred Mormon Fundamentalists who belong to the UEP [United Effort Plan] and answer unconditionally to Prophet Rulon Jeffs. Girls from Bountiful are regularly sent south across the international border to be married to men in Colorado City, and even greater numbers of girls from Colorado City are brought north to marry Bountiful men" (2004, 29). Krakauer's book was published in 2003 when Rulon Jeffs was still alive. He has since served as one of the executive producers of the documentary *Prophet's Prey* (2015), which updates the FLDS story through Warren Jeffs.

12. A 2010 documentary on Blackmore and the Bountiful FLDS compound put the figure at 121 children and twenty-four wives. It ran on the National Geographic Channel in Britain, touting that number with the title *The Man with 121 Children (and 24 Wives)*. In the U.S., the documentary also aired through National Geographic, under the title *Inside Polygamy: National Geographic Special*. The failed prosecution prompted the BC government to launch a constitutional reference case, asking the province's Supreme Court to examine whether the criminal code provisions ban-

ning polygamy were consistent with the Charter of Rights and Freedoms. The court issued a ruling in 2011, upholding the law as constitutional, so long as it isn't used to prosecute child brides.

13. Daphne Bramham, an investigative reporter for the *Vancouver Sun*, titles her exposé on the FLDS *The Secret Lives of Saints: Child Brides and Lost Boys in Canada's Polygamous Mormon Sect*, while *20/20*, a prime-time U.S. news program on ABC, features its report under the title "Breaking Polygamy: The Secrets of the Sect" (Rorbach 2012).

5. GENDER TROUBLE IN HAPPY VALLEY

1. Eternal sealings are available to temple-worthy heterosexual couples only. This is not to say, however, that sealings necessarily uphold monogamy. While the mainstream church officially forbade the practice of plural marriage in 1890, plural marriage is an open question for the afterlife. Indeed, many mainstream LDS folk believe that "the principle" will be a part of the marriage economy of heaven. In earthly terms, the politics of sealing bear this out. If a Mormon man's wife dies or they become divorced, he may remain sealed to the first wife and to any subsequent wives. A Mormon woman may only be sealed once. If her husband dies or they divorce and she seeks to remarry, she may not be sealed again unless the church offers to break the sealing, a spiritual divorce that is quite difficult to obtain. If a woman remarries and has children with her new husband, those children are considered sealed to her first husband. As Stacey Solie (2013) writes in a blog post otherwise on the stigma Mormonism attaches to sex, "Polygamy has long been outlawed from mainstream Mormonism in this life, but, to the discomfort of most current and former Mormon women I know, who thoroughly embrace monogamy, it lives on in the next" (see also Pearson 2016).

2. Here I must be clear that Mormonism does not acknowledge transgender subjects, so trans men are not eligible for membership, much less the leadership roles of priesthood status or bishoprics. Those assigned male at birth receive their rewards early. At age twelve, boys are anointed into the Aaronic Priesthood, which grants them privileges of authority over all girls and women (including their mothers). At age eighteen, they are eligible for the more exalted Melchizedek Priesthood, which allows men to offer blessings and healings.

3. A few representative examples are Broadly (2017); *Salt Lake Tribune* (2017); and a 2017 series on the podcast *Mormon Stories* about transgender Mormons coming to terms with their identities and their faiths.

4. Osmond is the mother of eight children, three biological and five adopted.

5. See chapter 2 for a fuller discussion on the studies alluded to here.

6. See the blog *The Sarcastic Molly Mormon*, whose tag line is "Reflections of a humble, incredibly attractive, nearly perfect LDS blogger & realist" (http://thesarcasticmollymormon.com/#gs._ptRAlY).

7. See the documentary *Happy Valley* (Williams 2014), which offers a heartbreaking account of LDS drug addiction, pinning the cause largely on Mormonism's insistence

on cheer. On the more humorous side, there's *Mobsters and Mormons* (Moyer 2005), a feature film depicting the culture clash between a tightly knit Mormon community and a Mafioso, who is put in the witness protection program in the fictional Happy Valley, Utah.

8. For a spirited debate on the meanings of LDS modesty culture, in both biblical and cultural terms, see Jana Riess's (2015) blog post, "Beauty Pageant Shows Mormons Missing the Point of Modesty—Again." Be sure to read the comments section.

9. Indeed, media outlets were not only invasive, they were suspicious, speculating that the nine months of Elizabeth's abduction might very well have allowed for the convenient coverup of a teen pregnancy. Why does she look heavy and bloated post-abduction, people wondered? And if her captors conveyed her openly through major urban areas, such as Los Angeles and Salt Lake City, why didn't she identify herself or attempt to flee?

10. The Amazon page selling *My Story* ranks it with a composite score of 4.7 stars out of 5. As of this writing in May 2019, there are 2,083 reviews (a significant response). Those giving her five stars (77 percent) consistently note the role model she presents of enduring "a horrible ordeal" and emerging, as Jill F puts it, "happy, and well adjusted" (https://www.amazon.com/My-Story-Elizabeth-Smart-ebook/dp/B00C74VCIG/ref=sr_1_1?s=books&ie=UTF8&qid=1541168373&sr=1-1&keywords=elizabeth+smart+my+story&dpID=51E5LsEyw2L&preST=_SY445_QL70_&dpSrc=srch).

11. *People*'s "Dream Wedding" article not only described Smart as "radiant," "effervescent," her smile "beaming," it also included a sidebar about her wedding in the Laie Hawaii Temple in Oahu. Only worthy Mormons might marry in the temple—and worthiness typically requires sexual purity, meaning that the church had determined Elizabeth was guilt free in the loss of her virginity through rape (Free and Dennis 2012).

12. Given the extremely fraught circumstances surrounding the F/LDS culture of patriarchal authority, female submission, and silence around sex, it is difficult to assess the rate at which sexual abuse may happen. Nationwide, we do know that one in four girls and one in six boys are likely to experience sexual abuse. Mediated Mormonism is riddled with survivors of sexual assault and childhood sexual abuse. This, of course, does not mean that Mormons, whether mainstream or fundamentalist, are more at risk of sexual assault but that those who have experienced such violence often seek healing by telling their stories.

13. In 2017, on the heels of a rash of sexual harassment scandals and the #MeToo campaign that gave substance to the widespread issue of sexual predation, the *Guardian* reported the particular issues mainstream Mormon women experience around acknowledging sexual assault (Smardon 2017). This connection was made all the more salient in early 2018, when Rob Porter, a member of the LDS Church and a political aide in the Trump White House, resigned his post after it was revealed that he could not get a high-level security clearance. Twice divorced, Porter had been accused by his former wives, Jennifer Willoughby and Colbie Holderness, of verbal and physical assault. Both Willoughby and Holderness spoke of having been counseled by LDS bishops to suppress their concerns. They strongly discouraged divorce (see Burke and Lee 2018).

14. Many feminist Mormon scholars, such as Janet Bennion, Claudia Bushman, and Laurel Thatcher Ulrich, might well agree with these sentiments, arguing that polygamy created dynamic communities where women's choices and sex radicalism, or the capacity to choose when and with whom to bear children, prevailed. See, in particular, Laurel Thatcher Ulrich (2018), *A House Full of Females*.

15. John Dehlin, founder of the podcast series *Mormon Stories*, was also excommunicated, his hearing occurring the day before Kelly's. As with Kelly, it was largely Dehlin's crime of publicity that doomed him in his love court.

6. "PRAY (AND OBEY) THE GAY AWAY"

Note on epigraph: John Dehlin is the founder and creator of *Mormon Stories*. His January 15, 2015, press release discussing his disciplinary hearing ultimately led to his excommunication.

1. The authors cite a much-mentioned study on the capacity of four-year-old children to delay gratification as a piece of evidence to support their claims. Mischel, Shoda, and Peake (1988) conducted an experiment whereby children were offered one reward now or a more preferred reward later if they could wait. The research team then longitudinally correlated success in life, finding that those subjects able to forestall gratification as four-year-olds accomplished more as teenagers. While Forgas, Baumeister, and Tice (2009) attribute success to capacities for self-control, Mischel's study emphasized what his team called "cognitive and social coping competence" or "the ability to deploy attention flexibly" and "metacognitive understanding of the behavioral and subjective consequence of alternative types of thoughts or objects of attention" (Mischel, Shoda, and Peake 1988, 688). In other words, successful self-control here equated to self-distraction—or ways to divert desire rather than to alter it.

2. In *Squirrel Cage*, Cindi Jones's memoir of Mormonism and gender transition, Jones recounts a meeting with a member of the Seventy (a major governing body of the LDS Church): "Brother Steele," says the elder to Jones, using her previous name and sex. "You were not born with this problem. You have been taught this immoral thing. What are you doing to overcome this problem?" Jones relates her personal journey of effort and sacrifice, which includes daily sessions for prayer, serving a mission, attending church meetings, marrying a woman, teaching gospel doctrine in Sunday school, working with the Boy Scouts, directing the church choir, volunteering at the church farm, and going to temple as often as possible. But, she concedes, "The problem only grows stronger." The elder intones, "Brother Steele, that is not enough!" (Jones 2011, 163).

3. Brynn Tannehill, director of advocacy for SPARTA, succinctly and persuasively makes the case for why LGB and T belong together: (1) We all violate gender norms; (2) sociologists categorize all of us as sexual minorities; (3) familial rejection is a common theme; (4) LGB and T persons go through similar processes of denial, awakening, and (hopefully) self-acceptance; (5) coming out is a rite of passage for members of both communities; (6) the psychiatric world still pathologizes people within the LGBT+ spectrum; (7) marriage equality persists as an issue for all; (8) we

all face potential discrimination and lack of protection at work; (9) LGB peoples tend to be more comfortable with gender fluidity; (10) "We must all hang together, or we will assuredly hang separately" (Tannehill 2013).

4. A fascinating counterstudy is Karma Lochrie's (2005) impressive *Heterosyncracies: Female Sexuality When Normal Wasn't*, which considers a politics of sexuality in the European medieval period. Lochrie persuasively argues that scholars must understand the overlapping but distinct meanings of heterosexuality and heteronormativity: "Neither concept is as transparent as we often assume it to be, but neither are the two identical or interchangeable. 'Heterosexuality' expands on a specific desire for the opposite sex and sexual intercourse to include moral and social virtue. 'Heteronormativity,' in brief, is heterosexuality that has become presumptive, that is, heterosexuality that is both descriptive and prescriptive, that defines everything from who we think we are as a nation, to what it means to be human, to 'our ideal, our principles, our hopes and aspirations.' It is also a heterosexuality that excludes others from these same meanings and communities" (2005, xii).

5. Interestingly, Mormon policies related to transgender identification allow for some small degree of difference. "Gender is central to both LDS doctrine and practice," notes the *Salt Lake Tribune* in a conversation on transgender Mormons streamed live and later archived on their YouTube channel, Trib Talk. "Women have distinct and eternal characteristics, men gather in priesthood meetings while women attend Relief Society, etc. This makes it especially difficult for transgender Mormons to find a space within their faith" (Napier-Pearce 2015). But transgender identification also provides a potentially safe space within Mormonism (depending on the attitudes of the local church authorities), since for some people it might allow for male-female union and marriage, though not a temple wedding (which, in turn, means there is no promise of celestial heaven for trans people).

6. Fales is here paying homage to his former mother-in-law Carol Lynn Pearson's *Good-bye, I Love You*. In that book, Pearson quotes church president Spencer W. Kimball's book *The Miracle of Forgiveness*, which is anything but forgiving: "There it was in black and white," writes Pearson in shock and anger as she reads Kimball's book for guidance. "Homosexuality was 'an ugly sin . . . repugnant . . . embarrassing . . . perversion . . . sin of the ages . . . degenerate . . . revolting . . . abominable and detestable crime against nature . . . carnal . . . unnatural . . . wrong in the sight of God . . . deep, dark sin'" (1986, 78).

7. As I discuss throughout the book, shame culture for boys is equally insistent. The 2018 documentary *Believer*, otherwise about the need for gay acceptance within the church, offers a moving account of a young man who died by suicide after he was expelled from BYU. The shame of perceived failure led him to take his own life. His sin? Having sex with his girlfriend.

8. Evergreen International, Inc. was a 501(c)(3) nonprofit organization located in Salt Lake City, Utah, whose stated mission was to assist "people who want to diminish same-sex attractions and overcome homosexual behavior." It adhered to Christian and particularly LDS teaching, but was independent of the Church of Jesus Christ of Latter-day Saints. The organization stated this task could be accomplished with the

help of the Lord and, in some cases, psychological counseling. Though not affiliated with the church, the organization adhered to its teachings "without reservation or exception." Evergreen dissolved into North Star on January 1, 2014.

9. This PSA, which was created by students at BYU-Idaho in 2014, went viral after national magazines and comedians got wind of it. The video is no longer available through BYU-Idaho, but many copies of it exist on YouTube, as cited in the text.

10. As one example, see the comments section to Green (2015).

11. An excellent history is Compton (1997).

CONCLUSION

Note on epigraph: Obituaries of Mormon leaders do not go uncontested. When church president Thomas S. Monson passed in January 2018, for example, the *New York Times* was assailed by angry readers, who felt its obituary spent too much time on controversial topics related to Mormonism (Takenaga 2018).

1. Titles of her book include *Tell It All: The Story of a Life's Experience in Mormonism* (Utah Lighthouse Ministry, 2000); *Tell It All: The Tyranny of Mormonism; or, An Englishwoman in Utah* (Praeger, 1971); *"Tell It All": The Story of Life's Experience in Mormonism: An Autobiography* (Worthington and Co., 1875); *"Tell It All": The Story of Life's Experience in Mormonism: An Autobiography* (Sampson Law and Co., 1880); *"Tell It All": The Ordeals of a Woman against Polygamy within the Mormon Church during the 19th Century* (Leonaur, 2010); *Exposé of Polygamy: A Lady's Life among the Mormons* (Utah State University Press, 2008); *Tell It All* (Rare Books Club, 2012); *Exposé of Polygamy: A Lady's Life among the Mormons. A Record of Personal Experience as One of the Wives of a Mormon Elder during a Period of More Than Twenty Years* (American News Company, 1972); *Tell It All, a Woman's Life in Polygamy* (Kessinger Publishing, 2003); TELL IT ALL: *The Story of a Life's Experience in Mormonism* (Forgotten Books, 2015); *The Great Sensation: The Most Fascinating and Interesting Book Ever Published. "Stranger than Fiction—More Thrilling than Romance."—A genuine Autobiography—Presenting a Vivid Picture of Married Life Among the 'Saints'"* (Worthington and Co., 1874).

2. Green's letter was sent to two publications, the *Park Record* (Letters to the Editor, February 15–17, 2017) and the *Wasatch Wave* (Letters to the Editor, February 15, 2017).

3. According to the National Women's Law Center, in Utah in 2017, white women make 71 cents for every dollar a white man earns, while black and Latina women make 56 cents and 47 cents for every dollar a white man makes.

EPILOGUE

1. My friend Stacey, to whom this book is dedicated, sent me a post written by Renee on the *Laughs Like Thunder* blog that just about says it all:

Dear Mormon Neighbors, Having lived in Gilbert for most of my life, we have been visited by many young, passionate, Mormon missionaries throughout the years. Recently they have been offering their help with anything we may need assistance with. These exchanges always include the typical pleasantries where I thank them for their generous offer, and add that, "no, we don't need help with anything at this time." After their last visit however, as the young men pedaled away, I realized that I do have a request. A request that has been bubbling beneath the surface, unspoken for quite some time now. A desire that began formulating in my grade school years and has been refined since having children of my own. The next time a Mormon missionary asks if there's anything they can do for me, I'm going to humbly and vulnerably reply as follows:

- Please teach your children to be inclusive of my non-mormon children and please guide them to carry that inclusion past grade school, into middle school, and throughout high school.
- Please encourage your children to sit with mine in the lunchroom.
- Please permit your kids to invite my kids to their slumber parties, birthday parties, and weekend get togethers even AFTER my child has made it clear that he or she is not interested in attending fireside, seminary, or church with your family.
- Please allow your teen to go with mine to school dances, athletic events, and group dinners trusting that just like you, my husband and I have done the best we know how to raise a teenager who knows right from wrong.
- Please welcome my children into your homes and permit your children to visit ours.
- Please ask your kids to consider how isolating it must be on "Seminary (extra credit) Days" for those kids who do NOT come to school dressed for church.
- Please reflect on the fact that adolescents spend the majority of their waking hours comparing themselves to their peers, so when they recognize that it would never be "acceptable" to date your son or daughter or be your son or daughter's best friend, it is, at best, damaging to their delicate self-esteem.
- Please call to mind your younger years when your primary objective was to be loved and accepted for who you were without having to pretend you were someone else.
- Please understand that my family's faith also emphasizes the importance of loving others, giving of ourselves, forgiving those who have wronged us and seeking forgiveness when we wrong others, doing what is right and turning from evil, seeking a relationship with God, spending time in prayer, and living a life inspired by Jesus.
- Please support your children in having open, vulnerable, honest, transparent, loving, kind, accepting conversations with my children about what they believe and why. In fact, while our kids are having that "grown-up" conversation, I also hope to enter into this depth of sharing with you . . . the Mormon parent.
- Please know that I hold your child in the same regard as any other child who shares my family's faith or who prescribes to no religion at all. Your child is special, and beautiful, and worthy of my love and caring regardless of doctrine or theology.

- Please believe that I see our differences as an opportunity for us to grow together in loving-acceptance. God did not call us to tolerate our neighbors. I love and welcome you, your family, and your faith because we are all children of God made in His image. Your faith is a sizable component of who you are, and you are God's creation with gifts and beauty and a soul that has the ability to positively transform my life with each encounter.
- As these hopes for my children spill out, I realize that these are the same yearnings I had when I was too young to express them and they remain yearnings for me now. . . . For decades now I have felt an invisible yet palpable partition between my family and our mormon neighbors . . . a silent criterion that has said, "we can't be <u>that</u> close . . . we can't walk this life together <u>too</u> often, we can't be <u>intimate</u> friends unless we share the same faith." I want to tear down this barricade and abolish this silent destroyer of fellowship. I fear we are forfeiting valuable friendships and life-changing communion with one another as we allow religion to segregate our lives. We are not that different. Our children are not that different. We are all living in a beautiful yet broken world doing the best we can with what we have. With inclusion and acceptance we can lighten each other's burdens and love each other through the brokenness. We are all damaged humans, so let's be damaged together. As our fractured pieces are assembled together, we will transform into a magnificent and vast tapestry of vibrant hues and unity . . . we can weave our hearts into a community of "us" . . . dynamic threads of surviving souls stretching out to reach each other, love each other, understand each other. . . . staying true to ourselves while supporting one another. Loved and loving! Fully belonging! (LittleT. 2017)

    2. For a version of the chastity message that young boys would have received during my childhood in the 1970s, see "Message to Young Men," found on the LDS website: https://www.lds.org/general-conference/1976/10/media/session_5_talk_1/2680671857001?lang=eng By most accounts, this is still the message (and the material) being used to instruct preadolescent boys about sexual health and desire.

    3. Throughout this book, I discuss many secrets associated with both mainstream and fundamentalist Mormons, ranging from endowment ceremonies to underwear to notions of the end times. Yet this capacity for telling and keeping secrets has also provided the F/LDS with a handy revenue stream, reinforced by the notion that Mormons are patriotic, conscientious, and ethical. So, for instance, many credit card companies, such as American Express and Discover Card, are located in Salt Lake City. The National Security Agency (NSA) houses a massive data center, code-named the Bumblehive, at which it conducts a good deal of its surveillance on the nation ("Utah Data Center" 2018). The CIA and the FBI also have Mormon recruitment centers, considering Mormons incorruptible, as compared to non-Mormon recruits (Laskow 2015).

REFERENCES

Abele, Robert. 2015. "'Prophet's Prey' Takes Chilling Look at Polygamous Sect Leader Warren Jeffs." *Los Angeles Times*, September 24. http://www.latimes.com/entertainment/movies/la-et-mn-prophets-prey-review-20150925-story.html.

Alameddine, Rabih. 2011. Promotional endorsement of *The Lonely Polygamist: A Novel*, by Brady Udall. New York: Vintage.

Applegate, Debby. 2006. *The Most Famous Man in America: The Biography of Henry Ward Beecher*. New York: Doubleday.

Aran, Isha. 2015. "Inside the World of Mormon Porn." *Splinter*, July 17. https://splinternews.com/inside-the-world-of-mormon-porn-1793849262.

Bachelard, Gaston. 2014. *The Poetics of Space*, rev. ed. New York: Penguin.

Bady, Aaron. 2016. "Libertarian Fairy Tales: The Bundy Militia's Revisionist History in Oregon." *Pacific Standard*, January 7. https://psmag.com/libertarian-fairy-tales-the-bundy-militia-s-revisionist-history-in-oregon-8e81c0a6d5db#.yaekmwjgz.

Banet-Weiser, Sarah. 2012. *Authentic: The Politics of Ambivalence in a Brand Culture*. New York: New York University Press.

Baty, S. Paige. 1995. *American Monroe: The Making of a Body Politic*. Berkeley: University of California Press.

Bauer, Carlene. 2013. "Losing Her Religion." *New York Times*, September 21. www.nytimes.com/2013/09/22/books/review/nicole-hardys-confessions-of-a-latter-day-virgin.html.

Beam, Alex. 2014. *American Crucifixion: The Murder of Joseph Smith and the Fate of the Mormon Church*. New York: PublicAffairs.

Bednars_Gay_Son. 2017. "From Heber Utah Newspaper 'Equal Pay for Women Has Consequences'—You Guys Have Got to Read This." *Reddit*, February 16. https://www.reddit.com/r/exmormon/comments/5ufn1g/from_heber_utah_newspaper_equal_pay_for_women_has/.

Bennett, Isaiah. 2011. "What's the Real Story on Mormon Beliefs and Race?" *Catholic Answers*, August 4. https://www.catholic.com/qa/whats-the-real-story-on-mormon-beliefs-and-race.

Bennion, Janet. 1998. *Women of Principle: Female Networking in Contemporary Mormon Polygyny*. New York: Oxford University Press.

Bennion, Janet. 2012. *Polygamy in Primetime: Media, Gender, and Politics in Mormon Fundamentalism*. Boston: Brandeis University Press.

Bentley, Paul, and Rachel Quigley. 2011. "Jurors Weep as Court Hears Twisted Tape of Sexual Instructions Warren Jeffs Gave Child Brides Threatening That God Would 'Reject Them' before Having Sex by Baptism Pool." *Daily Mail Online*, August 9. https://www.dailymail.co.uk/news/article-2023887/Warren-Jeffs-trial-Twisted-tape-sexual-instructions-polygamist-gave-child-brides.html#ixzz4LfCden44.

Berger, John. 1990. *Ways of Seeing*. New York: Penguin.

"Best Bets on TV." 2016. *Hoosier Times*, August 14.

Bille, Mikkel, and Tim Flohr Sørensen. 2007. "An Anthropology of Luminosity." *Journal of Material Culture* 12 (3): 263–84. doi:10.1177/1359183507081894.

Bloom, Harold. 1992. *The American Religion: The Emergence of the Post-Christian Nation*. New York: Simon and Schuster.

Boedeker, Hal. 2015. "'My Husband's Not Gay' Bombs." *Orlando Sentinel*, January 14. https://www.orlandosentinel.com/entertainment/tv/tv-guy/os-my-husbands-not-gay-bombs-20150114-post.html.

Bosker, Bianca. 2014. "Hook of Mormon: Inside the Church's Online-Only Missionary Army." *Huffington Post*, April 9. https://www.huffingtonpost.com/2014/04/09/mormon-church-online_n_5024251.html.

Bowler, Kate. 2013. *Blessed: A History of the American Prosperity Gospel*. New York: Oxford University Press.

Bowler, Kate. 2016. "Death, the Prosperity Gospel and Me." *New York Times*, February 13. https://www.nytimes.com/2016/02/14/opinion/sunday/death-the-prosperity-gospel-and-me.html?_r=0.

Bowman, Matthew. 2012. *The Mormon People: The Making of an American Faith*. New York: Random House.

Brachear, Manya. 2009. "'Big Love' in Big Trouble with Mormons." *The Seeker*, March 15. http://newsblogs.chicagotribune.com/religion_theseeker/2009/03/big-love-in-big-trouble-with-mormons.html.

Brodie, Fawn M. 1995. *No Man Knows My History: The Life of Joseph Smith*, 2nd ed. New York: Vintage.

Brooks, David. 2017. "Jeff Flake Plants a Flag." *New York Times*, July 28. https://www.nytimes.com/2017/07/28/opinion/columnists/jeff-flake-plants-a-flag.html.

Brooks, E. Marshall. 2018. *Disenchanted Lives: Apostasy and Ex-Mormonism among the Latter-day Saints*. Rutgers: Rutgers University Press.

Brooks, Joanna, Rachel Hunt Steenblik, and Hannah Wheelwright, eds. 2015. *Mormon Feminism: Essential Writings*. New York: Oxford University Press.

Brostrom, Jennifer. 1997. "The Time-Management Gospel." In *Commodify Your Dissent: Salvos from the Baffler*, edited by Thomas Frank and Matt Weiland, 112–20. New York: Norton.

Brown, Sarah. 2016. "What BYU's New Immunity Clause Could Mean for Sex-Assault Victims." *Chronicle of Higher Education*, October 28. https://www.chronicle.com/article/What-BYU-s-New-Immunity/238211.

Burke, Daniel, and M. J. Lee. 2018. "Rob Porter and Mormonism's #MeToo Moment." CNN, February 11. https://www.cnn.com/2018/02/09/politics/rob-porter-mormonism-metoo/index.html.

Burris, Sarah K. 2016. "Inside the Bizarre World of Mormon Porn—Which Is Freaking Out the Church and Utah Lawmakers." *Raw Story*, April 28. https://www.rawstory.com/2016/04/inside-the-bizarre-world-of-mormon-porn-which-is-freaking-out-the-church-and-utah-lawmakers/.

Bushman, Richard L. 2005. *Joseph Smith: Rough Stone Rolling*. New York: Alfred A. Knopf.

Byrne, Rhonda. 2006. *The Secret*. New York: Atria.

Campbell, Mary. 2016. *Charles Ellis Johnson and the Erotic Mormon Image*. Chicago: University of Chicago Press.

Cart, Julie. 2002. "Study Finds Utah Leads Nation in Antidepressant Use." *Los Angeles Times*, February 20. http://articles.latimes.com/2002/feb/20/news/mn-28924.

Cather, Willa. 2013. *The Selected Letters of Willa Cather*. Edited by Andrew W. Jewell and Janis P. Stout. New York: Knopf.

Chambers, Samuel Allen. 2009. *The Queer Politics of Television*. New York: I. B. Tauris.

Chen, Chiung Hwang, and Ethan Yorgason. 1999. "'Those Amazing Mormons': The Media's Construction of Latter-Day Saints as a Model Minority." *Dialogue: A Journal of Mormon Thought* 32 (2): 107–28.

Compton, Todd M. 1997. *In Sacred Loneliness: The Plural Wives of Joseph Smith*. Salt Lake City: Signature Books.

Cooper, Chet. 2018. "Marie Osmond Interview by Chet Cooper." *ABILITY Magazine*, accessed May 3. https://www.abilitymagazine.com/osmond.html.

Coppins, McKay. 2017. "Jeff Flake's Gamble." *The Atlantic*, September. https://www.theatlantic.com/magazine/archive/2017/09/jeff-flakes-gamble/534201/.

Cortez, Marjorie. 2007. "Marjorie Cortez: Is Salt Lake Vainest City? Maybe We're Just Insecure." *Deseret News*, December 18. https://www.deseretnews.com/article/695236923/Is-Salt-Lake-vainest-city-Maybe-were-just-insecure.html?pg=all.

Cott, Nancy F. 2002. *Public Vows: A History of Marriage and the Nation*. Cambridge, MA: Harvard University Press.

Couldry, Nick. 2010. *Why Voice Matters: Culture and Politics after Neoliberalism*. Thousand Oaks, CA: Sage.

"Court Releases Warren Jeffs Audio Sex Tapes." 2011. CNN, August 12. http://www.cnn.com/2011/CRIME/08/12/texas.polygamist.jeffs/index.html.

Coviello, Peter. 2014. "How the Mormons Became White: Polygamy, Indigeneity, Sovereignty." Lecture, Ohio State University, April 18.

Cowdery, Oliver. 1836. "The Abolitionists." *Messenger and Advocate*, April, 299–301.

Crawford, Amanda J. 2009. "Leaving the Flock." *Running for a Life*, azcentral.com. http://archive.azcentral.com/news/specials/runningforalife/sunday.html.

Crawford, Amanda J. 2014. "Trying to Fit In." *Running for a Life*, azcentral.com, accessed June 14. http://archive.azcentral.com/news/specials/runningforalife/monday.html.

Dalton, Elaine S. 2010. "Remember Who You Are!" Church of Jesus Christ of Latter-day Saints, April. https://www.lds.org/general-conference/2010/04/remember-who-you-are?lang=eng.

Dawson, Mackenzie. 2016. "Are Mormons the Happiest People in America?" *New York Post*, November 3. https://nypost.com/2016/11/03/are-mormons-the-happiest-people-in-america/.

Debord, Guy. 1967. *The Society of the Spectacle*. Detroit: Black and Red.

DeGeneres, Ellen. 2013. "Donny and Marie Osmond Talk Marriage." *The Ellen DeGeneres Show*, December 27. https://www.youtube.com/watch?v=XhTKPh6Mwb8.

Deleuze, Gilles. 1988. *Foucault*. Minneapolis: University of Minnesota Press.

Dobner, Jennifer. 2015. "Mormon Leader Joseph Smith's 34 Wives Inspire Utah Artist." *New York Times*, August 17. https://www.nytimes.com/2015/08/18/us/mormon-leader-joseph-smiths-34-wives-inspire-utah-artist.html.

Dodge, Ethan. 2018. "Commentary: Two Mormon Petitions Show the Contrasting Priorities of Members." *Salt Lake Tribune*, January 13. https://www.sltrib.com/opinion/commentary/2018/01/13/commentary-two-mormon-petitions-show-the-contrasting-priorities-of-members/.

Dominguez, Alex. 2013. "Elizabeth Smart Speaks on Human Trafficking." *Christian Science Monitor*, May 4. https://www.csmonitor.com/USA/Latest-News-Wires/2013/0504/Elizabeth-Smart-speaks-on-human-trafficking.

Doty, Alexander. 2007. *Fabulous! Divas, Part 1*. Camera Obscura: Feminism, Culture, and Media Studies. Durham, NC: Duke University Press.

Duke, Alan. 2013. "Elizabeth Smart: 'I Couldn't Be Happier.'" CNN, October 9. https://www.cnn.com/2013/10/08/us/elizabeth-smart-anderson-cooper/index.html.

Dyer, Richard. 1979. *Stars*. London: British Film Institute.

Dyer, Richard. 1997. *White*. New York: Routledge.

Dyer, Richard. 2004. *Heavenly Bodies: Film Stars and Society*. 2nd ed. New York: Routledge.

Edwards-Stout, Kergan. 2012. "Steven Fales: A Gay Mormon Boy Grows Up." *Huffington Post*, April 21. https://www.huffingtonpost.com/kergan-edwardsstout/steven-fales-a-gay-mormon_b_1439055.html.

Einstein, Mara. 2008. *Brands of Faith: Marketing Religion in a Commercial Age*. New York: Routledge.

Emery, Debbie. 2013. "From Devout Mormon to Serial Dater: The Secret Double Life of Travis Alexander Exposed in Jodi Arias Trial." *Radar Online*, April 11. https://radaronline.com/exclusives/2013/04/from-devout-mormon-dating-multiple-women-double-life-travis-alexander/.

Epstein, Ethan. 2014. "Are Conservative Cities Better?" *Politico*, September 17.

Fagan, Gabrielle. 2017. "Donny Osmond: 'I Truly Feared I'd Never Sing Again.'" BT, January 24. https://home.bt.com/lifestyle/health/wellness/donny-osmond-i-truly-feared-id-never-sing-again-11364138050693.

Forgas, Joseph P., Roy F. Baumeister, and Dianne M. Tice. 2009. *Psychology of Self-Regulation: Cognitive, Affective, and Motivational Processes*. New York: Psychology Press.

Foucault, Michel. 1978. *The History of Sexuality, vol. I: An Introduction.* New York: Vintage.

Foucault, Michel. 1991. *Discipline and Punish: The Birth of the Prison.* New York: Penguin.

Free, Cathy, and Alicia Dennis. 2012. "Elizabeth Smart, Happily Ever After." *People*, March 5, 65–70.

Friedan, Betty. 1964. *The Feminine Mystique.* New York: Dell.

"Gay Polygamy and Open Borders." 2013. YouTube, April 3. https://www.youtube.com/watch?v=Pu7baWMMQnk.

"Genesis Group." 2017. Wikipedia, November 7. https://en.wikipedia.org/wiki/Genesis_Group.

Giddens, Anthony. 1991. *Modernity and Self-Identity: Self and Society in the Late Modern Age.* London: Polity.

Gillespie, L. Kay. 1976. "Cancer Quackery in the State of Utah." Utah Department of Social Services, Office of Comprehensive Health Planning.

Givens, Terryl L. 1997. *The Viper on the Hearth: Mormons, Myths, and the Construction of Heresy.* New York: Oxford University Press.

Givens, Terryl L. 2002. *By the Hand of Mormon: The American Scripture That Launched a New World Religion.* New York: Oxford University Press.

Goodstein, Laurie. 2013. "Some Mormons Search the Web and Find Doubt." *New York Times*, July 20. https://www.nytimes.com/2013/07/21/us/some-mormons-search-the-web-and-find-doubt.html.

Goodstein, Laurie. 2014. "Mormons Expel Founder of Group Seeking Priesthood for Women." *New York Times*, June 23. https://www.nytimes.com/2014/06/24/us/Kate-Kelly-Mormon-Church-Excommunicates-Ordain-Women-Founder.html.

Green, Emma. 2015. "The Profound Lack of Empathy in *My Husband's Not Gay*." *The Atlantic*, January 12. https://www.theatlantic.com/entertainment/archive/2015/01/the-profound-lack-of-empathy-in-my-husbands-not-gay/384414/.

Green, Rebecca. 2017. "Vice Chair of Wasatch County GOP Apologizes for Letter on Equal Pay for Women." Fox 13, Salt Lake City. https://fox13now.com/2017/02/16/vice-chair-of-wasatch-county-gop-apologizes-for-letter-on-equal-pay-for-women/.

Gregory, Alice. 2017. "Why So Many of Your Favorite Beauty Personalities Are Mormon." *Allure*, October 11. https://www.allure.com/story/why-so-many-beauty-bloggers-are-mormon.

Grossman, Cathy Lynn. 2012. "Elie Wiesel to Romney, Mormons: Don't Baptize Dead Jews." *USA Today*, February 14. https://content.usatoday.com/communities/Religion/post/2012/02/mitt-romney-mormon-baptism-elie-wiesel-holocaust/1#.WmS9LiOZNsM.

Gruen, J. Philip. 2014. *Manifest Destinations: Cities and Tourists in the Nineteenth-Century American West.* Norman: University of Oklahoma Press.

Gutjahr, Paul C. 2012. *The Book of Mormon: A Biography.* Princeton, NJ: Princeton University Press.

Haglund, Kristine. 2014. "What the 'Mormon Moment' Actually Accomplished." *Slate Magazine*, December 1. https://www.slate.com/articles/life

/faithbased/2014/12/mormon_moment_is_over_but_it_changed_mormon_culture_for_good.html.

Hahn, Gregory. 2007. "Mormons Growing Used to Spotlight." *Pop Matters*, June 27. Accessed July 22, 2017. https://www.popmatters.com/article/mormons-growing-used-to-spotlight/.

Hahn, Kate. 2011. "Marie Osmond: 'The Best Prevention Is a Positive Attitude.'" *Prevention*, November 3. https://www.prevention.com/health/healthy-living/marie-osmond-exclusive-interview-prevention.

Halberstam, J. Jack. 2012. *Gaga Feminism: Sex, Gender, and the End of Normal*. Boston: Beacon.

Halperin, David M. 2003. "The Normalization of Queer Theory." *Journal of Homosexuality* 45 (2–4): 339–43. doi:10.1300/j082v45n02_17.

Hampton, Morgan. 2015. "Study Shows 'Mormon Glow' Is Real." *Mormon Hub*, May 8. https://lds.net/blog/buzz/study-glow-mormons/.

Henderson, Peter. 2012a. "LDS Church Makes Money by Mormon Donations." *Huffington Post*, August 12. https://www.huffingtonpost.com/2012/08/12/insight-mormon-church-mad_n_1769539.html.

Henderson, Peter. 2012b. "Mormon Church Earns $7 Billion a Year from Tithing, Analysis Indicates." NBC News, August 13. http://investigations.nbcnews.com/_news/2012/08/13/13262285-mormon-church-earns-7-billion-a-year-from-tithing-analysis-indicates.

Hitt, Tarpley. 2019. "The 'Hypersexualized' Mormon Church President Imposter Angering LDS Twitter." *Daily Beast*, January 15. https://www.thedailybeast.com/the-hypersexualized-mormon-church-president-impersonator-angering-lds-twitter.

Hogan, Mike. 2015. "Amy Berg Is Seriously Worried about What Warren Jeffs Might Do Next." *Vanity Fair*, October 9. https://www.vanityfair.com/news/2015/10/amy-berg-warren-jeffs-prophets-prey.

Hoover, Stewart M. 2010. *Religion in the Media Age*. New York: Routledge.

Horowitz, Jason. 2012. "The Genesis of a Church's Stand on Race." *Washington Post*, February 28. https://www.washingtonpost.com/politics/the-genesis-of-a-churchs-stand-on-race/2012/02/22/gIQAQZXyfR_story.html#comments.

Houghton, Adrienne, Loni Love, Jeannie Mai, Tamera Mowry-Housley. 2013. "'The Real Speaks with 'Sister Wives.'" *The Real*, July 17. http://thereal.com/videos/the-real-speaks-with-sister-wives/. Telepictures Productions.

Houston, Pam. 2011. Promotional endorsement of *The Lonely Polygamist: A Novel*, by Brady Udall. New York: Vintage.

Hyde, Jesse. 2011. "Inside 'The Order,' One Mormon Cult's Secret Empire." *Rolling Stone*, June 15. https://www.rollingstone.com/culture/news/inside-the-order-one-mormon-cults-secret-empire-20110615.

Iati, Marisa. 2018. "Buy a Goat or a Soccer Ball from a Mormon Vending Machine—for Charity." *Washington Post*, December 24. https://www.washingtonpost.com/religion/2018/12/24/buy-goat-or-soccer-ball-mormon-vending-machine-charity/?noredirect=on&utm_term=.8af9bab355b8.

The Jeff Probst Show. 2012. "The Stars of 'Sister Wives.'" Season 1, Episode 58. November 29. Sunset Bronson Studios.

JKC. 2016. "The Pride Cycle, the Prosperity Gospel, and Grace." *By Common Consent*, August 15. https://bycommonconsent.com/2016/08/15/the-pride-cycle-the-prosperity-gospel-and-grace/.

Jordan, Benjamin Rene. 2016. *Modern Manhood and the Boy Scouts of America: Citizenship, Race, and the Environment, 1910–1930*. Chapel Hill: University of North Carolina Press.

"Joseph Smith." n.d. Church of Jesus Christ of Latter-day Saints, accessed March 15, 2016. https://www.lds.org/topics/joseph-smith?lang=eng.

Joyce, Kathryn. 2015. "The Coming Crackdown on Mormon Liberals." *Daily Beast*, January 19. https://www.thedailybeast.com/articles/2015/01/19/the-coming-crackdown-on-mormon-liberals.html.

Katz, Alyssa. 2015. *The Influence Machine: The U.S. Chamber of Commerce and the Corporate Capture of American Life*. New York: Spiegel and Grau.

Katz, Jonathan Ned. 2005. *The Invention of Heterosexuality*. Chicago: University of Chicago Press.

Kearney, Mary Celeste. 2015. "Sparkle: Luminosity and Post-Girl Power Media." *Continuum* 29 (2): 263–73.

"Kidnap Victim Elizabeth Smart, My Untold Story." 2008. *People*, June 23.

Kimmel, Michael S. 1997. *Manhood in America: A Cultural History*. New York: Free Press.

King, Karisa. 2016. "Polygamist Diary Describes Secret Bed Used for Sex Assaults." *San Antonio Express-News*, March 4. https://www.mysanantonio.com/news/local_news/article/Polygamist-diary-describes-secret-bed-used-for-4078569.php#item-38489.

Kirkland, Dennis. 2008. *Mormons and Muslims: A Case of Matching Fingerprints: Mormons and Muslims Are More Alike Than You Might Think*. Maitland, FL: Xulon Press.

Kirn, Walter. 2011. "The Mormon Moment." *Newsweek*, July 14. https://www.newsweek.com/mormon-moment-67951.

"'Kissing Can Be Very Dangerous': Sister Wives Star Kody Brown Shares Conservative Views in 'Man Talk' with a Boy Dating His Daughter." 2014. *Daily Mail Online*, June 8. https://www.dailymail.co.uk/tvshowbiz/article-2652402/Sister-Wives-star-Kody-Brown-shares-conservative-views-man-talk-boy-dating-daughter.html.

"Kody Brown Net Worth." 2015. Celebrity Net Worth, October 6. https://www.celebritynetworth.com/richest-businessmen/business-executives/kody-brown-net-worth.

Kolodny, Annette. 1987. *The Lay of the Land: Metaphor as Experience and History in American Life and Letters*. Chapel Hill: University of North Carolina Press.

Krule, Miriam. 2015. "Faced with More and More Press, the Mormon Church Is Once Again Walling Itself Off." *Slate Magazine*, January 19. https://www.slate.com/blogs/browbeat/2015/01/19/john_p_dehlin_facing_excommunication_mormon_critic_lobbying_for_gay_marriage.html.

Kuruvilla, Carol. 2017. "Mormon Scholars Are Reaching Back into Church History to Support Muslims." *Huffington Post*, April 27. https://www.huffingtonpost.com/entry/mormon-muslim-ban_us_5901e7bde4b0026db1deb4d4.

Laskow, Sarah. 2015. "Why Mormons Make Great FBI Recruits." Atlas Obscura, November 4. https://www.atlasobscura.com/articles/why-mormons-make-great-fbi-recruits.

LDS Living Staff. 2016. "LDS Newlyweds to Be Featured in New Reality Show." *LDS Living*, June 18. https://www.ldsliving.com/LDS-Newlyweds-to-Be-Featured-in-New-Reality-Show/s/82150.

Lee, Allyssa. 2011. "'Big Love' Creators Discuss the Finale: 'We Didn't Want It to Be a Downer.'" *Los Angeles Times*, March 21. https://latimesblogs.latimes.com/showtracker/2011/03/big-love-creators-on-the-series-finale-we-never-felt-oh-now-the-women-could-finally-be-free-of-that-.html.

"Legal Victory for Sister Wives as Judge Rules Utah Law on Bigamy Is Unconstitutional." 2013. *Daily Mail Online*, December 14. https://www.dailymail.co.uk/news/article-2523604/Legal-victory-Sister-Wives-judge-rules-Utah-law-bigamy-unconstitutional.html#ixzz2risId1yw.

Leonard, Wendy. 2010. "Antidepressants Flow Freely in Utah as 1 in 5 Women Partakes." *Deseret News*, September 16. https://www.deseretnews.com/article/700066056/Antidepressants-flow-freely-in-Utah-as-1-in-5-women-partakes.html?pg=all.

"Letters to the Editor, Feb. 15–17, 2017." 2017. *Park Record*, February 14. https://www.parkrecord.com/opinion/letters/letters-to-the-editor-feb-15-17-2017/.

Levin, Sam. 2016. "Rebel Cowboys: How the Bundy Family Sparked a New Battle for the American West." *The Guardian*, August 29. https://www.theguardian.com/us-news/2016/aug/29/oregon-militia-standoff-bundy-family.

Lochrie, Karma. 2005. *Heterosyncracies: Female Sexuality When Normal Wasn't*. Minneapolis: University of Minnesota Press.

Lopez Tonight. 2011. "Kody Brown, Meri Brown, Christine Brown, Robyn Sullivan." March 11. 2.2 Productions.

Lythgoe, Dennis. 2005. "Nibley Siblings Outraged over Sister's Book." *Deseret News*, February 5. https://www.deseretnews.com/article/600109810/Nibley-siblings-outraged-over-sisters-book.html.

Malkin, Marc. 2012. "*Sister Wives* Stars Support Gay Marriage: Let Individuals Choose Who They Love." *E! News*, May 10. https://www.eonline.com/news/315316/sister-wives-stars-support-gay-marriage-let-individuals-choose-who-they-love.

M&M_Vlogs. 2014. "Outlaw Prophet Viewing Party." YouTube, June 30. https://www.youtube.com/watch?v=E04RAkP2Gn0.

"Many Polygamists Blend into Modern Society." 2008. Fox News, April 18. https://www.foxnews.com/story/many-polygamists-blend-into-modern-society.

Marsh, Jodi. 2018. "Reinvention Leads to Rejuvenation." *Healthy Living Made Simple*. http://healthylivingmadesimple.com/reinvention-leads-rejuvenation/.

Martin, Denise. 2008. "'Twilight' Countdown: Catherine Hardwicke Talks about the Meadow and Making Robert Pattinson 'Dazzle.'" *Los Angeles Times*, November 4.

https://latimesblogs.latimes.com/entertainmentnewsbuzz/2008/11/twilight-coun-2.html.

Mauss, Armand L. 1994. "Refuge and Retrenchment: The Mormon Quest for Identity." In *Contemporary Mormonism: Social Science Perspectives*, edited by Marie Cornwall, Tim B. Heaton, and Lawrence A. Young. Champaign: University of Illinois Press.

Mauss, Armand L. 2003. *All Abraham's Children: Changing Mormon Conceptions of Race and Lineage*. Champaign: University of Illinois Press.

Maynes, Richard J. 2017. "The First Vision: Key to Truth." *Ensign*, June. https://www.lds.org/ensign/2017/06/the-first-vision-key-to-truth?lang=eng.

McCarter, Melissa Miles. 2010. "'Sister Wives': Overcoming Feminism." *Salon*, October 12. Accessed April 14, 2005. https://open.salon.com/blog/lissahoop/2010/10/12/sister_wives_overcoming_feminism.

McClelland, Nicholas Hegel. 2011. "Happy Valley, Utah: Brian Shumway Reflects on His Mormon Upbringing." *Time*, December 5. https://time.com/3783335/happy-valley-a-photographer-reflects-on-his-mormon-upbringing/.

McCombs, Brady. 2013. "'My Five Wives': TLC's Newest Polygamous Family Favors Buddhism." *Huffington Post*, September 18. Accessed April 4, 2014. https://www.huffingtonpost.com/2013/09/16/my-five-wives-tlc.

McFadden, Cynthia. 2013. "Modern Polygamy: One Husband, Chosen by Multiple Wives." ABC News, YouTube, June 4. https://www.youtube.com/watch?v=vcH3XyobtBw.

McGee, Micki. 2005. *Self-Help, Inc.: Makeover Culture in American Life*. New York: Oxford University Press.

McGraw, Phil. 2012. "Donny Osmond." *Dr. Phil*, February 8.

McRobbie, Angela. 2012. *The Aftermath of Feminism: Gender, Culture and Social Change*. Thousand Oaks, CA: Sage.

"'Meet the Mormons' Pulls in Audiences Nationwide." 2014. Newsroom, Church of Jesus Christ of Latter-day Saints, October 11. https://www.mormonnewsroom.org/article/theatrical-release-of-meet-the-mormons--has-exceeded-all-expectations-.

Mencimer, Stephanie. 2012. "Get-Rich-Quick Profiteers Love Mitt Romney, and He Loves Them Back." *Mother Jones*, May–June. https://www.motherjones.com/politics/2012/04/mitt-romney-nu-skin-multilevel-marketing-schemes.

Metcalfe, Brent, and Jan Shipps. 2014. "001: Jan Shipps—New History of the Prairie and Mountain Saints; Race and Gender." *Mormon Studies*, November 24. http://www.mormonstudiespodcast.org/jan-shipps/.

Mischel, Walter, Yuichi Shoda, and Philip K. Peake. 1988. "The Nature of Adolescent Competencies Predicted by Preschool Delay of Gratification." *Journal of Personality and Social Psychology* 54 (4): 687–96.

Mooallem, Jon. 2013. "When Hollywood Wants Good, Clean Fun, It Goes to Mormon Country." *New York Times*, May 23. https://www.nytimes.com/2013/05/26/magazine/when-hollywood-wants-good-clean-fun-it-goes-to-mormon-country.html.

Moore, R. Laurence. 1987. *Religious Outsiders and the Making of Americans*. New York: Oxford University Press.

Moore, R. Laurence. 1995. *Selling God: American Religion in the Marketplace of Culture*. New York: Oxford University Press.

Mormon Channel. 2018. "I'm a Mormon," accessed December 19. https://www.mormonchannel.org/watch/series/im-a-mormon.

"Mormon Church Addresses Past Racism." 2013. *The Guardian*, December 10. https://www.theguardian.com/world/2013/dec/10/mormon-church-addresses-past-racism.

"Mormon Church Applauds Stars of TLC Show Who Are Attracted to Men but Married to Women as 'True to Their Religious Convictions.'" 2015. *Daily Mail Online*, January 7. https://www.dailymail.co.uk/news/article-2900643/Gay-advocates-assail-new-TV-My-Husbands-Not-Gay.html.

"Mormon Welfare Program." 2016. *Religion and Ethics Newsweekly*, June 24. https://www.pbs.org/wnet/religionandethics/2016/06/24/mormon-welfare-program/31091/.

"Mormon Women's Group Founder Kate Kelly Excommunicated." 2014. NBC News, June 24. https://www.nbcnews.com/news/us-news/mormon-womens-group-founder-kate-kelly-excommunicated-n138746.

Nagourney, Adam. 2014. "A Defiant Rancher Savors the Audience That Rallied to His Side." *New York Times*, April 23, 2014. https://www.nytimes.com/2014/04/24/us/politics/rancher-proudly-breaks-the-law-becoming-a-hero-in-the-west.html?_r=0.

Napier-Pearce, Jennifer. 2015. "Trib Talk: Transgender and Mormon." *Salt Lake Tribune*, April 6. Accessed May 15, 2016. http://archive.sltrib.com/article.php?id=2336521&itype=CMSID.

Negra, Diane. 2008. *What a Girl Wants: Fantasizing the Reclamation of Self in Postfeminism*. New York: Routledge.

Neilson, Reid Larkin. 2011. *Exhibiting Mormonism: The Latter-Day Saints and the 1893 Chicago World's Fair*. New York: Oxford University Press.

Nelson, James. 2012. "Elizabeth Smart, Former Kidnapping Victim, Marries Matthew Gilmour in Hawaii." *Huffington Post*, February 18. https://www.huffingtonpost.com/2012/02/18/elizabeth-smart-marries_n_1287016.html.

Nugent, Walter. 2004. "The Religious Demography of an Oasis Culture." In *Religion and Public Life in the Mountain West: Sacred Landscapes in Transition*, edited by Jan Shipps and Mark Silk, 19–47. New York: AltaMira.

Nussbaum, Emily. 2007. "'Big Love': Utah Gets Kinky." *Vulture*, July 31. https://www.vulture.com/2007/07/big_love_utah_gets_kinky.html.

O'Dell, Nancy. 2014. "Tony Goldwyn—Outlaw Prophet (ET Online)." YouTube, June 17. https://www.youtube.com/watch?v=tHg0swBhEXQ.

"The Old Mormon Fort: Birthplace of Las Vegas, Nevada." 2017. National Parks Service, U.S. Department of the Interior, accessed March 15. https://www.nps.gov/nr/twhp/wwwlps/lessons/122fort/.

Ouellette, Laurie, and James Hay. 2008. *Better Living through Reality TV: Television and Post-welfare Citizenship*. Boston: Wiley-Blackwell.

Pakman, David. 2013. "Glenn Beck and Rand Paul Wonder If Gay Marriage Leads to Zoophilia and Polygamy." *David Pakman Show*, YouTube, June 27. https://www.youtube.com/watch?v=8Yzpwqwm6jc.

Parker, Theodore. 1853. *Ten Sermons of Religion, of Justice and the Conscience*. Boston: Crosby Nichols.
Passey, Brian. 2013. "Mormon Liberals: A 'Minority within a Minority.'" *USA Today*, October 30. https://www.usatoday.com/story/news/politics/2012/10/30/mormon-liberals-minority/1669155/.
Pellot, Brian. 2014. "Gay Mormon, Gay Catholic, Gay Activist: 'Book of Mormon' Star Rory O'Malley on Faith, Rights, and Religious Freedom." Religion News Service, January 22. https://brianpellot.religionnews.com/2013/09/24/gay-mormon-gay-catholic-gay-activist-book-mormon-star-rory-omalley-faith-rights-religious-freedom/.
Peterson, Sarah, and Alison Moore. 2014. "17 Mormon References in Movies and Sitcoms." *Deseret News*, January 22. https://www.deseretnews.com/top/2240/6/oCheers1-198917-Mormon-references-in-movies-and-sitcoms-Part-1.html.
Petrey, Taylor G. 2015. "A Mormon Leader Signals New Openness on Transgender Issues. This Could Be Huge." *Slate Magazine*, February 13. https://www.slate.com/blogs/outward/2015/02/13/mormons_and_transgender_elder_dallin_h_oaks_says_the_lds_church_is_open.html.
Phillips, Adam. 2009. "Introduction." In *A Philosophical Enquiry into the Origin of Our Ideas of the Sublime and Beautiful*, by Edmund Burke. New York: Oxford University Press.
Phillips, Kim, and Barry Reay. 2011. *Sex before Sexuality: A Premodern History*. New York: Polity.
Phillips, Kristine. 2017. "Utah Republican Argues against Equal Pay for Women: It's 'Bad for Families' and Society." *Washington Post*, February 19. https://www.washingtonpost.com/news/post-nation/wp/2017/02/19/utah-republican-argues-against-equal-pay-for-women-its-bad-for-families-and-society/?utm_term=.0168b7f0c79d.
Pinsky, Drew. 2012. "3 Wives, 24 Children: 'We All Work Really Hard.'" *Dr. Drew*, HLN, YouTube, December 3. https://www.youtube.com/watch?v=mBIzzVIHnZ0.
Poovey, Mary. 1988. *Uneven Developments: The Ideological Work of Gender in Mid-Victorian England*. Chicago: University of Chicago Press.
Prescott, Marianne Holman. 2016. "Meet the Mormons: New Faces, New Stories." *Church News and Events*, August 1. https://www.lds.org/church/news/meet-the-mormons-new-faces-new-stories?lang=eng.
"Prevalence of Prescription Drug Abuse in Utah." 2012. Turning Point Centers, October 24. https://turningpointcenters.com/blog/prevalence-of-prescription-drug-abuse-in-utah/.
Projansky, Sarah. 2014. *Spectacular Girls: Media Fascination and Celebrity Culture*. New York: New York University Press.
"Prop 8 Documentary 'The Case against 8' Wins Sundance Prize." 2014. *On Top Magazine*, January 26. https://www.ontopmag.com/article.aspx?id=17618&MediaType=1&Category=4.
Pugsley, Mark. 2017. "Another Former LDS Stake President Indicted for Affinity Fraud." Ray Quinney and Nebeker, November 8. https://rqn.com/blog/utahsecuritiesfraud/category/affinity-fraud/#.WPJ2zrGZPvo.

Purtill, James. 2016. "The Oregon Siege Is Finally Over. What Actually Happened?" Triple J Hack, Australian Broadcasting Corporation, February 12. https://www.abc.net.au/triplej/programs/hack/the-oregon-siege-is-over-what-actually-happened/7164530.

Quinn, D. Michael. 1994. *The Mormon Hierarchy: Origins of Power*. Salt Lake City: Signature Books.

Quinn, D. Michael. 1997. *The Mormon Hierarchy: Extensions of Power*. Salt Lake City: Signature.

Quinn, D. Michael. 2017. *The Mormon Hierarchy: Wealth and Corporate Power*. Salt Lake City: Signature.

Quinn, Jennifer. 2013. "Jodi Arias: How Sex and Murder Created a Tabloid Trial and Killer Ratings." *The Star*, May 4. https://www.thestar.com/news/world/2013/05/04/jodi_arias_how_sex_and_murder_created_a_tabloid_trial_and_killer_ratings.html.

"Reality TV Show Polygamist and His Four Wives Challenge Utah's Bigamy Laws—with Support from Their Fellow 'Sister Wives.'" 2013. *Daily Mail Online*, January 18. https://www.dailymail.co.uk/news/article-2264326.

Reeve, W. Paul. 2015. *Religion of a Different Color: Race and the Mormon Struggle for Whiteness*. New York: Oxford University Press.

Rodriguez, Jennifer. 2013. "Victims of Polygamy Face TLC's 'Sister Wives.'" *The Virtual Rebel*, May 11. Accessed April 15, 2015. https://virtual-rebel.com/2013/ . . . of-polygamy-face-tlcs-sister-wive.

Romig, Rollo. 2012. "'Julie through the Glass': The Rise and Fall of the Mormon TV Commercial." *The New Yorker*, January 20. https://www.newyorker.com/culture/culture-desk/julie-through-the-glass-the-rise-and-fall-of-the-mormon-tv-commerical

Rose, Nikolas. 1993. "Government, Authority, and Expertise in Advanced Liberalism." *Economy and Society* 22: 283–99.

Roth, Max. 2015. "Multi-level Mecca: Utah's MLMs Are Big Business, but Few Make Money." Fox 13, November 11. https://fox13now.com/2015/11/10/multi-level-mecca-utahs-mlms-are-big-business-but-few-make-money/.

Ruiz, Rebecca. 2012. "America's Vainest Cities." *Forbes*, July 24. https://www.forbes.com/2007/11/29/plastic-health-surgery-forbeslife-cx_rr_1129health.html.

Rule, Nicholas O., James V. Garrett, and Nalini Ambady. 2010. "On the Perception of Religious Group Membership from Faces." *PLOS ONE*, December 7. https://journals.plos.org/plosone/article?id=10.1371%2Fjournal.pone.0014241#s3.

Sanders, Josh. 2017. "Cancel Your Upcoming TV Show, 'My Husband's Not Gay.'" Change.org, accessed November 1. https://www.change.org/p/tlc-cancel-your-upcoming-tv-show-my-husband-s-not-gay.

Schott, Bryan. 2017. "Wasatch County GOP Leader Blows Up Facebook Arguing against Equal Pay for Women." Utah Policy, February 16. https://utahpolicy.com/index.php/features/today-at-utah-policy/12390-wasatch-county-gop-leader-blows-up-facebook-arguing-against-equal-pay-for-women.

Scott, Joan. 1986. "Gender: A Useful Category of Historical Analysis." *American Historical Review* 91, no. 5 (December): 1053–75.

Sedgwick, Eve Kosofsky. 1990. *Epistemology of the Closet*. Berkeley: University of California Press.

Segal, Victoria. 2016. "The Pursuit of Happiness and Why It's Making Us Anxious by Ruth Whippman." *Sunday Times*, March 13. https://www.thetimes.co.uk/article/the-pursuit-of-happiness-and-why-its-making-us-anxious-by-ruth-whippman-ddwfck2j9.

Seppi, Greg. 2015. "Gruen, 'Manifest Destinations: Cities and Tourists in the Nineteenth-Century American West' [review]." *Dawning of a Brighter Day*, accessed February 3. https://associationmormonletters.org/blog/reviews/older-reviews/gruen-manifest-destinations-cities-and-tourists-in-the-nineteenth-century-american-west-reviewed-by-greg-seppi/.

Shipps, Jan. 2012. "Our Mormon Moment: A Roundtable on Mormonism in Contemporary America, in Honor of Paul Gutjahr's *The Book of Mormon: A Biography*." Paper presented at Indiana University, College Arts and Humanities Institute, Bloomington, Indiana, October 31.

Shire, Emily. 2014. "Thank God! To the Church, This Transgender Woman Is Just a Skank." *Daily Beast*, October 22. https://www.thedailybeast.com/articles/2014/10/22/thank-god-to-the-church-this-transgender-woman-is-just-a-skank.html.

Siegler, Kirk. 2017. "With National Monuments under Review, Bears Ears Is Focus of Fierce Debate." *All Things Considered*, NPR, May 5. https://www.npr.org/2017/05/05/526860725/with-national-monuments-under-review-bears-ears-is-focus-of-fierce-debate.

Singer, T. Benjamin. 2011. "Towards a Transgender Sublime: The Politics of Excess in Trans-specific Cultural Production." PhD diss. Rutgers University, Department of Literatures in English.

"Sister Wives." 2017. Wikipedia, December 17. https://en.wikipedia.org/wiki/Sister_Wives.

"'Sister Wives' Stars Win Legal Victory against Utah Polygamy Law." 2013. Radar Online, December 14. https://radaronline.com/exclusives/2013/12/sister-wives-polygamy-legal-ruling-victory/.

Skoloff, Brian, and Jacques Billeaud. 2013. "Jodi Arias Trial: An Over-the-Top Media-Spectacle." *Huffington Post*, May 23. Accessed November 11, 2015. https://www.huffingtonpost.com/2013/05/23/jodi-arias-trial-media-coverage_n_3324549.html.

Skousen, Royal. 2009. *The Book of Mormon: The Earliest Text*. New Haven, CT: Yale University Press.

Smardon, Andrea. 2017. "For Mormon Women, Saying #MeToo Presents a Particular Challenge." *The Guardian*, November 29. https://www.theguardian.com/world/2017/nov/29/mormon-women-metoo-particular-challenge-sexual-abuse.

Smith, N. Lee. 1979. "Herbal Remedies. God's Medicine?" *Dialogue: A Journal of Mormon Thought* 12 (3): 37–60.

Smith-Rosenberg, Carroll. 1986. *Disorderly Conduct: Visions of Gender in Victorian America*. New York: Oxford University Press.

Solie, Stacey. 2013. "Unlearning the Mormon Sex Stigma." Crosscut, October 15. https://crosscut.com/2013/10/nicole-hardy-mormon-confessions-virgin/.

Sontag, Susan. 2001. *Against Interpretation: And Other Essays*. New York: Picador.

Stacey, Judith. 2011. *Unhitched: Love, Marriage, and Family Values from West Hollywood to Western China*. New York: New York University Press.

Stack, Peggy Fletcher. 2015a. "Picture This: Mormon Women Giving Blessings (Ordained Women Can)." *Salt Lake Tribune*, January 10. http://archive.sltrib.com/story.php?ref=/2036330-155/#&ui-state=dialog.

Stack, Peggy Fletcher. 2015b. "Where Mormon Feminists Stand a Year after Kate Kelly's Excommunication." *Huffington Post*, June 27. https://www.huffingtonpost.com/2015/06/27/mormon-feminists-excommunication_n_7647696.html.

Stephens, Stephanie. 2014. "Marie Osmond Shares the Life-Changing Final Lesson She Learned from Her Mother." *Parade*, April 18. https://parade.com/280911/stephaniestephens/marie-osmond-shares-the-life-changing-final-lesson-she-learned-from-her-mother/.

Stephenson, Kathy. 2015. "Mormon Vice: Utah Buys More Candy Than Any Other State." *Washington Post*, May 19. https://www.washingtonpost.com/national/religion/mormon-vice-utah-buys-more-candy-than-any-other-state/2015/05/19/a85f2744-fe48-11e4-8c77-bf274685e1df_story.html.

Stewart, Dodai. 2011. "*Sister Wives*' Greatest Fear: Feminists!" Jezebel, November 14. https://jezebel.com/5859341/sister-wives-greatest-fear-feminists.

Stout, David. 2015. "Boyd K. Packer, Advocate of Conservative Mormonism, Dies at 90." *New York Times*, July 4. https://www.nytimes.com/2015/07/05/us/boyd-k-packer-advocate-of-conservative-mormonism-dies-at-90.html.

Stryker, Susan. 2017. *Transgender History: The Roots of Today's Revolution*. Thousand Oaks, CA: Seal.

Takenaga, Lara. 2018. "Our Obituaries Editor on Coverage of Former Mormon Leader Thomas Monson." *New York Times*, January 8. https://www.nytimes.com/2018/01/08/reader-center/thomas-monson-obituary.html.

Tannehill, Brynn. 2013. "Why 'LGB' and 'T' Belong Together." *Huffington Post*, February 25. https://www.huffingtonpost.com/brynn-tannehill/why-lgb-and-t-belong-together_b_2746616.html.

Turley, Jonathan. 2011. "Brown Family to File Challenge to the Criminalization of Polygamy in Utah." *Jonathan Turley*, July 12. https://jonathanturley.org/2011/07/12/brown-family-to-file-challenge-to-the-criminalization-of-polygamy-in-utah/.

Turner, John G. 2012. *Brigham Young, Pioneer Prophet*. Cambridge, MA: Harvard University Press.

Ulrich, Laurel Thatcher. 2018. *A House Full of Females: Plural Marriage and Women's Rights in Early Mormonism, 1835–1870*. New York: Vintage.

"Utah Data Center." 2018. Domestic Surveillance Directorate, accessed October 18. https://nsa.gov1.info/utah-data-center/.

"Utah Doctor Found Guilty of Murdering Wife." 2013. *New York Daily News*, November 9. https://www.nydailynews.com/news/crime/utah-doctor-found-guilty-murdering-wife-article-1.1511590#ixzz2lfs7uLoo.

Valentine, David. 2007. *Imagining Transgender: An Ethnography of a Category*. Durham, NC: Duke University Press.

Vandereycken, Walter, and Ron van Deth. 1994. *From Fasting Saints to Anorexic Girls: The History of Self-Starvation*. New York: New York University Press.

Van Noord, Roger. 1988. *King of Beaver Island*. Champaign: University of Illinois Press.

Van Noord, Roger. 1997. *Assassination of Michigan King: The Life of James Jesse Strang*. Ann Arbor: University of Michigan Press.

Wallace, Irving. 1962. *The Twenty-Seventh Wife*. New York: Signet.

Warnke, Melissa Batchelor. 2016. "In Acquitting the Oregon Militants, a White Jury Determines That the Law Doesn't Apply to White Protesters." *Los Angeles Times*, October 28. https://www.latimes.com/opinion/opinion-la/la-ol-malheur-bundy-occupation-acquittal-20161028-story.html.

"Washing and Anointing." 2017. Wikipedia, December 11. https://en.wikipedia.org/wiki/Washing_and_anointing.

Weber, Brenda R. 2009. *Makeover TV: Selfhood, Citizenship, and Celebrity*. Durham, NC: Duke University Press.

Weber, Brenda R., ed. 2014. *Reality Gendervision: Sexuality and Gender on Transatlantic Reality Television*. Durham, NC: Duke University Press.

West, Brian. 2008. "Search: Were Beds in Temple Used for Teen Sex?" *Deseret News Utah*, April 10. https://deseretnews.com/article/1,5143,695269096,00.html.

"Who Is Flora Jessop and Why Is She Coming to Eldorado?" 2004. *Eldorado Success*, March 25.

Williams, Florence. 1997. "A House, 10 Wives: Polygamy in Suburbia." *New York Times*, December 10. https://www.nytimes.com/1997/12/11/garden/a-house-10-wives-polygamy-in-suburbia.html.

Williams, Troy. 2012. "When Mormons Were Socialists." *Salon*, April 16. https://www.salon.com/2012/04/15/when_mormons_were_socialists/.

Winter, Caroline. 2012. "How the Mormons Make Money." Bloomberg, July 18. https://www.bloomberg.com/news/articles/2012-07-18/how-the-mormons-make-money.

Wolf, Naomi. 2001. *The Beauty Myth: How Images of Beauty Are Used against Women*. New York: Harper Perennial.

Woodland, Cadence. 2014. "The End of the Mormon Moment." *The New York Times*, July 14. https://www.nytimes.com/2014/07/15/opinion/the-end-of-the-mormon-moment.html.

Woodruff, Emily. 2017. "Why Are So Many Mormons Getting Boob Jobs?" Total Beauty, accessed June 13. https://www.totalbeauty.com/content/blog/mormon-plastic-surgery-140502.

MEDIA ARCHIVE

In an intermedial project such as this, conventional citation schemas fall short. The following list of media texts are those that I examined or referenced. Other primary texts, such as television talk shows, are included in the general references since I consider them supplemental to my primary archive of materials.

Even if indicated by the title, I've added genre classification information to the end of each entry. I use the terms "feature film" and "feature documentary" to indicate length rather than specific theatrical release. By contrast, "video" suggests media fare directly released to DVD or the internet. Interestingly, while many of the feature films and documentaries listed here had limited theatrical release or circulated through festivals, they are now widely available for the cost of membership with services such as Netflix and Amazon Prime Video. In general, I have termed a nonfiction television program "reality TV" if it appears to be unscripted and "TV documentary" if it does not have a director credited through IMDB (Internet Movie Data Base).

This list is not meant to be encyclopedic of all Mormon-related media fare. Instead, it is a reference for the media I use in the book. Its breadth suggests the polyglossia in these latter-day screens.

Abney, Alice. 2017. *Sisters in Sin: A Forbidden Mormon Romance*. Amazon Digital Services. Novel.
"Agency." 2018. Church of Jesus Christ of Latter-day Saints, accessed April 14. https://www.lds.org/topics/agency?lang=eng&old=true. Church website.
Alexander, Jace, dir. 2013. *Jodi Arias: Dirty Little Secret*. City Entertainment. TV movie.
Alliegator. 2017. "When Striving for Perfection Just Makes Us Feel Bad about Ourselves." *Feminist Mormon Housewives*, January 16. http://www.feministmormonhousewives.org/2017/01/when-striving-for-perfection-just-makes-us-feel-bad-about-ourselves/. Blogpost.
Alpha House. 2014. Season 2. Sid Kibbitz Productions, Amazon Studios. TV series.
Anderreg, Adam Thomas, dir. 2002. *Jack Weyland's Charly*. Cinergy Films, Focused Light Films, Kaleidoscope Pictures. Feature film.

Andersen, Kurt. 2017. *Fantasyland: How America Went Haywire: A 500-Year History*. New York: Random House. Nonfiction book.

Anderson, Scott S., dir. 2004. *The Best Two Years*. Halestorm Entertainment. Feature film.

Argott, Don, dir. *Believer*. 2018. Live Nation Productions, 9.14 Pictures, Another Brother Productions. Feature documentary.

"Articles of Faith." 2018. Church of Jesus Christ of Latter-day Saints, accessed October 16. https://www.mormon.org/beliefs/articles-of-faith. Church website.

Azrieli, Avraham. 2012. *The Mormon Candidate*. CreateSpace Independent Publishing Platform. Novel.

Baker, Elna. 2010. *The New York Regional Mormon Singles Halloween Dance: A Memoir*. New York: Plume. Memoir.

"Baptism for the Dead." 2018. Wikipedia, Wikimedia Foundation, accessed January 23. en.wikipedia.org/wiki/Baptism_for_the_dead. Church website.

The Barbara Walters Special. 1978. "Donny and Marie Osmond." ABC News, August 9. TV news.

Barnes, Jane. 2012. *Falling in Love with Joseph Smith: My Search for the Real Prophet*. New York: TarcherPeregree. Memoir.

Batty, Garret, dir. 2013. *The Saratov Approach*. Saratov Films, Three Coin Productions. Feature film.

Baxley, Craig R., dir. 1985. *The Avenging Angel*. Esparza/Katz Productions. TV movie.

Beck, Martha. 2006. *Leaving the Saints: How I Lost the Mormons and Found My Faith*. New York: Broadway. Memoir.

Benedict, Jeff. 2007. *The Mormon Way of Doing Business: How Nine Western Boys Reached the Top of Corporate America*. New York: Warner Business Books. Nonfiction book.

Berg, Amy, dir. 2015. *Prophet's Prey*. Imagine Entertainment. Feature documentary.

Bernahard-Bubb, Heidi. 2016. "Make It Up Every Day." In *Baring Witness: 36 Mormon Women Talk Candidly about Love, Sex, and Marriage*, edited by Holly Welker. Kindle ed. Champaign: University of Illinois Press. Memoir.

Bernhard, Torben, dir. 2014. *Transmormon*. OHO Media. Documentary short.

The Book of Mormon. 2018. San Francisco Theater, accessed October 23. https://www.san-francisco-theater.com/theaters/curran-theater/the-book-of-mormon.php. Playbill.

Boyd, Gale. 2014. "So You're in Love with a Mormon Girl: 5 Things to Watch Out For." *Mormon Hub*, January 23. https://mormonhub.com/blog/life/relationships/youre-love-mormon-girl-5-things-watch/. Website.

Bramham, Dorothy. 2009. *The Secret Lives of Saints: Child Brides and Lost Boys in Canada's Polygamous Mormon Sect*. Toronto: Vintage Canada. Memoir.

Breaking the Faith. 2013. Hot Snakes Media. Reality TV series.

Broadly. 2017. "Being Transgender in the Mormon Church." YouTube. https://www.youtube.com/watch?v=Zzyr0z1OgSA. YouTube video.

Brooks, Joanna. 2012. *The Book of Mormon Girl: A Memoir of an American Faith*. New York: Free Press. Memoir.

Brooks, Joanna. 2013. "Traditional Mormon Sexual Purity Lessons Contributed to Captivity, Elizabeth Smart Tells University Audience." *Religion Dispatches*, May 8. http://religiondispatches.org/traditional-mormon-sexual-purity-lesson-contributed-to-captivity-elizabeth-smart-tells-university-audience/. Online periodical.

Brower, Sam. 2012. *Prophet's Prey: My Seven-Year Investigation into Warren Jeffs and the Fundamentalist Church of Latter-day Saints*. New York: Bloomsbury. Memoir.

Brown, Kody, Meri Brown, Janelle Brown, Christine Brown, and Robyn Brown. 2012. *Becoming Sister Wives: The Story of an Unconventional Marriage*. New York: Gallery. Memoir.

Bullock, Nicole. 2013. "TMI Friday: Mormon Beauty, Modesty, and Shame." *Cute Culture Chick*, March 1. http://www.cuteculturechick.com/2013/03/tmi-friday-mormon-beauty-modesty-and-shame/. Website.

Burnham, Kimberly. 2017. "Lesbian Mormon Poetry," accessed March 14. https://www.pinterest.com/KimberlyBurnham/lesbian-mormon-poetry/. Pinterest.

Burrows, James, dir. 1989. "Call Me Irresponsible." *Cheers*, Season 7, Episode 20. Charles/Burrough/Charles Productions, Paramount Television. TV series.

Butterfly Expressions, LLC. 2018. Accessed April 4. https://butterflyexpress.net. Website.

Cain, Christopher, dir. 2007. *September Dawn*. Black Diamond Pictures. Feature film.

Card, Orson Scott. 2007. *Saints: A Novel*. New York: Tom Dougherty Associates. Novel.

Carrier, Scott. 2011. *Prisoner of Zion: Muslims, Mormons, and Other Misadventures*. Berkeley: Counterpoint. Memoir.

Chase, Zoe. 2017. "Flake News." In "Things I Mean to Know." *This American Life*, Episode 630. American Public Radio, October 27. Radio.

Chase, Zoe. 2018. "The Impossible Dream." *This American Life*, Episode 642. American Public Radio, April 6. Radio.

Christensen, T. C., dir. 2011. *17 Miracles*. Excel Entertainment, Remember Films. Feature film.

Church Educational System. 2003. "Plan of Salvation." In *Eternal Marriage Student Manual*. Church of Jesus Christ of Latter-day Saints. https://www.lds.org/manual/eternal-marriage-student-manual/plan-of-salvation?lang=eng. Church website.

Clark, Tom, dir. 2015. *Elder: A Mormon Love Story*. *New York Times* Op-Doc. Documentary short.

Clarkson, Heather. 2014. "85: Mormons and Money—the Prosperity Doctrine." *The Mormon Expositor*, December 10. Accessed September 20, 2017. https://podtail.com/en/podcast/mormon-expositor-podcast/85-mormons-and-money-the-prosperity-doctrine/. Podcast.

"Code of Conduct." 2013. Mesa Easter Pageant, accessed April 25, 2014. www.easterpageant.org/auditions2013/CodeofConduct.asp. Church website.

Condon, Bill, dir. 2011. *Twilight Saga: Breaking Dawn, Part 1*. Summit Entertainment. Feature film.

Condon, Bill, dir. 2012. *Twilight Saga: Breaking Dawn, Part 2*. Summit Entertainment. Feature film.

Cooper, Alex. 2016. *Saving Alex: When I Was Fifteen I Told My Mormon Parents I Was Gay, and That's When My Nightmare Began*. New York: HarperOne. Memoir.

Covey, Stephen R. 1982. *The Divine Center*. Salt Lake City, UT: Deseret. Nonfiction book.

Cowan, Reed, and Steven Greenstreet, dirs. 2010. *8: The Mormon Proposition*. David v. Goliath Films. Feature documentary.

Cox, C. Jay, dir. 2003. *Latter Days*. Funny Boy Films, Davis Entertainment Filmworks. Feature film.

DaCosta, Neil. 2018. *Mormon Missionary Positions*. Neil DaCosta, accessed November 9. http://neildacosta.com/mormon-missionary-positions/. Website.

Darger, Joe, Alina Darger, Vicki Darger, Valerie Darger, and Brooke Adams. 2012. *Love Times Three: Our True Story of a Polygamous Marriage*. New York: HarperOne. Memoir.

The Darger Family. 2019. Facebook, accessed January 10. https://www.facebook.com/TheDargers/. Social media.

TheDargerFamily. 2019. Twitter, accessed January 10. https://twitter.com/thedargerfamily?lang=en. Social media.

Davis, Mitch, dir. 2001. *The Other Side of Heaven*. 3Mark Entertainment. Feature film.

DeBlasi, Anthony, dir. 2013. *Missionary*. Poiley Wood Entertainment, Missionary Film Production. Feature film.

Dehlin, John. 2006a. "019–021: Mormon, Married, Gay and Facing Discipline—an Interview with Buckley Jeppson." *Mormon Stories*, March 17. https://www.mormonstories.org/mormon-stories-019–020-and-021-mormon-married-gay-and-facing-discipline-an-interview-with-buckley-jeppson/. Podcast.

Dehlin, John. 2006b. "026: Blacks and the LDS Priesthood—an Interview with Darius Gray and Margaret Young." *Mormon Stories*, April 12. https://www.mormonstories.org/mormon-stories-026-blacks-and-the-lds-priesthood-an-interview-with-darius-gray-and-margaret-young/. Podcast.

Dehlin, John, creator. 2015a. "#518: Clark Johnsen—Broadway Book of Mormon Musical—Part 1." *Mormon Stories*, January 21. https://www.mormonstories.org/podcast/clark-johnsen-from-byu-to-broadways-book-of-mormon-musical/. Podcast.

Dehlin, John, creator. 2015b. "588–589: Laura Roper Andreasen—Granddaughter of LDS Apostle M. Russell Ballard." *Mormon Stories*, November 18. https://www.mormonstories.org/laura-roper-andreasen-granddaughter-m-russell-ballard/. Podcast.

Dehlin John, creator. 2015c. "Disciplinary Council." *Mormon Stories*, January 15. https://www.mormonstories.org/disciplinary-council/. Podcast website.

Dehlin, John, creator. 2017a. "735–738: Kimberly Anderson's Journey from Living 45 Years as a Mormon Man to Living Openly as a Woman." *Mormon Stories*, May 4. https://www.mormonstories.org/podcast/kimberly-anderson/. Podcast.

Dehlin, John, creator. 2017b. "#739 Mormon Transgender Experiences." *Mormon Stories*, May 12. https://www.mormonstories.org/podcast/mormon-transgender-experiences/. Podcast.

Dehlin, John, creator. 2017c. "#740: Alex Autry—Transitioning from Female to Male as a Post-Mormon Teen." *Mormon Stories*, May 16. https://www.mormonstories.org/podcast/london-flynn/. Podcast.

Dehlin, John, creator. 2017d. "#743: London Flynn—Transitioning from Male to Female as a Post-Mormon Teen." *Mormon Stories*, May 22. https://www.mormonstories.org/podcast/london-flynn/. Podcast.

Denton, Katherine Jean. 2015. *Breaking Free: Gay Mormon Guilt Free*. Kindle ed. Createspace. Memoir.

The District. n.d. Lds.org. https://www.lds.org/callings/missionary/the-district?lang=eng. Web series.

The Doctrine and Covenants of the Church of Jesus Christ of Latter-day Saints. 2018. Church of Jesus Christ of Latter-day Saints, accessed October 17. https://www.lds.org/scriptures/dc-testament?lang=eng. Church website.

Douglas, Jerry, and John Rutherford, dirs. 2004. *BuckleRoos Part II*. Buckshot Productions, Colt Studio Group. Video.

Draga, Jeffrey. 2011. "The 101 Mormon Commandments." *Mormon411*, April 7. http://mormon411.blogspot.com/2011/04/101-mormon-commandments.html. Website.

Eagleston, Paul, dir. 2003. *It's Latter-day Night! Live*. Halestorm Entertainment. Feature film.

Ebershoff, David. 2008. *The 19th Wife: A Novel*. New York: Random House. Novel.

Elizabeth Smart: Autobiography. 2017. Asylum Entertainment, Marwar Junction Productions. TV documentary miniseries.

Elizabeth Smart: Questions Answered. 2017. Asylum Entertainment, Marwar Junction Productions. TV documentary.

"Entertainment and Media." 2018. Church of Jesus Christ of Latter-day Saints, accessed October 17. https://www.lds.org/youth/for-the-strength-of-youth/entertainment-and-media?lang=eng. Church website.

Escaping Polygamy. 2014–present. RIVR Media. Reality TV series.

Escaping the Prophet. 2014. Screaming Flee Productions. Reality TV series.

Evans, Robert, and Anonymous. 2015. "5 Things I Learned as a Mormon Polygamist Wife." *Cracked*, January 21. http://www.cracked.com/personal-experiences-1224-5-things-i-learned-as-mormon-polygamist-wife.html. Website.

Fabris, T., and C. Jay Cox. 2004. *Latter Days: A Novel*. New York: Alyson. Novel.

Fales, Steven. 2003. "Confessions of a Mormon Boy: An Autobiographical One-Man Play Written, Created, and Performed by Steven Fales." *Sunstone*, December. https://www.sunstonemagazine.com/pdf/130-40-56.pdf. Periodical.

Fales, Steven. 2006. *Confessions of a Mormon Boy: Behind the Scenes of the Off-Broadway Hit*. New York: Alyson. Memoir/play.

"The Family: A Proclamation to the World." 1995. Church of Jesus Christ of Latter-day Saints, September 23. https://www.lds.org/topics/familyproclamation?lang=eng&_r=1. Website.

Faust, James E. 2000. "Womanhood: The Highest Place of Honor." Church of Jesus Christ of Latter-day Saints, April. https://www.lds.org/general-conference/2000/04/womanhood-the-highest-place-of-honor?lang=eng. Website.

Finding Your Roots. 2012–present. PBS. Kundhart McGee Productions, Inkkwell Films, Ark Media. TV documentary series.

Finding Your Roots. 2018. Accessed December 12. http://www.pbs.org/weta/finding-your-roots/home/. Website.

Flake, Jeff. 2017. *Conscience of a Conservative: A Rejection of Destructive Politics and a Return to Principle*. New York: Random House. Memoir.

Fleischer, Ruben, dir. 2017. "We Can't Kill People," *The Santa Clarita Diet*. Season 1, Episode 2. Garfield Grove Productions. TV series.

Ford, John, dir. 1950. *Wagon Master*. Argosy Pictures. Feature film.

Freeman, Judith. 2016. *The Latter Days: A Memoir*. Kindle ed. New York: Pantheon. Memoir.

Freeman, Marnie. 2014. *To the One: You Don't Get to Be Mormon and Lesbian, Even If You Were Born Both*. Port Orange, FL: Ollin. Memoir.

"Frequently Asked Questions." 2015. Ordain Women, February 17. https://ordainwomen.org/faq/. Website.

Garcia, Jon, dir. 2013. *The Falls: Testament of Love*. Lake Productions. Feature film.

Garcia, Jon, dir. 2016. *The Falls: Covenant of Grace*. Lake Productions. Feature film.

Goldenberg, Rachel Lee, dir. 2013. *Escape from Polygamy*. Indy Entertainment. TV movie.

Gray, Darius A., and Margaret B. Young. 2008. *Nobody Knows: The Untold Story of Black Mormons*. Barton Productions. Feature documentary.

Grey, Mya. 2013. *Mormon Girl to Sex Slave: My Secret Memoir*. Kindle ed. Pennsauken, NJ: BookBaby. Memoir.

Hanson, C. L. 2016. "Its Own Reward." In *Baring Witness: 36 Mormon Women Talk Candidly about Love, Sex, and Marriage*, edited by Holly Welker. Kindle ed. Champaign: University of Illinois Press. Memoir.

Hanson, Doris, creator. 2008–present. *Polygamy: What Love Is This?* Salt Lake City KTMW-TV. TV series.

Hardwicke, Catherine, dir. 2008. *Twilight*. Summit Entertainment. Feature film.

Hardy, Nicole. 2013. *Confessions of a Latter-day Virgin: A Memoir*. New York: Hachette. Memoir.

Harrison, Mette Ivie. 2014. *The Bishop's Wife: A Linda Wallheim Mystery*. New York: Soho Crime. Novel.

Harrison, Mette Ivie. 2016. *His Right Hand*. New York: Soho. Novel.

Harrison, Mette Ivie. 2017. *For Time and All Eternities*. New York: Random House. Novel.

Hatewatch. 2016. "Ammon Bundy Responds to His Critics That He's Being Used by God." YouTube, January 7. https://www.youtube.com/watch?v=PeZ19MaQm2I. YouTube video.

Hathaway, Henry, dir. 1940. *Brigham Young*. Twentieth Century Fox. Feature film.

HLN after Dark: The Jodi Arias Trial. 2012–13. Cable News Network (CNN). TV news.

Holcomb, Rod, dir. 2010. *The 19th Wife*. Sony Pictures Television. TV movie.

"How to Date a Mormon." 2015. WikiHow, July 9. https://www.wikihow.com/Date-a-Mormon. Website.

Hughes, Garry John. 1997. *Osmond Family Values*. TV movie.

Hutchison, Darlene Chidester. 1992. "Sex Education." *The Encyclopedia of Mormonism*. https://eom.byu.edu/index.php/Sex_Education. Website.

I Am Cait. 2016. "Politically Incorrect." Season 2, Episode 1. Reality TV series.

Ives, Stephen, dir. 1996. *The West*. Florentine Films, Insignia Films. TV documentary series.

"Janelle Brown." 2015. Fundamentalists Wiki, accessed June 14. http://fundamentalists.wikia.com/wiki/Janelle_Brown. Website.

Jeffs, Brent W., and Maia Szalavitz. 2009. *Lost Boy: The Story of One Man's Exile from a Polygamist Cult and His Brave Journey to Reclaim His Life*. New York: Broadway. Memoir.

Jeffs, Rachel. 2017. *Breaking Free: How I Escaped Polygamy, the FLDS Cult, and My Father, Warren Jeffs*. New York: Harperluxe. Memoir.

Jessop, Flora, and Paul T. Brown. 2010. *Church of Lies*. Hoboken, NJ: Jossey-Bass. Memoir.

"Jodi Arias." 2016. *Murder with Friends*, Season 1, Episode 26. The Young Turks. Reality TV series.

"Jodi Arias." 2018. *In Defense Of*, Season 1, Episode 3. Magical Elves Productions. Reality TV series.

Johnston, Carol Shaw. 2008. "Elizabeth Smart Rises above Kidnapping." *The Media Sib*, September 10. Accessed September 14, 2014. https://themediasib.com/category/headlinescurrent-events/. Blogpost.

Jones, Cindi. 2011. *Squirrel Cage*. CreateSpace. Memoir.

Kimball, Heber C. 1857. "Faith and Works, Submission to Authority, the Lords Provision for His Saints, Etc." *Journal of Discourse*, volume 6, November 22, 68–74. West Valley City, Utah: Walking Lion Press, 2006. Nonfiction book.

Knoll, Berry. 2009a. "FLDS Beliefs 101—'Keep Sweet.'" *FLDS 101*, May 7. Accessed December 26, 2018. https://flds101.blogspot.com/2008/05/flds-101-keep-sweet.html. Blogpost.

Knoll, Berry. 2009b. "FLDS Beliefs 101—Obey the Prophet." *FLDS 101*, May 10. Accessed December 26, 2018. http://flds101.blogspot.com/2008/05/flds-beliefs-101-obey-prophet.html. Blogpost.

Knudsen, Jeff, dir. 2005. *American Mormon*. Nick Moe Productions. Feature documentary.

Krakauer, Jon. 2004. *Under the Banner of Heaven: A Story of Violent Faith*. New York: Anchor. Nonfiction book.

Kushner, Tony. 1991. *Angels in America*. Play.

Kushner, Tony. 1993, 2013. *Angels in America: A Gay Fantasia on National Themes*. New York: Theatre Communications Group. Playbook.

Lawrence, Gary C. 2008. *How Americans View Mormonism: Seven Steps to Improve Our Image*. Orange, CA: Parameter Foundation. Nonfiction book.

Lawson, Adam. 2003. *Day of Defense*. NuWorlds Productions. Feature film.

Ling, Lisa. 2011. "Modern Polygamy." *Our America with Lisa Ling*, Season 2, Episode 2, October 23. Creative Audio Post. TV news series.

LittleT. 2017. "A Letter to Mormons." *Laughs Like Thunder*, August 9. https://laughslikethunder.blog/2017/08/09/a-letter-to-mormons/. Blogpost.

Logan, Joshua, dir. 1969. *Paint Your Wagon*. Alan J. Lerner Productions, The Malpaso Company. Feature film.

Lopez, Robert, Matt Stone, and Trey Parker. 2011. *The Book of Mormon* [musical theater]. Live performance.

Lord, Stephen, dir. 1969. "Drop Out." *Death Valley Days*, Season 17, Episode 23. Filmmaster Productions, Flying 'A' Productions, Madison Productions Inc. TV series.

Mama Dragons. n.d. https://mamadragons.org. Website.

Manning, James David. n.d. *The Manning Report*. Atlah Media Network. https://atlah.org/amn4/category/atlah-on-demand/the-manning-report-featured-videos/page/4/. Radio.

Mansfield, Stephen. 2012. *The Mormonizing of America: How the Mormon Religion Became a Dominant Force in Politics, Entertainment, and Pop Culture*. Franklin, TN: Worthy. Nonfiction book.

Marceil, Lauren. 2014. "Mormon Parody Songs." YouTube. https:/www.youtube.com/playlist?list=PLTeII6w3-d0Wt6HepPalyUu0HU_O8xXUc. YouTube video.

"Marie Osmond's New Year's Resolution Is to Get 'Balanced.'" 2018. *First for Women*, January 15, 42–43. Periodical.

Mason, Patrick Q. 2015. *Planted: Belief and Belonging in an Age of Doubt*. Salt Lake City: Deseret Books. Nonfiction book.

McCain, Meghan, and Michael Ian Black. 2012. *America, You Sexy Bitch: A Love Letter to Freedom*. Boston: Da Capo. Nonfiction book.

McKay, Jim, dir. 2013. "Is It Safe?" *The Americans*, Season 1, Episode 9. Amblin Television, Dreamworks Television. TV series.

McEveety, Bernard, and Vincent McEveety, dirs. 1978. "Mormon Story." *How the West Was Won*, Season 2, Episode 2. MGM Television. TV series.

McGowan, Stuart E., dir. 1952–1970. "Sego Lilies," Season 1, Episode 16; "The Mormon's Grindstone," Season 3, Episode 15; "Miracle of the Seagulls," Season 4, Episode 5. *Death Valley Days*. Filmmaster Productions, Flying 'A' Productions, Madison Productions Inc. TV series.

Measom, Tyler, and Jennilyn Merten, dirs. 2010. *Sons of Perdition*. Chicken and Egg Pictures, Fork Films. Feature documentary.

Merrill, Joseph F. 1934. "Tabernacle Choir at Chicago Fair." *Millennial Star*, September 6, 568. Newspaper.

Meyer, Stephenie. 2011. *Twilight*. New York: Little, Brown. Novel.

Miller, Brent C., and H. Wallace Goddard. 2017. "Dating and Courtship." *The Encyclopedia of Mormonism*, accessed April 27. http://eom.byu.edu/index.php/Dating_and_Courtship. Website.

Miner, Allen H., dir. 1959. "The Flint McCullough Story." *Wagon Train*, Season 2, Episode 15. Revue Productions. TV series.

"Mission Statement." 2014. Ordain Women, March 18. https://ordainwomen.org/mission/. Website.

Moder, Dick, dir. 1960. "The Mormons." *Zane Grey Theater*, Season 5, Episode 10. Four Star Productions, Pamric Productions. TV series.

The Mormon Moment. 2011. Australian Broadcasting Company, Journeyman Pictures. TV documentary.

Morris, Errol, dir. 2010. *Tabloid*. Air Loom Enterprises, Moxie Pictures. Feature documentary.

Moyer, John E., dir. 2005. *Mobsters and Mormons*. South Jersey Productions. Feature film.

"Murderous Mormons." 2013. *Deadly Devotion*, Season 3, Episode 4. Investigation Discovery. TV documentary series.

Musser, Rebecca. 2014. *Red Flags for Girls*. Rebecca Musser, February 18. https://www.rebeccamusser.com/redflags/. Website.

Musser, Rebecca, and M. Bridget Cook. 2014. *The Witness Wore Red: The 19th Wife Who Brought Polygamous Cult Leaders to Justice*. New York: Grand Central. Memoir.

My Five Wives. 2013–present. Critical content. Reality TV series.

My Husband's Not Gay. 2015. Hot Snakes Media. Reality TV series.

"New Dermatological Study on Mormons Gives Scientific Reason for Self-Righteousness." 2015. *BunYion*, April 30. http://www.thebunyion.com/2015/04/30/mormon-glow-study/. Website.

Nichols, Mike, dir. 2003. *Angels in America*. Avenue Pictures, HBO Films, Panorama Films. TV miniseries.

Oaks, Dallin H. 1993. "The Great Plan of Happiness." Church of Jesus Christ of Latter-day Saints, October. https://www.lds.org/general-conference/1993/10/the-great-plan-of-happiness?lang=eng. Church website.

Oaks, Dallin H. 2015. "The Parable of the Sower." Church of Jesus Christ of Latter-day Saints, April. https://www.lds.org/general-conference/2015/04/the-parable-of-the-sower?lang=eng&_r=1. Church website.

Olsen, Mark V., and Will Scheffer, writers and creators. 2006. *Big Love*. Anima Sola Productions, Playtone Productions. TV series.

Osbourne, Brad, dir. 2015. "Jodi Arias." *Murder Made Me Famous*, Season 1, Episode 1. AMS Pictures. TV documentary series.

Osmond, Donny. 1999. *Life Is Just What You Make It: My Story So Far*. New York: Hyperion. Memoir.

Osmond, Donny. 2012. "Donny Osmond's Story of Protandim and Health." Donny Osmond website, January 1. Accessed January 12, 2017. https://donny.com/2012/01/donny-osmonds-story-protandim-health/. Website.

Osmond, Marie, and Marcia Wilkie. 2013. *The Key Is Love: My Mother's Wisdom, a Daughter's Gratitude: Essays to Move Us Forward*. New York: New American Library. Memoir.

Osmond, Marie, with Marcia Wilkie and Judith Moore. 2001. *Behind the Smile: My Journey out of Postpartum Depression*. New York: Grand Central. Memoir.

Oswaks, Molly. 2016. "'I'm a Person, and I Deserve More': What It's Like to Escape a Polygamous Cult." *Broadly*, September 21. https://broadly.vice.com/en_us/article/gyxbvb/im-a-person-and-i-deserve-more-what-its-like-to-escape-a-polygamous-cult. Blogpost.

Packer, Boyd K. 1976. "Message to Young Men." lds.org. https://www.lds.org/general-conference/1976/10/media/session_5_talk_1/2680671857001?lang=eng. Website.

Packer, Boyd K. 1993. "Talk to the All-Church Coordinating Council." *Zion's Best*, May 18. https://www.zionsbest.com/face.html. Website.

Palladino, Daniel, dir. 2018. "We're Going to the Catskills." *The Marvelous Mrs. Maisel*, Season 2, Episode 8. Amazon Studios. TV series.

Parker, Trey, dir. 1997. *Orgazmo*. Kuzui Enterprises, MDP Worldwide, Avenging Conscience. Feature film.

Parker, Trey, and Matt Stone, creators. 2003. "All About the Mormons." *South Park*, Season 7, Episode 12. Comedy Central. TV series.

Pearson, Carol Lynn. 1986. *Good-bye, I Love You: A True Story of a Wife, Her Homosexual Husband, and a Love That Transcended Tragedy*. New York: Random House. Memoir.

Pearson, Carol Lynn. 2016. *The Ghost of Eternal Polygamy: Haunting the Hearts and Heaven of Mormon Women and Men*. Chicago: Pivot Point. Nonfiction book.

Pearson, Emily. 2012. *Dancing with Crazy: A Memoir*. Kindle ed. Indianapolis: Hullabaloo. Memoir.

Perry, L. Tom. 2013. "Missionary Work in the Digital Age," accessed December 20, 2018. https://www.lds.org/broadcasts/article/worldwide-leadership-training/2013/06/missionary-work-in-the-digital-age?lang=eng. Website.

Petersen, Mark E. 1954. "Race Problems—as They Affect the Church." Tietoa mormonismista suomeksi, August 27. https://www.mormonismi.net/mep1954/10.html. Website.

Peterson, Leslie O. 2015. *The Forgotten Wives of Joseph Smith*. Watercolor series.

The Plan. 1973. The Osmonds. MGM Records. Music.

"Plural Marriage in Kirtland and Nauvoo." 2014. Accessed October 10. https://www.lds.org/topics/plural-marriage-in-kirtland-and-nauvoo?lang=eng. Website.

"Plural Marriage in Kirtland and Nauvoo—Response to LDS.org." 2015. *Mormon Think*, January 15. https://mormonthink.com/essays-plural-marriage-in-kirtland-and-nauvoo.htm. Website.

Podgursky, Peter. *M Is for Mormon Missionaries*. The ABC's of Death. Video short.

The Polygamy Store. 2015. Accessed August 12. polygamystore.com. Website.

Polygamy USA. 2013–present. part2 pictures. Reality TV series.

Post, Sue-Ann. 2005. *The Confession of an Unrepentant Lesbian Ex-Mormon*. Sydney: ABC. Memoir.

Postmormongirl. 2012. "Blessings and Tithing." *A Post-Mormon Life*, September 18. https://postmormongirl.blogspot.com/2012/09/blessings-faith.html. Blogpost.

Preece, Michael, dir. 1998. "Paradise Trail." *Walker, Texas Ranger*, Season 7, Episode 9. Norris Brothers Entertainment, The Ruddy Grief Company, CBS Productions. TV series.

The Progressive Mormons. https://theprogressivemormons.com. Website.

Quincy, Josiah. 1883. "Joseph Smith at Nauvoo." Book of Abraham Project. https://www.boap.org/LDS/Early-Saints/JQuincy.html. Church website.

"Race and the Priesthood." 2017. Church of Jesus Christ of Latter-day Saints, accessed November 15. https://www.lds.org/topics/race-and-the-priesthood?lang=eng&_r=1. Website.

Raju, Sharat, dir. 2017. "The Bad Girl." *The Catch*, Season 2, Episode 5. Shondaland. TV series.

Range, Gabriel, dir. 2014. *Outlaw Prophet: Warren Jeffs*. Sony Pictures Television. TV movie.

Ravenclaw, Malcolm. 2014. "How to Use the Mormon Glow to Attract and Influence People." *Single-Minded Determination*, January 28. https://malcolmravenclaw.com/spiritual-experiences/use-mormon-glow-attract-spouse-influence-people/#more-965. Blogpost.

"Remembering the Forgotten Wives of Joseph Smith." n.d. *Feminist Mormon Housewives*. https://www.feministmormonhousewives.org/?s=joseph%2Bsmith%2Bforgotten%2Bwives. Blogpost series.

Ricks, Bonnie. 2012. *The Mormon Woman . . . Goddess or Second Class Citizen?* Kindle ed. Amazon Digital Services. Nonfiction book.

Riedelbach, Dot, dir. 2005. *Banking on Heaven*. Over the Moon Productions. Feature documentary.

Riess, Jana. 2015. "Beauty Pageant Shows Mormons Missing the Point of Modesty—Again." Religion News Service, April 17. https://religionnews.com/2015/04/15/beauty-pageant-shows-mormons-missing-point-modesty/. Online periodical.

Rival Survival. 2014. Renegade 83. Reality TV series.

Roberts, Bryndis. 2015. "African American Mormon Convert: LDS Church Needs to 'Make Amends' for Past Racism." Religion News Service, March 19. https://religionnews.com/2015/03/19/african-american-mormon-convert-lds-church-needs-make-amends-past-racism/. Online periodical.

Robinson, Robert. 2017. *Muslim Mormon Koran*. Independently published. Nonfiction book.

Romney, Ann. 2013. *The Romney Family Table: Sharing Home-Cooked Recipes and Favorite Traditions*. Salt Lake City: Shadow Mountain Publishing. Nonfiction book.

Romney, Ann. 2015a. *In This Together: My Story*. New York: Thomas Dunne Books. Memoir.

Romney, Ann. 2015b. *Whatever You Choose to Be: 8 Tips for the Road Ahead*. Salt Lake City: Shadow Mountain Publishing. Nonfiction book.

Romney, Mitt. 2010. *No Apology: The Case for American Greatness*. New York: St. Martin's.

Rorbach, Amy. 2012. "Breaking Polygamy: The Secrets of the Sect." *20/20*, ABC News, November 23. TV news program.

Rosenberg, Drew Ann, dir. 2009. *Follow the Prophet*. Red Road Productions. TV movie.

Roth, Bobby. 2003. *The Elizabeth Smart Story*. Patricia Clifford Productions. TV movie.

RoyalzFamily YouTube channel. 2015. LGBT Topics, Season 7. YouTube series.

S, Andrew. 2009. "The Book of Mormon and the Prosperity Gospel." *Mormon Matters*, August 19. https://www.mormonmatters.org/the-book-of-mormon-and-the-prosperity-gospel/. Podcast.

The Salt Lake Tribune. 2017. "Former Mormon Leader Talks about Her Transition from Man to Woman." YouTube. https://www.youtube.com/watch?v=ZRwDdv_PN2A. YouTube video.

"Same-Sex Attraction." 2016. Church of Jesus Christ of Latter-day Saints, accessed November 5. https://www.lds.org/topics/same-gender-attraction?lang=eng. Website.

Secular Talk. 2014. "Hilarious Anti-masturbation Campaign Waged by BYU." YouTube, February 4. https://www.youtube.com/watch?v=Ueuz0-Rnd5c. YouTube video.

Seeking Sister Wife. 2018–present. Discovery Studios. Reality TV series.

"See the Stories." 2017. Protect LDS Children, accessed June 5, 2018. https://protectldschildren.org/see-the-stories/. Website.

"Shawna Cox Cell Phone Video from Inside LaVoy Finicum's Truck." 2016. *The Oregonian Channel.* YouTube, March 14. https://www.youtube.com/watch?v=eEswP_HSFV4. YouTube video.

Shelley, Elona K. 2013. *Confessions of a Molly Mormon: Trading Perfectionism for Peace, Fear for Faith, Judging for Joy.* Orem, UT: Summit View. Nonfiction book.

Short, Rex, dir. 2018. *Jodi Arias: An American Murder Mystery.* TV documentary series.

Shunn, William. 2015. "Mormonspeak." William Shunn Writer, accessed March 18. https://www.shunn.net/speak/. Blogpost.

Sister Wives. 2010–present. Puddle Monkey Productions, Figure 8 Films. Reality TV series.

16×9onglobal. 2012. "Inside Bountiful: Polygamy Investigation." YouTube, April 11. https://www.youtube.com/watch?v=UixdcBdOjNM. TV news series and YouTube video.

Slade, David, dir. 2010. *Twilight Saga: Eclipse.* Summit Entertainment. Feature film.

Smart, Elizabeth A. 2018. *Where There's Hope: Healing, Moving Forward, and Never Giving Up.* New York: St. Martin's. Memoir.

Smart, Elizabeth A., and Chris Stewart. 2014. *My Story.* New York: St. Martin's. Memoir.

Smith, Joseph. 1836. Letter to O. Cowdery. *Messenger and Advocate,* April, 289–91.

Smith, Joseph. 1920. *History of the Church of Jesus Christ of Latter-day Saints.* Board of Publication of the Reorganized Church of Jesus Christ of Latter-day Saints. Website.

Smith, Joseph, and Joseph Fielding Smith. 1993. *Teachings of the Prophet Joseph Smith.* Salt Lake City: Deseret. Nonfiction book.

Smith, Korey, and Marcus Joseph. 2016. "Adele—Hello (Mormon Missionary Parody)." YouTube, April 5. https://www.youtube.com/watch?v=ckLqfX62u_I. YouTube video.

Stanulis, Steve. 2013. "Is This Thing On?—'Sister Wives Recruiting a New Wife' [Segment]." YouTube, June 13. https://www.youtube.com/watch?v=HNdaGWGdCRc. YouTube video.

Stenhouse, Fanny. 1875. *Tell It All: The Story of a Life's Experience in Mormonism: An Autobiography.* New York: Worthington and Co. Memoir.

Stern, Howard. 1998. "Donny Osmond." *The Howard Stern Radio Show,* January 21. Eyemark Entertainment. Radio.

Stevenson, Russell. 2014. *Black Mormon: The Story of Elijah Ables.* CreateSpace. Nonfiction book.

Strasburg, Jilly. 2014. "Judgement Is of the Devil." *The Mormon Housewife Blog,* April 28. https://www.themormonhousewife.com/2014/04/judgement-is-of-devil.html. Blogpost.

"Strengthening Church Members Committee." 2017. Wikipedia, October 6. https://en.wikipedia.org/wiki/Strengthening_Church_Members_Committee. Website.

Studio C. 2012–present. BYUTV. TV series.

Taylor, Erika Martin. 2017. *The Sarcastic Molly Mormon*, accessed June 14. http://thesarcasticmollymormon.com/#gs._ptRAlY. Blogpost.

Teenage Newlyweds. 2016. A Smith and Co. Productions. Reality TV series.

Thomas, M. E. 2014. *Confessions of a Sociopath: A Life Spent Hiding in Plain Sight*. New York: Broadway. Memoir.

"Those Beautiful Mormon Girls." 2013. MormonWiki, November 4. https://www.mormonwiki.com/Those_Beautiful_Mormon_Girls. Website.

Three Wives, One Husband. 2017. KEO Films, The Complete Camera Company. TV documentary.

Townsend, Johnny. 2009. *Mormon Underwear*. Bangor, ME: BookLocker. Fiction book.

Transparent. 2015. "Raffles." Season 2, Episode 4. Amazon Studios. TV series.

True, Blair, dir. 2014. *Meet the Mormons*. Intellectual Reserves, The Church of Jesus Christ of Latter-day Saints. Feature documentary.

Turner, Lisa Ray. 1993. "Requiem for a Typical Mormon Woman." *Exponent II* 18 (1). https://web.archive.org/web/20081007002326/http://exponentii.org/articles/requiem_mormon_woman.html. Online periodical.

Udall, Brady. 1998. "The Lonely Polygamist." *Esquire*, February, 44–45. Magazine short story.

Udall, Brady. 2011. *The Lonely Polygamist: A Novel*. New York: Norton. Novel.

Vega, Cecilia. 2013. "One Woman, Chosen by Multiple Wives." *Nightline*. ABC, June 4. TV news series.

Vestal, Shawn. 2017. *Godforsaken Idaho*. New York: Little A. Short stories.

Vincent, Ali. 2009. *Believe It, Be It: How Being the Biggest Loser Won Me Back My Life*. Emmaus, PA: Rodale. Memoir.

Vuissa, Christian, dir. 2008. *The Errand of Angels*. Excel Entertainment Group. Feature film.

Yankovic, "Weird Al," and Donny Osmond. 2006. "White and Nerdy." *Straight Outta Lynwood*. Volcano Entertainment. Music video.

Walker, Sarah, dir. 2017. *I Am Elizabeth Smart*. Marwar Junction Productions. TV movie.

Wall, Elissa, and Lisa Pulitzer. 2012. *Stolen Innocence: My Story of Growing Up in a Polygamous Sect, Becoming a Teenage Bride, and Breaking Free*. New York: William Morrow. Memoir.

Watkins, Naomi. 2016. "Plan A." In *Baring Witness: 36 Mormon Women Talk Candidly about Love, Sex, and Marriage*, edited by Holly Welker. Kindle ed. Champaign: University of Illinois Press. Nonfiction book.

Webster, Nicholas, dir. 1969. "A Passage of Saints." *The Big Valley*, Season 4, Episode 20. Levee-Gardner-Laven Productions, Four Star Productions. TV series.

"We Have a Free Gift for You . . ." 2015. CTR Ring Shop, accessed December 3. https://ctrringshop.com/ctr-wallpaper. Web advertisement.

Weitz, Chris, dir. 2009. *Twilight Saga: New Moon*. Summit Entertainment. Feature film.

"Wellness Summits." 2017. DŌTERRA Essential Oils, December 11. https://doterra.com/US/en/wellness-prosperity-summits. Web advertisement.

Westover, Tara. 2018. *Educated: A Memoir*. New York: Random House. Memoir.

Weyland, Jack. 1980. *Charly*. Salt Lake City: Deseret Books. Novel.

Whippman, Ruth. 2016. *America the Anxious: How Our Pursuit of Happiness Is Creating a Nation of Nervous Wrecks*. New York: St. Martin's. Nonfiction book.

Whitaker, Judge, dir. 1963. *Windows of Heaven*. Brigham Young University. Feature film.

White, Adam, dir. 2014. *Inspired Guns*. Pitch White Entertainment. Feature film.

Whitely, Greg, dir. 2014. *Mitt*. One Potato Productions. Feature documentary.

Whitley, Helen, dir. 2007. *The Mormons, Parts I and II*. *American Experience*, Season 19, Episodes 13 and 14. WGBH. TV documentary series.

"Who We Are." 2015. Affirmation: LGBT Mormons, Families and Friends, accessed February 1. https://affirmation.org/who-we-are/. Website.

"Why Is It Better to Be Mormon?" 2016. Yahoo! Answers, accessed July 29. https://answers.yahoo.com/question/index;_ylt=A0LEVidItfNYLkgASaEPxQt.;_ylu=X30DMTByMjB0aG5zBGNvbG8DYmYxBHBvcwMxBHZ0aWQDBHNlYwNzYw—?qid=20120415073614AASKArn. Website.

Williams, Ron, dir. 2014. *Happy Valley*. Forever Green Pictures. Feature documentary.

Williams, Terry Tempest. 1991. *Refuge: An Unnatural History of Family and Place*. New York: Pantheon. Memoir.

Williams, Terry Tempest. 2013. *When Women Were Birds: Fifty-Four Variations on Voice*. New York: Picador. Memoir.

Williams, Terry Tempest. 2017. "Will Bears Ears Be the Next Standing Rock?" *New York Times*, May 6. https://www.nytimes.com/2017/05/06/opinion/sunday/will-bears-ears-be-the-next-standing-rock.html. Newspaper opinion.

Winfrey, Oprah. 2007. "Oprah and the Osmonds." *The Oprah Winfrey Show*. Season 23, Episode 174, November 9. Harpo Productions. TV talk show.

Winfrey, Oprah. 2009. "Oprah Goes Inside the Yearning for Zion Polygamist Ranch." *The Oprah Winfrey Show*, March 30. OWN. TV talk show.

Winston. 2013. "Are Utah Mormon Girls a Good Option?" Happier Abroad Forum Community, June 14. http://www.happierabroad.com/forum/viewtopic.php?t=19114. Website.

Witney, William, dir. 1959–1973. "The Pursued: Part 1," Season 8, Episode 4; "The Pursued: Part 2," Season 8, Episode 5. *Bonanza*. National Broadcasting Company. TV series.

Young, Ann Eliza. 1875. *Wife No. 19: The Story of a Life in Bondage, Being a Complete Expose of Mormonism, and Revealing the Sorrows, Sacrifices and Sufferings of Women in Polygamy*. Hartford, CT: Dustin, Gilman, and Co. Memoir.

Young, Brigham. 1858. *Journal of Discourses by President Brigham Young, His Two Counsellors, and the Twelve Apostles*. Volume 5. Liverpool: Asa Calkin. Nonfiction book.

Young, Brigham. 1860. *Journal of Discourses by President Brigham Young, His Two Counsellors, and the Twelve Apostles.* Volume 7. Liverpool: Amasa Lyman. Nonfiction book.

Young, Brigham. 1872. *Journal of Discourses by President Brigham Young, His Two Counsellors, and the Twelve Apostles.* Volume 14. Liverpool: Albert Carrington. Nonfiction book.

Young, Brigham. 2014. "Brigham Young on Race: Later Comments." Institute for Religious Research, March 6. http://bib.irr.org/brigham-young-on-race-later-comments. Website.

Young, Steve. 2016. QB: *My Life behind the Spiral.* New York: Houghton Mifflin. Memoir.

INDEX

Adam/God theory, 8, 190, 309n1
affinity fraud, 64–65, 66, 77–78, 315n4
Alameddine, Rabih, 125–26
Alpha House, 273
Americanness: and affect, 39, 51, 231, 246, 251, 294; and appeals to egalitarianism, 158; and the Boy Scouts of America, 78, 312–13n15; and celebrity, 119, 135–36, 158; and coalition against Mormons, 166; and commodification, 136, 138, 160; and freedom of choice, 14, 43–44, 54, 66–67, 79, 86–86, 166, 204, 240, 262, 266; and freedom of religion, 166; gender codes, 74–75; and imperialism, 39–41; and Joseph Smith the All-American prophet, 189, 192, 195–97; and land, 39; and marketplace, 60–61, 63, 65–66; and meritocracy, 16, 40, 44, 54–54, 60, 61, 65–67, 75, 204, 211, 223, 246, 281; and models of masculinity, 25–26, 53–54, 126, 156–57, 281, 317n5; and Mormons, 6, 26, 54, 123; neoliberal mandate, 58; nineteenth-century celebrity appeal of, 195–96; and plurality, 93, 95, 134–35, 159; and polygamists as quintessential Americans, 25–26, 132, 134, 159–60; resistance to government, 111–13; as role models, 16, 18, 25–26, 51, 61, 85, 86, 123, 156, 158, 162–63; and self-improvement, 75, 79, 119, 208, 244–47; and sexuality, 17, 35. *See also* race; separatism; spiritual neoliberalism; whiteness
Americans, The, 84
Andersen, Kurt, 195–96
Angels in America: A Gay Fantasia on National Themes, 42
apostasy, 280, 315–16n11; and excommunication, 59, 238–39; and LGBT+ lives, 21, 241
Apostolic United Brethren (AUB), 10, 127, 160, 169

Applegate, Debby, 193
Arias, Jodi, 34–35, 42, 259, 312n12
Avenging Angel, The, 8
Azrieli, Avraham, 311n7, 313n16

Bachelard, Gaston, 108, 109
Bady, Aaron, 113
Baker, Elna, 27, 33
Banet-Weiser, Sarah, 62
baptism for dead, 10–12, 50, 57, 297
Barbara Walters Special, The, 36–38
Barnes, Jane, 196–97
Baty, Paige S., 126
Bauer, Carlene, 235
Baumeister, Roy F., 245–46, 323n1
Beam, Alex, 105, 195, 196
beauty, 26, 151, 200, 214; as evidence of spiritual goodness and recruitment tool, 103–5, 212–14, 224; and Marie Osmond, 118–19, 208–9; and modesty culture, 321n8; and plastic surgery, 220–24; and postfeminist glamour, 109–10; as prerequisite for women's eternal progression, 220; and prettiness, 46, 91, 188f, 220, 223; and regulation of body, 208–10, 240. *See also* glow; modesty
Beck, Martha, 14, 82, 178, 241, 291
Believer, 20, 21
Benedict, Jeff, 312n14
Bennett, Isaiah, 98
Bennion, Janet, 140, 150, 168–69, 266, 323n14
Bentley, Paul, 180
Berger, John, 224
Bernahard-Bubb, Heidi, 233
Best Two Years, The, 24

Big Love, 3, 5, 34–35, 41–42, 45, 57, 72, 82, 92, 120–27, 130, 131, 134–36, 139, 147, 152, 163, 269, 290, 303, 311n12, 318n6; as an element of mediated Mormonism, 146, 161, 236; as feminist provocation, 237; as queer text, 140, 144–45
Black, Michael Ian, 91, 92, 245
Blackmore, Winston, 197–200, 320–21n12, 321n13
bloggernacle, 26, 62, 103
blood atonement, 8, 9, 190, 192, 273
Bloom, Harold, 6, 315n6
Boedeker, Hal, 264
Bonanza, 314n22
Book of Mormon, The, 42, 51, 52, 59, 93, 251–54, 294, 295, 312n13; and parodica, 85–90. *See also* Johnsen, Clark; Lopez, Robert; Parker, Trey; Stone, Matt
Bosker, Bianca, 85
Bowler, Kate, 75
Bowman, Matthew, 37, 78, 252
Boyd, Gale, 212–13
Boy Scouts of America, 27–28, 98, 286, 312n15, 323n2
brainwashing, 151, 163, 166–68, 187–88, 234, 262, 302n6, 311n7, 320n6
brand culture and religion, 62
branding and F/LDS faith, 12, 17, 27; brand currency, 142, 145; and forever families, 8, 56, 309n2; as "just like you," 159, 160; management of, 78; and monetization of identity, 44, 138; and progressivism as brand, 154; and rebranding, 122, 176; self-aware cultivation of, 78, 85–90; as sexually restrictive, 33, 56, 85–90; as those who endure, 158; as upbeat, 39, 56, 75, 76*f*
Brigham Young, 41, 310n3
Brigham Young University (BYU), 11, 12, 27, 39, 42, 80, 98, 99, 213, 250, 256, 294–95; and code of conduct, 82, 232, 265, 324n7, 325n9; and restricted education, 252; and settler colonialism, 39, 40*f*, 310n4; and TV, 24
Brodie, Fawn M., 22
Brooks, David, 25, 26, 111–12
Brooks, Joanna, 27, 123, 289–90, 318n3; and compulsory virginity, 33–34, 261; and feminism, 32; and Marie Osmond, 208–10; and media control, 84
Brooks, Marshall E., 313n17
Brostrom, Jennifer, 316n13
brother husbands (polyandry), 154–55, 162, 269, 310n6
Brower, Sam, 176
Brown, Christine, 13, 122, 130, 137, 143–44, 148, 154, 158, 257–58. *See also Sister Wives*
Brown, Janelle, 13, 58, 122, 130, 144, 148, 151, 155, 257. *See also Sister Wives*
Brown, Kody, 3, 10, 13, 14, 21, 30, 120, 122, 127–28, 137; as American everyman, 158–59; and families by choice, 130, 143, 310n1; and management savvy, 158, 182; net worth, 136, 316n6; plural marriage as progressive, 132, 134, 156; polygamists as oppressed, 140, 274–75; and race, 318n8; and sexual ecosystem, 29, 144, 146, 154–55, 257–58; and trope of (beleaguered) polygamous patriarch, 131, 147, 148, 151, 153, 157, 160; and his wives without him, 149*f*, 156–57. *See also Sister Wives*
Brown, Meri, 13, 122, 156, 310n1; and business platforms, 136–37; and catfish scandal, 128; and infertility, 158; and privacy, 258; and sexual economy of polygamy, 146, 152–53, 154–55, 257–58
Brown, Robyn, 13, 122, 129, 136, 146, 148, 149*f*, 153, 158, 257, 310n1; polygamists as oppressed, 134–35, 143; polygamy as feminist friendly, 154; polygamy as progressive system, 156
Buckleroos, 52
Bullock, Nicole, 221–22
Bun Yion, 105
Burris, Sarah K., 280
Bushman, Claudia, 323n14
Bushman, Richard L., 96

camp, 85–90, 110, 192–94, 197, 252
Campbell, Mary, 23, 26
Card, Orson Scott, 24, 270
Cassidy, Butch (Robert LeRoy Parker), 314n12
Cather, Willa, 284, 295
celebrity, 44, 45, 114, 124, 127–28, 137, 145, 183, 193; and celebrity theory, 53, 136, 141–42, 158, 276; and charismatic appeal, 185–88; and Elizabeth Smart, 226–32; and Flora Jessop, 174–75, 320n7; and gender, 193; and Joseph Smith, 192–97; and the Osmonds, 27, 115, 118–19, 207; as a means for social justice, 162–63, 165; Mormon celebrities, 76*f*, 194, 302n7, 312n12, 315n7
Chaffetz, Jason, 66, 115
Chambers, Samuel Allen, 144–46
charisma, 27, 107, 136; and fundamentalism, 163, 175, 176, 185–87; and Joseph Smith, 4–5, 16, 188, 190, 192–97
Charly, 319n9
Chase, Zoe, 25, 312n13
chastity, 15–16, 28, 31–34, 51, 56, 59, 84, 95, 103, 202, 214–16, 231–32, 250, 259, 280, 291, 302, 315–16n11, 324n7; and law of, 29–30, 33–34, 57, 259–60; and lessons, 33–34, 221–23, 260–61, 292, 327n2; and virgin status, 35, 55, 59, 225, 278, 309–10n2, 322n11. *See also* Choose the Right; sexuality
Cheers, 84
choice: absence of, 161, 162, 166, 173, 230, 234, 266; choosing wisely, 54, 56, 57, 201, 234; as compromised, 127, 132, 151–52, 156–57, 173, 256, 262, 275;

362 Index

families created by, 15, 124, 130, 143, 147, 151–52, 157, 162, 323n14; freedom of religion, 166, 204; free will/free agency as American and religious value, 14, 43–44, 54, 79, 85–86, 166, 198, 204, 233, 262–63; and glow, 214; between the godly and the satanic, 97; between the godly and the worldly, 66–67, 239; and happiness, 202, 230; LGBT+ lives, 242, 247, 266; and neoliberalism, 58, 62, 71, 162–63, 133, 202; politics of, 121–22, 138, 129, 140, 149–50, 161, 200–205, 221, 234, 266, 283; as a precursor to modernity, 233, 240; and sexuality, 154, 247, 264, 266. *See also* Choose the Right; conscience; consent

Choose the Right, 56, 214, 259–60. *See also* choice; conscience

Church of Lies, 9, 167, 168, 174, 189, 320n6. *See also* Jessop, Flora

City Creek Center, 65

closet, 15, 44–45, 86, 140–46, 153, 249, 258, 264, 268, 271, 274–75

code of conduct, 36, 172, 248, 301; at BYU, 232

conscience, 46, 166–67, 188, 204, 241, 242, 251; vs. creed, 239, 247, 268; crisis of, 234, 239, 253, 266, 275

consent, 1, 233; as American value, 166, 262; complications around, 181, 184, 234; and plural families, 15, 124, 127, 129, 139, 147, 163, 166; and proxy baptism, 10; and sex, 258

Cooper, Alex, 41, 205

Cooper, Anderson, 226, 320n7

Coppins, McKay, 25

correlation, 78

Cortez, Marjorie, 221

Cott, Nancy, 16, 166

Court of Love (Council of Love), 82–83, 237, 239, 241, 242–43, 275. *See also* disciplinary council

Covey, Stephen R., 24, 49, 83, 316n13

Coviello, Peter, 244

Cowdery, Oliver, 95

Crawford, Amanda J., 170, 174

critical thinking, 219, 220, 252–53; and doubt, 178; and threat of intellectuals, 29, 84, 92, 276, 277, 312n10. *See also* apostasy

DaCosta, Neil, 86, 87f

Dalton, Elaine S., 103

Dancing with Crazy: A Memoir, 41, 253. *See also* Pearson, Emily

Darger, Joe, 133–34, 137–39, 146, 160. *See also* Dargers

Darger, Valerie, 141

Darger, Vicki, 141

Dargers, 137–39, 146, 151

David Pakman Show, 142

Dawson, Mackenzie, 75–76

Day of Defense, 52

Death Valley Days, 314n22

Debord, Guy, 109

Dehlin, John, 3, 89–90, 92, 101, 219, 241, 251–52, 255, 275, 323n15. *See also Mormon Stories*

Deleuze, Gilles, 108, 109

Denton, Katherine Jean, 205, 260–61

depression, 306; and antidepressants, 217–18; and Donny Osmond, 37, 116; and Marie Osmond, 207; and women, 217, 218, 235, 294

Deseret, 39, 40f, 57, 61, 65

Deseret News Utah, 221

Dialogue: A Journal of Mormon Thought, 93

disciplinary council, 241, 242–43. *See also* Court of Love

District, The, 24

Divine Center, The, 49

Doctrine and Covenants of the Church of Jesus Christ of Latter-day Saints, The (D&C), 33, 59, 60, 81, 195, 251; D&C 132 (on principle of plural marriage), 7, 269

Donny and Marie (Osmond), 27, 36–38, 115–19. *See also* Osmond, Donny; Osmond, Marie; Osmond Family

dōTERRA, 67–72, 104f, 105, 315n5

Doty, Alexander, 197

Draga, Jeffrey, 81

Dr. Drew, 138, 146

Dr. Phil, 118, 138

Dyer, Richard, 44, 53, 94, 247

Educated: A Memoir, 315n5. *See also* Westover, Tara

8: The Mormon Proposition, 20

Elder: A Mormon Love Story, 52

Ellen DeGeneres Show, The, 37–38, 136, 153

epistemology of light, 44, 94, 109–11, 209–10

equal-opportunity oppression, 139–40

essential oils, 64, 67, 71–73; and Dr. Mom, 73, 315n5; as God's medicine, 66–67. *See also* dōTERRA; sacred oil; separatism

eternal companion, 56, 103, 204, 212, 259

eternal marriage, 8, 55–56, 74–75, 103, 250, 309–10n2; and eternal polygamy, 59, 192, 321n1. *See also* eternal progression; forever families

eternal progression, 8, 74, 75, 213, 219, 220

Facebook, 15, 24, 33, 80–82, 84, 112–13, 128, 136, 138, 174, 220, 245, 264, 274, 282, 317n2

Fales, Steven, 254–55, 324n6; on smiling through the pain, 251, 275

Falls: Covenant of Grace, The, 52

Falls: Testament of Love, The, 52

Index 363

feminism, 19, 21, 29, 82, 124, 130, 149–50, 152, 204, 224; and desires for whole personhood, 172, 235, 236, 240; and fundamentalist Mormons, 150–57, 167–76, 236, 237; and mainstream Mormons, 17, 93, 118, 215, 223, 233, 235, 240, 253, 276, 278, 315–16n11; and political consciousness, 46, 188, 206, 221, 281–83; as strong-minded women, 148, 173, 176, 215. *See also* choice; Ordain Women; voice; women's empowerment

Feminist Mormon Housewives, 206, 270–71

financial holdings, of LDS Church, 65

Finding Your Roots, 11–12

First for Women, 115, 117f, 118

Flake, Jeff, 25–26, 112, 312n13

Follow the Prophet, 121, 165

forever families, 8, 37, 56, 71, 204, 300, 309n2. *See also* eternal marriage

Forgotten Wives of Joseph Smith, The, 270–71, 272f

Foucault, Michel, 244–45, 247, 318n5

Freeman, Judith, 203, 208, 216

Freeman, Marnie, 82, 205, 234, 251, 274–75

Friedan, Betty, 218

garments (Mormon underwear), 3, 31, 72, 84, 265, 290, 302, 327n3; and the Mormon smile, 84, 85f

gender roles, 37; as divinely preordained, 74, 203, 204, 237; division by, 77, 197–200, 203, 204, 218–19, 249, 281–83, 321n2, 324n5; as part of meritocratic order, 75, 281; restrictions based on, 71–73, 77, 203, 208–9, 235–40

gender stereotypes: as exemplified by Donny and Marie Osmond, 36–38, 115–19; Molly Mormon, 36, 216–25, 240, 321n6; Peter Priesthood, 36

Giddens, Anthony, 210

Givens, Terryl L., 78, 96

glow, 44, 71; and countenance, 103–8; defined, 94; and Elizabeth Smart, 322n11; and female beauty, 209–15; and luminosity, 108–11; as proselyting tool, 103, 214; as racialized signifier explained, 106; and shimmering, 108, 110

God Squad, 168, 173

Goldwyn, Tony, 183–88

Google Apostasy, 315–16n11

Gray, Darius, 100, 101

Great Plan of Happiness (Plan of Salvation), 73–75

Gregory, Alice, 26

Grey, Mya, 262

Gruen, J. Philip, 195

Gutjahr, Paul C., 23, 158

Haglund, Kristine, 93, 102–3

Hahn, Gregory, 92

Halberstam, Jack, 163

Halperin, David M., 144

Hanson, C. L., 224

happiness: as aspirational affect, 202; as compulsory, 216–25, 225–31, 244–47, 251, 322n11; as proof of good choices, 75; as reason for depression, 217–18, 294, 321n7; as technology of spiritual neoliberalism, 75–78, 202. *See also* Great Plan of Happiness; Mormon smile

Happy Valley, 39–41, 46, 321n7; and feminism, 206; and imperatives for female perfectionism, 216–25, 254; and modesty culture, 221–23; and plastic surgery, 220–24; as sheltered, 255–56

Hardy, Nicole, 27, 216, 235

Harrison, Mette Ivie, 311n8

Hatch, Orrin, 115

hegemony, 257, 273, 275; and hegemonic structures of Mormonism, 1, 2, 47, 250, 273, 284–307; made visible through mediated Mormonism, 46, 256–57, 273; and neoliberalism, 58; and patriarchy, 161, 168, 197; with respect to gender, 42, 127, 151, 183, 192–93, 203, 210–11, 219, 224, 312n14; with respect to sexuality, 146, 197, 205–6, 247; with respect to whiteness, 42, 197; those on margins, 139, 197. *See also* choice; masculinity; toxic femininity

Heisenberg Theory of Mediation, 146

Henderson, Peter, 63, 65

heterosexuality, 20, 28, 34, 42, 46, 75, 140, 144, 158, 167, 193, 203, 207, 212, 218, 234, 242, 248, 259, 263–70; as social construction, 247, 324n4

Hitt, Tarpley, 314n23

homosexuality: homophobia, 19, 247, 265–66; and reparative therapy, 254, 266, 324–25n8; as sin, 21, 324n6. *See also* pray the gay away

Horowitz, Jason, 100

Houston, Pam, 126

Hyde, Jesse, 120

I Am Cait, 10

indigenous peoples, 47, 113–14; and Bears Ears, 114–15; Paiutes, 191, 310n4. *See also* Lamanites

Inspired Guns, 52

Instagram, 136, 317n2

Jack Weyland's Charly, 309–10n2

Jankowiack, William, 128

jealousy, 35, 129–30, 132, 154–56, 280

Jeff Probst Show, The, 148

Jeffs, Brent W., 9, 177–79, 181–83, 320n7

Jeffs, Rachel, 178, 311n7

Jeffs, Rulon, 164, 177, 320n11

364 Index

Jeffs, Warren Steed, 9, 21–22, 24, 45–46, 163–64, 176–92, 198, 258; and body, 176, 183, 184–85; as charismatic, 181–82, 186; as conflated with Joseph Smith and Brigham Young, 45, 188–92, 200; and connections to Osama bin Laden, 17, 165, 166, 177, 187, 311n7; as dangerous cult leader, 165, 170, 172, 177; and demands for absolute control, 172, 177–79, 192, 251; as epitome of evil, 124, 125, 167, 168, 176–83, 319–20n5; and *Outlaw Prophet*, 42, 165, 183–88, 189, 192; and retribution against, 174, 230, 233, 320n6; and sexual assault, 177–78, (heavenly sessions) 179–83, 230; and stereotypes about, 120–21; and voice, 167, 176, 180, 181–83, 184, 185. *See also* keep sweet; polygamy

Jessop, Flora 9, 165–70, 173–76, 189, 320nn6–7
Johnsen, Clark, 88–89, 251–52, 275, 316n1
Johnston, Carol, 231
Jones, Cindi, x, 205, 275, 323n2
Joyce, Kathryn, 84, 241

Katz, Alyssa, 28
Katz, Jonathan Ned, 247
Kearney, Mary Celeste, 109, 110
keek, 18
keep sweet, 167, 172, 250–52
Kimball, Heber C., 268
Kimball, Spencer W., 29, 36, 98, 268, 324n6
Kimmel, Michael, 131
King, Martin Luther, Jr., 18, 311–12n9
Kingston Clan (Kingston Group), 125, 170–73, 310–20n5, 320n8
Kirn, Walter, 78, 92
Kolob, 93, 316n1
Krakauer, Jon, 8, 320n11
Krule, Miriam, 102–3
Kuruvilla, Carol, 18

Lamanites, 96, 97–98, 105
latter-day screens: defined, 18, 108–9, 146, 276–77; and its evils, 273, 276; as motivated by Warren Jeffs, 176–77; and not-knowingness, 252–57; and sexuality, 267, 273–75; as site of resistance, 275, 281–83; and toxic femininity, 207, 224–25; as transmedia, 53
Lawrence, Gary C., 79, 315n9
Leaving the Saints: How I Lost the Mormons and Found My Faith, 241, 291. *See also* Beck, Martha
LGBT+, 46, 247–48; and choice, 204; as community, 323–24n3; and human rights, 82; as a minority within the church, 93, 102; and modern polygamy, 139–48; as threats to the church, 19, 20–21, 42

Lochrie, Karma, 324n4
Lonely Polygamist: A Novel, The, 39, 124–25, 129–30, 139, 147, 151, 155–56, 161
"Lonely Polygamist, The," 148
Lopez, Robert, 51
Lopez Tonight, 136, 153
Lost Boy, 9, 126, 177, 236, 320n7
lost boys, 130, 156
Love, Loni, 318
LuLaRoe, 64, 136, 137

Mama Dragons, 20, 274
Manning Report, The, 142
marginalization of Mormons, 2, 27, 44, 47, 93, 123, 126, 132, 139, 140, 144–46, 169, 197. *See also* separatism; unique/alike axis
marriage, 42; and antibigamy laws, 13–14, 140–41, 164, 310n5; forced, 122, 162, 172, 179, 320n8; and housewives, 216, 227; and interracial unions, 29, 99; importance of, 250; LDS critiques of, 234; marital rights, 114–15; open, 16; as required for highest heaven, 28, 263, 266, 316n3; same-sex, 18, 24, 44, 102, 140, 143, 323–24n3; and sealing, 31, 59, 205, 298–99, 300, 309–10n2, 321n1; and sex, 30, 35, 259–61, 293, 302, 314n22; therapy and, 121; what makes a good or bad, 127–29, 169, 268. *See also* eternal marriage; polygamy; Proclamation of the Word on the Family
Marriott International, 69–71; Center, 79–80, 300
Marvelous Mrs. Maisel, The, 316n14
masculinity, 19; as absolute authority, 36–38, 178, 192, 204, 219; and appeals to conventional, 25–26, 35, 42, 62–63, 81, 132, 199, 224; as artifice, 193; and audacity, 192–93; and Donny Osmond, 119, 317n5; and godhead, 7, 8, 31, 54, 93, 107, 156, 205, 220, 281, 288; and hierarchical power relations, 37, 109, 156, 183, 192–93, 197, 204, 205; and polygamy, 131, 155–57; and missionary, 52, 54; and obligations as a patriarch, 131; and possibility for postpatriarchal relations, 150, 155, 157, 182–83; and sexuality, 131
Mason, Patrick Q., 315–16n11
Masons (Freemasons), 313n18
masturbation, 33, 83, 259, 260, 265–66, 292, 314n23, 325n9
Mauss, Armand L., 96, 99, 159, 276
Maynes, Richard J., 194–95
McCain, Meghan, 91–94, 245
McCarter, Melissa Miles, 153–54
McClelland, Nicholas Hegel, 252
McGee, Micki, 210
McRobbie, Angela, 109

Index 365

mediated Mormonism: as analytic, 3, 52–53; defined, 1–3, 15, 18; gender and sexuality, 15–16, 248, 278–80; as meme, 3, 52–53, 277; in nineteenth century, 16–17, 22–24; and progressivism, 19–20, 29, 277; and rise of the church, 20–38; as transmediated, 53, 276–77; as trope, 52–54, 163–64, 169

Meet the Mormons, 79

Mencimer, Stephanie, 66–67

Merrill, Joseph F., 23

Metcalfe, Brent, 9, 10

#MeToo, 322n13. *See also* obedience; sexual abuse

Meyer, Stephenie, 24, 30, 76f, 107, 312n12

M is for Mormon Missionaries, 52

missionaries: as colonizers, 310n4; as excellent salespeople, 66; as gods in training, 75, 103, 254; and marriage, 215, 220, 294–95; media related to, 24, 34, 42, 51–52; as mediated figure, 2, 23, 44, 49–54, 93, 286, 287, 290, 312n13; as models of persuasion and perseverance, 21, 64, 66, 78, 79, 84–85, 280, 285, 289, 302, 304, 325–26; as polysemic signifiers, 52; regulation of, 80, 81, 83; and sexuality, 86–90, 248, 252, 278; and social media, 79–81, 83–85; as super nice, 302, 325–27n1; and testimonials, 118; women, 50, 305–6, 314n1

Missionary, 52

modern polygamy (progressive polygamy), 44–45; and beset patriarch, 131, 147, 148–56; as better than monogamy, 129, 131, 132, 139; as good for women, 131, 149; as indistinguishable from others, 120, 122–23, 162–63; and LGBT+ politics, 139–48; and parallel monogamies, 147; practitioners as "normal" Americans, 121–22, 124, 126, 132, 147, 148; and sexual economy within, 129–30, 146–47; and social justice through visibility, 120–21, 123, 142; and spiritual neoliberalism, 124–25; as very unlike FLDS, 122, 124. *See also* Americanness; *Big Love*; polygamy; *Sister Wives*

modesty, 34, 75, 172, 202, 214, 221–23, 232, 240, 322n8

Molly Mormon, 36, 216–25, 240, 321n6

Mollywood, 23

mommy blogs, 26, 36, 76, 254, 318n6

Monson, Thomas, 80, 81, 325

Moore, R. Laurence, 17, 84, 195, 316n11, 321n3, 323n15

Mormon Candidate, The, 311n7, 313n16

Mormon history, 3–8, 16, 94–98, 268–73, 319n1. *See also* race; Smith, Joseph, Jr.; Young, Brigham

MormonLeaks, 315–16n11

Mormon Missionary Positions, 86, 87f

Mormon moment, 92, 103; and *The Mormon Moment*, 137–38, 146

Mormon Problem, 78

Mormons and Muslims, 17–18, 23, 232, 311n7

Mormon smile: as brand of the faith, 36, 37, 39, 50f, 57, 68, 75, 76f, 83, 212, 246, 257, 267, 275, 287, 291, 294, 298, 306, 307; and compulsory happiness, 216–25, 244–47, 251, 322n11; and the Osmonds, 27, 118, 207, 208; as underwear, 84, 85f. *See also* Happy Valley

Mormon Stories, 3, 89–90, 92, 101, 219, 241, 251–52, 255, 275, 323n15. *See also* Dehlin, John

Mormon War, 5, 160, 231, 310n4

Mormon welfare, and Desert Industries, 57, 61, 65; and the Bishop's Storehouse, 61, 64, 315n3. *See also* United Order

Moroni, Angel, 4, 54, 71, 189

Moroni, Captain, 112–13

Mountain Meadows Massacre, 191, 315–16n11

multilevel marketing (MLM), 64, 66–73, 105; and Donny Osmond, 116–17, 118, 317nn6–7. *See also* dōTERRA; LuLaroe; NuSkin, Young Living

Musser, Rebecca, 165–66, 185–86, 197, 233–34, 258

My Five Wives, 130, 139, 146, 317

My Husband's Not Gay, 263–68

My Sisterwife's Closet, 136, 137f

Napier-Pearce, Jennifer, 324n5

Negra, Diane, 153

Neilson, Reid Larkin, 23

Nelson, James, 225

Nelson, Russell M., 314

neoliberalism, 109, 132. *See also* spiritual neoliberalism

niceness, 25, 41–42, 57, 70, 172, 220, 293, 302, 304

non-Mormon in a Mormon world, 1, 27, 47, 284–307, 325–27n1

normal/abnormal, 145, 273; as enviable, 26; and marriage, 56, 122–23, 227, 267–69; and polygamy, 122–24, 138, 146, 158; questioning, 25; semiotic work of, 35, 68, 158, 160–61, 172; and sexuality, 144, 227, 242–43, 323n4

normativity, 12, 62, 78, 211, 250, 277; and beauty, 26, 221, 249; cultural work of, 268–69; and gender, 36, 202, 220; heteronormativity, 42, 46, 86, 144–47, 160–61, 204, 207, 220, 234, 240, 323n4; and personhood, 14, 139, 172, 310n2; and rule culture, 250; and sex and sexuality, 28, 35, 144, 195, 242–44, 248–50, 268, 271, 278–79, 323n4; and whiteness, 41–42, 109, 210

not-knowingness, 252–57, 269, 271, 273, 277

Nugent, Walter, 39

NuSkin, 66, 105

Nussbaum, Emily, 131

Oaks, Dallin H., 62, 74, 75

obedience, 2, 52, 59, 82–83, 175, 200, 241, 251, 273–74; and disobedience, 160, 253, 255–56, 274; and not-knowingness, 252–57; and sexual abuse, 43, 177–81, 261–62, 322n12; and striving for perfection, 75, 82, 244, 251, 256, 281; as unquestioned and absolute, 166, 177, 178, 192, 204, 252–57, 268, 274–75; and women, 206, 209–10, 218, 219, 237, 288–89. *See also* keep sweet

Olsen, Mark V., 127, 152

Ordain Women, 237–40

ordinances, 11, 57, 99, 313n18

Orgazmo, 42, 52, 86

Osmond, Donny, 27, 36–38, 76f; and glow, 115–19, 317n8; and masculinity, 119, 317n5; and MLMs, 117–18, 317nn6–7. *See also* Donny and Marie; Osmond Family

Osmond, Marie, 27, 36–38, 76f; and body/beauty, 118–19, 208–9; and glow, 115–19; as meme for Mormonism, 118; as mother, 321n4; and ruminations on Mormon beliefs, 36–37, 60; and sexual abuse, 232; and toxic femininity, 207–10, 232. *See also* Donny and Marie; Osmond Family

Osmond, Olive, 118, 209

Osmond Family, 27, 37, 41, 75, 316n1

Other Side of Heaven, The, 27, 52

Ouellette, Laurie, 318n5

Our America with Lisa Ling, 130, 131, 135, 151, 156

Outlaw Prophet, 42, 165, 183–92, 311n7. *See also* Jeffs, Warren Steed

Packer, Boyd K., 80, 81, 276; and "enemies of the church," 29, 277, 312n10

Paint Your Wagon, 311n6

Pakman, David, 142

Parker, Theodore, 311–12n9

Parker, Trey, 51, 86, 254, 316n1

parodica, 52, 85–90

Pearson, Carol Lynn, 59, 235, 255–56, 321n1, 324n6

Pearson, Emily, 20, 212, 219, 253–54, 257, 260, 275

perfectionism, 106, 254; and Molly Mormon, 216–25; and women, 204, 205, 206, 209–10, 215, 217–19, 221, 232, 241, 254, 256. *See also* gender stereotypes; toxic femininity

Perry, L. Tom, 80, 81

Peter Priesthood, 36

Petersen, Mark E., 97

Peterson, Leslie O., 271, 272f

Petrey, Taylor G., 249

Phillips, Adam, 110

Phillips, Kim, 247

Pioneers (Mormon settlers), 40–41, 99, 231, 253, 254–55, 298, 312n14, 313n21; handcarts, 40, 191

polygamy (plural marriage, the principle), 7–10; and abuse of women, 172, 180; as American Taliban, 17, 166, 225; as Anti-American, 164, 166–67; as cult, 120, 148, 166; and dress, 319n1; in early church, 268–73; as evil, 169, 225; as feminist space, 153, 154, 167–76, 323n14; gendered labor within, 199–200; and law, 13–15; and media use, 168, 319n4; and Muslims, 17–18, 124, 166; prejudices about, 141, 148, 150; and premortal existence, 318n4; and race, 316n3, 318n7; as sexual morality tale, 35; stereotypes about, 120–21, 163; as subjects of oppression, 134–35, 139–40; as threat, 16, 142, 163, 166; outside U.S., 124; as queer, 24f, 244, 319n4. *See also* Jeffs, Warren Steed; modern polygamy; preexistence

polygamy-visibility, 163, 164–67

Poovey, Mary, 144

pornography, 30, 34, 37, 52, 86, 91, 253, 260, 265–66, 273, 304, 318

Post, Sue-Ann, 205

postfeminism, 42, 109–10, 148–57

Postmormongirl, 63–64

pray the gay away, 242, 267; working oneself straight, 244–47, 254–55, 274, 323n2

preexistence, 74, 97, 303–4, 318n4

Proclamation of the Word on the Family, 204, 238, 248

progressive polygamy. *See* modern polygamy

Projansky, Sarah, 109

prophecy: as contemporary, 44, 280–81, 313n16; and polygamy, 127, 236, 269; and race, 98, 318n7. *See also* revelation

Prophet's Prey, 41, 165, 167, 168, 176, 181, 311, 320n11

Proposition 8 (California), 15, 20

prosperity gospel, 44, 54–65; and ties to Mormonism, 61–62

publicity, 275; as crime, 14, 239, 241, 249, 323n15; favorable, 23, 58; to leverage political gain, 102, 174; and privacy, 44; as stunt, 112, 175

public relations, 23–24, 84, 315n8; beauty as, 26; to counter image as "peculiar people," 78–79, 315nn9–10; and diversity, 104; and perceptions of racism, 94, 98–99; as response to *Book of Mormon* musical, 88–90; and self-improvement, 79; and social media, 79–85; and tight control, 84. *See also* publicity

Pugsley, Mark, 64–65

queer practices, 242–44; church restrictions on, 248–49

queer visibility, 274

Quincy, Josiah, 196

Quinn, D. Michael, 64

Quinn, Jennifer, 35

Index 367

race: civil rights, 35, 36, 111, 122, 128; 1978 ruling on black church members, 20, 29, 36, 77, 93, 94, 96, 98–99, 246, 273, 286, 318n7; in nineteenth century, 94–95; Orientalizing of Mormons, 23; and phenotypes, 110–11; and polygamy, 318n8; racism, 94–98, 113–14, 318n7. *See also* glow; whiteness

Ravenclaw, Malcolm, 103–4

reality television: and issues of authenticity, 170, 317n2; as genre of the real, 164, 277

Reay, Barry, 247

Reeve, W. Paul, 95, 96

representation in media: as both friendly and authoritarian, 83–84; as racially devolved, 95–96

revelation, 5, 6, 9, 20–21, 28–29, 36, 44, 59, 81, 194–95; as contemporary phenomenon, 78; as personal testimony, 118; as related to gender, 50, 54, 192, 249; as related to LGBT+ folks, 21; as related to marriage, 162, 269; as related to race, 98. *See also* prophecy

Reynolds, Dan, 21, 205

Ricks, Bonnie, 232

Riess, Jana, 100, 322n8

righteous resistance, 111–13, 133–34, 160, 200, 203, 239, 275; dangers of, 219–20; and LGBT+ lives, 249–50, 274–75. *See also* siege at Malheur National Wildlife Refuge

RLDS (Reformed Church of Jesus Christ of Latter-day Saints), 10

Roberts, Bryndis, 100–101

Romig, Rollo, 23

Romney, Ann, 312n11

Romney, Marion G., 28

Romney, Mitt, 24, 42, 61, 76f, 83, 85f, 91, 93, 312nn11–12

Romney Family, 41

Rorbach, Amy, 172, 319n4

RoyalzFamily, 267

sacred oil: anointing with, 72–73, 259; healing with, 70, 238, 239f, 321. *See also* essential oils

same-sex attraction (SSA), 19, 35, 42, 86, 263–68, 276

Santa Clarita Diet, The, 316n14

Saratov Approach, The, 52

Saturday Night Live, 12, 41

Scheffer, Will, 127, 152

Scott, Joan, 53

Sedgwick, Eve Kosofsky, 152

Seeking Sister Wife, 310n2, 317n1

Segal, Victoria, 77

self-regulation, 244–47

separatism, 16, 17, 23, 44–45, 79, 112, 123–24, 159, 250, 307; and medicine, 66–67, 315n5, 318–19n8

September Six, 84

settler colonialism, 113–14, 115, 191, 310n4

sexual abuse: bishopric interviews, 314n23; incest, 122, 142, 178, 189, 232; issues about reporting, 232, 322n13; pedophilia, 33, 35, 176–88, 189, 234, 251, 270, 324n23; rape, 33, 34, 52, 122, 148, 166, 174, 177, 180f, 181, 184, 186, 189, 225, 227, 230, 246, 251; and sexual assault culture, 261–62; trigger warning, 43. *See also* obedience; Smart, Elizabeth

sexuality: and naïveté, 34, 41–42, 51, 52, 57, 181, 255–56, 261, 267; and non-normative sex practices, 259, 268, 311n6; and not talking about it, 257–58, 261; public fascinations with, 258; as reason for leaving, 234–35, 251–52; restrictions on sexual behavior, 21, 28, 29–38, 33–34, 233, 250–52; and selfhood, 247–50

Shelley, Elona K., 216–17

Shipps, Jan, 9, 10, 78

siege at Malheur National Wildlife Refuge, 111–19

Singer, T. Benjamin, 110

Sister Wives (Kody Brown Family), 10; and appeals to normalcy, 146, 158, 159, 120–22; and gay pride arguments, 139–48; and home birthing, 144; and prosecution, 13–15; relative queerness of, 144–46; and religion, 159–60; and social justice, 21, 28. *See also* Americanness; Brown, Kody; modern polygamy; polygamy

social media, as proselyting tool, 83–84; for distribution of liberal ideas, 84, 93

Smart, Elizabeth, 3, 24, 35, 46, 165; and compulsory happiness, 225–34; and compulsory virginity, 33–35, 322n9; and glow, 322n11; rumors about. *See also* Happy Valley

Smith, Emma, 3, 152

Smith, Joseph, Jr., 3–7, 16, 20, 24; and blood atonement, 9; and bloodline, 82, 177, 270–71; as camp figure, 192–97; and celebrity, 195–97; as ceremonial general, 6, 196; and charisma, 4–5, 16, 188, 190, 192–97; and conceptualization of heaven, 59; and the Danites, 6; and death, 5–6, 15–16, 193–94; as diviner, 18, 108; and egalitarianism, 158; and founding of the church, 3–7, 178, 189; as fraud, 194, 315n4; in the grove, 4, 71, 178; and Jesus Christ, 5–6, 177, 192, 194–97, 286, 289; and the Masons, 313n18; and media, 22–23, 108; and multiple mortal probation, 303; and the perfect city, 296–97; and personal testimony, 112, 178, 189; and polygamy, 7, 20, 45, 59, 164, 188–92, 268–73, 303, 318n4; as presidential candidate, 24, 94, 195; as quintessential American, 195–96; and race/racism, 94–95; in relation to Brigham Young, 45, 60, 188–92; and United Order, 60–61; and Word of Wisdom, 31. *See also Forgotten Wives of Joseph Smith, The*; Smith, Emma

Smith, N. Lee, 66–67

Smith-Rosenberg, Carroll, 153
Snow, Lorenzo, 63
sons of perdition, 45, 59
Sons of Perdition, 165
Sontag, Susan, 86
South Park, 5, 41–42, 51, 57, 86
sovereign nation, the church as its own, 64
spiritual neoliberalism, 43–44, 54–65; as anchored by heavenly reward, 62, 85, 204; and appearance, 220; and brand recognition, 62; and glow, 115–19; and governance, 81, 133, 152, 208, 239–40, 250; and happiness, 75–78, 202; and management of the self, 57, 67, 74–75, 132–33, 202–3, 208–9, 217, 244–47; and meritocracy, 16, 40, 44, 53–54, 60, 61, 65–67, 75, 204, 211, 223, 246, 281; and reduced reliance on government, 57–58, 67, 78; and resourcefulness, 319n10; and time management, 83, 208, 316n13. *See also* choice; prosperity gospel; toxic femininity
Squirrel Cage, 205, 323
Stacey, Judith, 122, 132, 140, 150
Stack, Peggy Fletcher, 240
Stenhouse, Fanny, 190–91, 280–81, 325n1
stereotypes about Mormons, 41–42, 51–52, 246; as polygamists, 21, 120–23, 198–99, 267–68; as secretive, 327
Stevenson, Russell, 100
Stewart, Dodai, 154
Stone, Matt, 51, 86, 254, 312n13
Stout, David, 276
Strange, James Jesse (and the Strangites), 105
Strasburg, Jilly, 201–4
Stryker, Susan, 247
Sunstone, 274
surveillance and espionage, 327n3; through media, 168, 245, 319n4; methods for subverting, 223; as protection, 166; to reinforce "good choices," 57, 244–45; and selfhood, 244–47; and social rules, 81; and Strengthening Church Members Committee, 81–82, 245; and technology, 168; and time management, 83

Tabloid, 34, 52
Tannehill, Brynn, 323–24n3
Teenage Newlyweds, 54–59
temple worthy, 57, 63, 64, 300; and temple recommends, 261, 309
testimonial/testimony: as coerced, 256–57, 275; as epistemology of affect, 25, 83, 178, 204, 241–42, 255; for MLM products, 64, 66, 71–73, 116–18; for principle of plural marriage, 151–52; as proof of truth, 46, 112, 113, 257, 275, 314n23
Thomas, M. E., 294
Tice, Diane M., 245–56, 323n1

tithing, 56, 59, 65, 67, 244, 281, 288, 315n3; as mandatory for blessings, 61, 63–64
Townsend, Johnny, 29
toxic femininity, 202–3, 206–25; and Elizabeth Smart, 225–31; and Rebecca Musser, 233–34; and sexual assault, 232, 261–62
transgender, 247–48, 249–50, 321nn2–3, 323n2, 323–24n3, 324n5
Transmormon, 249–50
Transparent, 279–80
Turley, Jonathan, 14, 140–41
Turner, John G., 310
Twilight, 24, 30–31, 32f; and glow, 106–8
Twitter, 128, 174, 245, 264, 317n2

Udall, Brady, 39, 120–21, 124–25, 129–30, 140, 148–49, 151, 155–57, 318n4
Ulrich, Laurel Thatcher, 323n14
unique/alike axis, 44, 123, 92–93, 158–59
United Effort Plan (UEP), 320n11
United Order, 60–61

Valentine, David, 248
Vega, Cecilia, 135, 149, 151, 156, 319n10
Vestal, Shawn, 8
Vincent, Ali, 292–93
visibility: and cameras as weapons, 174; as recruitment strategy, 55–56, 133–34; as tool for social justice, 120–21, 123, 142, 175
voice: as feminist, 170, 176, 200, 203, 233, 235, 253, 275; for oppressed peoples, 45, 93, 100, 102, 123–24, 142, 205, 252, 274

Wallace, Irving, 194, 196
Wagon Master, 41
Walker, Texas Ranger, 41
Wall, Elissa, 162, 164, 203, 261
Warnke, Melissa Batchelor, 114
Watkins, Naomi, 220
West, 39–41, 64, 72, 113, 126, 284, 314n22; Arizona, 46–47, 284, 295–96; and Mesa, 1, 2, 30, 34, 46–47, 54–55, 59, 285–91, 292–304; and polygamy, 164, 165, 168; and television
Westerns, 314n22; and the Western frontier, 113–14
Westover, Tara, 315n5
Weyland, Jack, 309–10n2, 319n9
"White and Nerdy," 317n8
whiteness, 6, 29, 36, 41–42, 44, 52, 57, 71, 81, 86; and nineteenth century, 94–100; and notions of America, 140; as related to glow, 103, 105–7, 109, 116–19; and white panic, 166; and white privilege, 111–15. *See also* Americanness; race

Whippman, Ruth, 75–77
Williams, Terry Tempest, 3, 39, 115, 236
Williams, Troy, 60, 61
windows of heaven, 63
Windows of Heaven, 63
Winter, Caroline, 65
Wolf, Naomi, 209
women's empowerment, 203, 207; through essential oils, 70–73; in polygamy, 150–54, 167, 168–69, 176. *See also* feminism; voice
Woodland, Cadence, 92–93
Woodruff, Emily, 221
Word of Wisdom, 31, 33, 57, 106, 302, 317n4

Yankovic, "Weird Al," 317n8
Yearning for Zion, 45, 177, 179, 180f, 183, 319nn3–4

Young, Ann Eliza, 190–91, 196, 281
Young, Brigham, 6, 310, 316n4; and Adam/God theory, 309n1; and amusements, 84; and attitude toward women, 197; and beauty, 105; and blood atonement, 9; and *Brigham Young*, 40, 310n3; critique of, 190–91; as celebrity, 196; and the Danites, 6; and journey westward, 6, 191; Mountain Meadows Massacre, 191, 315–52n11; and polygamy, 45, 164, 188–92, 270, 273, 281, 320n10; and racism, 96–97, 303, 316n2; in relation to Joseph Smith, 188–92; United Order, 60
Young, Margaret B., 101
Young, Steve, 3, 73, 317n4
Young Living, 64
YouTube, 18, 27, 51, 72, 112, 113, 145, 198, 205, 206, 239–40, 249, 264, 267, 324n5, 324n9

www.ingramcontent.com/pod-product-compliance
Lightning Source LLC
Chambersburg PA
CBHW061342300426
44116CB00011B/1960